ASIAN DEVELOPMENT OUTLOOK 2018 UPDATE

MAINTAINING STABILITY AMID HEIGHTENED UNCERTAINTY

SEPTEMBER 2018

ASIAN DEVELOPMENT BANK

ADB

© 2018 Asian Development Bank
6 ADB Avenue, Mandaluyong City, 1550 Metro Manila, Philippines
Tel +63 2 632 4444; Fax +63 2 636 2444
www.adb.org

Some rights reserved. Published in 2018.

ISBN 978-92-9261-334-1 (print), 978-92-9261-335-8 (electronic)
ISSN 1655-4809
Publication Stock No. FLS189567-3
http://dx.doi.org/10.22617/FLS189567-3

The views expressed in this publication are those of the authors and do not necessarily reflect the views and policies of the Asian Development Bank (ADB) or its Board of Governors or the governments they represent.

ADB does not guarantee the accuracy of the data included in this publication and accepts no responsibility for any consequence of their use. The mention of specific companies or products of manufacturers does not imply that they are endorsed or recommended by ADB in preference to others of a similar nature that are not mentioned.

By making any designation of or reference to a particular territory or geographic area, or by using the term "country" in this document, ADB does not intend to make any judgments as to the legal or other status of any territory or area.

Notes:
In this publication, "$" refers to US dollars.
ADB recognizes "China" as the People's Republic of China and "Vietnam" as Viet Nam.
Corrigenda to ADB publications may be found at http://www.adb.org/publications/corrigenda.

Cover artwork by Ana Verayo/2018.

Contents

Foreword

Developing Asia is set to lead global growth with an outlook that remains resilient despite external headwinds. The growth forecast for the region this year is 6.0%, while growth excluding the high-income newly industrialized economies is forecast at 6.5%— both projections retained from *Asian Development Outlook 2018* published in April. Healthy domestic demand buttressed large economies in the region, while higher oil prices buoyed oil and gas exporters.

The growth prospect for 2019 is slightly lower, however, revised down by 0.1 percentage points as risks sharpen for financial and trade shocks. A US interest rate higher than market expectations could induce capital outflow from Asia and increase financial sector vulnerability from private debt. Volatile oil prices stirred up by geopolitical developments will further stress financial markets. The biggest risk, however, is disruption to international production linkages should trade tensions continue to ratchet up between the US and the PRC.

Taking a lesson from the Asian financial crisis of 1997–1998, Asia built sound domestic macroeconomic fundamentals, which shored up regional resilience during the global financial crisis of 2008–2009. A decade of low interest rates and large direct asset purchases by central banks helped the region become the major contributor to global growth. As advanced economies normalize their monetary policies, new pockets of vulnerability threaten to erode Asian resilience with capital flow reversals, pressures on regional currencies, unsustainable private debt buildup, elevated housing prices, and heightened contagion and spillover effects.

Fortunately, Asian policy makers have a variety of tools to maintain macroeconomic stability, ranging from conventional fiscal, monetary, and exchange rate policies to less conventional macroprudential policy and capital flow management.
To be effective, policy interventions need to conform to the nature, size, and duration of the shock and be appropriate in combination for the economy's structure and prevailing phase in the business cycle. To safeguard the region against heightened uncertainty, vulnerabilities must be carefully monitored, and economic fundamentals further strengthened, to ensure a stable macroeconomic environment able to sustain future growth.

TAKEHIKO NAKAO
President
Asian Development Bank

Acknowledgments

Asian Development Outlook 2018 Update was prepared by staff of the Asian Development Bank (ADB) in the Central and West Asia Department, East Asia Department, Pacific Department, South Asia Department, Southeast Asia Department, and Economic Research and Regional Cooperation Department, as well as in ADB resident missions. Representatives of these departments constituted the Regional Economic Outlook Task Force, which met regularly to coordinate and develop consistent forecasts for the region.

The authors who contributed the sections are bylined in each chapter. The subregional coordinators were Kenji Takamiya, Lilia Aleksanyan, and Fatima Catacutan for Central Asia, Akiko Terada-Hagiwara for East Asia, Masato Nakane for South Asia, Kwang Jo Jeong and Dulce Zara for Southeast Asia, and Rommel Rabanal and Cara Tinio for the Pacific.

A team of economists in the Economic Research and Regional Cooperation Department, led by Joseph E. Zveglich, Jr., director of the Macroeconomics Research Division, coordinated the production of the publication, assisted by Edith Laviña. Technical and research support was provided by Shiela Camingue-Romance, Cindy Castillejos-Petalcorin, Nedelyn Magtibay-Ramos, Pilipinas Quising, Aleli Rosario, Dennis Sorino, Lea Sumulong, Priscille Villanueva, and Mai Lin Villaruel. Additional research support was provided by Emmanuel Alano, Zemma Ardaniel, Kristina Baris, John Arvin Bernabe, Donald Jay Bertulfo, Feliciano Paul Neilmer, Jade Laranjo, Jesson Pagaduan, and Michael Timbang. The economic editorial advisors Robert Boumphrey, Joshua Greene, Srinivasa Madhur, Richard Niebuhr, and Reza Vaez-Zadeh made substantive contributions to the country chapters and regional outlook.

The theme chapter benefited from the insightful comments of discussants and other participants at the workshops held at the ADB headquarters on 30–31 May 2018 and 17 August 2018. The valuable support and guidance of Yasuyuki Sawada, Juzhong Zhuang, and Abdul Abiad throughout the production process is gratefully acknowledged. Josef Yap provided editorial advice on the theme chapter, as well on the regional outlook.

Peter Fredenburg advised on ADB style and English usage. Alvin Tubio handled typesetting and graphics generation, in which he was assisted by Heili Ann Bravo, Fermirelyn Cruz, and Elenita Pura. Art direction for the cover design was by Anthony Victoria, with artwork from Ana Verayo. Critical support for the printing and publishing of the report was provided by the Printing Services Unit of the ADB Office of Administrative Services and by the publications and web teams of the ADB Department of Communications. Fermirelyn Cruz and Rhia Bautista-Piamonte provided administrative and secretarial support. The Department of Communications, led by Vicky Tan and John Larkin, planned and coordinated the dissemination of *Asian Development Outlook 2018 Update*.

Definitions

The economies discussed in *Asian Development Outlook 2018 Update* are classified by major analytic or geographic group. For the purposes of this publication, the following apply:

- **Association of Southeast Asian Nations** comprises Brunei Darussalam, Cambodia, Indonesia, the Lao People's Democratic Republic, Malaysia, Myanmar, the Philippines, Singapore, Thailand, and Viet Nam.
- **Developing Asia** comprises the 45 members of the Asian Development Bank listed below.
- **Newly industrialized economies** comprises Hong Kong, China; the Republic of Korea; Singapore; and Taipei,China.
- **Central Asia** comprises Armenia, Azerbaijan, Georgia, Kazakhstan, the Kyrgyz Republic, Tajikistan, Turkmenistan, and Uzbekistan.
- **East Asia** comprises Hong Kong, China; Mongolia; the People's Republic of China; the Republic of Korea; and Taipei,China.
- **South Asia** comprises Afghanistan, Bangladesh, Bhutan, India, Maldives, Nepal, Pakistan, and Sri Lanka.
- **Southeast Asia** comprises Brunei Darussalam, Cambodia, Indonesia, the Lao People's Democratic Republic, Malaysia, Myanmar, the Philippines, Singapore, Thailand, and Viet Nam.
- **The Pacific** comprises the Cook Islands, the Federated States of Micronesia, Fiji, Kiribati, the Marshall Islands, Nauru, Palau, Papua New Guinea, Samoa, Solomon Islands, Timor-Leste, Tonga, Tuvalu, and Vanuatu.

Unless otherwise specified, the symbol "$" and the word "dollar" refer to US dollars. *Asian Development Outlook 2018 Update* is generally based on data available up to **7 September 2018**.

Abbreviations

ADB	Asian Development Bank
ADO	Asian Development Outlook
AFC	Asian financial crisis
APEC	Asia-Pacific Economic Cooperation
ASEAN	Association of Southeast Asian Nations
BIS	Bank for International Settlements
CPEC	China–Pakistan Economic Corridor
EMP	exchange market pressure
EU	European Union
FDI	foreign direct investment
FSM	Federated States of Micronesia
FY	fiscal year
GDP	gross domestic product
GFC	global financial crisis
GST	goods and services tax
IMF	International Monetary Fund
IT	information technology
Lao PDR	Lao People's Democratic Republic
Libor	London interbank offered rate
LNG	liquefied natural gas
M1	money that includes cash and checking accounts
M2	broad money that adds highly liquid accounts to M1
M3	broad money that adds time accounts to M2
mbd	million barrels per day
NFRK	National Fund of the Republic of Kazakhstan
NIE	newly industrialized economy
NPL	nonperforming loan
OECD	Organisation for Economic Co-operation and Development
OPEC	Organization of the Petroleum Exporting Countries
PMI	purchasing managers' index
PNG	Papua New Guinea
PRC	People's Republic of China
Q	quarter
QE	quantitative easing
RMI	Republic of the Marshall Islands
ROK	Republic of Korea
RPC	Regional Processing Centre (Nauru)
saar	seasonally adjusted annualized rate
SMEs	small and medium-sized enterprises
SOE	state-owned enterprise
SST	sales and services tax
US	United States of America
VAT	value-added tax
WTO	World Trade Organization

ADO 2018 Update—Highlights

Growth in developing Asia has so far held up against external headwinds. While the region is expected to meet the *Asian Development Outlook 2018* forecast of 6.0% growth in 2018, the projection for 2019 has been trimmed by 0.1 percentage points to 5.8%. Excluding Asia's high-income newly industrialized economies, the region is expected to expand by 6.5% this year and 6.3% in 2019.

The forecast for rising inflation is tempered despite higher global fuel and food prices. Consumer prices are projected to rise by 2.8% in both 2018 and 2019, or by 0.1 percentage points less than earlier forecast.

Downside risks to the outlook are intensifying. Any escalation of the trade conflict could disrupt cross-border production links. If tightened more than investors expect, US monetary policy could accelerate capital outflow from Asian economies and put further depreciation pressure on regional currencies. Most economies remain robust, but policy makers must be ready to respond.

The changing global landscape poses challenges to macroeconomic stability in developing Asia. Policy makers have at their disposal an array of policy tools with which to manage pockets of vulnerability and maintain stability, but they must be applied carefully. Continued efforts are needed to promote sound fiscal policies, the independence of central banks with careful internal policy coordination, strong financial sectors, market-oriented structural reform, and adequate social safety nets.

Yasuyuki Sawada
Chief Economist
Asian Development Bank

Cross-currents test Asia's resilience

External forces cast uncertainty on growth

- **Growth in the region has so far prevailed over external challenges.** This Update maintains the 2018 forecasts from *Asian Development Outlook 2018 (ADO 2018)* of growth at 6.0% for developing Asia as a whole and at 6.5% excluding the high-income newly industrialized economies. Robust domestic demand supported the region's large economies, and oil prices above expectations boosted prospects for many oil and gas exporters. The growth forecast for 2019 is trimmed by 0.1 percentage points to 5.8% regionwide and to 6.3% excluding the newly industrialized economies. Escalating trade tensions and tighter global liquidity are causes for concern in the coming year.

  » **Growth in the industrial economies has held up.** The aggregate growth forecast for the major industrial economies of the United States, the euro area, and Japan are retained at 2.3% in 2018 and 2.0% in 2019. Growth in the US remains robust, supported by strong private spending, fiscal expansion, and job creation. However, recovery in the euro area and Japan stalled somewhat in the early part of the year, prompting slight downward revisions to their 2018 growth projections. The US and euro area are expected to gradually normalize monetary conditions to preempt inflation.

  » **Growth in Asia's largest economy is on track but with clouds looming.** The 2018 growth forecast for the People's Republic of China (PRC) remains unchanged at 6.6%. Growth is bolstered by strong economic performance in the first half of the year, notably robust domestic consumption and solid expansion of services. The forecast for 2019 is revised down from 6.4% to 6.3% in light of slower demand growth and the implementation of US tariffs and PRC countermeasures. Supply-side reform amid monetary and fiscal support will nevertheless ensure that growth remains on track.

  » **India's growth rebound is solidifying.** With economic activity recovering as expected from the temporary effects of the demonetization of large banknotes and the introduction of a national goods and services tax, growth forecasts remain unchanged at 7.3% for 2018 and 7.6% for 2019. Robust domestic demand and growing exports, particularly manufactures, counteract import growth driven in large part by rising oil prices. The changing external environment poses some challenges ahead for India. Depreciation of the rupee, volatile external financial markets, and risks of inflation will require vigilance from monetary authorities, but tighter fiscal policy will help to quell inflationary pressures.

  » **Growth is moderating in 6 of the 10 economies in Southeast Asia.** The subregion is now expected to grow by 5.1% in 2018, or 0.1 percentage points less than forecast in *ADO 2018*. Investment in Malaysia was weaker than expected in the first half amid a transition to a new government, and policies going forward are expected to favor consumption over investment. Net exports moderated growth in Indonesia, the Philippines, Thailand, and Viet Nam as imports surged to support government investments in infrastructure. The growth forecast of 5.2% for 2019 is maintained as prices for export commodities recover and infrastructure investment rises.

» **Paths diverge for large Central Asian and Pacific commodity exporters.** This *Update* raises the growth forecast this year for Central Asia by 0.1 percentage points to 4.1%. Higher global oil prices boosted oil and natural gas production in Kazakhstan, adding to already positive contributions to growth from exports and investment. In contrast, the Pacific is now projected to expand by just 1.1%, half the rate forecast in *ADO 2018*. An earthquake in February in Papua New Guinea, the largest Pacific economy, temporarily interrupted liquefied natural gas production there, while shortfalls in fiscal spending undercut growth in Timor-Leste.

■ **The inflation forecast is tempered despite rising global fuel and food prices.** Prices in developing Asia should rise from 2.2% in 2017 on higher global fuel costs (with oil expected to average $74 per barrel in 2018), currencies weakening against the dollar in the first half of 2018, and disrupted food supply. Yet country-specific factors have kept the regional average in check such that aggregate forecasts are revised down by 0.1 percentage points to 2.8% in both 2018 and 2019. These domestic factors include relatively moderate food price inflation in India and the PRC, fuel subsidies in Indonesia and Malaysia, and currency stabilization in Tajikistan and Uzbekistan. However, inflation was higher than expected in the Philippines, prompting the central bank to tighten monetary policy there.

■ **The regional current account surplus will narrow.** Strong import growth caused the PRC to record a current account deficit in the first half of 2018, the first such deficit since it joined the World Trade Organization 18 years ago. Meanwhile, rising demand for capital and consumption goods widened trade deficits in some of the region's other larger economies. Developing Asia's current account surplus is now forecast to drop to the equivalent of 1.0% of GDP in 2018, or 0.4 percentage points lower than in *ADO 2018*, despite upwardly revised industry forecasts for manufactured exports such as electronics. Currency depreciation will support some economies' exports next year, but uncertainty from intensifying trade conflict may drag on growth in intermediate trade. This *Update* forecasts the current account surplus narrowing further to 0.7% in 2019.

■ **The region faces risks to its outlook from financial and trade shocks.** If the US economy shows signs of overheating, the Federal Reserve might raise interest rates beyond market expectations, which could intensify capital outflow from Asian economies, putting further pressure on regional currencies. Moreover, if interest rates in Asia rise further, economies with a lot of private debt could see more vulnerability in their financial sectors. Exchange rate turbulence in emerging markets outside of developing Asia could spill over into the region as well. Oil prices made volatile by geopolitical developments such as the US withdrawal from the multilateral deal with Iran deepen uncertainty about demand and heighten jitters in financial markets. However, the most prominent risk, analyzed below, comes from the disruption of international production linkages that could result from escalation in the trade conflict. While regional economies have responded to external shocks so far with resilience, policy makers must remain vigilant.

The impact of the trade conflict on developing Asia

- **Trade conflict is escalating, especially between the PRC and the US.**
  ADO 2018 reported that import tariffs the US imposed globally in January 2018—30% on solar panels, 20% on washing machines, 25% on steel, and 10% on aluminum—so far had little impact on growth in developing Asia. Subsequently, the US imposed 25% tariffs on $50 billion worth of imports from the PRC in two phases, to which the PRC retaliated with 25% tariffs on an equal value of imports from the US. In September, the US levied 10% tariffs on an additional $200 billion worth of PRC imports, to be raised to 25% in January 2019, further stating that it has under consideration targeting an additional $267 billion worth of goods. The PRC responded with a 10% tariff on $60 billion worth of US goods, also to be raised to 25% at year-end. Meanwhile, both sides are also tightening investment restrictions.

- **Further conflict between the US and PRC would spread through cross-border production networks.** Estimates show a moderate impact from measures implemented or proposed by 24 September, lowering GDP in the PRC by 0.5 percentage points and in the US by 0.1 percentage points but having a negligible effect on the rest of developing Asia. However, any further escalation, such as 25% tariffs on all bilateral trade between the US and PRC, would have greater consequences. The immediate impact would be particularly hard on the PRC, estimated to shave 1.0 percentage point off GDP, while the US would suffer a 0.2 percentage point shortfall. Other economies in developing Asia would initially feel the pinch as production slowed across global value chains. However, these players may gain over the medium term as trade is redirected within global supply chains to economies producing similar goods, benefitting in particular Southeast Asia and the newly industrialized economies. With trade conflict escalation, the US trade deficit with the PRC would shrink, but the overall US trade deficit would not change much as US imports would be redirected to other countries while US exports to the PRC declined.

- **Prolonged trade conflict could damage confidence and deter investment.** This indirect fallout would be large for many economies in the region and globally, especially if automobiles and other parts became embroiled in the trade conflict. Estimates of impacts do not fully capture possible disruption to production units as overseas business networks are severed and investment plans are cancelled amid a reallocation of global production, nor do they gauge the negative impact of heightened economic uncertainty more generally. Such disruptions could be substantial as the conflict drags on, escalates, or spills over into financial markets. Ongoing efforts by Asian governments to forge trade agreements within the region and beyond are welcome.

Outlook by subregion

- **Revisions to growth forecasts for developing Asia are roughly balanced.**
Growth projections for 45 regional economies in 2018 are upgraded from
April forecasts in *ADO 2018* for 14 economies, downgraded for 16, and
unchanged for 15. Looking ahead to 2019, the balance tips toward downward
adjustment, with moderation in East Asia weighing on the regionwide average.

- **East Asia remains buoyant amid escalating trade tensions.** Subregional GDP
will expand by 6.0% in 2018, as forecast in April, and by only 5.7% in 2019,
slightly lower than the *ADO 2018* projection. Growth in the PRC will slow from
6.9% in 2017 to 6.6% in 2018, unchanged from the previous forecast, and to
6.3% in 2019, revised down from 6.4% because of slower demand growth and a
worsening trade conflict with the US. In Hong Kong, China and in Taipei,China,
growth will be higher in 2018 than earlier projected but unchanged in 2019, with
domestic demand supporting growth. Surging consumption and exports raise
growth prospects in Mongolia substantially beyond earlier forecasts, but growth
in the Republic of Korea will be lower in both years as exports suffer under
higher tariffs imposed by two of its largest trade partners. Meanwhile, consumer
inflation will be, at 2.1% in both 2018 and 2019, slightly lower than forecast
in April. In the PRC, slow recovery for food prices and only mild pass-through
from currency depreciation will hold inflation at 2.2% in both years, less than
previously forecast.

- **South Asia sustains its growth momentum.** This *Update* retains subregional
growth forecasts published in April at 7.0% for 2018 and 7.2% for 2019. Similarly,
it retains for India growth forecasts at 7.3% for 2018 and 7.6% for 2019 despite
growth much faster than expected in the April–June first quarter of fiscal 2018.
Pakistan is estimated to have grown by 5.8% in the fiscal year to June 2018,
higher than forecast in *ADO 2018*, but the outlook is clouded by a large budget
deficit, a deteriorating current account deficit, and falling foreign exchange
reserves. In Bangladesh and Nepal, robust investment pushed estimated growth
in fiscal 2018 higher than forecast, but in Bhutan and Sri Lanka weaker domestic
demand lowers growth expectations for both 2018 and 2019. Drought and
scant improvement in security appears to hold growth in Afghanistan below the
forecast for 2018, and slower tourism requires a downgrade to the 2019 forecast
for Maldives. Subregional inflation forecasts are revised up from 4.7% to 4.9%
for 2018 and from 5.1% to 5.2% for 2019 on closing output gaps, weakening
currencies, and higher global oil prices, with a sharper upward revision for India
in 2018.

- **Southeast Asian growth is now forecast to dip slightly this year.** Subregional
growth is expected at 5.1% in 2018. This is slightly slower than the *ADO 2018*
forecast as a combination of factors—moderation in export growth, softer
domestic demand, subdued agriculture, higher inflation, net capital outflow,
and a worsening balance of payments—dim the growth outlook for this year in
6 of the 10 economies in the subregion: Indonesia, the Lao People's Democratic
Republic (Lao PDR), Malaysia, Myanmar, the Philippines, and Viet Nam.
Brunei Darussalam and Thailand, by contrast, look set to outperform earlier
forecasts, while Cambodia and Singapore will likely meet April projections.
Growth is still forecast to return in 2019 to the 2017 rate of 5.2%.

Subregional inflation is now projected marginally lower at 2.9% this year and next, the forecast revised down by 0.1 percentage points despite inflation pressures far stronger than projected in *ADO 2018* in Brunei Darussalam, the Lao PDR, the Philippines, Thailand, and Viet Nam.

■ **Central Asia benefits from higher oil prices and remittances.** The growth forecast for the subregion in 2018 is revised up by 0.1 percentage points to 4.1%. In the first half of the year, higher oil prices and petroleum production boosted growth in Kazakhstan, and Armenia and Georgia also exceeded growth expectations. By contrast, 2018 forecasts are now lower for the Kyrgyz Republic as mining output slows, for Turkmenistan in the expectation of fiscal tightening, and for Uzbekistan with protracted adjustment to a new exchange rate regime. The subregional growth projection for 2019 remains at 4.2%, with upgrades for Armenia, Georgia, and Kazakhstan offsetting lower forecasts for Turkmenistan and Uzbekistan. The inflation forecast for 2018 is cut by 0.1 percentage points to 8.4% as improved exchange rate stability has helped contain price pressures in Azerbaijan. Inflation below expectations in the first half of 2018 motivates lower 2018 forecasts for Georgia, the Kyrgyz Republic, and Tajikistan. With extended favorable conditions in Azerbaijan, the inflation forecast for 2019 is trimmed from 7.9% to 7.7%.

■ **Pacific growth prospects remain positive despite a setback in 2018.** The growth forecast for 2018 is reduced from *ADO 2018* after a slowdown in Papua New Guinea caused by an earthquake in February exceeded earlier assumptions. Projected growth is also lower in Palau, with a decline in tourism, and substantially lower in Timor-Leste as continuing political uncertainty undermines government expenditure and investment. The forecast for 2019 is slightly higher on projected recovery in Papua New Guinea, the largest economy in the subregion. Forecasts for most other economies in 2019 are unchanged from *ADO 2018*, the exceptions being lower forecasts for Timor-Leste and Palau and a higher forecast for Tuvalu in light of increased government spending. Inflation is now projected to be marginally higher in 2018 with several economies expecting higher food and fuel prices and Fiji raising taxes on alcohol and tobacco. The inflation forecast for 2019 is unchanged.

Maintaining stability amid heightened uncertainty

Gathering clouds of uncertainty and vulnerability

- **Developing Asia has enjoyed a good run since the Asian financial crisis.**
  Most remarkable is how well it weathered the global financial crisis of
  2008–2009 (GFC). As an engine of the global economy, developing Asia
  now accounts for more than 60% of global growth. With growth averaging
  6.8% since the GFC, and moderating trends for inflation and output volatility
  since the Asian financial crisis of 1997–1998 (AFC), the region has created
  stable economic conditions that reinforce development and poverty reduction.
  Sound domestic macroeconomic fundamentals and buoyant external conditions
  have contributed to these trends.

  » **Restructuring and reform strengthened resilience after the AFC.**
    The region's macroeconomic fundamentals improved with its moves toward
    greater exchange rate flexibility and central bank independence, and with
    its implementation of financial and fiscal reform. When the GFC struck,
    Asian economies were able to endure its impact with timely fiscal and
    monetary countermeasures to stimulate growth. A large PRC fiscal stimulus,
    in particular, supported the region.

  » **Buoyant external conditions further lifted Asia's performance.** Rapid
    growth in the volume of global trade before the GFC provided strong external
    demand for Asian exports. After the GFC, unprecedented easing of monetary
    policy in the advanced economies, in the form of sustained low interest
    rates and sizeable direct asset purchases by central banks, sent investors
    in search of higher yields and, consequently, large-scale capital flows
    into developing Asia. This fueled credit growth in the region that further
    supported the good run and boosted asset market valuations.

- **Changing external circumstances may disrupt the good run.** As the US
  and other advanced economies unwind their asset purchase programs and
  normalize their interest rates, the end of the era of super-low interest rates could
  reverse capital flow heretofore into the region. In addition, new risks previously
  unforeseen, notably escalating global trade tensions, now loom on the horizon.
  These factors could combine to undermine future growth and stability.

- **Internal and external conditions interact to expose pockets of vulnerability.**
  Complex interactions in the current environment that entwine the financial
  sector, the real economy, domestic policy, and the external sector pose new
  challenges to the maintenance of macroeconomic stability, necessitating careful
  monitoring as they generate tradeoffs between stabilization in the short term and
  sustainability over the long run. The theme chapter of this *Update* explores the
  key pockets of vulnerability and the policy options available to manage them.

Pockets of vulnerability

- **Sudden capital flow reversals may disrupt financial and economic stability.**
  Net capital inflow to developing Asia increased rapidly post-AFC, reversed
  sharply during the GFC, rebounded quickly in the GFC aftermath to reach a peak

of $391 billion in 2010, and declined from 2013, after which outflow started to outpace inflow. Such volatility is closely associated with pressure on exchange rates and domestic credit cycles that often generate vulnerability in the economy.

■ **Regional currencies are under pressure from changes in global liquidity.** Emerging economies are susceptible to steep currency depreciation caused by financial shocks, the extent of the pressure determined partly by their dependence on short-term capital. Large and abrupt changes in liquidity flow can translate into volatility in foreign exchange and financial markets, run down finite foreign currency reserves, and constrain monetary policy options.

■ **Unsustainable private debt buildups can weigh on the real economy.** The ratio of debt to GDP in Asia stood at 186% in 2016, driven mainly by a rapid accumulation of private debt, which increased in the preceding decade by over 60 percentage points in an environment of low interest rates, strong growth, and financial deepening. Changes in global liquidity conditions may curtail access to credit and raise borrowing costs, causing nonperforming loans to proliferate. Empirical analysis showed that slowdowns preceded by rapid buildups of private debt tended to be more severe than normal slowdowns, the effect being stronger in emerging economies than in advanced ones.

■ **Elevated housing prices threaten severe growth downturns if prices reverse abruptly.** Analysis showed escalating ratios of house purchase price to rent in major Asian cities, notably in Hong Kong, China; Malaysia; the PRC; the Republic of Korea; and Taipei,China. Contributing to these price spikes are such factors as economic booms, rural-to-urban migration, banks loosening credit policies, accommodative monetary conditions, and, more recently, capital inflow surges. Housing prices that have undergone sharp and sudden reversals, empirical studies showed, tended to be associated with longer and deeper slowdowns.

■ **Heightened contagion and spillover compound susceptibility to shocks.** Asian trade and financial markets have grown in the past 20 years in both absolute and relative terms, with deeper integration both globally and within the region. The issues of volatility transmission and the risk of contagion during periods of stress have come to the fore. Evidence shows rising financial market spillover from the PRC and the US, both between each other and to other Asian economies. This underlines the region's greater susceptibility to spillover from shocks through portfolio investment, balance sheets, or trade.

Tools available for maintaining stability

■ **Policy must be implemented carefully to manage multiple risks.** Policy makers have at their disposal a range of tools, from conventional fiscal, monetary, and exchange rate policies that target aggregate economic activity, to less conventional macroprudential policy and capital flow management that aim to control systemic risks. Customized and hybrid policy tools have evolved to tackle country-specific issues. How effectively these tools stabilize an economy depends on many factors: the economy's structure, its financial sector development, the phase of its economic cycle, and the nature, size, and duration of the shocks prompting the response.

■ **Effective countercyclical fiscal policy requires ample fiscal space.** Responsible policy preserves fiscal space during economic booms to allow countercyclical interventions during downturns. Procyclical fiscal policy, by contrast, amplifies vulnerability to shocks by consuming fiscal space in the good times, leaving little for the bad times when it is needed. To enable discretionary countercyclical fiscal policy, governments should expand fiscal space by reducing debt and widening the tax base—and further by investing in countercyclical fiscal buffers like sovereign wealth funds, as many resource-rich economies do, and ensuring that they are well governed. Equally important are improvements in economic, social, and political fundamentals that underpin broad macroeconomic management, as well as social safety nets that protect the most vulnerable.

■ **Monetary policy should pay attention to both credit and business cycles.** Monetary policy is a powerful tool to navigate macroeconomic currents. In some Asian economies, there were negative correlations between the credit and business cycles. Monetary policy focused solely on stabilizing business cycles risks amplifying swings in the credit cycle that can induce another wave of instability in the business cycle. When business cycles and credit cycles are not synchronized, monetary policy may be more effective if combined with appropriate microprudential and macroprudential policies.

■ **A more flexible exchange rate better insulates against shocks.** The exchange rate regime matters. Research shows that a fully flexible exchange rate regime tends to insulate the domestic economy from adverse external shocks more effectively than either a fixed exchange rate regime or an intermediate regime. In particular, economies with less flexible regimes tend to suffer greater deterioration in financial conditions and economic growth induced by global financial shocks than do economies with fully flexible regimes. In practice, regardless of the type of exchange rate regime formally espoused, monetary authorities have acted to smooth volatility caused by external shocks and thereby manage market sentiment.

■ **Capital flow management can contain volatility from external shocks.** Asian economies have managed capital flow by selectively using the measures available. Some of them are more effective than others at influencing flow volume and composition. Capital flow management can, however, lead to substitution and complementary effects between different components of capital flow, both within an economy and across borders, that may have unintended effects on the volume of untargeted capital flows. Policy makers need to bear in mind the risk of unintended consequences. For instance, when they try to stabilize bank lending, they may inadvertently undermine foreign direct investment if the two forms of capital are complementary. Policy makers may nevertheless consider restrictions on capital flow to mitigate pressure on the exchange rate or to achieve greater monetary policy independence.

■ **Macroprudential policies have gained popularity since the GFC.** Microprudential regulation became the norm in the region after the AFC, but regulations specific to firms or institutions do not guarantee the stability of the entire financial system. For example, requiring a minimum capital adequacy ratio can enhance the financial viability of an individual bank, but reducing the lending ability of many banks can end up curbing credit supply across the economy, inviting systemic risk. To address such risk, a policy framework has evolved that includes macroprudential measures such as caps on the loan-to-value ratio and on the debt-to-income ratio, as well as capital adequacy and liquidity requirements for systematically important financial institutions. Since 2008, Asia has relied more than any other region on macroprudential measures, especially policies to stabilize housing markets.

Safeguarding Asia against heightened uncertainty

- **Macroeconomic management requires close monitoring of vulnerability.** Pockets of vulnerability—such as volatile capital flows, elevated debt levels, large and unexpected changes in exchange rates, sharp housing price increases, and contagion between economies—are risks to macroeconomic and financial stability that require careful and constant monitoring. Such vigilance facilitates preemptive measures to mitigate existing imbalances and new ones as they arise.

- **Policy tools are plentiful, but favorable results require coordination.** The application of different policy tools may entail tradeoffs and complementarities, both domestically and across borders. Taking these factors into account may improve policy performance.

  » **Domestic policy coordination to boost effectiveness and target conflicting objectives.** Close links between business and financial cycles mean that effective responses depend critically on domestic policy coordination. Countercyclical fiscal policy, for instance, benefits from accommodative monetary policy to promote private investment and enhance growth. Similarly, macroprudential policy is more effective when coordinated with monetary policy. When lowering the interest rate to stimulate economic activity, for example, tighter macroprudential measures on housing can prevent overly rapid home price escalation. When, on the other hand, monetary policies are tightened to counter excessive borrowing or economic overheating, governments can consider measures for financial inclusion to avoid imposing onerous constraints on smaller borrowers.

  » **Cross-border cooperation to avoid unwanted external spillover.** One country implementing capital flow measures can alter net flows in other economies. With cross-border cooperation, the authorities can productively raise awareness of the unwanted consequences of policy spillover. Considering the cross-border effects of their own policies enables governments to help promote global stability. While monetary policy is generally understood to be oriented toward domestic objectives such as price stability and a sound financial system, the authorities, in particular those in larger economies, should be mindful of cross-border spillover.

- **Stabilization policies work best where fundamentals are strong.** To maintain stability under the current environment of heightened uncertainty, Asia may need to deploy the full range of policy tools at its disposal. These policies work best when fundamentals that support economic, social, and political stability are strong. Continued efforts are needed to promote sound fiscal policies, independent central banks, strong financial sectors, market-oriented structural reform, and adequate social safety nets.

GDP growth rate and inflation, % per year

	Growth rate of GDP					Inflation				
	2017	2018		2019		2017	2018		2019	
		ADO 2018	Update	ADO 2018	Update		ADO 2018	Update	ADO 2018	Update
Central Asia	**4.3**	**4.0**	**4.1**	**4.2**	**4.2**	**9.2**	**8.5**	**8.4**	**7.9**	**7.7**
Armenia	7.5	4.0	5.3	4.2	4.5	1.0	2.7	2.7	2.2	2.5
Azerbaijan	0.1	1.7	1.7	2.0	2.0	12.9	7.0	4.5	8.0	5.0
Georgia	5.0	4.5	4.9	4.7	5.0	6.0	3.5	3.0	3.0	3.0
Kazakhstan	4.1	3.2	3.7	3.5	3.9	7.4	6.8	7.0	6.2	6.5
Kyrgyz Republic	4.6	3.5	2.5	4.0	4.0	3.2	4.0	3.8	4.5	4.5
Tajikistan	7.1	6.0	6.0	6.5	6.5	6.7	7.5	6.5	7.0	7.0
Turkmenistan	6.5	6.5	6.2	6.7	6.0	8.0	8.0	9.4	8.0	8.2
Uzbekistan	5.3	5.5	4.9	5.6	5.0	14.4	16.0	16.0	14.0	14.0
East Asia	**6.3**	**6.0**	**6.0**	**5.8**	**5.7**	**1.6**	**2.3**	**2.1**	**2.2**	**2.1**
Hong Kong, China	3.8	3.2	3.7	3.0	3.0	1.5	2.2	2.3	2.1	2.2
Mongolia	5.3	3.8	6.4	4.3	6.1	4.3	8.0	7.2	7.0	7.0
People's Republic of China	6.9	6.6	6.6	6.4	6.3	1.6	2.4	2.2	2.3	2.2
Republic of Korea	3.1	3.0	2.9	2.9	2.8	1.9	1.9	1.8	2.0	1.8
Taipei,China	2.9	2.9	3.0	2.8	2.8	0.6	1.1	1.4	1.1	1.3
South Asia	**6.5**	**7.0**	**7.0**	**7.2**	**7.2**	**4.0**	**4.7**	**4.9**	**5.1**	**5.2**
Afghanistan	2.5	2.5	2.2	2.5	2.5	5.0	5.0	3.5	5.0	5.0
Bangladesh	7.3	7.0	7.9	7.2	7.5	5.4	6.1	5.8	6.3	6.3
Bhutan	7.5	7.1	6.7	7.4	7.1	4.3	4.6	3.6	5.4	4.9
India	6.7	7.3	7.3	7.6	7.6	3.6	4.6	5.0	5.0	5.0
Maldives	6.9	6.7	6.7	6.8	6.4	2.8	3.1	1.2	3.0	1.7
Nepal	7.4	4.9	5.9	5.5	5.5	4.5	5.5	4.2	6.0	6.0
Pakistan	5.4	5.6	5.8	5.1	4.8	4.2	4.5	3.9	4.8	6.5
Sri Lanka	3.3	4.2	3.8	4.8	4.5	7.7	5.2	4.5	5.0	4.7
Southeast Asia	**5.2**	**5.2**	**5.1**	**5.2**	**5.2**	**2.8**	**3.0**	**2.9**	**3.0**	**2.9**
Brunei Darussalam	1.3	1.5	2.0	2.0	2.0	−0.2	0.1	0.2	0.1	0.2
Cambodia	6.9	7.0	7.0	7.0	7.0	2.9	3.2	2.6	3.5	3.0
Indonesia	5.1	5.3	5.2	5.3	5.3	3.8	3.8	3.4	4.0	3.5
Lao People's Dem. Rep.	6.9	6.8	6.6	7.0	6.9	0.8	2.0	2.5	2.5	3.1
Malaysia	5.9	5.3	5.0	5.0	4.8	3.8	2.6	1.4	1.8	2.0
Myanmar	6.8	6.8	6.6	7.2	7.0	4.0	6.2	6.2	6.0	6.0
Philippines	6.7	6.8	6.4	6.9	6.7	2.9	4.0	5.0	3.9	4.0
Singapore	3.6	3.1	3.1	2.9	2.9	0.6	0.9	0.7	1.4	1.4
Thailand	3.9	4.0	4.5	4.1	4.3	0.7	1.2	1.3	1.3	1.4
Viet Nam	6.8	7.1	6.9	6.8	6.8	3.5	3.7	4.0	4.0	4.5
The Pacific	**2.4**	**2.2**	**1.1**	**3.0**	**3.1**	**4.2**	**4.1**	**4.2**	**3.9**	**3.9**
Cook Islands	3.5	3.5	3.5	3.0	3.0	−0.1	0.5	0.5	1.0	1.0
Federated States of Micronesia	2.0	2.0	2.0	2.0	2.0	0.5	1.0	1.0	1.0	1.0
Fiji	3.9	3.6	3.6	3.3	3.3	3.3	3.0	3.5	3.0	3.0
Kiribati	2.5	2.3	2.3	2.3	2.3	2.2	2.5	3.0	2.5	2.7
Marshall Islands	3.6	2.5	2.5	2.5	2.5	0.0	1.0	1.0	1.0	1.0
Nauru	4.0	−4.0	−3.0	0.5	0.5	5.0	2.0	2.0	2.0	2.0
Palau	−3.7	3.0	1.0	3.0	1.0	0.9	1.5	1.5	1.5	1.5
Papua New Guinea	3.0	1.8	0.5	2.7	3.0	5.4	5.0	5.0	4.5	4.5
Samoa	2.5	0.5	0.5	2.0	2.0	1.4	2.0	3.5	3.0	3.0
Solomon Islands	3.2	3.0	3.2	3.0	3.0	0.1	2.5	2.5	3.0	3.0
Timor-Leste	−5.3	3.0	0.6	5.5	4.5	0.6	2.0	2.0	3.0	3.0
Tonga	2.8	−0.3	−0.3	1.9	1.9	7.4	3.8	5.5	0.5	3.0
Tuvalu	3.2	3.0	3.8	3.0	3.5	4.4	2.5	4.0	2.8	3.4
Vanuatu	3.5	3.2	3.2	3.0	3.0	3.1	4.8	3.0	2.5	2.5
Developing Asia	**6.1**	**6.0**	**6.0**	**5.9**	**5.8**	**2.2**	**2.9**	**2.8**	**2.9**	**2.8**
Developing Asia excluding the NIEs	**6.6**	**6.5**	**6.5**	**6.4**	**6.3**	**2.3**	**3.0**	**2.9**	**3.0**	**3.0**

GDP = gross domestic product, NIEs = newly industrialized economies (Hong Kong, China; the Republic of Korea; Singapore; and Taipei,China).

1

CROSS-CURRENTS TEST ASIA'S RESILIENCE

Cross-currents test Asia's resilience

Growth in developing Asia has withstood mounting external challenges in 2018, its momentum drawing on robust demand—both domestic in the region's large economies and external, fortified by an upswing in the major industrial economies. For oil and gas exporters, fuel prices above expectations provided an added boost. The favorable performance enabled progress toward structural reform in several economies in the region. This *Update* maintains the forecasts published in April in *Asian Development Outlook 2018* (*ADO 2018*) for growth in developing Asia as a whole at 6.0% and, excluding the high-income newly industrialized economies (NIEs), at 6.5% (Figure 1.0.1). However, escalating trade tensions and tighter global liquidity have dampened prospects for 2019. Growth forecasts for next year have been trimmed by 0.1 percentage points to 5.8% for the whole region and 6.3% without the NIEs.

Uncertainty has mounted as the global trade situation deteriorated much faster than foreseen in *ADO 2018*. At this juncture, 60% of PRC imports from the US and 87% of US imports from the PRC are affected by new and higher tariffs. The forecast scenario for bilateral escalation in the trade conflict assumes that targeting will reach 100% on both sides. Applying a 25% tariff, the bilateral escalation scenario yields a 1.0 percentage point reduction in the GDP of the PRC and a 0.2 percentage point reduction in the GDP of the US over some years. Moreover, the conflict threatens to disrupt trade relations in the region and sour investor sentiment. There is already an additional threat of global tariffs on US imports of automobiles and auto parts looming over the next few months that, along with any ensuing global retaliation, would directly affect other economies in developing Asia. To address these external challenges, the PRC and the rest of developing Asia should strengthen their intraregional trade networks, and their monetary authorities should work together to enhance vigilance of and responses to tighter global financial conditions and mounting inflationary pressure.

1.0.1 GDP growth outlook in developing Asia

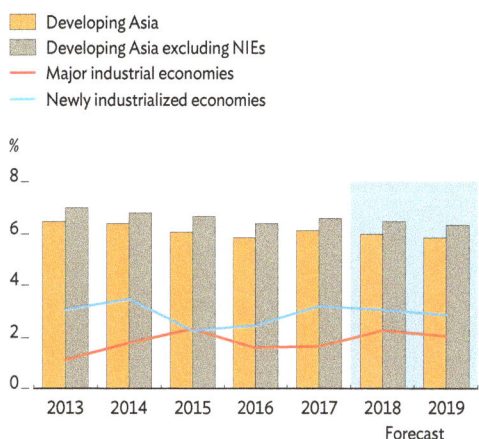

GDP = gross domestic product, NIE = newly industrialized economy.
Note: The major industrial economies consists of the United States, the euro area, and Japan.
Source: *Asian Development Outlook* database.

This chapter was written by Valerie Mercer-Blackman, Abdul Abiad, Mahinthan Joseph Mariasingham, Benno Ferrarini, Donghyun Park, Arief Ramayandi, Shu Tian, Madhavi Pundit, Shiela Camingue-Romance, Cindy Castillejos-Petalcorin, Nedelyn Magtibay-Ramos, Pilipinas Quising, Dennis Sorino, Priscille Villanueva, and Michael Timbang, consultant. All authors are in the Economic Research and Regional Cooperation Department, ADB, Manila.

External forces cast uncertainty on growth

Developing Asia has had a solid first half of 2018 as external contributions to growth from the industrial economies held up despite policy uncertainties emanating from the US in particular. Economic growth should remain healthy as domestic demand takes center stage despite trade growth facing downside risks from the intensifying US–PRC trade conflict. Developing Asia is projected to grow by 6.0% this year, the forecast unchanged from *ADO 2018* but down from its 2017 performance. Excluding the NIEs, growth should reach 6.5% in 2018, also unchanged from *ADO 2018*. Tailwinds from 2017 will have dissipated by 2019, and an external environment likely to be less favorable calls for lower growth forecasts for next year: 5.8% for the whole region and 6.3% excluding the NIEs. The outlook for the major industrial economies of the United States, the euro area, and Japan is retained at 2.3% in 2018 and 2.0% in 2019, with higher forecast growth in the US in both years offsetting slight downward revisions for the European Union and Japan in 2018 (Box 1.1.1). The forecasts for the region in this *Update* are likely the rosiest realistic prospect, given that global and regional risks are firmly on the downside.

Consumption driving 2018 growth

The pattern of economic growth among the subregions of developing Asia is expected to remain the same in 2018 and 2019 (Figure 1.1.1). South Asia will continue to lead the way but with a significant increase in its aggregate growth largely because of India's strong recovery from growth moderation in 2017. The Pacific will lag with growth in all its economies below the regional average. The growth trajectory of the heavily weighted PRC is steady, as expected, and as such will dictate the forecast regional trend as well. Looking further ahead, the PRC is the economy most vulnerable to emerging global risks. This vulnerability is tempered, however, by the substantial resources available to policy makers there to counter any eventuality. The other major exporters in Southeast Asia and among the NIEs continue to thrive as a group despite minor country-specific setbacks.

   Developments in the first half of 2018 show domestic demand driving growth in the largest economies in the region (Figure 1.1.2). By subregion, Central Asia benefitted from rising prices for oil and gas, the principal exports of its largest and third-largest economies, Kazakhstan and Azerbaijan.

1.1.1 GDP growth by subregion

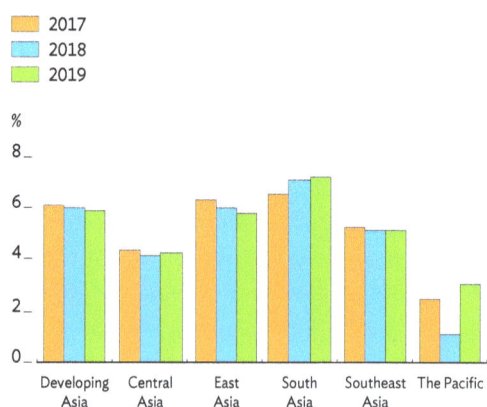

Source: *Asian Development Outlook* database.

1.1.1 Continued growth momentum despite policy uncertainty

Growth in the major industrial economies of the United States, euro area, and Japan remained strong, picking up by a notch in the second quarter (Q2) of 2018. Aggregate growth forecasts are retained from *ADO 2018* at 2.3% in 2018 and 2.0% in 2019 (box table).

GDP growth in the major industrial economies (%)

Area	2016 Actual	2017 Actual	2018 ADO 2018	2018 Update	2019 ADO 2018	2019 Update
Major industrial economies	1.6	2.3	2.3	2.3	2.0	2.0
United States	1.6	2.2	2.7	2.8	2.3	2.4
Euro area	1.8	2.5	2.2	2.0	1.9	1.9
Japan	1.0	1.7	1.4	1.1	1.0	1.0

ADO = Asian Development Outlook.

Notes: Average growth rates are weighted by gross national income, Atlas method. More details in Table A1.1.

Sources: US Department of Commerce, Bureau of Economic Analysis, http://www.bea.gov; Eurostat, http://ec.europa.eu/eurostat; Economic and Social Research Institute of Japan, http://www.esri.cao.go.jp; ADB estimates.

US growth achieved a solid seasonally adjusted annualized rate (saar) of 3.2% in the first half of 2018. GDP grew by 2.2% saar in Q1, driven mainly by private investment, then a strong rebound in consumption and exports generated Q2 growth at 4.2% saar, a 4-year high. Exports rose as trade partners of the US frontloaded their imports in anticipation of higher tariffs. Strong consumer confidence and retail sales suggest that consumption should remain the pillar of growth. The labor market remained tight as unemployment dipped below 4.0% in April and was sustained at 3.9% in July and August, the lowest since 2000. Strong aggregate demand has stirred inflationary pressure, lifting both headline and core inflation. Headline inflation rose to 2.9% in June and July, the highest since March 2012, and averaged 2.5% in the first 7 months of 2018. This rate is expected to be the full year average in 2018, but inflation will likely ease to 2.2% in 2019 in response to monetary tightening. Fiscal expansion, however, and a drift toward trade protectionism amid significant policy uncertainty pose downside risks to the US outlook.

The euro area lost growth momentum, slowing to 1.6% saar in Q1 of 2018 from 2.5% a year earlier. The strong expansion in Q4 of 2017 was stalled by a stronger euro, inducing a negative contribution to growth from net exports in Q1 of 2018. However, economic growth stabilized at 1.5% saar in Q2. Labor market conditions in the region further improved, with the unemployment rate dropping to 8.2% in July, the lowest since the global financial crisis of 2008–2009. Economic prospects in the region remain optimistic, backed by a solid domestic economy and adequate fiscal support. Assuming a gradual pickup in the second half of the year, the growth forecast for 2018 is still revised down to 2.0% from 2.2% in *ADO 2018*, then maintained at 1.9% for 2019. Headline inflation rose to a 6-year high of 2.1% in July from 2.0% in June, just above the European Central Bank target of under 2.0%. The central bank announced in June that it was winding down its massive bond-buying program. Adding to uncertainty are risks to major European banks from their heavy exposure to the financial sector of Turkey, which is reeling from a depreciating lira and balance of payments problems.

Japan saw economic growth recover strongly in Q2 as GDP increased by 3.0% saar, reversing contraction by 0.9% in the previous quarter. This decline had followed 8 consecutive quarters of growth, one of Japan's longest runs of expansion since the 1980s. Although consumption improved, net exports, which had propelled the previous expansion, dragged GDP growth down by 0.5 percentage points in Q2. Industrial production rebounded in Q2, and wage growth surged in June. When combined with continued low unemployment rates, standing at 2.4% in June, higher wages should continue to boost consumers' income and spending power. Spending should get a further positive jolt in the short term from public anticipation of a hike in the consumption tax. Even so, price pressures are building rather slowly, with the inflation rate well under the Bank of Japan target of 2%. Consumer price inflation picked up from 0.7% year on year in June to 1.0% in July, driven partly by higher energy costs. In its latest meeting, the central bank maintained its accommodative monetary policy. Growth is expected to slow to 1.1% in 2018 and further to 1.0% in 2019, down from 1.7% expansion in 2017 partly because of the impending consumption tax hike.

More prudent monetary policies have helped cut inflation in Tajikistan and Uzbekistan. GDP growth in several economies accelerated in the first half of 2018, outpacing their performance in the same period of last year. Growth in Armenia was the highest, reaching 8.3% on a sharp rise in investment and private consumption. Azerbaijan reversed contraction by 1.3% in the first half of 2017 to achieve 1.3% growth, with all sectors expanding and agriculture posting the largest increase.

Robust growth was observed in all five economies of East Asia in the first half of 2018. Consumption was a common major driver of growth, most especially in Hong Kong, China. Mongolia accelerated to 6.3% growth with mining investment as the main contributor. In the Republic of Korea (ROK), GDP grew moderately at 2.8% in the first half of 2018, matching the growth rate in the same period last year thanks to buoyant consumption and external demand. The projection for GDP growth in 2018 is revised upward for Hong Kong, China; Mongolia; and Taipei,China.

Economic growth in South Asia is generally upbeat. Bangladesh attained its highest rate of GDP growth in 47 years, estimated at 7.9% in fiscal year 2018 (FY2018, ended 30 June 2018) and propelled by a surge in private consumption. The same factor spurred 5.8% expansion in Pakistan in FY2018, the highest rate in 13 years. Meanwhile, GDP growth exceeded the *ADO 2018* projection in Nepal on government expenditure that exceeded expectations. Growth projections are revised down for Bhutan, with industry and tourism performing below expectations, and for Sri Lanka, where Q1 witnessed tightening government consumption, stagnant fixed investment, and lower net exports.

Growth momentum has been broadly maintained in Southeast Asia, with Viet Nam and Cambodia still the fastest growing economies. However, growth in six economies was slower than expected in the first half of 2018 as exports moderated and domestic demand weakened. Lower agricultural output subtracted from growth in the Philippines and Viet Nam. Meanwhile, Brunei Darussalam and Thailand grew faster than forecast. Higher oil prices spurred more investment in Brunei Darussalam to expand gas and oil production capacity. Thailand outperformed expectations on robust exports, buoyant domestic demand, and revived agriculture. Despite strong first-half export growth in Malaysia, a transition to a new government and a resulting shift in policy priorities put a damper on public and private investment. This was aggravated by weaker agriculture adversely affected by bad weather and falling international palm oil prices. Consumption in Malaysia will likely be spurred in Q3 of 2018 as a new sales and services tax replaces a broader goods and services tax following a 3-month sales tax holiday.

1.1.2 Demand-side contributions to growth, selected economies

- Private consumption
- Government consumption
- Total consumption
- Total investments
- Net exports
- Gross domestic product

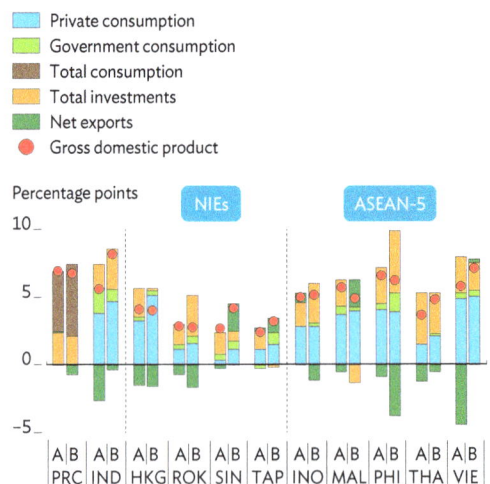

A = first half 2017, B = first half 2018, ASEAN-5 = five larger economies in the Association of Southeast Asian Nations (Indonesia, Malaysia, the Philippines, Thailand, Viet Nam), HKG = Hong Kong, China, IND = India, INO = Indonesia, MAL = Malaysia, NIE = newly industrialized economy, PHI = Philippines, PRC = People's Republic of China, ROK = Republic of Korea, SIN = Singapore, TAP = Taipei,China, THA = Thailand, VIE = Viet Nam.

Note: For India, data is for the first quarter (April–June) of the corresponding fiscal year.

Sources: Haver Analytics; CEIC Data Company (both accessed 17 September 2018); ADB estimates.

Growth in the Pacific has slumped because of weaker activity in Papua New Guinea (PNG) and Timor-Leste. Damage from a February 2018 earthquake in PNG turned out to be worse than initially estimated. Production of liquefied natural gas for export in 2018 is expected to be at least 10% lower than in 2017. Meanwhile, a decrease in public spending in Timor-Leste has adversely affected private consumption and commerce. The growth projection for Palau in FY2018 (ending 30 September 2018) is revised down because flights from Hong Kong, China and from Japan have been discontinued, causing visitor arrivals to drop. The outlook has improved, by contrast, for Solomon Islands, as logging, agriculture, and bauxite and nickel mining performed better than expected, and for Tuvalu, as windfall fishing license revenue is being used to finance fiscal stimulus this year.

Steady consumer and business expectations

Indicators at the sector level support the forecast for moderating economic growth in 2018 compared with 2017. The leading indicators among them show some dampening in recent months, which is consistent with a slightly more subdued economic growth forecast for developing Asia in 2019 than presented by the *ADO 2018* assessment in April.

Underlying robust consumption growth, retail sales in the region rose rapidly in Q1 of 2018 but declined in Q2 (Figure 1.1.3). Higher sales connected with festive holidays and booming e-commerce drove sales in East Asia. Strong consumer sentiment and buoyant inbound tourism, particularly from the PRC, provided an additional boost in Hong Kong, China. In Taipei,China this trend was combined with solid demand for vehicles, fuel, and information and communication devices, with the latter responding to aggressive promotions. A similar trend but at a lower trajectory was observed in the ROK, slowing slightly in Q2 as wavering confidence affected spending. The PRC experienced the opposite cycle. As consumers waited for import tax cuts to be implemented in July 2018, sales of cars; foodstuffs; and clothing, footwear, and accessories moderated. Sales of construction material grew more slowly with what was likely a delayed reaction to slower property sales growth.

As in East Asia, online purchases and spending on festival goods boosted Q1 sales in some Southeast Asia economies. Despite a very mild GDP growth slowdown, retail sales remained strong in Malaysia and Viet Nam because of improving incomes. In Thailand, strong retail sales could be traced to the entry of some large international retail chains. Retail sales exceeded expectations in Indonesia with higher

1.1.3 Retail sales, selected economies in developing Asia

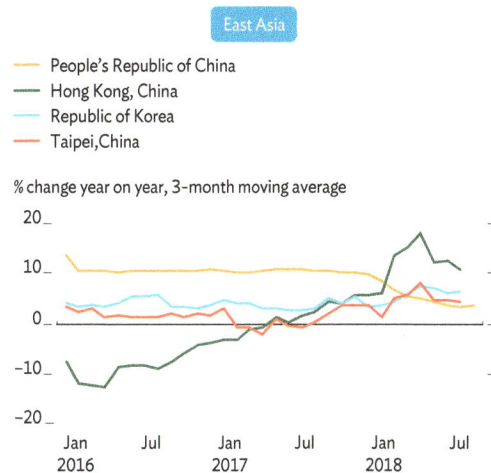

East Asia

— People's Republic of China
— Hong Kong, China
— Republic of Korea
— Taipei,China

% change year on year, 3-month moving average

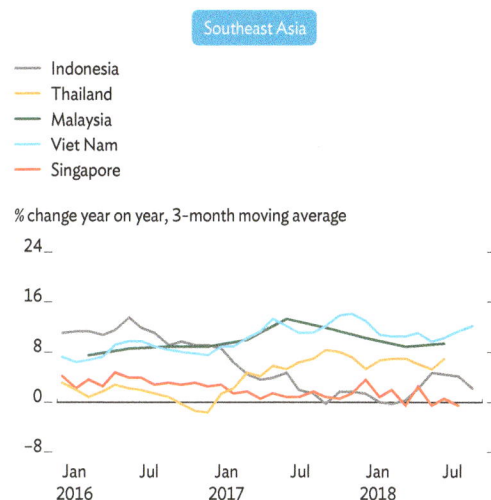

Southeast Asia

— Indonesia
— Thailand
— Malaysia
— Viet Nam
— Singapore

% change year on year, 3-month moving average

Note: Data for Malaysia are quarterly.
Source: Haver Analytics (accessed 17 September 2018).

purchases of fuel, and food sales received a significant boost from Ramadan. Retail sales fluctuated in Singapore as caution affected vehicle purchases amid rising global trade tensions.

Consumer confidence was mixed in the first 8 months of 2018 as the region's consumer outlook became clouded by the escalating US–PRC trade conflict and its spillover on domestic jobs and incomes. Confidence indexes in most economies remained in positive territory, indicating optimism. Malaysia and, to a lesser extent, Thailand saw improvement in confidence, largely reflecting internal factors, while consumers in the Philippines and the ROK became more pessimistic about prospects (Figure 1.1.4). In Malaysia, uncertainty connected with a national election was resolved in May with a change in government, causing the consumer index to soar to 133 in June, the highest in 21 years. Other contributory factors included bullish sentiment on the employment outlook and, as mentioned above, the 3-month sales tax holiday ahead of the change to a lower tax.

Meanwhile, consumer confidence has steadily strengthened in Thailand since July 2017, largely tracking rising growth in tourism. Indonesian consumer optimism is flat, by contrast, but remained in positive territory. In India, teething problems last year following demonetization late in 2016 are mostly resolved, and consumer confidence, though still in negative territory, continues to rise with improving sentiment, notably in rural households. In the Philippines, the confidence index improved in Q2 of 2018 in tandem with better household income, reversing declines in the previous 3 quarters. The index remains in negative territory, however, as concern over rising food prices continues to dampen sentiment.

Consumer confidence in East Asia took a turn toward pessimism in Q2 of 2018 as global trade tensions started to escalate. While the PRC consumer confidence index remains in optimistic territory, it has been falling since March 2018. One factor is consumer confidence shaken by trade tensions, and another is an increase in personal income tax that affected household real disposable income. Consumer confidence in Taipei,China strengthened in August 2018 relative to a year earlier but was down from the start of this year. Accommodative monetary policy and wages driven higher in a tightening labor market continue to support household spending. Consumer confidence in the ROK sank rapidly this year amid worsening unemployment and a falling stock market. The ROK is further affected by the intensifying trade conflict between the US and the PRC, its two largest trade partners, and geopolitical tensions between the US and the Democratic People's Republic of Korea.

1.1.4 Consumer confidence and expectations, selected economies in developing Asia

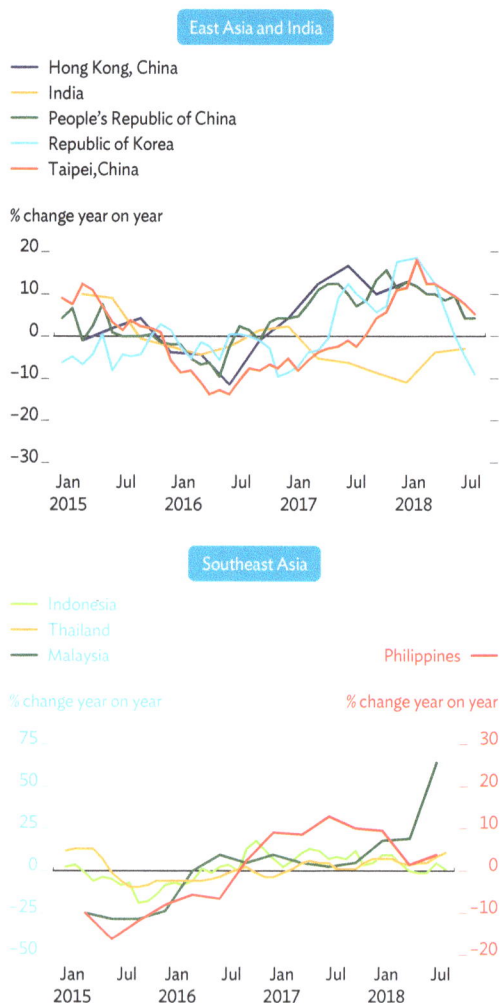

East Asia and India

— Hong Kong, China
— India
— People's Republic of China
— Republic of Korea
— Taipei,China

Southeast Asia

— Indonesia
— Thailand
— Malaysia
Philippines —

Note: A rating >100 indicates rising optimism, and a score <100 means deepening pessimism. Data for Hong Kong, China; India; Malaysia; and the Philippines are quarterly. Data for Hong Kong, China use January 2000 as the base year. For the Philippines, the index refers to consumer expectations, computed as the percentage of households that expressed a favorable view less the percentage that expressed an unfavorable view.

Sources: Haver Analytics; CEIC Data Company (both accessed 28 August 2018).

1.1.1 Markit purchasing managers' index

Economy	2017												2018					
	Q1			Q2			Q3			Q4			Q1			Q2		
Developing Asia																		
India	50.4	50.7	52.5	52.5	51.6	50.9	47.9	51.2	51.2	50.3	52.6	54.7	52.4	52.1	51.0	51.6	51.2	53.1
Indonesia	50.4	49.3	50.5	51.2	50.6	49.5	48.6	50.7	50.4	50.1	50.4	49.3	49.9	51.4	50.7	51.6	51.7	50.3
Malaysia	48.6	49.4	49.5	50.7	48.7	46.9	48.3	50.4	49.9	48.6	52.0	49.9	50.5	49.9	49.5	48.6	47.6	49.5
PRC	51.0	51.7	51.2	50.3	49.6	50.4	51.1	51.6	51.0	51.0	50.8	51.5	51.5	51.6	51.0	51.1	51.1	51.0
Philippines	52.7	53.6	53.8	53.3	54.3	53.9	52.8	50.6	50.8	53.7	54.8	54.2	51.7	50.8	51.5	52.7	53.7	52.9
Rep. of Korea	49.0	49.2	48.4	49.4	49.2	50.1	49.1	49.9	50.6	50.2	51.2	49.9	50.7	50.3	49.1	48.4	48.9	49.8
Taipei,China	55.6	54.5	56.2	54.4	53.1	53.3	53.6	54.3	54.2	53.6	56.3	56.6	56.9	56.0	55.3	54.8	53.4	54.5
Thailand	50.6	50.6	50.2	49.8	49.7	50.4	49.6	49.5	50.3	49.8	50.0	50.4	50.6	50.9	49.1	49.5	51.1	50.2
Viet Nam	51.9	54.2	54.6	54.1	51.6	52.5	51.7	51.8	53.3	51.6	51.4	52.5	53.4	53.5	51.6	52.7	53.9	55.7

PRC = People's Republic of China, Q = quarter.

Note: Pink to red indicates contraction (<50). White to green indicates expansion (>50).

Source: Bloomberg (accessed 14 September 2018).

Better business conditions are reflected in the Markit purchasing managers' index (PMI), which remained above 50 in seven of nine economies in developing Asia in Q2 of 2018 (Table 1.1.1). Viet Nam was the top performer, with a PMI consistently above the 50 threshold since January 2016 and improving throughout 2018. Its reading of 55.7 in June 2018 reflected high manufacturing output, notably in the export-oriented telecommunications, electronics, and textile industries. The indexes of Malaysia and the ROK stayed below 50 in most months in 2018. Malaysia's performance improved somewhat as performance in manufacturing, mining and quarrying, and construction became less sluggish. In the ROK, manufacturing growth eased as higher input costs constrained production. Data to June show sales picking up in that month without noticeable impact from the trade conflict, though this may change in the next few months as the PMI is a leading indicator of business plans. However, some early signs of weakness are evident in the PRC, which has data beyond June. The Caixin China General Manufacturing PMI fell to a 14-month low of 50.6 in August 2018 from 50.8 in the previous month, as new export orders shrank for the fifth month in a row.

The monthly industrial production index rose in 2018 for members of the Association of Southeast Asian Nations (ASEAN), particularly Viet Nam, and NIEs, particularly Hong Kong, China (Figure 1.1.5). The index for the Philippines posted a sharp recovery to 16.4% in June from a large drop in December 2017 powered by strength in construction and continuing growth in manufacturing. Meanwhile, the index for the ROK languishes on the low side because of sluggish manufacturing.

Domestic demand drives growth in India and the People's Republic of China

Recent growth trends in India and the PRC have moved very much as expected, with domestic consumption, particularly services, as the largest contributors to growth. On the supply side, industrial production grew at a rate above 6% in both countries in July, suggesting that production remains healthy (Figure 1.1.5). Although the growth outlook for 2018 remains roughly the same as in *ADO 2018*, at 6.6% for the PRC and 7.3% for India, external developments pose some challenges ahead.

The main challenge facing India is depreciation of the rupee coupled with accelerated inflation with high oil prices, and for the PRC it is the trade conflict with the US. Export growth and the PMI, a leading indicator, suggest that growth should be steady, though early reports suggest some dampening of the PMI for the PRC in Q2 of 2018 (Figure 1.1.6). Structural reform will continue to deepen in both economies, albeit gradually. The robust growth pickup in India so far this year suggests resolution of the problems from demonetization in 2016 and the implementation of the goods and services tax in 2017.

Growth is recovering strongly in India, accelerating to 8.2% in Q1 of fiscal year 2018 (April–June 2018) on improved domestic demand and aided by reduced drag from net exports. Investment grew by 10% mostly on growth in infrastructure and housing construction and a better business environment, as reflected by improvement in "doing business" rankings, which fueled a sharp rise in net foreign direct investment (FDI) by 38% in the first half. In general, those worst affected by the shocks of demonetization (such as cash-dependent rural areas) and the introduction of the goods and services tax (manufacturers) have recovered well. Nonetheless, inflation, both headline and core, has risen steadily, with headline inflation exceeding the central bank's medium-term target of 4%.

With healthy growth, the goods and services tax firmly on track, progress on the bankruptcy code, and some deleveraging by state-owned enterprises, domestic factors now support sustained growth, putting India firmly on track to grow by 7.3% in 2018. The schedule for medium-term fiscal consolidation has been stretched slightly, now targeting a reduction of the budget deficit to 3.3% of GDP instead of 3.0%, but the effort is still moving in the right direction. Growth in exports, notably of manufacturing goods, grew by 10%. India got caught in the trade conflict as the US levied a tariff on its steel exports, and it retaliated in kind, but the impact on economic growth will be minimal.

1.1.5 Industrial production indexes

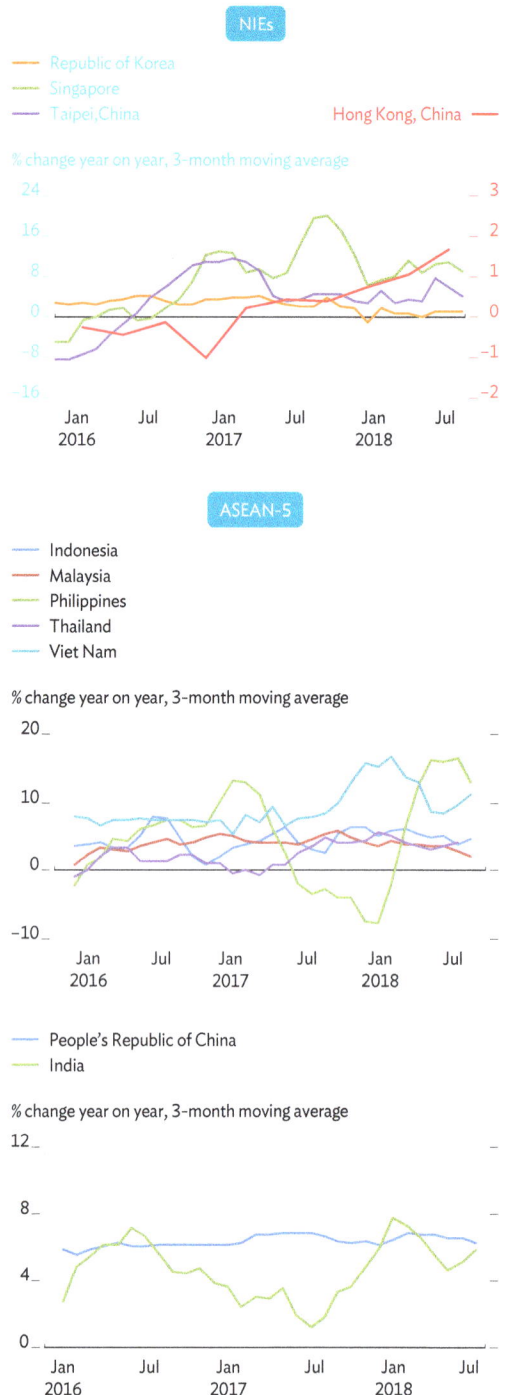

NIEs

Republic of Korea
Singapore
Taipei,China   Hong Kong, China

% change year on year, 3-month moving average

ASEAN-5

Indonesia
Malaysia
Philippines
Thailand
Viet Nam

% change year on year, 3-month moving average

People's Republic of China
India

% change year on year, 3-month moving average

ASEAN-5 = five larger economies in the Association of Southeast Asian Nations (Indonesia, Malaysia, the Philippines, Thailand, Viet Nam), NIE = newly industrialized economy.
Note: Data for Hong Kong, China and Malaysia are quarterly.
Sources: CEIC Data Company; Haver Analytics (both accessed 17 September 2018).

Domestic demand will remain the driver of growth this year, particularly in rural areas. Despite an uptick of inflation, proactive adjustments to monetary policy and the consolidation of fiscal policy will help quell any inflationary pressures that may arise.

The PRC continues its gradual economic restructuring away from industry and toward services. The service sector was again the main growth driver in the first half of 2018 with 7.6% growth year on year, though marginally down from 7.7% a year earlier. Strong increases in consumer and high-tech manufacturing, and in manufacturing for export, partly offset deceleration in mining and raw materials, where production was subject to retrenchment targets. On the demand side, consumption remained, in line with *ADO 2018* projections, the major driver of growth in the first half of 2018 as growth in household consumption accelerated to 6.7% from 6.1% a year earlier. As anticipated in *ADO 2018*, investment growth weakened further in the first half of 2018, contributing only 2.1 percentage points to growth, or 0.3 points less than in the same period of 2017. Net exports dragged on growth amid high consumption demand. Meanwhile, financial reform continued on track. The Ministry of Finance proposed in June 2018 an amendment to the personal income tax law that would adjust tax brackets upward, raise the standard personal allowance, and allow additional specified deductions. The proposed amendment aims to encourage private consumption in the short run and, over the longer run, help alleviate income inequality.

The softening GDP growth trend in Q2 of 2018 is expected to continue in the second half of 2018, given a downtrend in the housing market, ongoing tight conditions for nonbank lending, and lower export growth relative to imports. However, supportive monetary and fiscal policies are likely to mitigate the impact of these factors. Consumption will remain the main driver of growth in 2018 and 2019 with solid wage growth in a tight market for skilled blue-collar workers, resilient consumer confidence reinforced by a reduced personal income tax burden, and higher government spending on social priorities. In heavy industry, excess capacity and high debt will continue to limit investment, while investment in services and in emerging and consumer-oriented industries is expected to persist.

Net exports are now forecast to drag on GDP growth in both 2018 and 2019, given the trade conflict with the US and worsening impediments to global trade and investment. The adverse impact of US tariffs on PRC exports will likely be mitigated by a weaker renminbi and/or lower profit margins for producers and exporters. The government announced in July 2018 fiscal measures including the speeding up of special bond issuance and, to counteract the dampening effect of

1.1.6 Production indicators

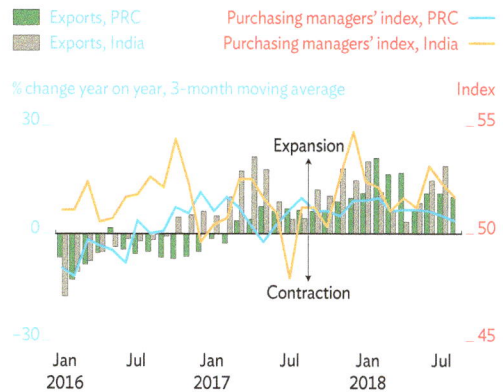

PRC = People's Republic of China.

Note: A survey reading of >50 for the purchasing managers' index shows expansion and <50 contraction.

Source: CEIC Data Company (accessed 12 September 2018).

tariffs on trade, a reduction in taxes and fees for businesses. This development and the reduced personal tax burden indicate that fiscal policy will be more expansionary in the remainder of 2018.

Subregional growth mostly on track

While *ADO 2018* growth forecasts for most subregions are broadly maintained, there is less certainty about the sustainability of the growth outlook. Growth varies across regions. Forecasts are largely retained for East Asia and South Asia but downgraded for Southeast Asia and the Pacific. Central Asia is the only region with an upgraded forecast, in line with acceleration in Armenia, Georgia, and especially Kazakhstan, the subregion's largest economy. Higher oil prices should benefit oil-exporting economies, but expansion in Azerbaijan, Turkmenistan, and Uzbekistan is constrained by lower domestic demand, water deficits, and the lingering impact of currency devaluation from last year. The growth forecast for the subregion as a whole improves slightly in 2018 to 4.1% from 4.0% forecast in *ADO 2018* and is maintained at 4.2% for 2019.

The outlook for growth in East Asia is unchanged from April, at 6.0% this year and 5.7% next, mirroring the forecast for the PRC. The PRC is likely to meet its growth target of 6.6% in 2018, as forecast in April, then slow slightly more than earlier forecast to 6.3% growth in 2019, when it will face ever stiffer headwinds from US tariffs on its exports. The US–PRC trade conflict is expected to spill over into the rest of the subregion, but accommodative monetary and fiscal policies and resultingly strong domestic demand will serve as cushions. As exports have held up despite global trade friction, growth forecasts are upgraded for Hong Kong, China; Mongolia; and Taipei,China, but not for the ROK, where they are slightly downgraded.

South Asia is similarly on track to meet the 7.0% subregional growth forecast in *ADO 2018* with continued recovery in India, and to accelerate as forecast to 7.2% in 2019 with faster expansion in the rest of the region. Continued expansion in manufacturing and construction supports the earlier 7.6% growth forecast for these sectors this year. Growth forecasts for Bangladesh, Nepal, and Pakistan are upgraded on higher domestic demand and supportive government policies, including currency devaluation and, in Pakistan, the imposition of new tariffs on imported goods. Meanwhile, the growth forecast for Pakistan in 2019 is downgraded in light of a pressing need to deal with large budget and external imbalances. Meanwhile, the Sri Lanka growth forecast is downgraded for both this year and next on weak investment and exports, and as the government implements structural reform to lift its fiscal performance.

Growth in Southeast Asia is now forecast to dip to 5.1% in 2018, not sustaining the 2017 growth rate of 5.2% as projected in *ADO 2018* with 6 of 10 subregional economies underperforming April forecasts. Domestic factors will deduct from growth in some of the bigger economies, but exports are likely to hold up well on surprisingly resilient demand for electronics and higher oil prices. The subregion occupies with East Asia the heart of global value chains for electronics, and many Southeast Asia economies compete directly with the PRC in various manufacturing capacities. Energy-exporters should benefit from a pickup in global commodity prices. Meanwhile, private consumption and public spending on infrastructure will add to growth, particularly in Malaysia, the Philippines, and Thailand. The growth forecast for the subregion is retained at 5.2% in 2019 as growth in Indonesia, Thailand, and Viet Nam picks up.

The Pacific is now projected to grow by 1.1% in 2018 and 3.1% in 2019. The revised forecast for 2018 is lower by half from the forecast in *ADO 2018* because of weaker prospects for Papua New Guinea (PNG) following an earthquake in February and for Timor-Leste. Conversely, the 2018 outlook for Solomon Islands and Tuvalu is upgraded on better logging, agriculture, and mining output. Looking ahead to 2019, the aggregate forecast for the Pacific is upgraded to 3.1% from 3.0% in *ADO 2018* as recovery in production of liquefied natural gas and reconstruction should improve growth in PNG, and despite lower forecasts for Palau and Timor-Leste.

Inflation pressures tempered

Regional inflation in the first 7 months of 2018 soared on external and domestic factors but remained broadly stable and below 3% (Figure 1.1.7). A combination of higher global oil prices (see the Annex), weaker local currencies, food supply disruptions, and domestic factors helped to push prices up in some economies, while increased domestic activity and rising wages added to price pressures in others.

In Central Asia, inflation was lowest in Azerbaijan and the Kyrgyz Republic thanks to stabilized currencies, and in Georgia and Armenia with lower food prices. The receding impact of earlier excise tax hikes kept prices hikes below those in 2017 in Georgia, while currency appreciation in early 2018 helped to contain imported inflation in Kazakhstan. In East Asia, higher oil prices and inflation expectations raised prices in Taipei,China, while higher prices for food, electricity, gas, and water pushed up prices in Hong Kong, China. Inflation also picked up in the PRC as food prices recovered from a decline in 2017, but it remained below target.

1.1.7 Inflation forecasts in *ADO 2018 Update* versus year-to-date results

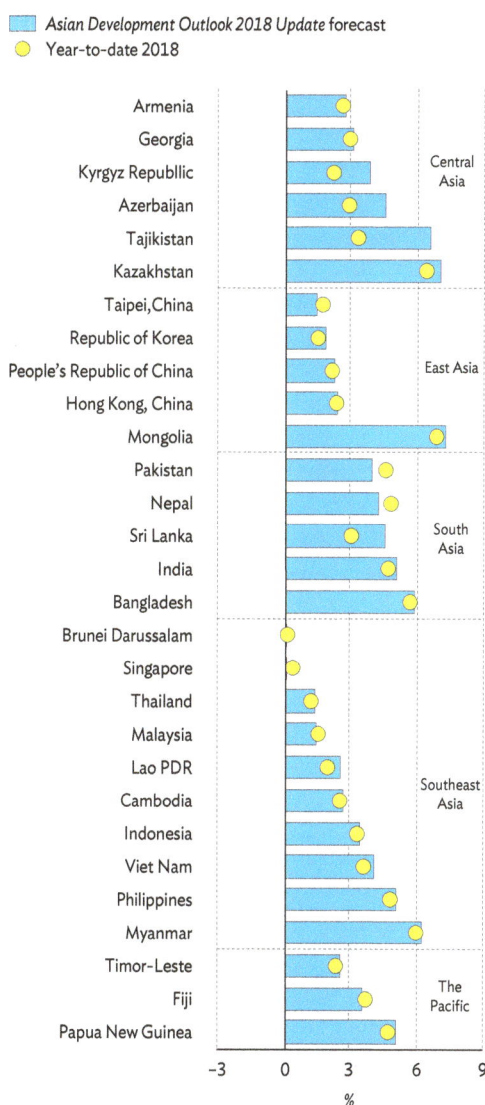

Lao PDR = Lao People's Democratic Republic.
Source: *Asian Development Outlook* database.

Inflation rates in Southeast Asia are mostly stable, except in the Philippines, where the rate more than doubled to 6.4% in the first 8 months of 2018. A confluence there of cost-push factors—mainly elevated oil prices, food supply disruptions, and a new tax reform program—drove transport, electricity, and food prices higher. By contrast, inflation in Malaysia reached record lows with the reintroduction of fuel subsidies and a 3-month tax holiday following the suspension in June of a 6% goods and services tax and before its replacement by a lower sales and services tax. Tighter monetary policy kept prices contained in Indonesia, which has accommodated a policy rate rise by 125 basis points since January 2018. In South Asia, inflation has quickened to reach a 4-year high in Pakistan and a 2-year high in India, driven by rising oil and food prices. Both economies are big oil importers, and the depreciation of their currencies against the US dollar has caused oil import costs to surge. By contrast, inflation moderated in Sri Lanka with easing food prices and the statistical base effect from last year's high prices. Inflation in the Pacific has accelerated on higher oil prices.

As global economic activity remained strong and geopolitical developments caused some volatility in oil prices and financial markets, the price of Brent crude oil reached $80.9 per barrel on 25 September 2018, the highest in 46 months. The region is also beset by widespread currency depreciation against the US dollar, with rising US interest rates further motivating some important capital outflows, notably from Indonesia and the Philippines. Foreign currency reserves have fallen precipitously in Pakistan. Depreciation may create upward pressure on prices, but exchange rates in Asia have moved much less in effective terms. Adjusted for depreciation against the currencies of trade partners, currency values have remained mostly stable, except possibly in India, Indonesia, and the Philippines (Figure 1.1.8). The currencies of most Pacific countries are tied to the Australian dollar, which has appreciated against the US dollar. Despite higher inflation, real effective exchange rates have not changed much since the beginning of the year compared with nominal effective exchange rates because inflation gaps across trade partners have not widened notably (Figure 1.1.9). Some countries have responded with tighter monetary policy, while others have made exchange rates more flexible (Table 1.1.2). These factors and the impact of rising demand and of food supply disruptions prompt upward revisions to inflation forecast for a number of countries.

1.1.8 Local currency movements against the US dollar

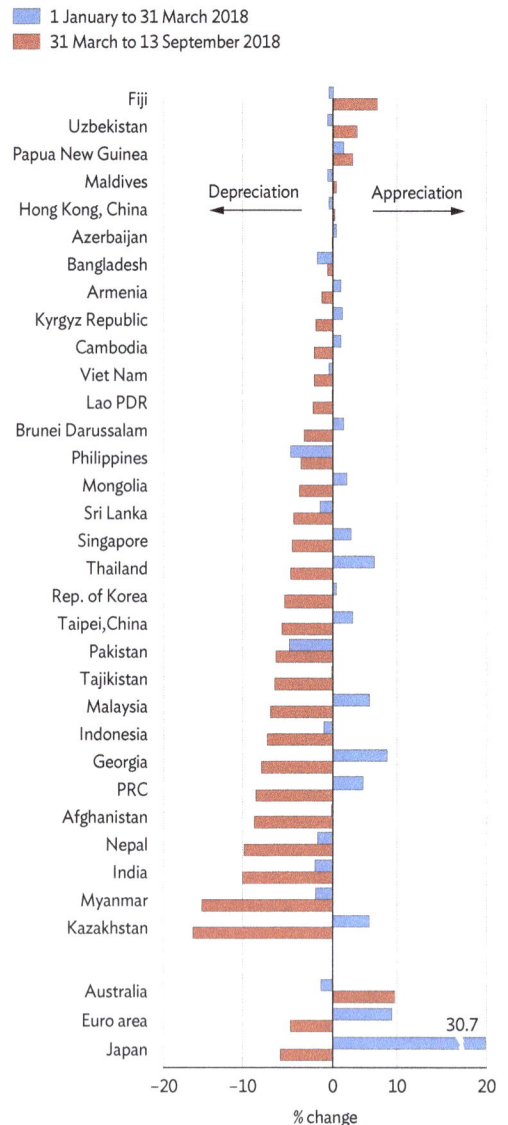

Lao PDR = Lao People's Democratic Republic, PRC = People's Republic of China.
Source: Bloomberg (accessed 19 September 2018).

1.1.9 Effective exchange rate movements

— Hong Kong, China	— Indonesia
— Republic of Korea	— Malaysia
— Singapore	— Philippines
— Taipei,China	— Thailand

— People's Republic of China
— India

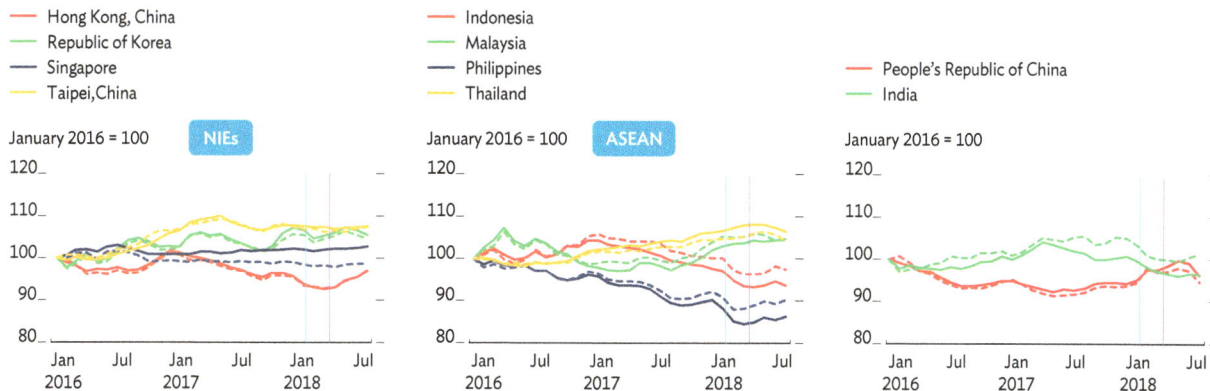

ASEAN = Association of Southeast Asian Nations, NIE = newly industrialized economy.

Notes: Broken lines refer to real effective exchange rates and solid lines refer to nominal effective exchange rates. Vertical blue lines refer to 22 January 2018, when the US imposed 30% tariff on imports of solar panels and 20% taxes on imports of washing machines. Vertical violet lines refer to 23 March 2018, when the US imposed additional 25% tariffs on steel and 10% tariffs on aluminum imports.

Sources: CEIC Data Company; Haver Analytics (both accessed 17 September 2018).

Domestic factors such as a tax holiday in Malaysia, currency stabilization and the reinstatement of fuel subsidies in Azerbaijan and Uzbekistan, the fading impact of previously introduced taxes in India, and other price-control measures in various countries have quelled inflationary pressures. Yet external pressures are stronger.

Inflation across the region is now expected to be 0.1 percentage points lower than forecast in *ADO 2018*, rising from 2.2% in 2017 to 2.8% in 2018 and 2019 (Figure 1.1.10). Regional inflation thus remains firmly below the 10-year average of 3.7%, but fluctuations in financial and currency markets are likely to occur given global uncertainty, requiring vigilance on the part of monetary authorities.

The inflation forecast for Central Asia is trimmed from 8.5% to 8.4% in 2018 and from 7.9% to 7.7% in 2019, reflecting slower inflation in most economies in the first half of 2018. In Uzbekistan, continued tight monetary policy and exchange rate interventions will contain inflation, while in Turkmenistan cuts in subsidies, higher imported prices, and expansionary credit policy necessitated upward changes to inflation forecasts.

Inflation in East Asia is now expected to be lower than forecast, reflecting moderating prices for food and downward revisions for the PRC. Expectations of weaker GDP growth and moderate pass-through of the renminbi depreciation are prompting downward revision to projected inflation in the PRC to 2.2% in both 2018 and 2019, still up from 1.6% in 2017. Inflation forecast downgrades for Indonesia and Malaysia prompt the same for the Southeast Asia

1.1.10 Subregional inflation

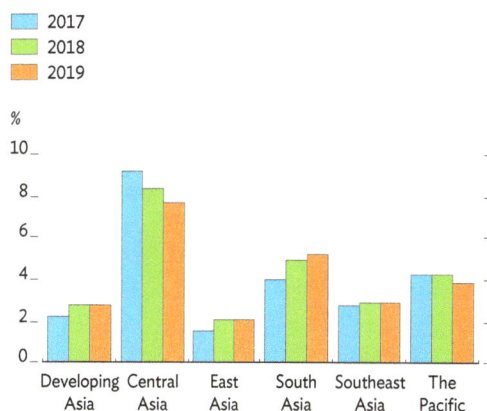

Source: *Asian Development Outlook* database.

1.1.2 Policy and exchange rates, selected economies in developing Asia

Economy	Policy rate (as of 19 September 2018)			Exchange rate		
	% per annum	Date of decision	% change since January 2018	LCU/$ as of 1 January 2018	LCU/$ as of 19 September 2018	% change (1 January 2018 vs 19 September 2018)
Malaysia	3.25	25 January 2018	0.25	4.000	4.1	−2.4
Philippines	4.00	9 August 2018	1.00	49.900	54.1	−7.7
People's Republic of China	4.35	23 October 2015	0.00	6.500	6.9	−5.7
Indonesia	5.50	15 August 2018	1.25	13,568.000	14,896.0	−8.9
Japan	−0.10	19 September 2018	0.00	112.600	112.3	0.3
Republic of Korea	1.50	30 November 2017	0.00	1,070.700	1,121.6	−4.5
Thailand	1.50	19 September 2018	0.00	32.600	32.6	−0.1
India	6.50	1 August 2018	0.50	63.675	72.7	−12.4
Pakistan	7.50	16 July 2018	1.75	110.310	124.2	−11.2
Sri Lanka	8.50	4 April 2018	−0.25	153.500	165.6	−7.3

LCU = local currency unit.

Sources: CEIC Data Company; Bloomberg (both accessed 24 September 2018).

subregion, by 0.1 percentage points to 2.9% in both 2018 and 2019. With continued depreciation of local currencies in the subregion, imports may put upward pressure on inflation this year and next, but this will likely be tempered by countercyclical monetary policies and government support measures.

In South Asia, the projection for inflation in India in 2018 is revised up—in response to higher global oil prices and government procurement prices and to currency depreciation—by 0.4 percentage points to 5.0%, which is also the retained forecast for 2019. Forecasts for 2018 are revised down for every other economy in the subregion. Such is the weight of India in South Asia that the subregional inflation forecast for 2018 is raised by 0.2 percentage points to 4.9%. The subregional forecast for 2019 is raised from 5.1% in *ADO 2018* to 5.2%.

An upward revision to the 2018 inflation forecast for the Pacific reflects higher inflation in Fiji with increased taxes on alcohol and tobacco, local food supply bottlenecks in Tonga in the aftermath of Tropical Cyclone Gita, and the pass-through of higher global food and fuel prices in Kiribati, Samoa, and Tuvalu. Inflation forecasts for PNG and Timor-Leste are retained, with inflation in PNG remaining elevated at 5.0% this year and 4.5% next year but much lower in Timor-Leste, at 2.0% in 2018 rising to 3.0% in 2019.

Continued export growth in the wake of the trade conflict

Growth in external demand is expected to remain robust to the forecast horizon following a surprisingly sharp upswing in 2017. So far in 2018, both exports and imports have held up very well, with continued double-digit growth in many economies. Going forward, there is heightened uncertainty about the external environment and perhaps some early signs of the dampening impact on business sentiment from the intensifying US–PRC trade conflict.

Export growth remains positive

Exports and imports continued to grow by double digits in January–July 2018 as tailwinds from the strong global economy in 2017 provided demand momentum. The largest percentage increases came in commodity exporters. Growth in the 11 largest economies has been steady for almost 3 years (Figure 1.1.11). In the PRC and many ASEAN economies, the pickup reflected strong momentum derived from double-digit trade growth in the latter part of 2017. Growth in the PRC was steady for almost a year before it started slowing in March, while Indian export growth has fluctuated with a rebound in Q2, averaging healthy 11% growth for about 2 years. In the NIEs and the ASEAN-5, the annual export growth rate moderated slightly in the year to July, but exports still grew on average by 9% in the NIEs and 13% in the ASEAN-5.

Growth in exports and imports in 2018 remains broad-based and synchronized across regional economies (Figure 1.1.12). Some of the growth in exports in the first half of 2018 reflected recovery in business sentiment from one-off events in the first half of 2017, including political uncertainty in the ROK, seasonal impacts on retail sales in Indonesia, and a mining slowdown in Viet Nam. The Philippines, by contrast, saw exports decline by 3% in the year to date with moderation in demand for electronics and contraction in agricultural production and exports. The largest percentage increases were in commodity exporters, particularly Azerbaijan and Mongolia, as export prices improved. With respect to nominal growth in imports, high oil prices factored in on the upside and nominal currency depreciation against the dollar on the downside. The result has been import growth even stronger than export growth. In Cambodia, India, and Viet Nam, import growth to July doubled over the same period in 2017.

In real terms, the exports of the largest 12 economies, which accounted for 97% of all exports, grew by 5.0% in the first half of 2018, marginally down from 5.1% in the same period in 2017 (Figure 1.1.13), suggesting that trade growth

1.1.11 Export growth, selected economies

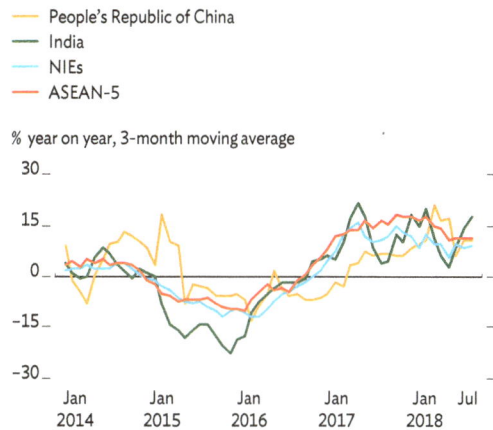

— People's Republic of China
— India
— NIEs
— ASEAN-5

% year on year, 3-month moving average

ASEAN-5 = five larger economies in the Association of Southeast Asian Nations (Indonesia, Malaysia, the Philippines, Thailand, Viet Nam), NIE = newly industrialized economy.

Note: Newly industrialized economies are Hong Kong, China; the Republic of Korea; Singapore; and Taipei,China.

Source: CEIC Data Company (accessed 11 September 2018).

1.1.12 Merchandise trade, selected economies

- 2016
- January to July 2017
- January to July 2018

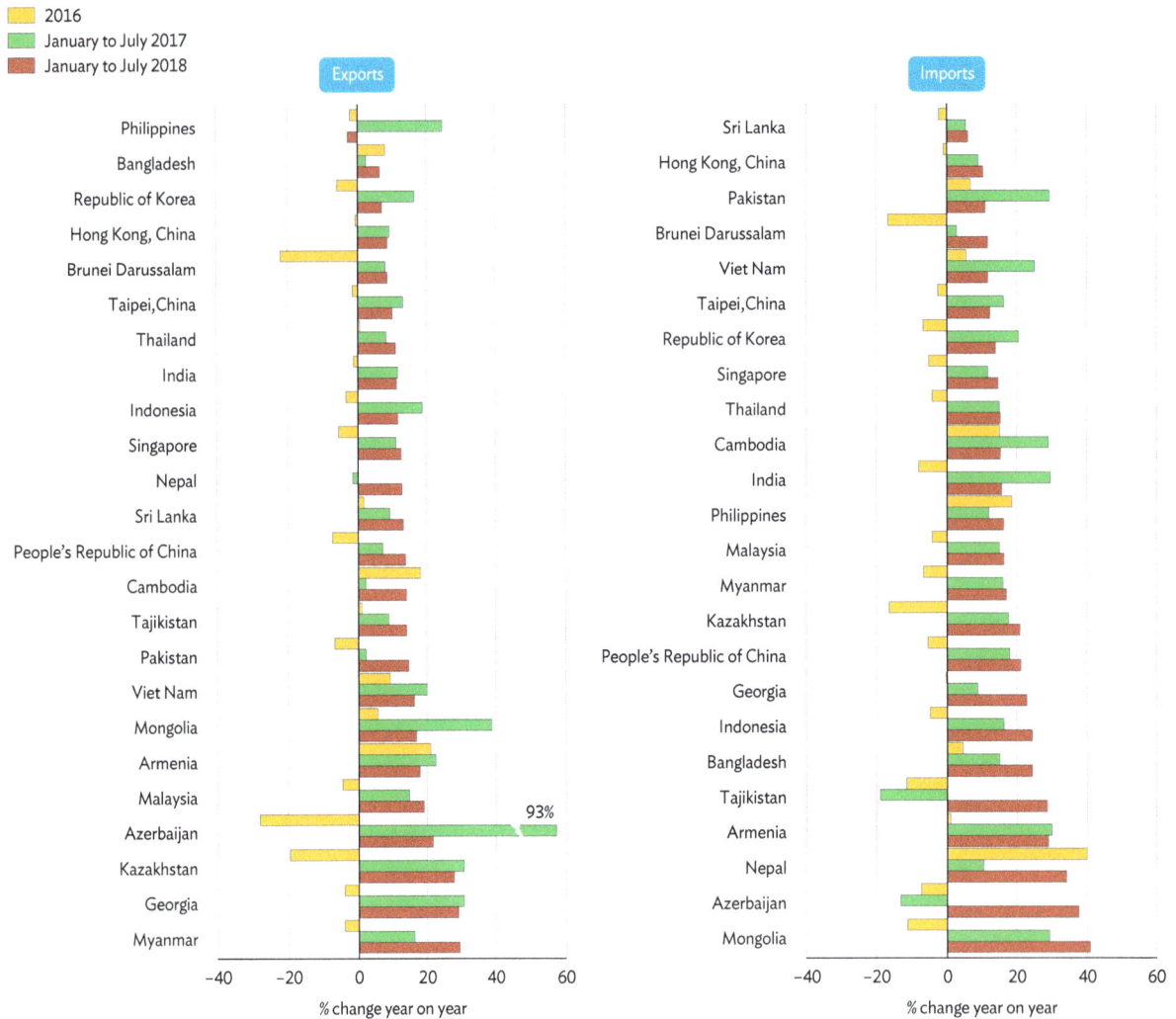

Exports

Imports

Philippines
Bangladesh
Republic of Korea
Hong Kong, China
Brunei Darussalam
Taipei,China
Thailand
India
Indonesia
Singapore
Nepal
Sri Lanka
People's Republic of China
Cambodia
Tajikistan
Pakistan
Viet Nam
Mongolia
Armenia
Malaysia
Azerbaijan
Kazakhstan
Georgia
Myanmar

93%

% change year on year

Sri Lanka
Hong Kong, China
Pakistan
Brunei Darussalam
Viet Nam
Taipei,China
Republic of Korea
Singapore
Thailand
Cambodia
India
Philippines
Malaysia
Myanmar
Kazakhstan
People's Republic of China
Georgia
Indonesia
Bangladesh
Tajikistan
Armenia
Nepal
Azerbaijan
Mongolia

% change year on year

Sources: CEIC Data Company; Haver Analytics (both accessed 11 September 2018).

1.1.13 Growth in export and import volume, selected regions

- Advanced economies
- Central and Eastern Europe
- Selected developing Asia
- World

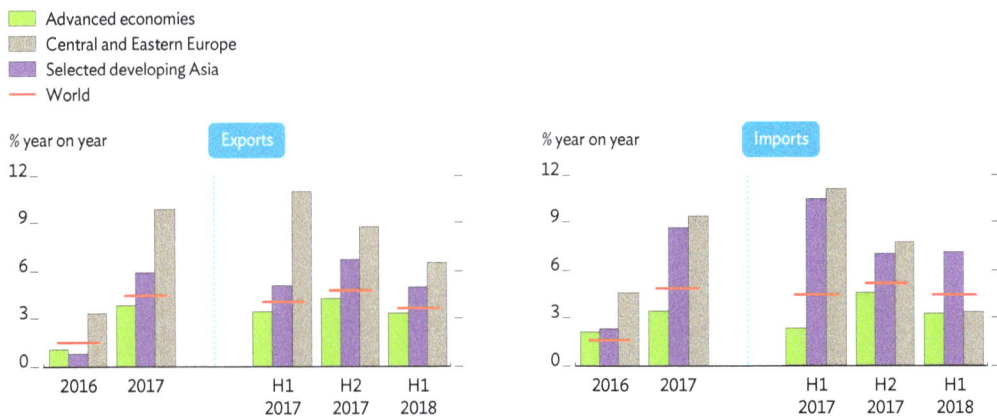

% year on year

Exports

% year on year

Imports

2016   2017   H1   H2   H1
                   2017 2017 2018

2016   2017   H1   H2   H1
                   2017 2017 2018

H = half.

Notes: Both exports and imports by volume are indexed to 2010 (2010 = 100). The advanced economies are Australia, Bulgaria, Canada, Croatia, the Czech Republic, Denmark, the euro area, Hungary, Iceland, Japan, New Zealand, Norway, Poland, the former Yugoslav Republic of Macedonia, Romania, Sweden, Switzerland, Turkey, the United Kingdom, and the US. The selected economies in developing Asia are Hong Kong, China; India; Indonesia; Malaysia; Pakistan; the People's Republic of China; the Philippines; the Republic of Korea; Singapore; Taipei,China; Thailand; and Viet Nam. Central and Eastern Europe include Belarus, Kazakhstan, the Russian Federation, and Ukraine.

Source: CPB Netherlands Bureau for Economic Policy Analysis. Available: https://www.cpb.nl/en/worldtrademonitor (accessed 16 September 2018).

remains strong despite exchange rate and price volatility. Import volumes also grew strongly, by 7.2%, though somewhat less than 10.5% growth in the same period of the previous year. In sum, trade growth continues with only slightly less momentum.

Early effects of the trade conflict

With only 1 month of data available since the ramping up in July of bilateral measures in the trade conflict between the US and the PRC, there is not yet any sign of falling exports. PRC export growth even accelerated slightly in July. However, survey reports and shipping data suggest that merchants have frontloaded trade, particularly imports of raw materials to the US and imports of soybeans and components to the PRC, ahead of tariff imposition dates. The frontloading of exports and imports was also reported in Hong Kong, China and in Malaysia.

Paradoxically, developing Asia's trade surplus with the US widened in the first 5 months of 2018, an unexpected consequence of greatly expansive fiscal policy in the US. Growth in imports from the US was 10.9% year on year (many of them going to Central Asia), decelerating from 18.9% in same period of 2017. In contrast, exports to the US grew by 10.9%, up from 7.7% growth in the previous year. Some of this growth could have been frontloading, but it is also consistent with the depreciation of most major currencies against the dollar (Figure 1.1.8). It is noteworthy as well that imports from other advanced economies accelerated slightly.

Very recently, signs of trade conflict effects are creeping into the data. Manufacturing in the PRC grew in August at its slowest pace in more than a year, with export orders shrinking for a fifth month, and the PRC manufacturing purchasing managers' index fell in August to its weakest reading since June 2017. Growth in Indian manufacturing unexpectedly slowed in August, suggesting a slight loss of momentum in an economy that had expanded in the April–June quarter at its fastest pace in more than 2 years. In the ROK, factory activity contracted in August for a sixth consecutive month as export orders shrank for the first time in 3 months. The PRC is expected to report low investment growth and weak retail sales in August, reinforcing views that domestic demand is vulnerable to US trade pressure. It is difficult to tell, however, whether it is a lull after the frontloading of trade in June and early July or the beginning of subdued consumer and business confidence brought about by the trade conflict.

Moreover, it is still too early to gauge when and how strongly the effect of the tariffs will show up in US data. As of the end of September, the US has levied tariffs on $298 billion worth of imports, equal to 1.3% of GDP, but as of

July, US purchasing managers' indexes, retail data, and business confidence indexes remained strong. However, retail sales in August showed some weakness, and, despite strong overall job numbers in August, employment in sectors affected by tariffs came in worse than expected. The auto industry, which is particularly exposed to trade, eliminated 4,900 jobs in August after cutting 3,500 in July. Soybean farmers have reported expected losses and complained in surveys that the loss of contracts with PRC importers threatens to create a serious economic dent.

Another early sign of the trade conflict would be the postponing of investment plans in response to lower business confidence. FDI flows had reportedly fallen for more than a year as of Q1 of 2018, while FDI in high-tech sectors, the original target of US grievances, continues to be restricted everywhere. However, the indirect impact on FDI from the trade conflict is likely to be worse than the direct restrictions imposed so far (Box 1.1.2).

Finally, fallout from the trade conflict has been evident in Asian financial markets. Lower business and consumer confidence because of concerns about global trade can adversely affect financial markets, which in turn can further dent economic activity. Empirical evidence shows that stock returns are significantly affected by announcements about key macroeconomic indicators such as GDP growth, inflation, unemployment, and trade balances. Indeed, as a result of trade tensions and other factors including deleveraging measures, the PRC stock market lost 17.6% of its value in 2018 to 25 September, with the SSE Composite Index declining from 3,369.1 on 3 January to 2,777.2.

Financial markets in Asia and elsewhere have nevertheless remained calm, as measured by the volatility index of the Chicago Board Options Exchange, though history has shown that calm can vanish very quickly if uncertainty becomes reflected in market activity. An analysis using a generalized autoregressive conditional heteroskedasticity model of stock market movements found that trade tension news from 18 July 2017 to 17 July 2018 had a statistically significant negative impact on returns in most Asian stock markets (ADB 2018a). Specifically, analysis indicated an abnormal return of –0.37% in the PRC, while stock indexes in Japan, Malaysia, the Republic of Korea, and Singapore witnessed abnormal and statistically significant returns ranging from –0.32% to –0.49% around the implementation date, when trade restrictions were confirmed, but not around the announcement date, when there was still uncertainty regarding the timing of implementation (Table 1.1.3).

1.1.3 Stock market reaction to trade tension news

Markets	Announcement date	Implementation date
Developed markets		
United States	–0.08	0.16
European Union	0.11	0.14
Japan	–0.15	–0.43
Selected developing Asian markets		
PRC	–0.41	–0.37
Indonesia	–0.03	0.02
Hong Kong, China	–0.51	–0.23
Republic of Korea	–0.30	–0.46
Malaysia	–0.49	–0.49
Philippines	–0.58	–0.04
Singapore	–0.34	–0.32
Thailand	–0.13	0.11

PRC = People's Republic of China.

Notes: Cells highlighted in green represent statistical significance at 1%, orange at 5%, and blue at 10%. Stock indexes used in this estimate include the Standard and Poor's 500 Index for the United States, STOXX Europe 600 for Europe, Nikkei 300 Index for Japan, CSI 300 Index for the People's Republic of China, KOSPI Index for the Republic of Korea, Jakarta Composite Stock Price Index for Indonesia, FTSE Bursa Malaysia KLCI Index for Malaysia, Philippine Stock Exchange PSE Index for the Philippines, Straits Times Index for Singapore, and Bangkok SET Index for Thailand.

Sources: Bloomberg (accessed 1 August 2018); ADB estimates.

1.1.2 Is the trade conflict affecting foreign direct investment?

FDI flows have abated since 2016, particularly flows between the US and the PRC. Data for 2017 show inward FDI to developing Asia down by 38.9% from 2016, and FDI into the PRC growing by a meager 3.6% while greenfield FDI fell by 13.7%. In 2017, 19% of FDI from the US went to developing Asia, with 5% going to the PRC. Most of it went into machinery and equipment manufacturing and into business services directly connected with the electrical and electronics equipment trade (though investment in oil and gas in Central Asia was also prominent). Conversely, the PRC, which spent an amount equal to only 0.2% of its GDP on FDI in the past 5 years, sent 9% of its FDI to the US in 2017 and almost 24% to developing Asia. Real estate and hospitality remained the largest recipient sectors of PRC capital flow into the US. Comprehensive FDI data are not available for 2018. However, the Organisation for Economic Co-operation and Development published preliminary data that suggest that global outward FDI declined in Q1, in large part because US profits held abroad were repatriated in response to lowered tax rates starting in 2018 (OECD 2018). Meanwhile, survey results estimate a 90% drop in

outward FDI from the PRC to the US in the first half of 2018 from the same period in 2017, following a 28% decline in 2017 (Hanemann 2018).

It is not clear how much US announcements about impending trade and investment restrictions caused the recent FDI declines. Restrictions specifically limiting Asian investment in communication technology in industrial countries continue to be imposed but have not escalated. As far back as March 2016, for example, the US administration preemptively blocked a very large merger and acquisition attempt between the Singaporean firm Broadcom Ltd. and the US company Qualcomm Inc., invoking national security concerns. But there were also concerns of being left behind in mobile technology as the Made in China 2025 technology program ramped up. Other less-visible nontariff measures continue in 2018 (box figure). ZTE Corporation, a prominent Chinese manufacturer of cellphones based in Shenzhen and a large employer, was almost barred from supplying to the US in April 2018 for not complying with the embargo on the Democratic People's Republic of Korea, though ultimately the penalty was reduced to a fine.

continued next page

Tariff and investment measures under the trade conflict

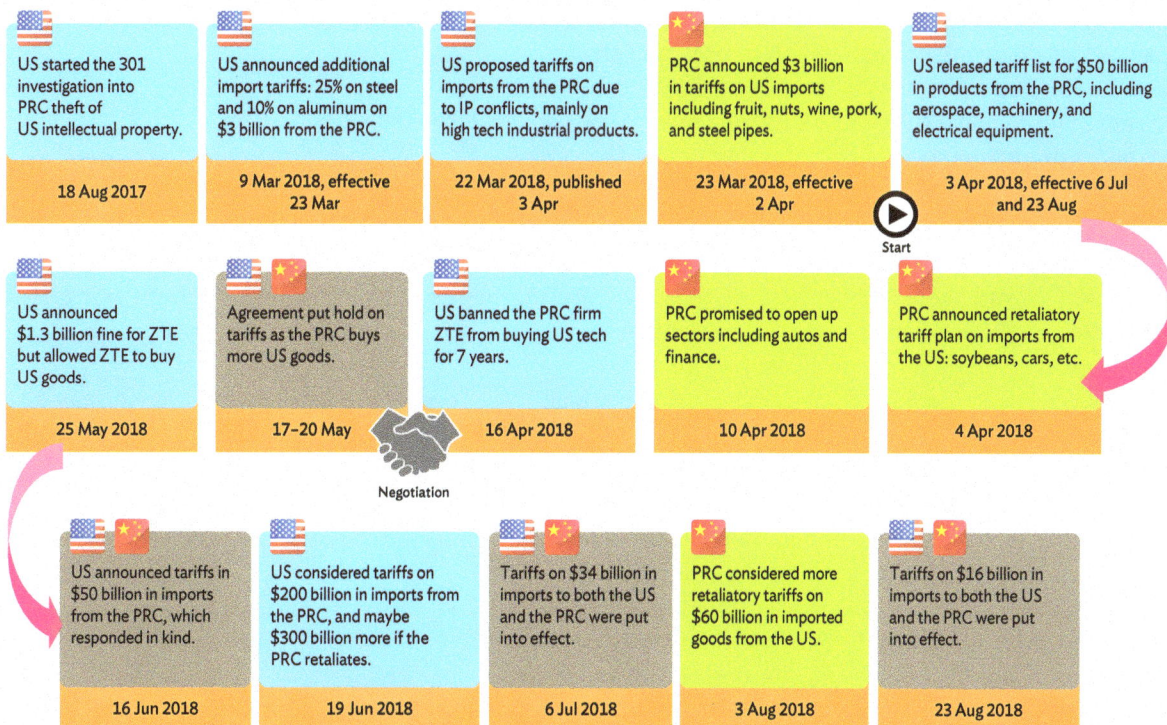

US started the 301 investigation into PRC theft of US intellectual property.	US announced additional import tariffs: 25% on steel and 10% on aluminum on $3 billion from the PRC.	US proposed tariffs on imports from the PRC due to IP conflicts, mainly on high tech industrial products.	PRC announced $3 billion in tariffs on US imports including fruit, nuts, wine, pork, and steel pipes.	US released tariff list for $50 billion in products from the PRC, including aerospace, machinery, and electrical equipment.
18 Aug 2017	9 Mar 2018, effective 23 Mar	22 Mar 2018, published 3 Apr	23 Mar 2018, effective 2 Apr	3 Apr 2018, effective 6 Jul and 23 Aug

Start

US announced $1.3 billion fine for ZTE but allowed ZTE to buy US goods.	Agreement put hold on tariffs as the PRC buys more US goods.	US banned the PRC firm ZTE from buying US tech for 7 years.	PRC promised to open up sectors including autos and finance.	PRC announced retaliatory tariff plan on imports from the US: soybeans, cars, etc.
25 May 2018	17–20 May	16 Apr 2018	10 Apr 2018	4 Apr 2018

Negotiation

US announced tariffs in $50 billion in imports from the PRC, which responded in kind.	US considered tariffs on $200 billion in imports from the PRC, and maybe $300 billion more if the PRC retaliates.	Tariffs on $34 billion in imports to both the US and the PRC were put into effect.	PRC considered more retaliatory tariffs on $60 billion in imported goods from the US.	Tariffs on $16 billion in imports to both the US and the PRC were put into effect.
16 Jun 2018	19 Jun 2018	6 Jul 2018	3 Aug 2018	23 Aug 2018

IP = intellectual property, PRC = People's Republic of China, US = United States.

Source: Gentile and Li, forthcoming.

1.1.2 *Continued*

In August 2018, the US passed legislation that strengthened national security reviews of PRC investment in the US, prohibiting PRC investment in key high-tech sectors such as aerospace and robotics on that grounds that some companies had stolen intellectual property in the past. In addition, outbound restrictions imposed by the PRC on the US have recently escalated amid tougher controls on investments by leveraged private investors in the US. European Union governments have also tightened restrictions on high-tech FDI from the PRC.

Even without FDI restrictions, international investment flows are likely to shrink, becoming collateral damage from the escalated trade dispute. So far, US tariff levies have been careful not to target popular consumer goods with components from the PRC, such as gadgets with Bluetooth capability. However, if threats to impose tariffs on all PRC imports are realized, this will eventually drive investment

toward domestic production. For example, a cellphone that is assembled in the PRC and shipped to US as a final consumption good, such as an Apple iPhone, was still immune to tariffs in mid-September. If the US imposes tariffs on all imports from the PRC, affected US companies will follow through on their announced plans to pass on the higher costs to consumers in the short term. Over the long term, such companies may choose divestment from labor-intensive component producers and assemblers in the PRC in favor of building highly automated assembly plants in the US. The PRC may ramp up domestic technology investment as well. FDI will thus fall substantially, regardless of whether there are direct restrictions on investment. Moreover, although large companies have sufficient market share to afford such transition costs, start-up companies introducing new products will find it hard to target a more limited domestic market. Thus, innovation is likely to suffer as well.

Current account balance

Current account balances in most economies in developing Asia will have smaller surpluses and bigger deficits than forecast in *ADO 2018* because of higher oil prices, as developing Asia is a net oil importer, and strong domestic consumption spurring growth in import demand. The aggregate regional surplus will narrow to the forecast horizon, shrinking its positive contribution to global balances from 0.47% of global GDP in in 2017 to 0.41% in 2018 and 0.36% in 2019 (Figure 1.1.14).

The aggregate current account forecast in this *Update* is thus revised down from a surplus equal to 1.4% of combined GDP to 1.0% in 2018 and from 1.3% to 0.7% in 2019. Excluding the NIEs, which historically post very large surpluses, the current account balance of developing Asia should be zero in 2018 and a small 0.3% deficit in 2019. The PRC largely drives this result, as the forecast for its current account surplus is now cut by half, to 0.7% in 2018 and 0.2% in 2019, largely owing to US import tariffs. PRC trade in intermediate and capital goods is almost 81% of its total trade in 2017 (Figure 1.1.15). The surpluses of Hong Kong, China and of the ROK are now expected to narrow in the next 2 years as trade disruption spills over into these economies and Southeast Asia. Meanwhile, currency depreciation in Taipei,China will temper import demand and encourage exports, causing its current account surplus to expand in both years.

1.1.14 World current account balance

- United States
- People's Republic of China
- Middle East
- Other industrial countries
- Japan
- Russian Federation
- Rest of developing Asia
- Rest of world

% of world GDP

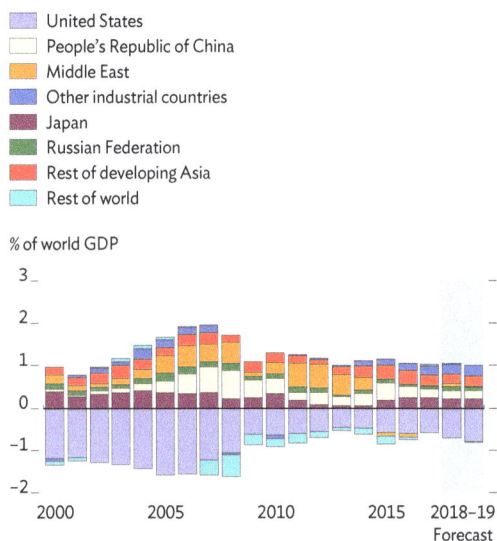

Source: Haver Analytics (accessed 17 September 2018).

External balances in the rest of the subregions are mostly revised to less favorable forecasts, but projections vary (Figure 1.1.16). The current account deficit projection for Central Asia is significantly revised to narrow from 2.1% of GDP to 1.3% in 2018 and from 2.2% to 1.2% in 2019, prompted by reassessed prospects for Azerbaijan, Kazakhstan, and Turkmenistan. The deficit projections for South Asia are revised to widen to 2.9% of GDP in both 2018 and 2019 as higher oil prices are expected to push up import bills in India and Sri Lanka, while continued imports of capital goods in Bangladesh, Maldives, and Nepal widen their current account deficits. Pakistan's current account deficit is expected to moderate as measures to restrict imports scale down import demand. In Southeast Asia, the forecast for the current account surplus is revised down from 2.7% of GDP to 2.5% in 2018 and 2.4% in 2019 as exports moderate faster than expected and import growth exceeds earlier expectations. Imports of capital goods for energy and transport infrastructure projects are escalating sharply in Indonesia and Philippines, and higher oil imports to Viet Nam undermine gains from manufacture exports. In Malaysia, higher international energy prices are seen to boost exports despite downward trends in palm oil prices. Meanwhile, swelling demand for consumer imports is likely to keep imports high, reducing the overall current account surplus. Singapore will sustain its expansion in pharmaceutical and biotechnology exports. Finally, the current account surplus in the Pacific is still expected to narrow in 2018 from the equivalent of 10.4% of GDP in 2017, to 9.4%, remaining 2.8 percentage points wider than projected in *ADO 2018*. The surplus is projected to be 8.2% of GDP in 2019.

Risks to the outlook

Risks to the outlook for developing Asia are firmly tilted to the downside. Regional economies have been strong, boosted by a recovery in trade in 2017 as growth rebounded in the advanced economies and by newly robust commodity prices. This gives them buffers to withstand shocks. Nonetheless, Asian economies face several risks, particularly from the escalating trade conflict.

First, increases to the US Federal Funds rate beyond market expectations could dampen growth. If the US economy shows signs of overheating, the Federal Reserve may raise interest rates faster than anticipated, spurring large capital flow reversals in Asian economies. Several currencies in developing Asia have already depreciated against the US dollar, generating higher domestic inflation. In response, some Asian monetary authorities have tightened monetary policy and raised interest rates.

1.1.15 Total merchandise trade, People's Republic of China

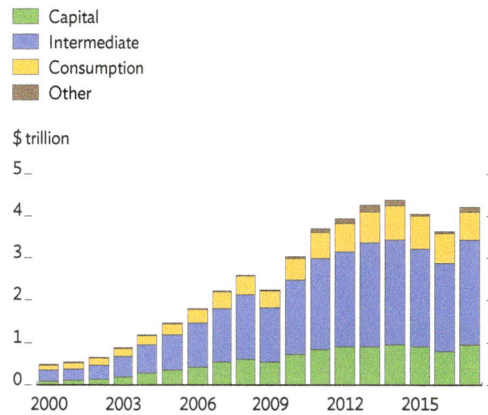

Note: Total merchandise trade is the sum of exports and imports.
Source: United Nations Statistics Division. UN Comtrade Database. Available: https://comtrade.un.org/data (accessed 15 September 2018).

1.1.16 Current account balance, developing Asia

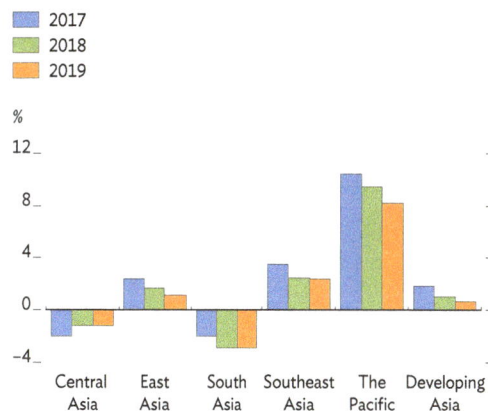

Source: *Asian Development Outlook* database.

Such action could dampen growth in their economies. In light of this, elevated private debt levels risk destabilizing the financial sector. Since the global financial crisis, many economies in developing Asia, such as Malaysia, the PRC, the ROK, and Thailand, have rapidly driven up private debt as a share of GDP, with possible destabilizing effects on their financial sectors.

Second, exchange rate turbulence in emerging markets outside of Asia has temporarily spilled over into developing Asia but apparently without serious contagion. In Q2 of this year, the Argentine peso and Turkish lira came under heavy pressure, triggering anxiety about a broader selloff of assets in emerging markets. Underlying these economies' vulnerabilities were public debt issues in Argentina and high foreign debt amid high and rising inflation in Turkey. The situation in Turkey was exacerbated by a diplomatic dispute with the US, which saw the US announce a doubling of tariffs on steel and aluminum imports from Turkey on 10 August and Turkey retaliating with tariffs on automobiles, alcohol, and tobacco from the US. Some spillover from Turkish lira turbulence was documented. For example, the 12 major emerging markets that are tracked daily by the Institute of International Finance experienced aggregate portfolio capital outflow of $1.4 billion from 9 to 15 August 2018. The Indian rupee and Indonesian rupiah lost value but have recovered somewhat. Fortunately, signs of contagion in other financial markets were short-lived, and markets responded favorably when the Turkish monetary authorities resolutely raised interest rates and Argentina entered into program negotiations with the International Monetary Fund. Nevertheless, issues that directly affect developing Asia, such as the impact of the trade conflict and investment restrictions, could rock financial markets further.

Third, geopolitical developments could stir up oil price volatility and trade disruption in the near term. Those with potentially explosive impacts, such as the US withdrawal from the multilateral deal with Iran, create additional oil price volatility. More serious sanctions targeting the Iranian oil industry are scheduled to take effect in November 2018. Iran was the fifth-largest oil exporter in the world in 2017, exporting 2.1 million barrels per day. As such, disruptions to Iranian supply caused by US sanctions will have significant repercussions on the global oil market and in neighboring Afghanistan, Pakistan, and Central Asia. Ratios of oil stocks to use have remained stable, however, and higher production agreed by the Organization of the Petroleum Exporting Countries and the Russian Federation in June 2018, and greater output from US shale oil producers, will likely more than cover the supply disruptions. Markets therefore anticipate that prices will likely stay below $80/barrel over the medium term.

Finally, the escalating trade conflict poses by far the most serious direct downside risk to the region, particularly to the PRC. Outlook projections incorporate trade measures implemented as of mid-September, but the course of the conflict can change at any time. Additional measures between the two countries and the possibility of US tariffs across the board on automobiles and auto parts would harm the growth outlook for other Asian economies going into 2019. Retaliation from other countries and disruption to trade and investment could have severe adverse effects. Strong economic links through global production chains could be weakened, prompting investors to postpone business plans for fear of future tariffs, and the prospect of higher prices for goods could sour consumer sentiment. Should producer and consumer sentiment turn significantly negative, financial markets and international capital flows would be hit.

The calm reaction so far suggests that financial markets have been able to adjust to uncertain global trade tensions as investors remain largely confident about strong macroeconomic fundamentals. However, calm could mask a wait-and-see attitude awaiting new policy announcements. The world takes for granted the benefits from global value chains and trade until they fall into jeopardy. The next section of this report presents a model that estimates the impact of a protracted trade conflict on developing Asia and globally.

The impact of the trade conflict on developing Asia

International trade drives growth in Asia. That makes the recent trade conflict worrisome. The two main protagonists, the US and the PRC, are the world's two largest economies and traders, together accounting for two-fifths of global GDP and a quarter of global trade. They are also the main hubs for global production chains (Figure 1.2.1). Further, the trade conflict is not just bilateral but global, with many countries hit by the first wave of tariffs on steel, aluminum, washing machines, and solar panels and retaliating against them, even as a new wave of tariffs is threatened against automobiles and auto parts. It is therefore important to understand and quantify the risks to Asian economies posed by the measures already implemented, as well as those that may follow.

1.2.1 Global production chains

Note: Includes the 61 economies in the Organisation for Economic Co-operation and Development–World Trade Organization Trade in Value-Added database. The figure shows only the most important bilateral flows in intermediate goods excluding oil. Line thickness indicates the size of bilateral flows, and blue lines indicate more important flows. Blue nodes are those with the highest degree of "PageRank centrality," as defined in Diakantoni et al. (2017).

Source: WB Group, IDE-JETRO, OECD, UIBE, and WTO. 2017.

The trade conflict unfolds

The first salvoes of the trade conflict occurred in the first quarter of 2018. On 22 January, the US imposed 20% tariffs on imports of large residential washing machines and 30% on solar panels, and on 23 March it imposed 25% tariffs on imports of steel and 10% tariffs on aluminum. Together these tariffs affected $58.3 billion worth of goods (Figure 1.2.2). The economies that were hit—the European Union, Canada, Mexico, the Russian Federation, Turkey, and, in developing Asia, India, and the PRC—retaliated with their own tariffs affecting $35.8 billion of US exports. The direct impact of these first measures on developing Asia was small, as they affected less than 0.1% of the region's exports.

The conflict escalated and became more bilateral in nature in the second and third quarters of this year. The US imposed in two steps tariffs on a wide range of imports from the PRC worth $50 billion: $34 billion on 6 July and another $16 billion on 23 August. The PRC immediately retaliated with tariffs on an equal amount of imports from the US. On 24 September, an additional $200 billion of PRC imports were hit with a 10% tariff scheduled to increase to 25% in January 2019. The PRC retaliated with tariffs of 5%–10% on $60 billion worth of imports from the US, effective the same day. The smaller amount reflected the fact that the PRC imports only about $130 billion in goods from the US, most of which are now subject to a tariff. The PRC exports some $500 billion in goods to the US.

1.2.2 A chronology of the trade conflict

- ▢ US imports
- ▢ PRC imports
- ▢ Other countries' imports

Value of imports affected by the tariff ($ billion)

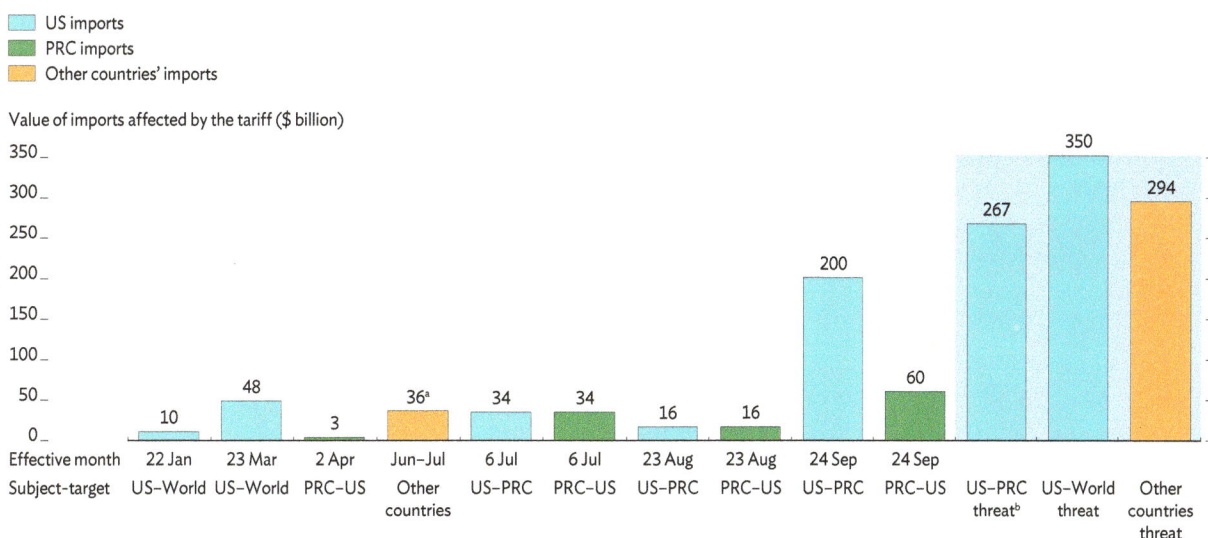

Effective month	22 Jan	23 Mar	2 Apr	Jun–Jul	6 Jul	6 Jul	23 Aug	23 Aug	24 Sep	24 Sep	US–PRC threat[b]	US–World threat	Other countries threat
Subject-target	US–World	US–World	PRC–US	Other countries	US–PRC	PRC–US	US–PRC	PRC–US	US–PRC	PRC–US			
Value	10	48	3	36[a]	34	34	16	16	200	60	267	350	294

PRC = People's Republic of China, US = United States.

[a] The $35.8 billion in retaliatory tariffs against US steel and aluminum tariffs excludes pending cases for $4.1 billion filed by the European Union and $1.9 billion by Japan through the World Trade Organization dispute settlement mechanism.

[b] The PRC has so far retaliated tit for tat. Continued tit for tat would require retaliation by $17 billion. The PRC has not yet announced a list, but such tariffs are assumed under the bilateral escalation scenario (Figure 1.2.3).

Source: ADB estimates.

Continued threats of even more trade measures, both bilateral and global, portend even greater escalation. On the bilateral front, the US has begun vetting tariffs on another $267 billion of imports from the PRC that, should they go into effect, would effectively mean all goods exported from the PRC to the US subject to a tariff. The PRC has threatened to retaliate with similar tariffs on all its merchandise imports from the US and is considering other avenues for retaliation. On the global front, the US administration has submitted for consideration a 25% tariff on US imports of autos and auto parts from all trade partners, which would affect $350 billion worth of goods. Here as well, the European Commission indicated that retaliatory tariffs would hit up to $294 billion worth of US exports.

Estimating the impact of the trade conflict

There are various channels through which the trade conflict can affect economies in developing Asia. The analysis presented here, based on an approach described in more detail in Box 1.2.1, focuses on three possible channels:

- Direct effects hit the products and countries that are subject to the tariffs. Purchasers of these goods in the country that imposed the tariff now have to pay more per unit, which reduces their demand for these products from the targeted countries.
- Indirect effects work through local and international supply chains. Producers that now sell fewer goods because of the tariffs respond by lowering production and buying fewer intermediate inputs from their suppliers, both domestic and foreign, with knock-on effects all the way along local and international supply chains.
- Trade redirection is possible toward suppliers that are not hit by the tariffs. These suppliers can be either domestic or in third countries that are exempt from the tariffs. Trade redirection may thus benefit other countries not directly involved in the trade conflict. This is particularly so for countries that already produce the goods targeted but are exempted from the tariffs now hitting their competitors. Redirection may benefit as well countries to which production may shift in a prolonged trade conflict.

The implications of two separate trade conflict scenarios are examined. The first scenario is the trade conflict as it currently stands, which includes all trade measures implemented as of September 2018. For the $200 billion in tariffs that the US imposed on the PRC, a 25% rate is assumed because the US has already declared that the tariff will rise to this rate in January 2019. The second scenario features bilateral escalation, with the trade conflict between the US and PRC intensifying further. Specifically, it assumes that both countries impose blanket tariffs of 25% on all merchandise imports from the other country.

1.2.1 Analyzing the impact of the trade conflict through various channels

The analysis here uses a combination of tools to estimate how the trade conflict will affect economies through the three channels: direct effects, indirect effects, and trade redirection. First, the direct effect of the tariffs is quantified at the product level using elasticities of demand in response to changes in prices. The results presented here use country-specific import price elasticities of demand from Tokarick (2010).[a]

The indirect impact of these changes working through local and global production chains is then analyzed using the 2017 version of the ADB Multi-Regional Input-Output Table, which documents trade and production links between economies and industries for 35 sectors in 62 economies, including 24 in developing Asia, plus an economy called the "rest of the world."[b] This approach allows the calculation of impact not just on broad regions, as is often the case with more sophisticated models, but on individual economies and even individual sectors and industries within economies.

Finally, the modeling of how trade is redirected toward other countries adopts the approach of Feenstra and Sasahara (2017), which reallocates trade toward other producers in proportion with their shares in the global market. The assumption is that only half of tariff-affected trade is redirected; should actual trade redirection be greater or smaller than this, so will potential positive spillover into third countries that produce the same goods. For further details on the methodology and additional results, see Abiad et al. (forthcoming).

[a] These elasticities can be refined further based on the characteristics of the specific product and its market. For example, the higher the exporting country's market share in the importing country for a specific product, the lower the elasticity because it is harder to find alternative suppliers. In addition, products that are more complex, as measured in Hidalgo and Hausmann (2009), tend to be less elastic than products that are simpler and more like commodities. Abiad et al. (forthcoming) showed how refining elasticity assumptions can affect the estimated impact of the trade conflict.
[b] The table is described in detail in ADB (2018b).

Following an examination of the implications for the two main protagonists, the US and the PRC, the study turns to the impact on the world economy and developing Asia, and finally on sectors within developing Asia.

Analysis estimates the percentage difference in GDP in three scenarios: without the trade conflict, with the current trade conflict, and with bilateral escalation of the trade conflict. It is important to emphasize that these effects may take longer than a year to manifest themselves. This is especially true of indirect effects through production links and trade redirection.

Under the current scenario, both the PRC and the US are negatively affected, with a larger impact on the PRC (Figure 1.2.3 top panel, blue bars). The trade measures already implemented will mean GDP in the PRC 0.5% lower than what it would have been in the absence of any trade conflict. The impact on the US is substantially smaller, erasing 0.1%–0.2% of GDP. For both economies, most of the negative impact arrives through the direct and indirect channels. Trade redirection toward domestic producers in these two economies provides only a marginal boost of less than 0.1% of GDP. The difference in effects across the two economies should not be surprising. As Figure 1.2.2 shows, the tariffs imposed by the US on the PRC are an order of magnitude larger than those imposed by the PRC on the US, and the PRC is more dependent on US demand for its goods than the US is on PRC demand.

1.2.3 GDP impact of trade conflict by economic region

- Current scenario
- US–PRC trade threats
- Bilateral escalation scenario

Impact on the PRC

% of GDP

- Direct and indirect effects: −0.51%, −0.58%, −1.08%
- Direct, indirect, and trade redirection effects: −0.48%, −0.55%, −1.03%

Impact on the US

% of GDP

- Direct and indirect effects: −0.16%, −0.10%, −0.26%
- Direct, indirect, and trade redirection effects: −0.12%, −0.08%, −0.20%

Impact on the world

% of GDP

- Direct and indirect effects: −0.15%, −0.13%, −0.28%
- Direct, indirect, and trade redirection effects: −0.08%, −0.07%, −0.15%

Impact on developing Asia excluding the PRC

% of GDP

- Direct and indirect effects: −0.05%, −0.03%, −0.09%
- Direct, indirect, and trade redirection effects: 0.06%, 0.16%, 0.22%

GDP = gross domestic product, PRC = People's Republic of China, US = United States.
Source: ADB estimates.

Should the bilateral trade conflict escalate to cover all goods traded between the two countries, the effect on output in the two countries would be significantly larger, with the PRC again hit harder (Figure 1.2.3 top left panel, red bars). GDP in the PRC would be smaller by just over 1%, with most of the effects again coming as direct effects of the tariffs and indirect effects delivered through domestic production links. The US would see its GDP smaller by 0.2% relative to a baseline of no conflict (Figure 1.2.3 top right panel).

The effect of the trade conflict on the rest of the world is relatively small, and the rest of developing Asia may actually benefit through trade redirection. Global GDP is lower by 0.08% under the current scenario and by 0.15% under the bilateral escalation scenario (Figure 1.2.3 bottom left panel). Most of the loss is through the negative impact on the PRC and US. Effects on Europe and Japan (not shown) are negligible.

Meanwhile, for the rest of developing Asia outside the PRC, the impact of the trade conflict through the direct effects of tariffs and the indirect effects conveyed via production links are negative but relatively small: 0.05% in the current scenario and 0.09% with bilateral escalation (Figure 1.2.3 bottom right panel). Allowing for trade redirection, the net effect on the rest of developing Asia turns positive. The potential gain from trade redirection is 0.11% of GDP under the current scenario and 0.31% with bilateral escalation. The economies in the region that stand to benefit the most are, in descending order, Viet Nam, Malaysia, and Thailand because they produce and export goods similar to those made by the PRC.

From a sector perspective, the negative impact on the PRC cuts across many sectors, but the gains in the rest of developing Asia are concentrated in only a few (Figure 1.2.4). Under the bilateral escalation scenario, for example, the PRC electronics industry is the hardest hit but still subtracts less than one-seventh of the whole loss of GDP. Other hard-hit sectors are wholesale trade, mining and quarrying, textiles and garments, agriculture, financial services, chemicals, and metals. The presence of wholesale trade and financial services in the list illustrates the significant role that production links play in transmitting the impact of the trade conflict throughout the economy. For the rest of developing Asia, the potential benefit from trade redirection is concentrated in sectors and industries where the region competes with the PRC. Foremost among them is electronics, which is boosted substantially in Southeast Asia (ASEAN-5) and the NIEs. Textiles also benefit in ASEAN-5 economies, and metals in the NIEs gain because the ROK is one of just a handful of countries exempted from US tariffs on steel. By contrast, the gains for other economies in developing Asia outside ASEAN-5 and the NIEs are primarily in textiles, agriculture, and wholesale trade.

Effects on current account balances

Under both scenarios, the impact on current account balances is mild (Figure 1.2.5). In the bilateral escalation scenario, for example, the current account surplus of the PRC is only marginally narrower, equal to 1.0% of GDP in 2019 rather than 1.2% as forecast in April *ADO 2018* around the time of the escalation announcements. While the decline in PRC exports is significant, imports are also lower because of both the tariffs imposed by the PRC and indirect effects that reduce demand in the PRC for imported intermediate inputs. In addition, as noted above, GDP is smaller. For the same reasons, the US sees only a marginally narrower current account deficit, equal to 3.3% of GDP in 2019 instead of 3.4% as forecast in *ADO 2018*.

1.2.4 Impact of the trade conflict by sector

- Agriculture
- Business services
- Chemicals
- Electronics
- Finance
- Machinery nec
- Metals
- Oil, mining, & quarrying
- Textiles & garments
- Wholesale trade
- Others

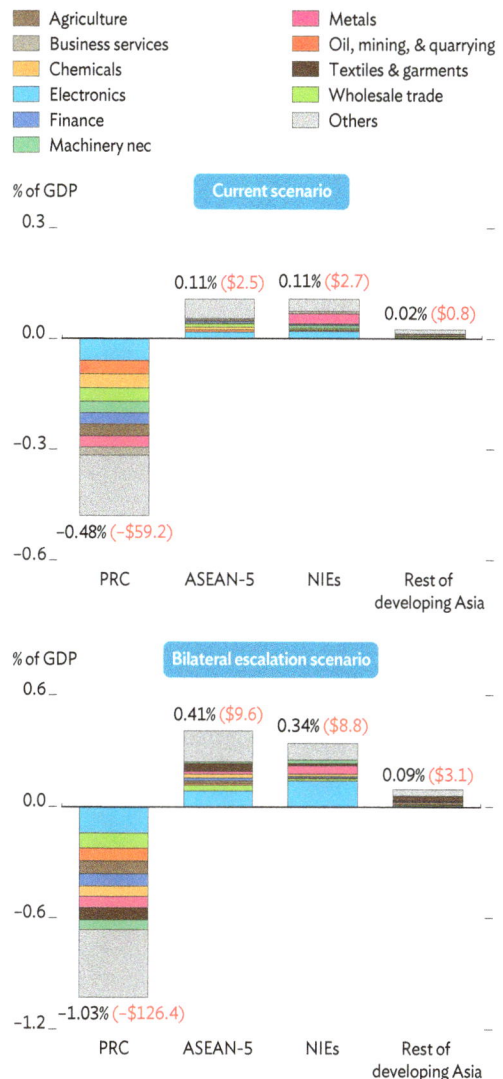

ASEAN-5 = five larger economies in the Association of Southeast Asian Nations (Indonesia, Malaysia, the Philippines, Thailand, Viet Nam), GDP = gross domestic product, nec = not elsewhere classified, NIE = newly industrialized economy (Hong Kong, China; the Republic of Korea; Singapore; Taipei,China), PRC = People's Republic of China. Rest of developing Asia = Bangladesh, Bhutan, Brunei Darussalam, Cambodia, Fiji, Kazakhstan, the Kyrgyz Republic, the Lao People's Democratic Republic, Maldives, Mongolia, Nepal, Pakistan, Sri Lanka.

Note: Numbers in parenthesis refer to the impact in billion dollars.

Source: ADB estimates.

1.2.5 Effects on current account balances

■ ADO 2018
— Current scenario
● Bilateral escalation scenario

ADO = Asian Development Outlook, ASEAN-5 = five larger economies in the Association of Southeast Asian Nations (Indonesia, Malaysia, the Philippines, Thailand, Viet Nam), GDP = gross domestic product, IND = India, NIE = newly industrialized economy (Hong Kong, China; the Republic of Korea; Singapore; Taipei,China), USA = United States of America.
Note: Data labels refer to the ratio of the current account surplus/deficit to GDP under the bilateral escalation scenario.
Source: ADB estimates.

Similarly, the rest of developing Asia sees only minor impacts on current account balances even in the bilateral escalation scenario. The NIEs see their 2019 current account surplus higher at 7.5% of GDP, not 7.1% as forecast earlier, and the ASEAN-5 current account surplus equals 1.1% of GDP in 2019, not 0.8%—the benefits to both groups coming from trade redirection. There is no discernible impact on India's current account deficit.

A time for concern? The region has options

The analytical model captures important intersectoral trade links but with unavoidable simplifications such that some channels of impact are not captured. Like other models, the exercise does not shed light on the timing of these effects. Some of the impact, particularly through the direct channel, may occur quickly, while effects through production links and especially trade redirection may take longer to appear. Further, the analysis is not a general equilibrium analysis, so it does not take into account the balancing of supply and demand in labor and other markets. However, analyses of the trade conflict using computable general equilibrium models—such as in Gentile and Li (forthcoming), which uses the ADB Multi-Regional Input-Output Table, and in Bollen and Rojas-Romagosa (2018)—find effects that are similar in magnitude to what is reported above.

The model also does not take into account the potential opening of new trade channels. As concern over collateral damage from the US–PRC trade dispute continues, Asian economies have called for stronger trade ties within the region.

Free trade initiatives that are pushing ahead include negotiations on the Regional Comprehensive Economic Partnership, supported by the PRC; the Asia-Pacific Trade Agreement, members of which receive tariff reductions from the PRC; and the Comprehensive and Progressive Agreement for Trans-Pacific Partnership, signed by 11 countries in March 2018 to replace the Trans-Pacific Partnership vacated by the US.

Most importantly, the model does not capture the effects of the trade conflict that work through confidence and future investment, which may be large and already taking effect (Box 1.2.1). The impact through greater economic uncertainty, and the extent of economic disruption that may occur as global production is reallocated is difficult to predict and not captured in the channels explored here. These effects could be substantial as the conflict escalates, drags on, or spills over into financial markets. In this regard, IMF (2018) uses a six-region model that incorporates trade and confidence channels but not spillovers through production links. These simulations show impact through trade channels similar in magnitude to what is reported above—an impact of 0.1%–0.2% of GDP in the US and small effects in Japan and the euro area—but fold the PRC into emerging Asia, impeding comparability. The effects calculated with an added confidence shock are large, with global GDP lower by 0.5% at peak impact and most of the loss working through the confidence channel and its negative effects on investment and consumption.

Finally, trade redirection assumes that relative prices across trade partners stay the same. However, if exchange rates or commodity prices change, the net effect could be smaller or larger trade reallocation. For example, the PRC renminbi has depreciated by 6.3% against the US dollar since the end of March 2018, when the trade conflict began, which counteracts the tariff-induced 25% higher import cost from the PRC, negating a quarter of the tariff in dollar terms, which is what matters for US buyers. Also, Asian stock markets have responded with losses to announcements in the short run (Table 1.1.3), potentially having large negative wealth effects by lowering asset prices.

To smooth some of the trade shocks that may be coming, governments in Asia have many tools at their disposal, ideally applied early and appropriately, using monetary, fiscal, or macroprudential policy. The theme chapter of this *Update* discusses these options for managing volatility.

References

Abiad, A., K. Baris, A. Bernabe, D. Bertulfo, S. Camingue-Romance, P. Feliciano, V. Mercer-Blackman, and J. M. Mariasingham. Forthcoming. The Impact of Trade Conflict on Developing Asia. *ADB Economics Working Paper Series.* Asian Development Bank.

ADB. 2018a. *Asia Bond Monitor.* September. Asian Development Bank. https://asianbondsonline.adb.org/documents/abm_sep_2018.pdf.

———. 2018b. *Key Indicators for Asia and the Pacific.* Asian Development Bank. http://dx.doi.org/10.22617/FLS189512-3.

Bollen, J. and H. Rojas-Romagosa. 2018. Trade Wars: Economic Impacts of US Tariff Increases and Retaliations—An International Perspective. *CBP Background Document.* Centraal Planbureau Netherlands Bureau for Economic Policy Analysis.

Diakantoni, A., H. Escaith, M. Roberts, and T. Verbeet. 2017. Accumulating Trade Costs and Competitiveness in Global Value Chains. *WTO Staff Working Papers* ERSD-2017-02. World Trade Organization.

Feenstra, R. and A. Sasahara. 2017. The 'China Shock', Exports and US Employment: A Global Input–Output Analysis, *NBER Working Papers* 24022. National Bureau of Economic Research, Inc. https://ideas.repec.org/p/nbr/nberwo/24022.html.

Gentile, E. and G. Li. Forthcoming. Assessing the Economic Impact of the US–PRC Tariff Conflict Using a Multiregional CGE Model. *ADB Economics Working Paper Series.* Asian Development Bank.

Hanemann, T. 2018. *Arrested Development: Chinese FDI in the US in 1H 2018.* 19 June. https://rhg.com/research/arrested-development-chinese-fdi-in-the-us-in-1h-2018.

Hidalgo, C. and R. Hausmann. 2009. The Building Blocks of Economic Complexity. *Proceedings of the National Academy of Sciences* 106(28).

IMF. 2018. G-20 Surveillance Note. G-20 Finance Ministers and Central Bank Governors' Meetings. International Monetary Fund. https://www.imf.org/external/np/g20/pdf/2018/071818.pdf.

OECD. 2018. *Global FDI Outflows Tumble 44% in the First Quarter of 2018 due to US Tax Reform.* Organisation for Economic Co-operation and Development. https://www.oecd.org/daf/inv/investment-policy/FDI-in-Figures-July-2018.pdf.

Tokarick, S. 2010. A Method for Calculating Export Supply and Import Demand Elasticities. *IMF Working Paper* No. 10/180. International Monetary Fund.

WB Group, IDE-JETRO, OECD, UIBE, and WTO. 2017. Global Value Chain Development Report 2017 : Measuring and Analyzing the Impact of GVCs on Economic Development. World Bank Group, Institute of Developing Economies-Japan External Trade Organization, Organisation for Economic Co-operation and Development, University of International Business and Economics, and the World Trade Organization. https://www.wto.org/english/res_e/booksp_e/gvcs_report_2017.pdf.

Annex: Growth resilient despite trade friction and pricier oil

Aggregate growth forecasts for the major industrial economies of the United States, the euro area, and Japan are retained from *Asian Development Outlook 2018* (*ADO 2018*) at 2.3% in 2018 and 2.0% in 2019. US tariffs and global countermeasures seem to be having little immediate impact on prospects in these economies. Supported by strong private spending, growth in the US remains robust and on track to exceed the *ADO 2018* growth forecast. Balancing this upgrade, recovery early in the year in the euro area and Japan stalled somewhat, prompting slight downward revisions to 2018 growth projections.
In the euro area, a strong currency dented exports, and rising inflation weighed on household expenditure. Although the Japanese economy rebounded in the second quarter (Q2) of the year, contraction in Q1 from weak domestic demand weighs on growth prospects.

A1.1 Baseline assumptions on the international economy

	2016	2017	2018		2019	
	Actual		ADO 2018	Update	ADO 2018	Update
GDP growth (%)						
Major industrial economies[a]	1.6	2.3	2.3	2.3	2.0	2.0
United States	1.6	2.2	2.7	2.8	2.3	2.4
Euro area	1.8	2.5	2.2	2.0	1.9	1.9
Japan	1.0	1.7	1.4	1.1	1.0	1.0
Prices and inflation						
Brent crude spot prices (average, $/barrel)	44.0	54.3	65.0	74.0	62.0	74.0
Food index (2010 = 100, % change)	1.5	0.3	1.2	3.0	1.2	2.0
Consumer price index inflation (major industrial economies' average, %)	0.7	1.7	1.8	2.0	1.7	1.9
Interest rates						
United States federal funds rate (average, %)	0.4	1.0	1.8	1.8	2.7	2.7
European Central Bank refinancing rate (average, %)	0.0	0.0	0.0	0.0	0.0	0.0
Bank of Japan overnight call rate (average, %)	0.0	0.0	0.0	0.0	0.0	0.0
$ Libor[b] (%)	0.5	1.1	1.8	1.8	2.7	2.7

ADO = Asian Development Outlook, GDP = gross domestic product.

[a] Average growth rates are weighted by gross national income, Atlas method.

[b] Average London interbank offered rate quotations on 1-month loans.

Sources: US Department of Commerce, Bureau of Economic Analysis, http://www.bea.gov; Eurostat, http://ec.europa.eu/eurostat; Economic and Social Research Institute of Japan, http://www.esri.cao.go.jp; Consensus Forecasts; Bloomberg; CEIC Data Company; Haver Analytics; and the World Bank, Global Commodity Markets, http://www.worldbank.org; ADB estimates.

This *Update* forecasts a stronger pickup in food and fuel prices than anticipated in *ADO 2018*. Inflationary pressures in the advanced economies have started to build. The US Federal Reserve is expected to proceed with its normalization of monetary policy. Meanwhile, the euro area and Japan may maintain steady monetary policies, though the European Central Bank has signaled its plan to end its asset purchase program at the end of this year.

Recent developments in the major industrial economies

United States

The US economy grew solidly by a seasonally adjusted annualized rate (saar) of 3.2% in the first half of 2018. GDP grew by 2.2% saar in Q1, driven mainly by private investment, which primed a strong rebound in consumption and exports that supported in turn remarkable growth acceleration in Q2 to a 4-year high of 4.2% saar. Private consumption was the main contributor to GDP growth in Q2, adding 2.6 percentage points, or 2.2 points more than in Q1. Net exports contributed 1.3 percentage points to GDP growth, following subtraction in Q1, as exports expanded by 9.1% saar and imports shrank by 0.4% saar. The 9.1% saar increase in exports included an 80.0% annualized jump in exports of food, animal feed, and beverages, which reflected a spike in soybean and maize shipments to the People's Republic of China (PRC) ahead of tariffs taking effect. Private investment added 0.1 percentage points, down from 1.7 points in Q1, while government spending edged up its contribution to GDP growth from 0.3 percentage points in Q1 to 0.4 points (Figure A1.1).

Consumer confidence and retail sales remained strong in the first half of 2018 (Figure A1.2), indicative of a continuing rebound in consumption, which grew by 3.8% in Q2 after being muted at 0.5% growth in Q1. The consumer confidence index remained high in the first half of 2018, climbing in August to as high as 129.1 (2007 = 100). Retail sales continued to improve throughout the first half of the year, reaching 133.9 in July. Strong consumer confidence and retail sales suggest that consumption will remain the pillar of future growth.

Private investment grew by only 0.4% in Q2, down from a solid 9.6% growth in Q1 as inventories dropped and residential investment weakened—with nonresidential investment growth still strong at 8.5%. The industrial production index continued to rise in the first half of 2018, from 100.9 in January to 103.4 in July, and the purchasing managers' index remained strong at 56.0 in July. Both indexes suggest that expansion in

A1.1 Demand-side contributions to growth, United States

- Private expenditure
- Private investment
- Government expenditure & investment
- Net exports
- Gross domestic product

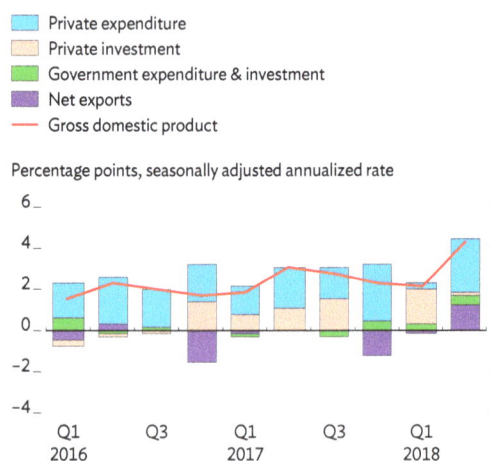

Percentage points, seasonally adjusted annualized rate

Q = quarter.
Sources: US Department of Commerce. Bureau of Economic Analysis. http://www.bea.gov; Haver Analytics (both accessed 4 September 2017).

US production will continue as this momentum and new tax incentives encourage domestic investment.

The labor market remained strong and the unemployment rate kept improving. Unemployment dipped below 4.0% in April and stayed in July and August firmly at 3.9%, one of the lowest rates in history. The economy added 147,000 nonfarm jobs in July and 201,000 in August. The average length of unemployment in the first 8 months of 2018 shortened to 23 weeks from 25 weeks in the same period of last year. Average weekly earnings rose by 3.1% in January–August 2018, improving on 2.5% in the same period of last year.

Continued strong growth in US economic activity has started to stir domestic inflation. Headline inflation reached 2.9% in June and July, the highest since March 2012, bringing average inflation to 2.5% in the year to July (Figure A1.3). Core inflation, which excludes food and energy, edged up from 2.3% in June to 2.4% in July. Rising inflation and a falling unemployment rate could give the Federal Reserve reason to proceed with its normalization of monetary policy and raise the benchmark interest rate further, bringing the Fed rate up to about 2.1% by the end of 2018. The speed with which this normalization progresses will depend on the growth and inflation rates realized during the year. Inflation is projected to accelerate to 2.5% in 2018 but ease to 2.2% in 2019 in response to monetary tightening.

With these developments, the US economy is now expected to grow by 2.8% in 2018, buoyed by its strong performance in Q2 as the short-term impact of tax cuts and higher spending were felt. Economic acceleration is seen to moderate to 2.4% in 2019 under anticipated tightening of monetary policy to prevent economic overheating. Meanwhile, a drift toward trade protectionism poses a downside risk to the forecast. Recently imposed tariffs on steel and aluminum may slow growth by inflating domestic production costs. Possible retaliation from trade partners could trigger a global trade war, creating serious downside risks to the global economy.

Euro area

Economic activity in the euro area lost momentum, slowing to 1.6% saar in Q1 from 2.5% growth in the whole of 2017. After propelling growth in Q4 of 2017, exports subtracted from growth in Q1. A stronger euro weighed down exports—which shrank by 2.9%, outpacing the decline in imports—and so weighed down growth. Softening growth in fixed investment, from 5.8% to 1.1%, and government consumption, from 0.8% to 0.4%, more than offset rising household spending (Figure A1.4).

A1.2 Business activity and consumer confidence indicators, United States

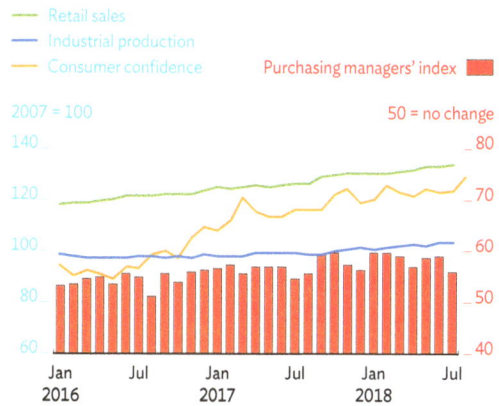

Note: A purchasing managers' index reading <50 signals deteriorating activity, >50 improvement.
Source: Haver Analytics (accessed 30 August 2018).

A1.3 Inflation, United States

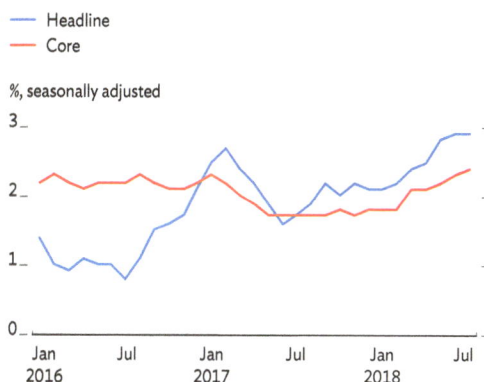

Source: Haver Analytics (accessed 30 August 2018).

Q1 softness in Germany, France, and Italy caused a slowdown in the euro area that was more pronounced than expected.

After the Q1 downshift, economic growth inched down further to 1.5% saar in Q2. Net exports continued to drag on growth for 2 consecutive quarters, contracting by 16.4% saar in Q2. Suffering from higher inflation, growth in private consumption braked to 0.7% saar from 2.0% in the previous quarter. Taking euro area economies individually, Germany helped to keep economic activity in the region on an even keel with growth at 1.8% saar in Q2, up from 1.5% in the previous quarter, growth in France was muted but steady at 0.6% saar, and growth in Italy slowed from 1.1% to 0.7%.

Assuming a gradual pickup in the second half of the year, the growth forecast for 2018 is still revised down to 2.0% from 2.2% in *ADO 2018* and maintained at 1.9% for 2019. Economic prospects in the region remain optimistic in light of a solid domestic economy, accommodative monetary policy, and adequate fiscal support. Consumer spending will go some way toward supporting activity, firmed by improving labor markets and a more positive jobs outlook. Investment is also set to contribute to growth, buoyed by favorable financing conditions, strong global demand, and high capacity utilization.

By and large, leading indicators remain supportive of continued growth in the currency bloc. Industrial production strongly rebounded in May before turning slightly negative in June (Figure A1.5). Similarly, retail trade resumed positive monthly readings in both May and June but turned slightly negative in July. The purchasing managers' index bounced back in June, ending its downward slide from January. Composite purchasing managers' indexes rose in France and Germany, and business conditions picked up broadly across the region, supported by improvements in the service sector. Economic sentiment weakened from an index reading of 114.9 in January to 111.6 in August but remains optimistic (Figure A1.6).

Labor markets in the region further improved as the unemployment rate dropped to 8.2% in July, the lowest since the global financial crisis of 2008–2009. Unemployment rates fell in Italy and Spain, remained unchanged in Germany and Portugal, and rose in France. Wage growth accelerated to 1.8% in Q1 from 1.6% in the previous quarter, which may spur inflation in the coming months.

With improving labor markets and higher oil prices, headline inflation was, at 2.0% in August, above the European Central Bank target of "under 2.0%" but slightly down from 2.1% a month earlier. Similarly, core inflation inched down to 1.2% in August from 1.3% in July. Low as it is, core inflation may soon rise steadily as wage growth firms.

A1.4 Demand-side contributions to growth, euro area

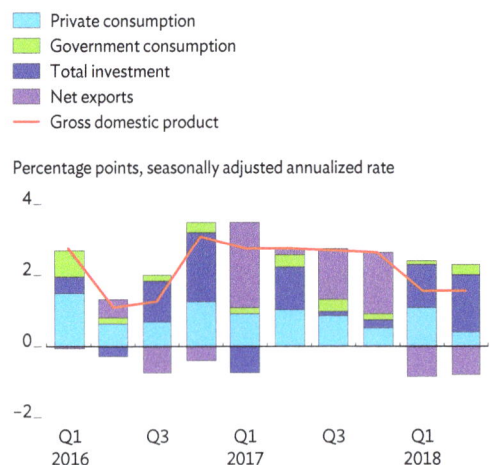

Private consumption
Government consumption
Total investment
Net exports
Gross domestic product

Percentage points, seasonally adjusted annualized rate

Q = quarter.
Source: Haver Analytics (accessed 10 September 2018).

A1.5 Selected economic indicators, euro area

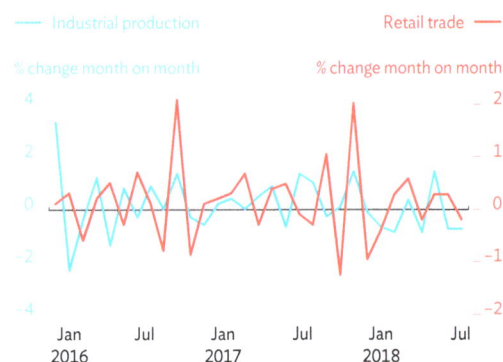

Industrial production   Retail trade

% change month on month   % change month on month

Source: Haver Analytics (accessed 13 September 2018).

The European Central Bank announced in June the winding down of its massive bond-buying program amid a healthy recovery and rising prices, signaling the beginning of the end for monetary stimulus in the euro area. The bank struck an accommodative tone, however, stating that it would leave interest rates unchanged until the end of summer 2019. Even so, inflation will pick up only gradually as the year progresses, so inflation forecasts are revised up slightly from *ADO 2018* to 1.5% for 2018 and 1.6% for 2019.

Risks to the outlook tilt to the downside. Trade is unlikely to support growth in the euro area with the euro strong and protectionism rising initially in the US and then elsewhere. Uncertainty surrounding Brexit negotiations, the deepening migration crisis, and member states' difficulty agreeing on euro area structural reform may dent market sentiment, worsen volatility, and sharpen lending conditions. In late August, Italian bond spreads over Germany's 10-year benchmark bond reached their highest since a large selloff in May as markets worried over government spending and potential fallout across Europe from member states' unwillingness to share responsibility for migrants arriving in Italy. A further risk is major European banks' heavy exposure to financial turmoil in Turkey, where pressure is growing on the lira and the balance of payments.

Japan

Recovery having stalled briefly in Q1 of 2018, Japan's return to growth in Q2 on improving domestic demand should limit this year's slowdown even as rising trade tensions and geopolitical uncertainties weigh on exports. The economy recovered strongly in Q2 as real GDP expanded by 3.0% saar, reversing contraction by 0.9% in the previous quarter. This dip had followed 8 consecutive quarters of growth, one of the longest runs of expansion since the 1980s. Growth in Q2 was driven by a rebound in private investment, which contributed 1.7 percentage points, and consumption, which contributed 1.6 points. Net exports, which had previously propelled the expansion, dragged on GDP growth by 0.5 percentage points in the latest quarter, owing partly to weakened exports and partly to robust growth in imports (Figure A1.7).

While strong business investment propelled growth in Q2, some monthly indicators suggest that business activity may have slowed slightly. In July, industrial production fell for a third consecutive month, by 0.1%. However, seasonally adjusted core machinery orders, a leading indicator of capital expenditure, rebounded in July by 11.0% from the previous month. The Nikkei Japan purchasing managers' index edged up from 52.3 in July to 52.5 in August, its value above the threshold of 50 suggesting that manufacturing continues to expand (Figure A1.8).

A1.6 Economic sentiment and purchasing managers' indexes, euro area

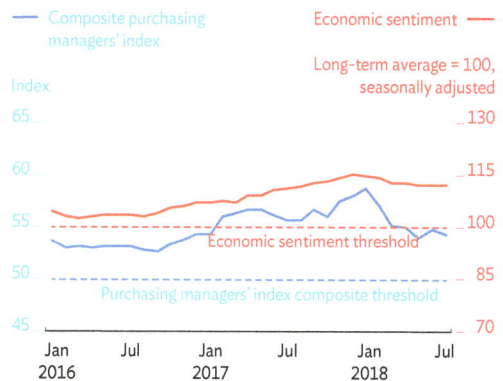

Sources: Bloomberg; Haver Analytics (both accessed 30 August 2018).

A1.7 Demand-side contributions to growth, Japan

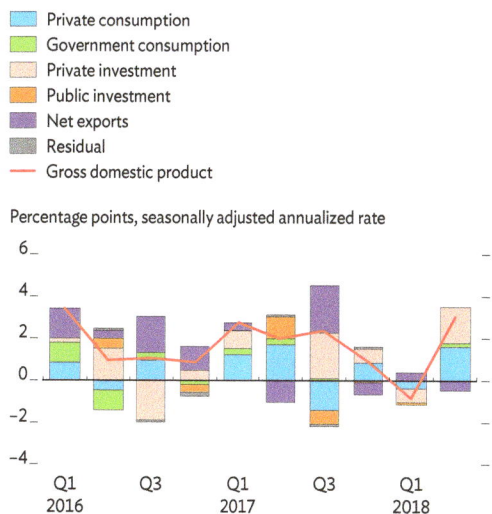

Source: Economics and Social Research Institute, Cabinet Office, Government of Japan. http://www.esri.cao.go.jp (accessed 10 September 2018).

Private consumption expanded strongly in Q2. However, a subdued increase of 0.1% in seasonally adjusted retail sales in July showed sluggishness in consumption demand at the start of Q3. This resonated with further weakening of the consumer confidence index from 43.3 in July to 43.2 in August, which may be reining in spending. On the other hand, the Bank of Japan's consumption activity index ticked up in June by 0.4% year on year. Wage growth improved in July, which, combined with a low unemployment rate hovering around 2.5% that month, should continue to boost consumer income and spending power. Anticipation of an imminent hike in consumption tax is also expected to raise spending in the short term.

Price pressures are building only slowly, however, and the inflation rate remains well under the Bank of Japan target of 2.0%. Consumer price inflation year on year picked up from 0.7% in June to 1.0% in July, partly driven by higher energy costs. Core inflation, which excludes fresh food and energy, crept into positive territory. At its latest meeting, the Bank of Japan maintained its accommodative monetary policy, with the short-term policy rate at –0.1% and 10-year Japanese government bond yields capped at about zero (but with slight adjustment of the band around zero to keep bond markets functioning).

Merchandise exports continued a run of growth that started in June 2016, though at a slower pace with exports up by 4.9% in July year on year but down from 7.6% in June. Weaker export growth in July reflected lower shipments to the US as demand fell for machinery and transport equipment. Import growth accelerated in July by 15.8%, well above the 3.4% growth in June. This swung the trade balance from a surplus of $6.5 billion in June to a deficit of $2.1 billion in July (Figure A1.9).

Notwithstanding the contraction in Q1 from weak domestic demand, the outlook is for moderate growth in 2018 supported by easy domestic financial conditions and a favorable labor market that can spur consumption growth. Gains in investment—buoyed by elevated business sentiment and supported by expenditure on preparations for the 2020 Summer Olympics in Tokyo—may be overshadowed, however, by rising trade tensions that squeeze the all-important external sector. Following GDP growth at 1.7% in 2017, growth is expected to slow to 1.1% in 2018 and further to 1.0% in 2019, partly in anticipation of the impending consumption tax hike.

A1.8 Consumption and business indicators, Japan

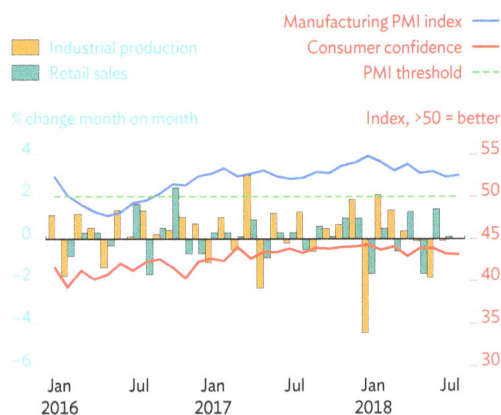

PMI = purchasing managers' index.
Notes: A purchasing managers' index reading <50 signals deteriorating activity, >50 improvement. A consumer confidence reading >50 signals better conditions. Data on industrial production are in quarters.
Sources: Haver Analytics; Bloomberg (both accessed 7 September 2018).

A1.9 Trade indicators, Japan

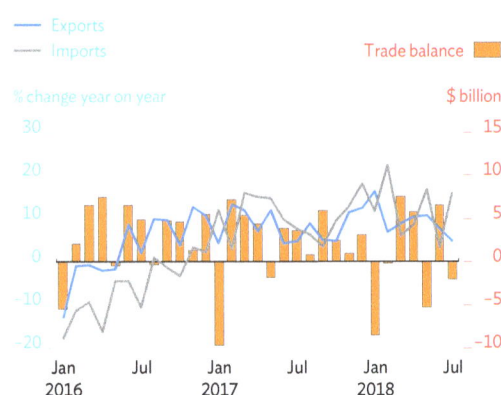

Sources: Haver Analytics; Bloomberg (both accessed 7 September 2018).

Australia and New Zealand

The Australian economy expanded by 3.5% saar in Q2 of 2018, slowing from 4.7% in Q1 (Figure A1.10). Consumption was the top contributor to growth, adding 2.3 percentage points, and net exports added 0.5 points, while fixed capital formation made no contribution and changes in inventory subtracted 0.1 points. Seasonally adjusted retail sales were stagnant in July 2018, but average monthly growth in the first 7 months of 2018 was 0.3%, up from 0.2% in the same period of 2017. The consumer sentiment index rose from 102.1 in June to 106.1 in July, the highest in 10 months and well above the 100 demarcation between optimism and pessimism. The business confidence index, which subtracts the percentage of pessimists from that of optimists, declined from 7 points in May to 6 points in June but remained above the zero threshold. The seasonally adjusted unemployment rate ticked down from 5.4% in June to 5.3% in July. The Australian Industry Group's manufacturing performance index increased from 52.0 points in July to 56.7 in August, well above the threshold of 50 points indicating expansion in manufacturing. Inflation increased from 1.9% in Q1 to 2.1% in Q2, entering the Reserve Bank of Australia target range of 2.0%–3.0%. In its 7 August 2018 monetary policy meeting, the central bank retained its all-time-low policy rate of 1.5%. With continuing expansion in retail sales and upbeat consumer sentiment, private consumption is expected to remain a major driver of economic growth, all the more so following income tax cuts approved by the Senate in mid-June. Portents of further economic growth are found in continued expansion in manufacturing, measures of business confidence that show optimism regarding future economic conditions, and a strong labor market. FocusEconomics panelists forecast GDP expanding by 2.9% in 2018 and 2.8% in 2019 on the expectation that exports will grow in a positive global environment and that business investment outside of mining will find support from accommodative monetary policy and encouraging business conditions.

New Zealand grew by 1.1% saar in Q1 of 2018, slowing from 1.7% growth in Q4 of 2017. This was the lowest rate in the past 19 quarters. Change in inventories was the biggest contributor to growth, adding 1.8 percentage points. Fixed capital added 0.7 points, and consumption added 0.3 points, while net exports subtracted 1.7 points (Figure A1.11). Retail sales expanded by 3.8% in Q2, up from 3.4% in the previous quarter. The seasonally adjusted performance of manufacturing index increased from 51.2 in July to 52.0 in August, further above the threshold of 50 indicating expansion. The business confidence index declined deeper into negative territory, from –44.9 in July to –50.3 in August.

A1.10 Demand-side contributions to growth, Australia

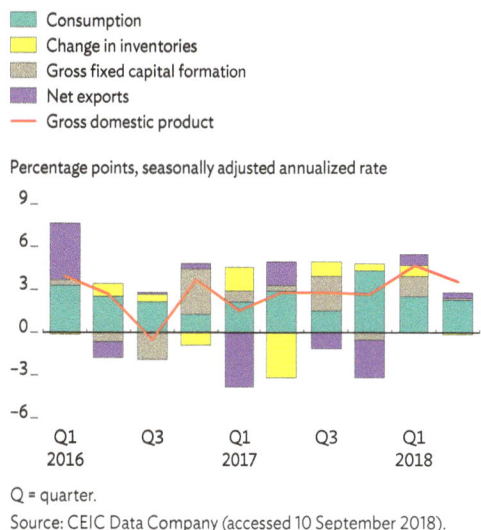

- Consumption
- Change in inventories
- Gross fixed capital formation
- Net exports
- Gross domestic product

Percentage points, seasonally adjusted annualized rate

Q = quarter.
Source: CEIC Data Company (accessed 10 September 2018).

A1.11 Demand-side contributions to growth, New Zealand

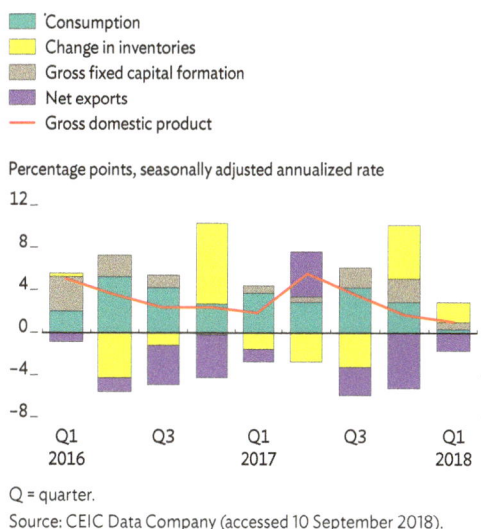

- Consumption
- Change in inventories
- Gross fixed capital formation
- Net exports
- Gross domestic product

Percentage points, seasonally adjusted annualized rate

Q = quarter.
Source: CEIC Data Company (accessed 10 September 2018).

However, consumer confidence remained positive at 120.0 in June, only slightly lower than 121.0 in May, with values above 100 indicating optimism. Inflation rose from 1.1% in Q1 to 1.5% in the following quarter, still well within the Reserve Bank of New Zealand target of 1.0%–3.0%. The seasonally adjusted unemployment rate ticked up from 4.4% in Q1 to 4.5% in Q2. In its 9 August 2018 meeting, the central bank retained the official cash rate at a record low of 1.75%. Consumer optimism, buoyed by a robust labor market and low interest rates, could boost private consumption, as indicated by higher retail sales. The tight labor market and persistent expansion in manufacturing support the prospect of steady growth. FocusEconomics panelists expect growth at 2.7% in both 2018 and 2019, underpinned by government plans to increase spending, an accommodative monetary policy, and favorable export prices.

Commodity prices

Commodities stirred in 2018 following subdued prices in recent years. Economic and geopolitical developments have caused wide fluctuations in oil prices, and rising demand in the face of declining production has put upward pressure on food prices.

Oil price movements and prospects

The price of Brent crude oil hovered around $70/barrel in the first 8 months of 2018 (Figure A1.12). Toward the latter part of May, prices reached their highest since 2014. Brent crude oil spot prices averaged $77/barrel in May, or $5 above the April average. Oil prices retreated slightly after Organization of the Petroleum Exporting Countries (OPEC) oil ministers and 10 non-OPEC oil ministers met on 22 June and agreed to increase oil production in view of an improved oil market. Consequently, OPEC crude oil production was higher in July than average production in the first half of 2018. Since then, oil prices have risen further as concerns mounted about US sanctions on Iran.

Prices have remained relatively high because of various supply concerns. The re-imposition of US sanctions on Iran is the key price driver in the near term. Market analysts estimate supply losses to be 0.6 million–1.5 million barrels per day (mbd). As the first wave of US sanctions suspended in January 2016 under the Iran nuclear deal were reinstated last 7 August, Brent crude prices rose to $74/barrel, up 50 cents, or 0.7%, from their last close. Another set of sanctions, this time more focused on Iran's energy sector, will be re-imposed in November 2018. In Venezuela, supply dropped to a record low of 1.3 mbd in July, or 0.7 mbd lower than a year earlier.

A1.12 Price of Brent crude

—— Spot
—— Annual average

Sources: Bloomberg; World Bank. Commodity Price Data (Pink Sheet). http://www.worldbank.org (both accessed 6 September 2018).

The reemergence of Libya as a risk factor affecting global supply follows a series of attacks on key infrastructure that saw production plummet to 0.7 mbd in July from more than 1.0 mbd a year earlier. Though improving, the situation remains unstable. Other geopolitical concerns—notably military escalation in Syria and tensions between Saudi Arabia and Iran—also support higher oil prices.

The upward pressure on oil prices has been countered by continued increases in US production. The US Energy Information Administration forecasts US crude oil production to rise from 9.4 mbd in 2017 to 10.8 mbd in 2018 and 11.8 mbd in 2019. If these forecasts are realized, production will surpass the previous record of 9.6 mbd set in 1970. Oil prices have been supported as well by strong consumption growth. The International Energy Agency (IEA) estimates in its August 2018 report that global oil consumption in the first half of 2018 was 1.3 mbd higher than in the first half of 2017, a rise of 1.3%. Some analysts warned that recent scorching summer temperatures in the northern hemisphere could affect oil demand by pushing up demand for air-conditioning.

In its August 2018 report, the IEA forecasts global oil demand to increase by 1.4 mbd in 2018 and 1.5 mbd in 2019, driven mostly by higher consumption in countries outside the Organisation for Economic Co-operation and Development (OECD). Non-OECD oil consumption is projected to rise by 1.0 mbd in 2018, less than the growth in 2017 as rising prices tamp down demand, then by 1.2 mbd in 2019 as the impact of higher prices subsides. Global oil supply rose to 99.4 mbd in July, or 1.1 mbd above a year earlier. OPEC compliance with agreed production cuts slipped to 97% in July as output cuts were relaxed. So far, there has been little impact on Iran's crude production from renewed US sanctions, but exports have fallen from the elevated levels of April and May. The IEA forecasts non-OPEC supply to expand by 2.0 mbd in 2018 and by 1.4 mbd in 2019.

The outlook for oil prices remains volatile. On the upside are further declines in Venezuelan production, cuts in Iranian crude oil exports larger than assumed with the re-imposition of sanctions, and emerging infrastructure constraints that could limit projected growth in US oil production. Oil prices could head much lower if Iran's trade partners do not significantly reduce their oil imports from Iran, US oil production ends up stronger than expected, Libyan production recovers, or demand growth slows in response to higher prices. Daily spot prices averaged $71.6/barrel in 2018 to the end of August, and the futures market shows Brent crude trading above $70/barrel for the next 2 years (Figure A1.13). This *Update* therefore raises the forecast for Brent crude to $74/barrel in both 2018 and 2019.

A1.13 Brent crude futures and spot prices

— Average spot price
-- Futures price (15 March 2018)
-- Futures price (6 June 2018)
--- Futures price (6 September 2018)

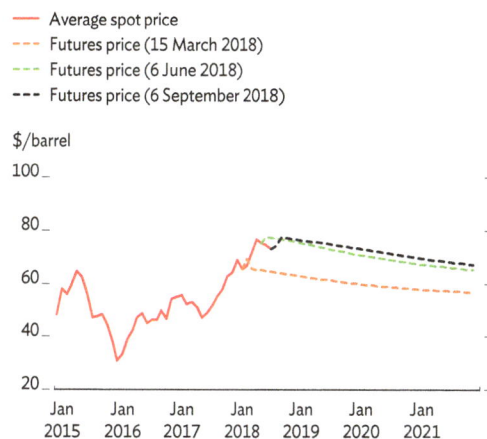

$/barrel

Source: Bloomberg (accessed 6 September 2018).

Food price movements and prospects

International food prices have been rising faster than forecast in *ADO 2018*. After a slight decline in July 2018 from a year earlier, the World Bank food price index averaged 88.6 points in August, 2.1% higher than in August 2017 (Figure A1.14). In the first 8 months of the year, food inflation averaged 2.6%. Two of the three World Bank price indexes tracking food prices, one for grain and another for edible oil and meal, rose while the "other food" index declined.

Grain prices increased by 11.1% from January to August. The grain index has followed an upward trend since July of last year, with prices for wheat, maize, and rice all gaining upward momentum in recent months. Wheat prices rose by a third in August as prolonged heat and dry conditions in the European Union and the Russian Federation took their toll on wheat crops. International prices for maize rebounded in August after two successive monthly declines. Lower maize shipments from Brazil and Argentina contributed to initially higher US maize quotations, and rising wheat prices further pushed up demand for maize. Rice prices rose in anticipation of higher demand from the PRC.

Prices for edible oil and meal edged up by 1.7% from January to August of this year. The latest price slide for edible oil and meal, importantly palm and soy oil, prevented the index from rising more markedly. International palm oil prices fell further in response to sluggish export demand, ample stocks held by leading producers, and expectations of higher production. Soy oil prices dropped because of weakness in the soybean market in general and persistently high production in the US and Brazil. The index for "other food" saw prices decline by 2.6% in the first 7 months of the year as a supply glut pushed down the price of sugar, the commodity with the highest weight in the index.

In its August assessment of global crop conditions, the United States Department of Agriculture (USDA) forecasts global grain production reaching 2,559 million tons in the current 2018/19 crop season. This is lower than estimated production in 2017/2018 but still above the 5-year average. Global wheat production is expected to decline, primarily with lower production in the European Union because of continuing drought. Rice production is forecast slightly lower than the USDA July assessment because of lower yields in the US. Lower production and higher global grain demand are expected to push the ratio of grain stock to use to its lowest since 2013/2014. The outlook for edible oil remains strong with the USDA forecasting higher production, exports, and ending stocks in 2018/19. The Agricultural Market Information System reported in August that the latter part of 2018 may witness El Niño weather disturbances but substantially weaker

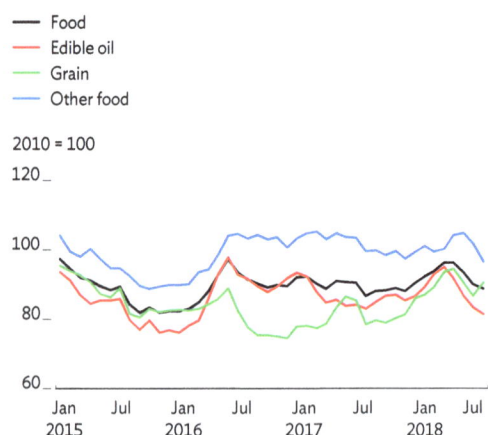

A1.14 Food commodity price indexes

— Food
— Edible oil
— Grain
— Other food

2010 = 100

Source: World Bank. Commodity Price Data (Pink Sheet). http://www.worldbank.org (accessed 10 September 2018).

than those in 2015 and 2016. Given higher projected oil prices, strong demand, and lower expectations for production, the forecast for higher food prices is raised to 3.0% in 2018 and 2.0% in 2019.

External environment in sum

Growth in the major industrial economies has so far been broadly in line with *ADO 2018* forecasts. Tariffs and countermeasures implemented to date have not notably affected demand growth, though data for August show some early signs of waning investor confidence, and there is a clear downside risk as tensions escalate. Although the PRC has been specifically targeted by the US, exports from developing Asia should enjoy strong demand buoyed by continuing economic strength in the advanced economies. While monetary policy in Japan will remain accommodative to the forecast horizon, continued US interest rate rises and the end of quantitative easing in the euro area will generally tighten global liquidity. Inflation in developing Asia is subject to some upward pressure from higher price rises for oil and food, but the uptick in commodity prices is unlikely to derail regional growth. While the external environment has deteriorated somewhat since *ADO 2018* was published in April, it remains broadly supportive.

2

MAINTAINING STABILITY AMID HEIGHTENED UNCERTAINTY

Maintaining stability amid heightened uncertainty

Two decades after the Asian financial crisis (AFC) in 1997–1998, the role of Asia and the Pacific as the main engine of growth in the global economy is firmly established. The crisis did not affect all Asian economies equally—as it was concentrated mainly in East and Southeast Asia, with Thailand worst affected, followed by Indonesia, the Republic of Korea, and Malaysia—but it was felt across the region. At the height of the AFC, economic growth in developing Asia plunged to below 2% after having averaged about 8% for 5 years prior to the crisis. This debacle slashed the regional share of global economic growth to below 30%. A strong economic rebound in subsequent years restored this contribution to 40%.

Rapid output expansion before the AFC was fueled by high investment rates in East and Southeast Asia that surpassed savings rates. The resulting current account deficits were financed by foreign borrowing that fueled faster economic growth. Deficits and credit were generally propped up by overvalued currencies in economies whose governments stuck to inflexible exchange rate regimes until they collapsed following the sudden stop in capital flows during the AFC. Sharp currency corrections and capital outflows drained liquidity in the affected economies and eventually decimated domestic investment. Lower rates of investment following the AFC slowed economic growth in many economies in developing Asia (Figure 2.0.1).

This chapter reviews the factors that contributed to Asia's recovery from the AFC. These factors were among those that helped developing Asia withstand the global financial crisis (GFC). The analysis then considers the region's emerging pockets of vulnerability that evolved along the way. Its observations and conclusions inform a discussion of policy options to address these pockets of vulnerability. The discussion addresses issues pertaining to the whole of developing Asia but illustrates some insights using analysis of smaller sets of economies selected for data availability.

2.0.1 Investment and GDP growth, emerging Asia

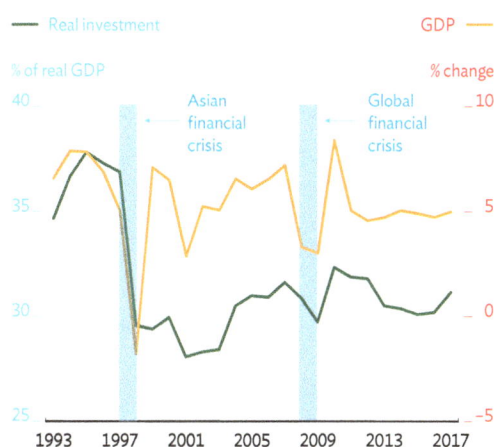

GDP = gross domestic product.

Note: Emerging Asia includes Hong Kong, China; India; Indonesia; Malaysia; the Philippines; the Republic of Korea; Singapore; Taipei,China; Thailand; and Viet Nam.

Sources: *Asian Development Outlook* database, Haver Analytics (accessed 7 September 2018), ADB estimates.

This chapter was written by Arief Ramayandi, Madhavi Pundit, Donghyun Park, and Hsiao Chink Tang of the Economic Research and Regional Cooperation Department, ADB, Manila. It draws on background papers listed at the end of the chapter.

A gathering cloud of uncertainty and vulnerability

In response to the AFC, Asian governments undertook several reforms to strengthen their economic fundamentals. Healthy external conditions further supported growth over the next several years such that, when the GFC struck, developing Asia was able to weather the storm well. However, in recent decades pockets of vulnerability have built up in the course of complex interactions between the financial sector and the real economy, as well as from other domestic and external developments. More lately, a cloud of uncertainty has begun to gather in the form of a changing global economic and political environment. This has unmasked the lurking vulnerabilities that threatens to affect the region's macroeconomic stability.

Asia as an engine of global growth

For the past 3 decades, developing Asia has been an increasingly important contributor to global economic growth (Figure 2.1.1). Its share of growth dipped in the aftermath of the AFC but has since been sustained. The global economy was shaken when the dot-com bubble burst in the early 2000s, but Asia was barely affected, continuing to recover from the AFC and growing at relatively stable pace, and meanwhile building up its fundamentals. When the GFC struck, developing Asia provided a crucial buffer, largely offsetting 3% economic contraction in the rest of the world in 2009. Global growth resumed in 2010, with the region providing the lion's share. As the engine of the global economy, developing Asia has grown since the GFC at an average pace of 6.8% annually, and it currently accounts for more than 60% of global growth.

Recovery from the AFC and subsequently stable economic growth were accompanied by moderating trends in inflation and output volatility. The favorable economic conditions brought significant progress in economic development, income growth, and poverty reduction. Strong development progress in Asia intensified economic activity in the region and also boosted Asian influence in the global economic arena. At the same time, the region has managed to improve the well-being of the broad majority of its people.

An example of how welfare has improved in developing Asia since its recovery from the AFC is the reduction in extreme poverty, defined as living on $1.90 per day in 2011

2.1.1 Contributions to global growth

— Developing Asia
— Rest of the world
— World GDP

Percentage points

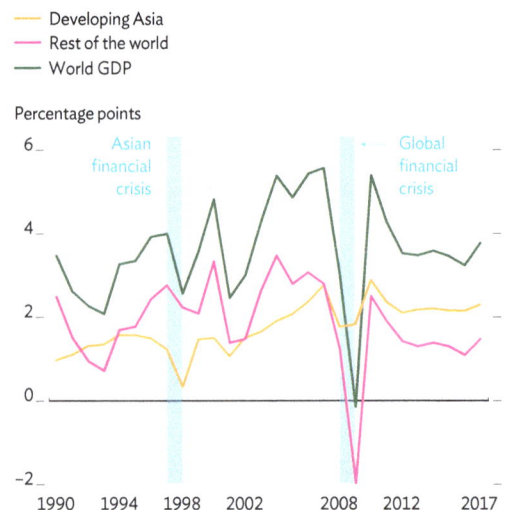

GDP = gross domestic product.
Sources: *Asian Development Outlook* database, Haver Analytics (accessed 7 September 2018), ADB estimates.

purchasing power parity (Figure 2.1.2). In 2002, over 1 billion people, or 33.7% of the regional population, lived in extreme poverty. This was slashed to 758 million people, or 21.5% of the population, only half a dozen years later in 2008. Five years after the GFC, the number fell substantially to only 331 million, or 8.9% of the population.

The geographic concentration of extreme poverty shifted during this time. In 2002, the incidence of poverty was greatest in South and East Asia, which together had 86.1% of the extreme poor in the region. The combined share remained the same in 2008, but extreme poverty skewed toward South Asia as East Asia managed much faster progress in reducing extreme poverty. South Asia still had the most extreme poverty in 2013, followed by Southeast Asia.

By 2013, East Asia was the subregion with the lowest incidence of extreme poverty, as only 1.8% of its population still lived below the $1.90 threshold. The Pacific has remained since 2002 the subregion with the highest density of extreme poverty, the incidence in 2013 at 30.3%. Despite the tremendous progress achieved so far, more than 300 million people in developing Asia still live in extreme poverty, so reducing poverty should remain a priority in the whole region.

Favorable economic conditions since the AFC are outcomes of both internal efforts within the economies of developing Asia, such as the pursuit of domestic reform, and a conducive external environment that has allowed developing Asia to expand its exports and enjoy the benefits of global financial liquidity. Reform and improved macroeconomic management across the region have established sound domestic fundamentals. Meanwhile, the GFC notwithstanding, external conditions have been for the most part beneficial to the region, especially in the immediate aftermath of both the AFC and the GFC.

Improvements in fundamentals

Macroeconomic fundamentals improved in developing Asia with economic restructuring and policy reform in the wake of the AFC. The painful experience of the crisis encouraged governments to move toward more flexible exchange rates, more independence for central banks, and the implementation of financial and fiscal reform. All these factors strengthened fundamentals, bringing better alignment to local currencies, lower and more stable inflation, less volatile output fluctuations, more favorable current account balances, and the accumulation of foreign exchange reserves. The improved fundamentals paid handsome dividends during the GFC, which the region weathered much better than it did the AFC.

2.1.2 Extreme poverty incidence in Asia

- 2002
- 2008
- 2013

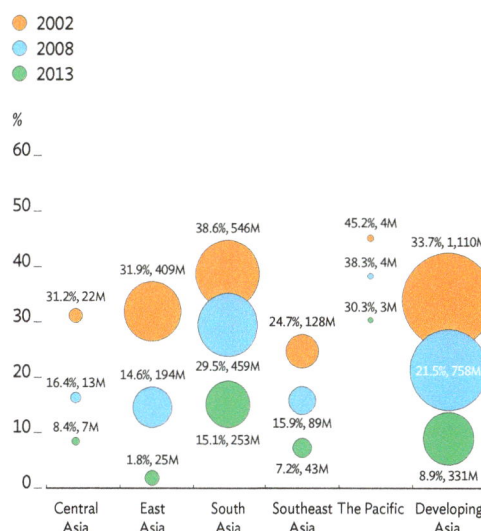

M = million.

Notes: The numbers next to the bubbles show the percentage of population in extreme poverty and the absolute number in millions. Central Asia includes Armenia, Azerbaijan, Georgia, Kazakhstan, the Kyrgyz Republic, Tajikistan, Turkmenistan, and Uzbekistan. East Asia includes the People's Republic of China and Mongolia. The Pacific includes Fiji, the Federated States of Micronesia, Kiribati, Papua New Guinea, Samoa, Solomon Islands, Timor-Leste, Tonga, Tuvalu, and Vanuatu. South Asia includes Bangladesh, Bhutan, India, Maldives, Nepal, Pakistan, and Sri Lanka. Southeast Asia includes Indonesia, the Lao People's Democratic Republic, Malaysia, Myanmar, the Philippines, Thailand, and Viet Nam.

Sources: ADB estimates using World Bank; PovcalNet Database: http://iresearch.worldbank.org/PovcalNet/home.aspx.

More flexible exchange rates allowed economies to avoid potentially damaging currency misalignment in the form of overvaluation, which could cause prolonged current account deficits. Exchange rates in Indonesia, Malaysia, the Republic of Korea, and Thailand experienced massive corrections after having limited movement prior to the AFC (Park, Ramayandi, and Shin 2014). After the AFC, many governments adopted more flexible exchange rate regimes but continued to acquire more international reserves. Although somewhat inconsistent with having more flexible exchange rates, these ample international reserves provided central bankers with plenty of ammunition to defend their currencies during the GFC.

Figure 2.1.3 illustrates a "fear of floating" tendency that remains strong among policy makers in developing Asia. It describes the discrepancy between *de facto* and *de jure* exchange rate regimes in nine economies. Scores indicate that declared regimes are more flexible than actual policy—that, after the authorities officially declare the adoption of more flexible regimes, they still intervene in markets to manage exchange rate volatility. The scores nevertheless indicate gradual movement toward greater exchange rate flexibility.

The trend toward more flexible exchange rates has contributed to greater resilience under external shock. Unlike the sharp currency depreciation seen during the AFC, there was less pressure for exchange rate correction during the GFC. The better-aligned currencies protected regional financial markets from speculative attacks that could have induced an exodus of capital from Asia.

In addition, less pressure for exchange rate correction has provided greater independence for monetary policy. Before the AFC, the massive pressure for currency depreciation experienced by several economies left their monetary authorities with no practical scope for easing interest rates to help stimulate slumping economies. By contrast, the scope for economic stimulation through monetary policy was relatively wide during the GFC, providing ways for the region to expand aggregate domestic demand at the height of the crisis.

Along with the move to more flexible exchange rates, regional economies have pursued more independence for monetary authorities. This can be gleaned from Figure 2.1.4, which shows how representative economies in East, South, and Southeast Asia have moved on average toward more independent monetary authorities, as indicated by the central bank independence index compiled in Garriga (2016). Progress has been relatively gradual but continuous in South and Southeast Asia and more stop-and-go in East Asia.

2.1.3 Trends in exchange regimes in Asia

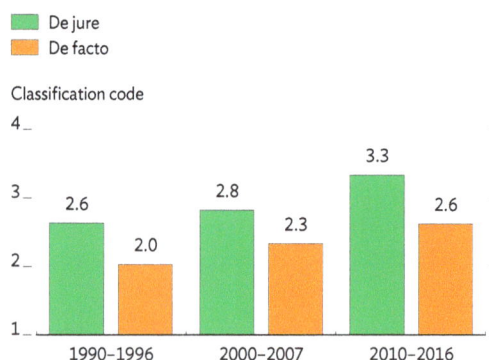

■ De jure
■ De facto

Classification code

1 = pre-announced peg, 2 = crawling peg, 3 = managed float, 4 = flexible.

Note: Average of the exchange rate regimes in India, Indonesia, Malaysia, the People's Republic of China, the Philippines, the Republic of Korea, Singapore, Thailand, and Viet Nam.

Sources: IMF Annual Report on Exchange Arrangements and Exchange Restrictions (AREAER) database; Ilzetzki, Reinhart, and Rogoff 2017.

2.1.4 Trend in the central bank independence index

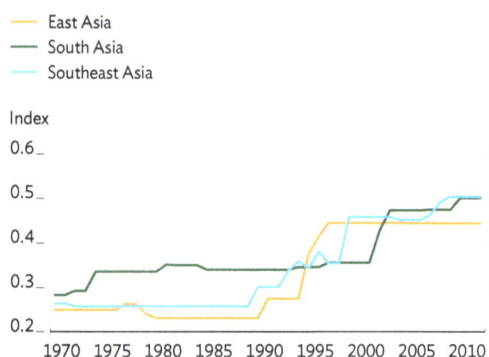

— East Asia
— South Asia
— Southeast Asia

Index

Notes: East Asia includes Mongolia, the People's Republic of China, the Republic of Korea, and Taipei,China. South Asia includes Afghanistan, Bangladesh, Bhutan, India, Maldives, Nepal, Pakistan, and Sri Lanka. Southeast Asia includes Cambodia, Indonesia, the Lao People's Democratic Republic, Malaysia, Myanmar, the Philippines, Singapore, Thailand, and Viet Nam.

Source: ADB estimates using data from Garriga 2016.

While East and Southeast Asia progressed most notably in the 1990s, South Asia made greater strides toward central bank independence in the early 2000s.

With more independence, central banks in the region have better control over the instruments they use to stabilize prices and/or output, such as policy interest rates, and over growth in the money supply. This adds to their credibility. Evidence of the positive impact of a more independent central bank is pervasive. More credible central banks mitigate macroeconomic uncertainties that undermine growth and stability.

The trend toward more independent central banks in developing Asia is consistent with the move toward more flexible exchange rates and with regional efforts to further deepen its financial sector. As such, central banks can act more independently to advance macroeconomic stability. Meanwhile, financial deepening occurs through the liberalization of domestic financial regulations. With these developments, investors and other economic agents can operate with greater certainty.

With regard to fiscal policy, measures introduced to instill more disciplined management practices have aimed primarily to contain fiscal deficits. These reforms worked by providing governments in the region with adequate fiscal resources to mitigate the adverse impacts of the GFC. For example, between 2003 and 2005, India, Indonesia, Pakistan, and Sri Lanka introduced rules intended to prevent government budget deficits and debt from becoming proportionately large (Budina et al. 2012).[1] Subsequently, Armenia implemented a rule on government debt in 2008, only after the GFC, and Maldives and Mongolia introduced similar rules in 2013 and 2014.

Mainly because of these measures, the ratio of public debt to GDP in the region has declined, thereby creating more fiscal flexibility. By 2016, average public indebtedness in Asia was the equivalent of only 29.3% of GDP. The trend varies, however, across the region (Figure 2.1.5). In East Asia it is generally flat, hovering around a low base, with some bumps around the GFC as governments implemented fiscal stimulus to cushion the crisis impact. The large fiscal stimulus in the PRC supported growth there and upheld its demand for imports from the region.

Southeast Asia experienced a buildup of public debt after the AFC, but the ratio subsequently declined and reached an average of 45% in 2016. The ratio of public debt to GDP in Central Asia dipped below 20% from 2005, following a rapid increase in global commodity prices, notably oil. The ratio gradually increased as the boom in oil prices subsided but was still below 20% in 2016. South Asia is the subregion with the highest public debt, but the ratio of public debt

2.1.5 Public debt

— Central Asia
— East Asia
— South Asia
— Southeast Asia
— The Pacific
— Developing Asia

% of GDP

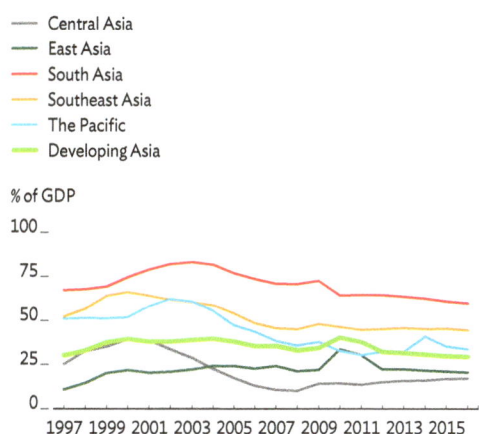

GDP = gross domestic product.

Sources: CEIC Data Company; Haver Analytics; International Monetary Fund (IMF) Article IV various years; IMF. World Economic Outlook online database. www.imf.org/external/pubs/ft/weo/2018/01/weodata/download.aspx; World Bank. World Development Indicators online database. data.worldbank.org/products/wdi (all accessed 1 August 2018); ADB estimates.

to GDP declined steadily to just below 60% in 2016, after peaking at 83% in 2003. The trend in the Pacific is somewhat similar to that of South Asia but with lower values.

There may be a limit to the amount of fiscal stimulus that economies in developing Asia can apply. This is because the average fiscal deficit in the region is just over 3%, which is an informal threshold that should not be breached (Figure 2.1.6). This deficit figure is an average and therefore not true for all subregions or for all economies. Nevertheless, there is a distinct possibility that many regional governments facing a crisis could apply adequate fiscal support only by ignoring the informal 3% threshold.

Buoyant external conditions

In the aftermath of the AFC, buoyant external demand helped several Asian economies export their way out of the crisis. Commodity exporters greatly benefited from the boom in international prices, particularly for oil. A sharp pickup in oil prices marked the accumulation of current account surpluses in developing Asia (Figure 2.1.7). Steady, rapid growth in the volume of global trade before the GFC provided to Asian economies strong external demand to absorb their exports. With sharp increases in export prices, the Asian current account went into surplus, peaking at 6.5% of GDP in 2007.

2.1.6 Fiscal balance of central government

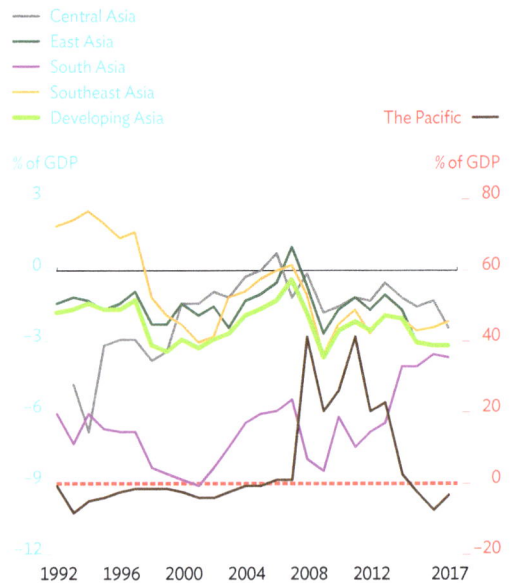

GDP = gross domestic product.
Source: *Asian Development Outlook* database.

2.1.7 World trade

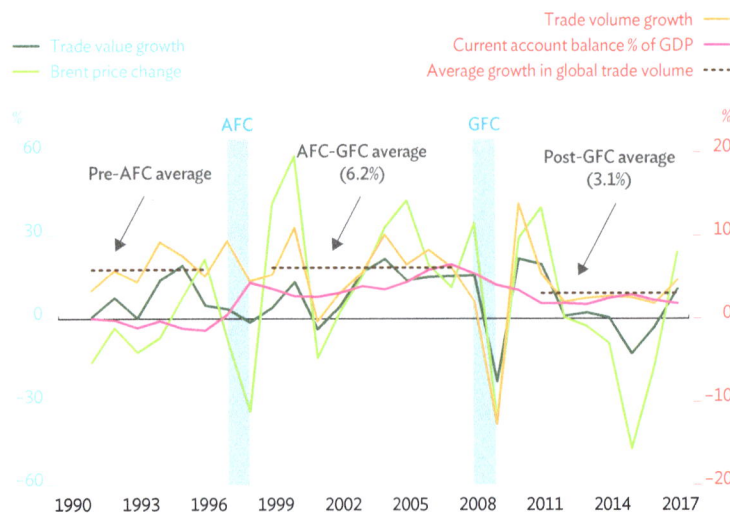

AFC = Asian financial crisis, GDP = gross domestic product, GFC = global financial crisis.
Sources: *Asian Development Outlook* database for current account balance, BP Statistical Review of World Energy June 2018 (www.bp.com/statisticalreview) for Brent prices, World Trade Organization (stat.wto.org) for trade.

Regional current account surpluses tended to narrow after the GFC brought a sudden collapse in global demand and then slower growth. Global demand volume slid by more than 12% at the height of the GFC in 2009 as the international oil price plunged by 37%. After briefly bouncing back in 2010, average growth in global demand fell by half from 6.2% in the years between the AFC and the GFC to 3.1% in the period 2011–2017. As a result, the aggregate current account surplus in developing Asia shrank.

In response to the subprime mortgage crisis that snowballed into the GFC, the US Federal Reserve proactively pushed down its reference interest rate, the federal funds rate, to nearly zero and poured massive amounts of liquidity into the economy through so-called quantitative easing. QE was intended to provide the stimulation needed to counter failing aggregate demand in the US. Central banks in the other advanced economies—the European Central Bank, Bank of England, and Bank of Japan—conducted their own QE programs to expand liquidity in their respective economies. The easing of monetary policy in the advanced economies, through long-sustained low interest rates and direct asset purchases by central banks, flooded the global economy with massive liquidity, driving investors in search of higher yields. A result was a surge in capital flows into emerging economies, including those in developing Asia.

The surge in capital inflows helped push up indebtedness as seen in accelerated growth in private credit across the region (Figure 2.1.8). Most of the growth in credit took place in East Asia. Similar trends were observed in other subregions but to a somewhat lesser degree. This contributed to economic growth after the GFC and boosted asset valuations in the region.

Changing external environment

Figure 2.1.9 is a graphical representation of the loose monetary policy implemented by the Fed to deal with the subprime mortgage crisis in the US and the GFC that ensued. It shows the drop in the federal funds rate from 5.25% in June 2006 to 0.125% in December 2008. Once the Fed was confronted by the liquidity trap (an interest rate too low to attract investors) it pushed beyond conventional monetary policy by regularly purchasing large amounts of US government and agency securities, to ensure that the long-term interest rate stayed low. The three rounds of QE— in November 2008, November 2010, and September 2012— had enlarged Fed asset holdings by more than a factor of 8 by the time the QE program ended in 2014.

2.1.8 Private debt

- Central Asia
- East Asia
- South Asia
- Southeast Asia
- The Pacific
- Developing Asia

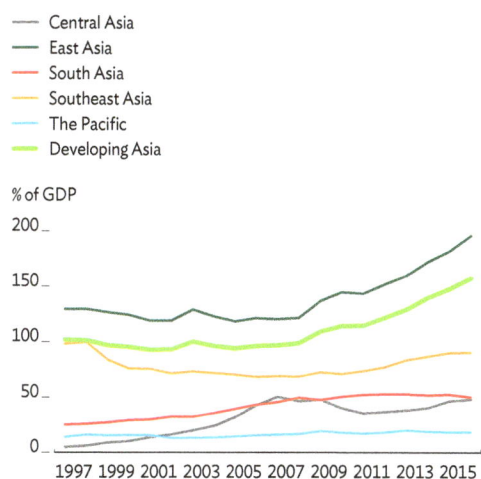

GDP = gross domestic product.
Sources: Haver Analytics (accessed 7 September 2018); ADB estimates.

2.1.9 US Federal Reserve balance sheet and the fed fund rate

- United States assets
- United States government and agency securities held outright
- Federal Reserve target rate

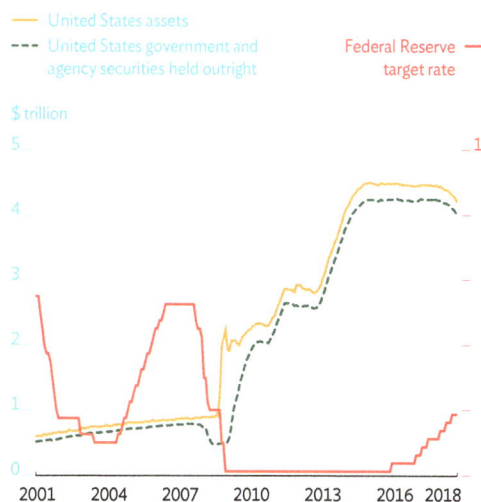

Source: Haver Analytics (accessed 7 September 2018).

As economic growth regains momentum in the US and other advanced economies, their central banks will eventually start normalizing monetary policy. The Fed is in the lead, already in the process of normalization. Since December 2015, it has raised policy rates seven times, bringing the rate up to 1.75%–2.00% from near zero. In September 2017, it announced that it would start the process of balance sheet normalization. Interest rate hikes in the US and potentially in other advanced economies, and their unwinding of QE policies, could reverse capital flows heretofore into Asia.

How much and how quickly the Fed further increases its interest rate will depend on the speed of the US economic recovery. Thus far, the US economy is growing robustly, with the unemployment rate at its lowest since 2000 and inflation showing signs of a solid pickup. A faster pickup in inflation might signal economic overheating, leaving the Fed with no choice but to accelerate its normalization of monetary policy through interest rate hikes and balance sheet normalization, moving faster than what analysts have so far projected.

Higher and faster hikes in US interest rates would, combined with robust economic growth, greatly strengthen the US dollar. Leaving aside for now any assumptions about the impact of trade friction, a stronger dollar would benefit the trade partners of the US, including economies in developing Asia. However, the benefits would not be shared uniformly (ADB 2017a). Those economies that manage their currencies to maintain a more stable exchange rate against the US dollar would tend to experience less currency depreciation than those with more flexible exchange rates. Consequently, the latter group, the economies with more market-oriented exchange rate regimes, would tend to benefit more than the former group as they would gain trade competitiveness through larger depreciation of their currencies in real effective terms.

This gain in trade, however, does not come without cost. Improvements in trade competitiveness would have to be balanced against potentially greater exchange rate volatility and resultingly higher inflationary pressure, especially in economies already operating at or above their technical potential. These factors might imperil domestic economic stability, requiring the authorities to tighten domestic liquidity to prevent capital outflows and to manage domestic inflation.

Meanwhile, the normalization of the Fed's burgeoning balance sheet since November 2017 would affect global capital flows. Total Fed assets have declined steadily since that time, albeit slowly. Because of its direct impact on the US money supply, balance sheet normalization has a greater impact on global liquidity than do the Fed's policy rate hikes. Further, a decline in total Fed assets tends to lower bond prices, thereby raising their interest rates.

Normalizing the Fed's balance sheet will mainly mean rolling up the unconventional part of the its monetary policy, the part that entails massive holdings of government securities. A study showed that changes in this unconventional monetary policy in the US tended to affect capital flows to and from emerging economies in Asia (ADB 2017b). The 2009 increase in Fed holdings of US government securities through QE brought higher net capital flows into the region, which is consistent with observations during the several episodes of US QE programs.

With ongoing balance sheet normalization, the issue of its potential impact on capital flows in developing Asia becomes relevant. Examining the issue quantitatively is not yet possible because data on the unwinding of QE are still scant. Assessment based on existing analysis suggests that if the impact of the changes in unconventional monetary policy is symmetrical, then the unwinding of the QE may drain capital flows from the region. However, there is no certain guarantee for this effect to hold. Asymmetrical impact is possible considering the implications that unwinding has for interest rates. While QE keeps the US interest rate on the floor, unwinding QE would allow it to rise. If the interest rate did rise at that point, QE unwinding in the US might not have an impact symmetrical with that of pursuing QE because the effects of unwinding may turn out to be similar to what happens under conventional monetary policy.

Nevertheless, either reducing Fed portfolio holdings or further hiking the policy rate would push up interest rates in the US, as would both actions simultaneously. This implies a stronger US dollar, which has mixed effects, and the potential for capital to drain from Asia. Higher US interest rates could spill over into emerging Asia by raising interest rates in the region, thereby posing a challenge to financial stability. The region would face higher financing costs for investment and higher effective discount rates, which would lower asset valuations and weaken the region's corporate balance sheets.

Meanwhile, there is little possibility that a global trade situation could emerge similar to the one seen in the aftermath of the AFC. Recent growth in the volume of global trade is much more modest than what occurred then. Instead, protectionist sentiment has emerged across the globe, introducing a new dimension of uncertainty regarding any pickup in global demand.

To summarize, despite internal efforts in developing Asia to achieve macroeconomic stability, the changing external environment is heightening uncertainty that may disrupt the good run of growth experienced by developing Asia since the AFC. Monetary policy developments in the US, potentially echoed in other advanced economies, suggest the end of the recent era of low interest rates with the unwinding of QE.

This could cause capital flows to reverse and flow out of developing Asia, challenging financial stability. In addition, new risks unseen in recent times, such as escalating global trade tensions, now loom.

Past events and current challenges

The past 2 decades of broad growth in developing Asia has seen ups and downs. Such business cycles are well known in economic literature. However, they are difficult to predict, and downturns sometimes snowball into major crises. Since 1990, Asia has weathered two major financial crises, the AFC and the GFC, both of which dragged output in most Asian economies well below their potential trend (Figure 2.1.10).

Recovery from the AFC was facilitated by internal reform to strengthen economic fundamentals and strong global demand that allowed growth led by exports. Post-GFC revival has benefitted from the further strengthening of economic fundamentals but also from super-loose global liquidity that allowed authorities to deploy timely fiscal, monetary, and financial stimulation to shield Asian economies from the worst of the GFC.

In Asian economies, the ratio of credit to output has risen in the past 2 decades, suggesting that economies rely increasingly on credit. Figure 2.1.11 shows the total credit average in all the included economies increased from the equivalent of 152% of GDP in 2000 to 189% in 2017. Private credit increased by 28 percentage points in the same time. It grew steadily in 2000–2008, paused with the GFC, and picked up again in 2010. Recently, however, the rate at which credit grows relative to GDP has slowed.

2.1.10 Output deviations from trend

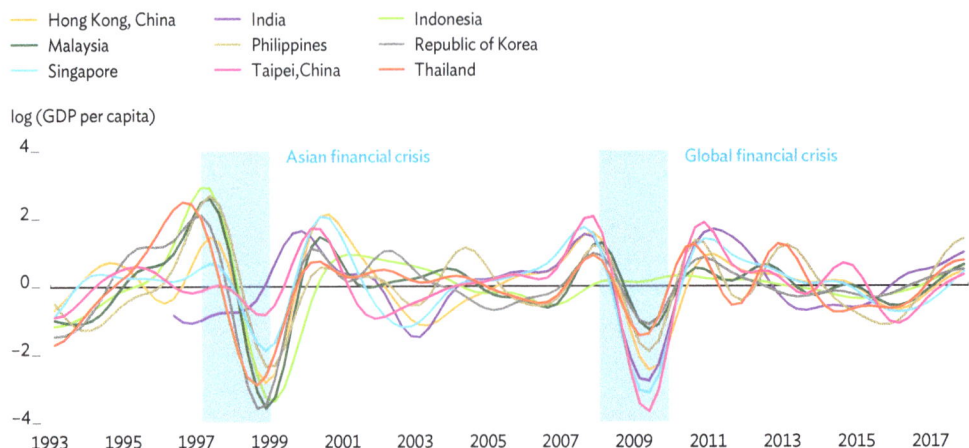

GDP = gross domestic product.

Note: Data in India started in the second quarter of 1996. The cycle, with a frequency between 8 and 32 quarters, is extracted from the log of real GDP per capita using the Cristiano-Fitzgerald filter.

Source: ADB estimates.

2.1.11 Credit ratios

◼ 2000   ◼ 2007   ◼ 2017

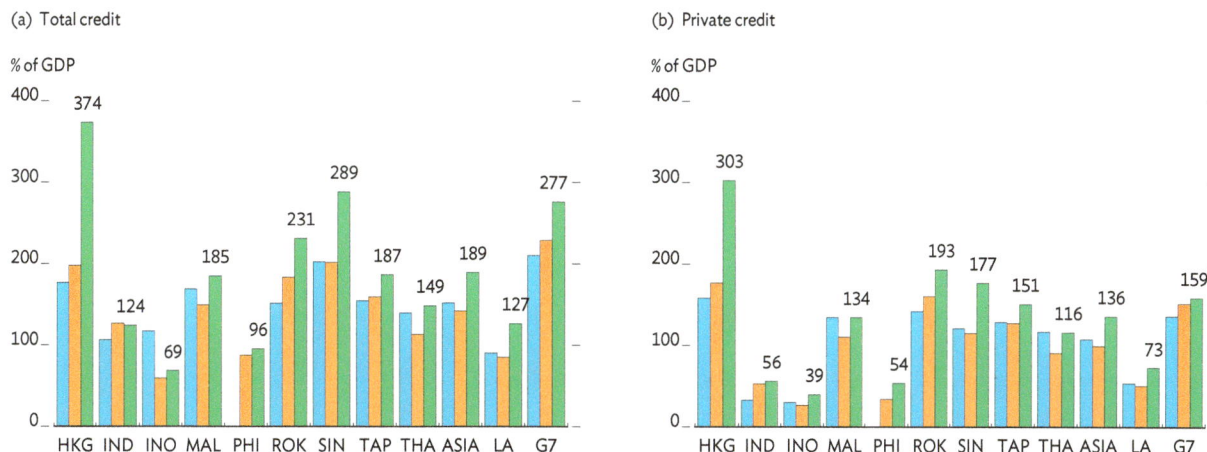

(a) Total credit

% of GDP

(b) Private credit

% of GDP

ASIA = the Asian economies shown individually, G7 = Group of Seven (Canada, France, Germany, Italy, Japan, the United Kingdom, and the United States), GDP = gross domestic product, HKG = Hong Kong, China, IND = India, INO = Indonesia, LA = Latin America (Brazil, Chile, Colombia, Mexico, and Peru), MAL = Malaysia, PHI = the Philippines, ROK = the Republic of Korea, SIN = Singapore, TAP = Taipei,China, THA = Thailand.

Notes: The series compiled by the Bank for International Settlements (BIS) calculates credit to the nonfinancial private sector as a percentage of GDP adjusted for breaks. It comprises of credit provided by domestic banks, all other sectors of the economy, and nonresidents to nonfinancial corporations, both privately and publicly owned, and to households and nonprofit institutions serving households, as defined in the System of National Accounts 2008 in terms of financial instruments, credit covers loans, and debt securities. The denominator is a 4-quarter moving sum of nominal GDP. The series for total credit to nonfinancial entities is obtained by adding general government debt.

Sources: BIS Total Credit Statistics; Haver Analytics; CEIC Data Company (all accessed 7 September 2018).

Increased reliance on credit has brought about interesting dynamics between the financial sector and the real economy. It is well known that dependence on credit has increased to finance investment, production, and consumption. One would therefore expect that a boom in credit would be associated with a boom in real economic activity. Actual data suggest otherwise. Consistent with observations in the advanced economies, the average contemporaneous correlation between swings in credit and real activity is negative in emerging economies, both in Asia and in Latin America. On average, the contemporaneous correlation between the credit and business cycles is –0.6 in the advanced economies of the Group of Seven (G7), –0.4 in Latin America, and –0.3 in Asia. Contrary to expectations, the credit cycle tends to move in the opposite direction from the business cycle.

The dynamic correlation between the credit and business cycles in Asia reveals similar patterns to those of the G7 and Latin America. Figure 2.1.12 shows the dynamic correlation between the two cycles over 16 quarters, with 8 quarters of lead and 8 of lag. Each point on the curve shows the strength and direction of correlation at any particular point of time within 8 lag and 8 lead quarters around that time. The contemporaneous correlation for each of the three regions is shown at the intersection between the dynamic correlation curve and the vertical line in the diagram for each of the regions. To the left of the vertical axis, the curve shows the correlation between the business cycle at a particular time and the credit cycle at its respective lag, or earlier time, from 1 to 8. Likewise, to the right of the vertical line, the curve shows the correlation between the business cycle and the credit cycle at its respective lead, or later time, from 1 to 8. In all three regions, the lag of the credit cycle tends to be negatively associated with the current business cycle, while the reverse relation is observed when it comes to the leads.

Figure 2.1.12 suggests complex interaction between the financial sector and real economic activity in Asia and elsewhere in the world. A boom in credit today is followed by a slowdown in economic activity about 1–2 years later. A boom in today's real economic activity, on the other hand, fuels acceleration in credit 2–3 quarters later, which eventually turns into an economic slowdown about a year later. These patterns are common to the three groups of economies considered, with G7 countries displaying the strongest pattern and Asia the weakest.

This observed dynamics between the credit and business cycles poses new challenges for maintaining macroeconomic stability. Intricate interactions between internal and external conditions have built up pockets of vulnerability in many economies, which requires in response careful evaluation of the policy tools available to maintain economic and financial stability.

The US example exhibited in Figure 2.1.9 is instructive. The Fed's move to push down the interest rate to as low as 1% in 2003 was justified to stimulate the economy after the burst of the dot-com bubble. This policy precipitated a boom in lending, however, that brewed a new internal problem that eventually evolved into the subprime mortgage crisis and the GFC.

Such cycles of events provide an illustration of the complex interaction between real economic activity, the financial sector, and policy to manage and stabilize the two. This underscores the dynamic correlation observed in Figure 2.1.12, which presents how a boom in one sector, or stabilization policy undertaken to deal with one event, may spawn evolving pockets of vulnerability that eventually pose future challenges. Developing Asia is not exempt from this conundrum and has been exposed to significant sources of vulnerability. These pockets of vulnerability need to be monitored carefully to keep them from evolving into unwanted events in the future.

2.1.12 Correlation between credit cycle and business cycle

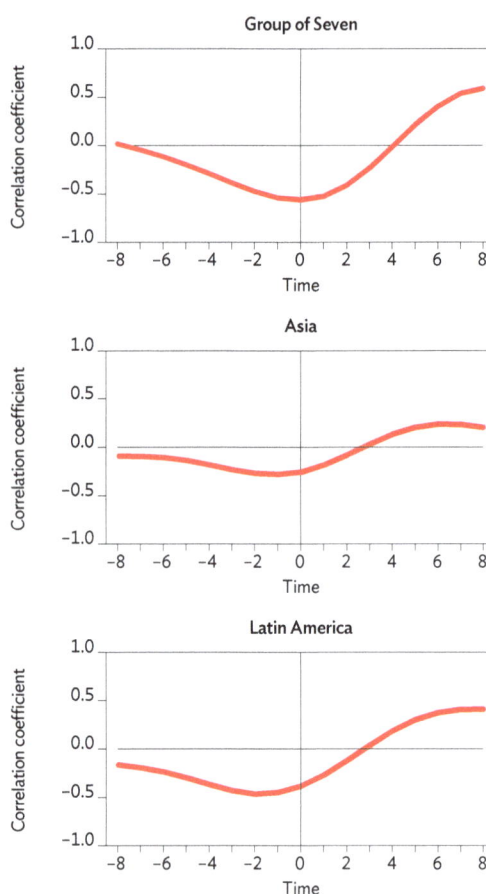

Source: ADB estimates.

Pockets of vulnerability

The preceding section describes the uncertainties and risks beginning to loom on the global economic horizon. In addition, several imbalances building up in developing Asia can threaten macroeconomic and financial stability: volatile capital flows, currency pressures, mounting debt, spikes in housing prices, and cross-border contagion. This section elaborates on the identified pockets of vulnerability that need to be carefully monitored for their impact on regional economies.

Volatile capital flows

Since 2000, there have been four distinct waves of capital flow into emerging Asia (Figure 2.2.1). The first major wave began in the early 2000s, after the AFC, and lasted until it was halted abruptly in 2008 by the GFC. The second was triggered by the QE episodes that began in mid-2009. This was followed by a third wave of declining inflow in 2013–2015 and, most recently, by a wave of revival since 2017.

Owing to the strength of the region's recovery after the AFC, its improved investment climate, and its growing importance in global value chains, capital flowed back into the region. Foreign direct investment (FDI) provided more than 40% of total inflow, mainly into the PRC. Other investment—the category other than FDI and portfolio, which includes trade credits, loans, currency and deposits, and other accounts receivable and payable—gradually increased as well. After reaching a peak of $1.1 trillion in 2007, total inflow dropped by 80% the next year, in the wake of the GFC. The decline was more pronounced than during the AFC and was led by outflow of portfolio and other investment mostly channeled through the banking system. Net FDI likewise declined but was more resilient.

With a remarkably quick rebound, the next wave of inflow took off in mid-2009. This was driven largely by QE in the US and other advanced economies, which left investors searching elsewhere for higher yields. Attracted by strong economic growth and positive interest rate differentials in emerging Asia, capital inflow reached unprecedented levels and surpassed outflow, such that net inflow peaked at $391 billion in 2010. FDI remained the most important inflow to Indonesia, the PRC, the Philippines, Thailand, and Viet Nam, while portfolio and other investment were dominant in Hong Kong, China; India; Malaysia; and the Republic of Korea.

2.2.1 Capital flows to selected Asian economies

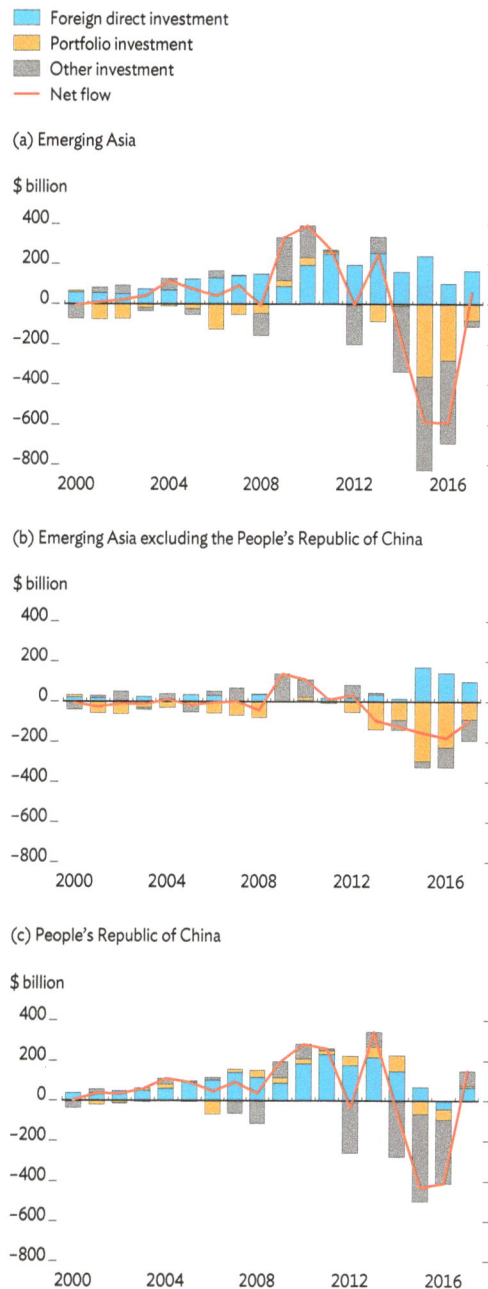

- Foreign direct investment
- Portfolio investment
- Other investment
- Net flow

(a) Emerging Asia

$ billion

(b) Emerging Asia excluding the People's Republic of China

$ billion

(c) People's Republic of China

$ billion

Notes: Emerging Asia consists of Hong Kong, China; India; Indonesia; Malaysia; the People's Republic of China; the Philippines; the Republic of Korea; Singapore; Taipei,China; Thailand; and Viet Nam. Charts are based on balance of payments data.
Source: Haver Analytics (accessed 7 September 2018).

Capital inflow declined in most Asian economies during the third episode, in 2013–2015, mainly with falling portfolio and other investment. The exception was Viet Nam, where continued inflow of FDI kept aggregate investment stable. A hint from the Fed of the possible unwinding of its QE program in May 2013 triggered a large reversal in capital flow, now away from developing Asia. This so-called "taper tantrum" was not followed by a systemic financial crisis or growth crash, however, thanks to the strengthened resilience of economies in emerging Asia. Nonetheless, concerns over slowing growth in the PRC and worsening uncertainty regarding global trade prospects further dampened market sentiment. Net inflow dipped into negative territory in 2014, reaching net outflow of $592 billion in 2016 as "other investment" flowed out of the PRC and portfolio investment flowed out of other economies in emerging Asia.

In the most recent wave, capital inflow, mainly "other investment" into the PRC and FDI into the rest of the region, recovered from a nadir in 2016 and continued to increase in 2017.

To summarize, in the past decade and a half, capital flow into emerging Asia went through cycles. It is commonly believed that the PRC dominated the pattern of flow, but the rest of emerging Asia also influenced movements in the past 5 years. The flow of capital was driven by volatile movements of "other investment" in the PRC, while other Asian economies experienced massive spurts and reversals mainly in volatile portfolio flows. The pronounced volatility was underpinned largely by changing global liquidity conditions, which raises concerns about economic and financial stability. The composition of inflow is also important with regard to its impact on the domestic economy. FDI has become less dominant since 2010, particularly in the PRC, raising the relative profile of other types of capital flow that are significantly more volatile.

Surging capital flow fueled credit expansion by augmenting domestic savings and boosting asset price valuations. The possibility of global liquidity drying up leaves economies vulnerable to sudden capital outflow. Large reversals are rightly blamed for sharp currency depreciation and financial market turbulence. They can also disrupt the trajectory of growth in credit to the private sector and induce asset price deflation, which can have damaging consequences for aggregate economic activity.

Currency pressures

Over the past decade, events related to the GFC and its aftermath have dominated the global economy. Asian economies have not been spared of the effects of these events, which are often reflected in changes in global liquidity that exert pressure on domestic exchange rates.

Two notable events are the initiation of QE in March 2009 and the signal in May 2013 that QE might be wound down.

2.2.2 Nominal exchange rate and reserves

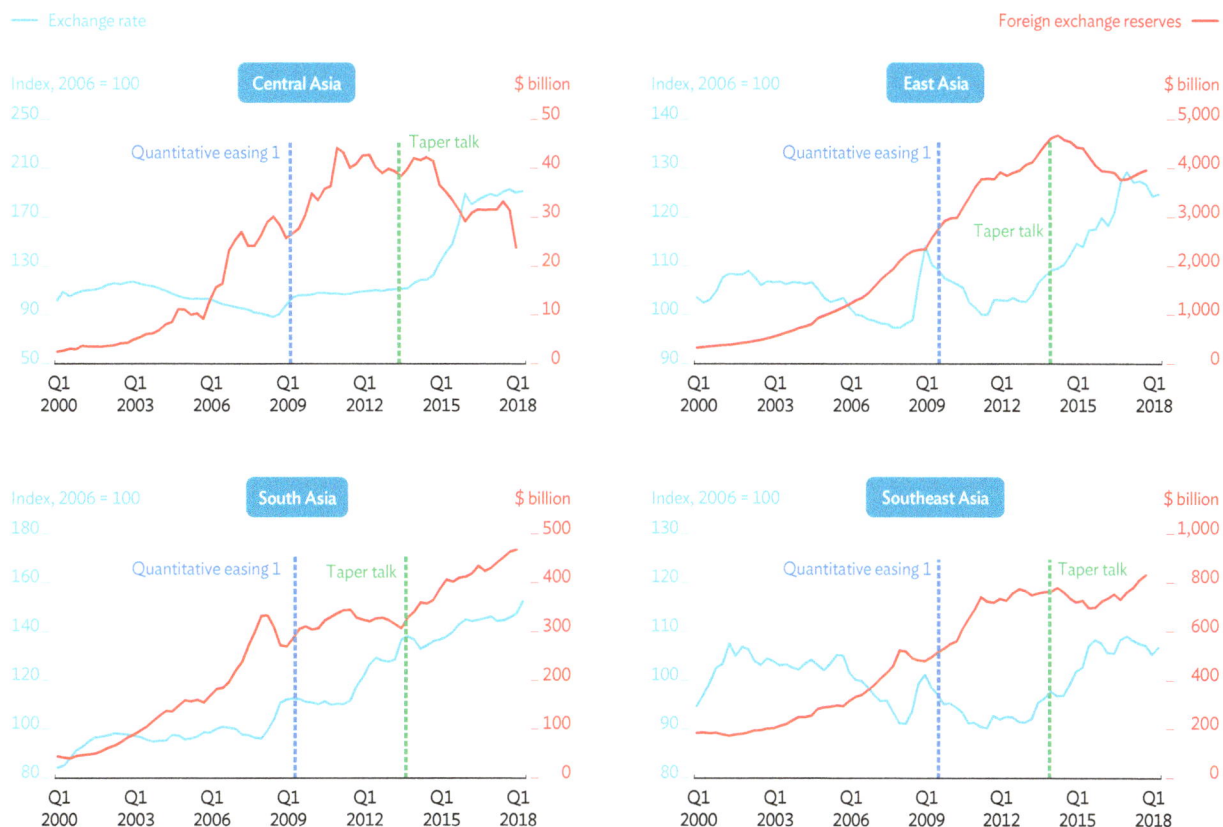

—— Exchange rate   Foreign exchange reserves ——

Central Asia

East Asia

South Asia

Southeast Asia

Q = quarter.

Note: Subregional nominal exchange rate indexes were computed as the average of quarterly nominal exchange rates in component economies, expressed as units of local currency per US dollar. Subregional foreign exchange reserves are the sum held by component economies. Southeast Asia excludes the Lao People's Democratic Republic and Myanmar.

Sources: CEIC Data Company (accessed 1 August 2018); ADB estimates.

Within 4 months of the initiation of QE, currencies appreciated by an average of 6.7% in East Asia, 4.5% in Southeast Asia, and 2.0% in South Asia as capital flowed into the region (Figure 2.2.2). The hint of tapering then reversed the capital flow and from May to August 2013 caused currencies to depreciate in South Asia by 6.9%, Southeast Asia by 4.2%, and East Asia by 2.7%. Since then, most regional currencies have continued to depreciate as the progressive strengthening of the US economy motivated the first tapering of bond purchases in December 2013, the eventual cessation of QE in October 2014, and the first fed funds rate hike in December 2015.

Many Asian economies restrained exchange rate movements by intervening in foreign exchange markets and/or changing their interest rates. Under such fixed or managed exchange rate regimes, the extent of pressure on a currency is not fully captured by the change in the nominal value of the exchange rate.

A more accurate picture is presented by a measure that combines the actual change in the nominal exchange rate and the change that would have taken place without the policy intervention: exchange market pressure (EMP) (Girton and Roper 1977).

Using a cross-economy dataset for EMP constructed in Patnaik, Felman, and Shah (2017), it is evident that developing Asia experienced higher appreciation pressure than other regions in the world after the initiation of QE, and it experienced significant depreciation pressure after the QE tapering announcement. However, experience across the 23 Asian economies studied is not uniform (Figure 2.2.3). During the first event, 17 economies experienced pressure to appreciate and 6 experienced pressure to depreciate. Then, in the second event, 15 economies experienced pressure to depreciate, which was greatest in India, Indonesia,

2.2.3 Exchange market pressure and exchange rate change by economy

■ Exchange market pressure
■ Change in exchange rate

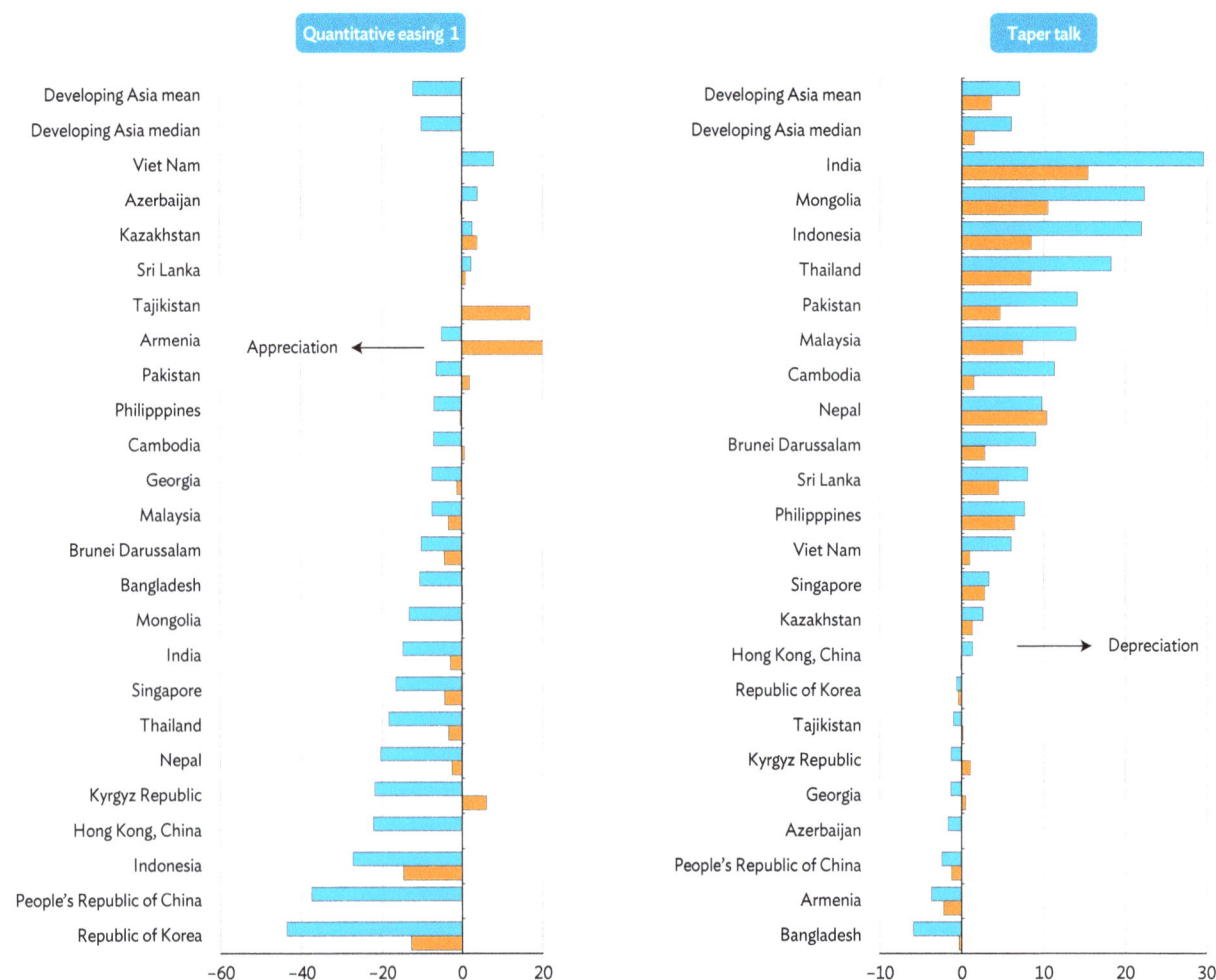

Note: Quantitative easing 1 covers March 2009–June 2009. Taper talk covers May–August 2013. As the exchange rate is local currency units per US dollar, positive values indicate local currency depreciation and negative values local currency appreciation. Exchange market pressure is defined as the combination of the actual change in the nominal exchange rate and the change that would have taken place without the policy intervention.

Sources: Patnaik, Felman, and Shah 2017; CEIC Data Company (accessed 1 August 2018).

and Mongolia. Interestingly, policy intervention was more pronounced during the first event than during the second. Policy makers seemed to intervene more actively against currency appreciation than depreciation, perhaps because countering depreciation drains foreign exchange reserves.

Recently, depreciation pressure has begun to intensify in several Asian economies (Figure 2.2.4). The determinants of EMP would be useful for identifying policies that could mitigate vulnerability in these economies.[1] For a broad group of economies, Patnaik and Pundit (forthcoming) estimated a model that shows factors representing domestic financial and macroeconomic conditions in an economy prior to the taper announcement that affected depreciation pressure from May to August 2013.

2.2.4 Exchange market pressure in Asian economies

- Exchange market pressure
- Change in exchange rate

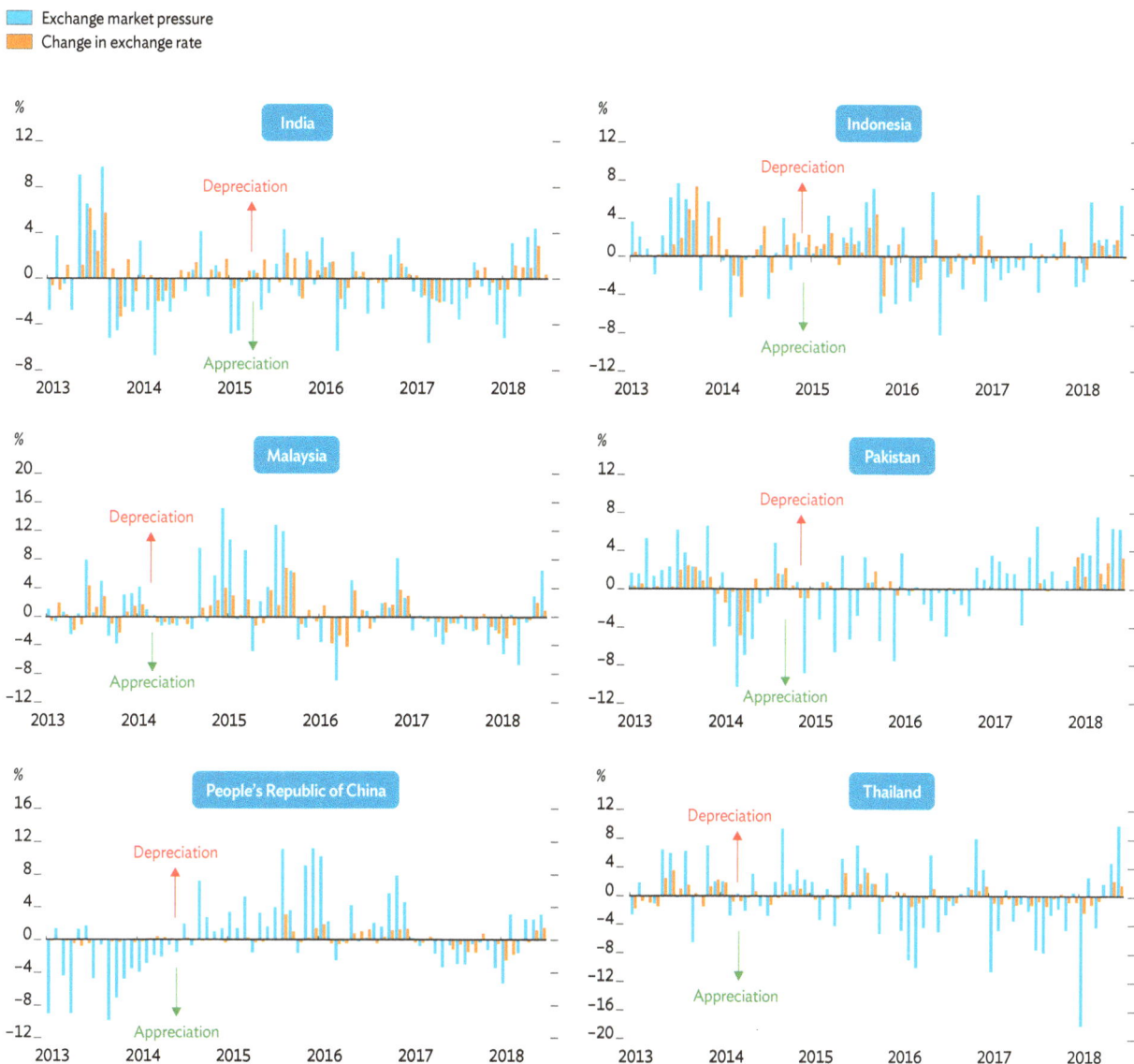

Sources: Patnaik, Felman, and Shah 2017; CEIC Data Company (accessed 1 August 2018).

The analysis found that emerging economies faced larger depreciation pressure than advanced economies. Their financial exposure, or the total of external private financing and the stock of portfolio liabilities, significantly heightened EMP. Because short-term portfolio investments are easily liquidated, the resulting outflow of capital can intensify depreciation pressure. This illustrates how the composition of capital flow matters.

Empirical results confirm that emerging markets remain exposed to the monetary policy of advanced economies. Allowing the exchange rate to absorb the full repercussions of sharp capital flow reversals is likely to disrupt an economy. Any central bank intervention will probably be limited because the foreign exchange reserves available to spend on it are also limited. Meanwhile, raising domestic interest rates to curb capital outflow will likely dampen economic activity, effectively pursuing a perversely procyclical policy. Past experience suggests, however, that spillover into emerging economies can be contained if monetary policy normalization in the advanced economies is gradual and adequately communicated to a wide range of investors to incorporate their expectations into the normalization process. The opposite approach, hiking interest rates higher and faster than expected, can pose a risk to vulnerable Asian economies. The risk is all the greater when the consequences of unprecedented actions are unknown or unanticipated, which is almost axiomatically the case when unwinding unconventional monetary policy.

Debt buildup

The tightening of global liquidity coincides with high indebtedness in Asian economies. Figure 2.2.5 shows that debt in developing Asia mounted after the GFC, reaching in 2016 the equivalent of 186.4% of aggregate GDP. Debt accumulation in itself is not necessarily a problem because debt allows governments and companies to finance productive investments and enables households to smooth their consumption over a lifetime. Notwithstanding the potential of debt to enhance people's welfare, it can cause macroeconomic instability when it builds up unsustainably and can even induce crises, as dramatically illustrated by the US subprime mortgage crisis, the gateway to the GFC. Asia's post-GFC debt buildup has been primarily private, incurred by households and corporations. The ratio of private debt to GDP increased by 60 percentage points from 2008 to 2016, rising even higher than immediately before the AFC. East Asia experienced the fastest growth, followed by Southeast Asia. In Central Asia, the ratio of public debt to GDP is climbing alongside that of private debt.

During the GFC, many advanced and emerging economies implemented policies to support banks and financial markets and to stimulate economic activity. Those policies catalyzed the rapid accumulation of public debt. In many emerging economies, low interest rates, strong growth, and financial deepening combined to excite a spurt in household and corporate debt as well. International capital flows abetted this trend by boosting the availability of credit to the private sector. Post-GFC monetary easing in the advanced economies brought an unprecedented decline in policy interest rates around the world. This reduced the cost of servicing the growing public and private debt, thus masking how vulnerability has deepened as growth in aggregate debt has outpaced that of GDP over the past 10 years.

Vulnerability now threatens to realize its damaging potential. Capital outflow and tighter liquidity under the unwinding of QE may exacerbate the financial burden on sovereign borrowers, households, and corporations by curtailing access to credit and raising borrowing costs. When high private sector debt combines with rising debt-servicing costs at a systemic level, nonperforming loans may proliferate and thus threaten the stability of the banking sector. Governments tend to step in and support banks when they come under pressure, thus taking on more contingent liability and jeopardizing fiscal sustainability.

All these factors have serious consequences for macroeconomic stability. Slowdowns can be divided into two types: financial versus normal (Box 2.2.1). Studying a set of 21 advanced economies and 17 emerging economies from 1960 to 2014, Park, Shin, and Tian (forthcoming) assessed the relative severity of the two types of slowdowns. The study found that, for advanced economies, a drop in output from the peak of the business cycle to the next trough is roughly 1.4 percentage points deeper if preceded by a financial peak—that is, if the drop in output comes after a large private debt buildup (Figure 2.2.6 and the table in Box 2.2.1). While investment decline is similarly deeper during financial slowdowns, there is no evidence of a difference in consumption decline between the two types of slowdowns.

When emerging economies are included in the sample, the difference in the magnitude of output and investment declines between financial versus normal slowdowns is even larger. Another notable difference is that consumption declines more during financial slowdowns. In the broader sample, annual output declines on average by 1.6 percentage points more following a financial peak than following a normal peak. The findings are true for all financial slowdowns, even those that do not coincide with crises.

2.2.5 Total debt

— Central Asia
— East Asia
— South Asia
— Southeast Asia
— The Pacific
— Developing Asia

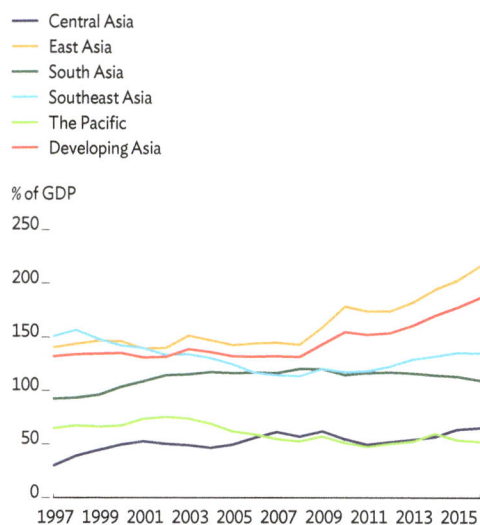

GDP = gross domestic product.
Note: For definitions of subregions, see page 12 of https://www.adb.org/sites/default/files/publication/411666/ado2018-highlights.pdf.
Sources: CEIC Data Company; Haver Analytics; International Monetary Fund (IMF) Article IV various years; IMF. World Economic Outlook online database. www.imf.org/external/pubs/ft/weo/2018/01/weodata/download.aspx; World Bank. World Development Indicators online database. data.worldbank.org/products/wdi (all accessed 1 August 2018); ADB estimates.

2.2.6 Depth of recession

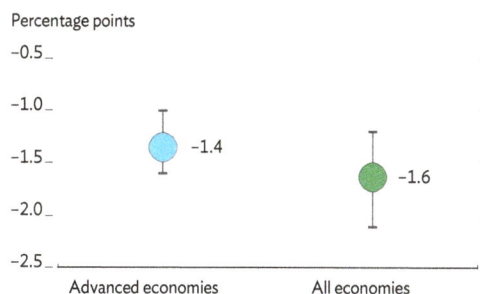

Sources: Park, Shin, and Tian forthcoming; ADB estimates.

2.2.1 Economic slowdowns and private debt buildup

Park, Shin, and Tian (forthcoming) obtained data on household and nonfinancial corporate debt from Bank for International Settlements' (BIS) Total Credit Statistics for 21 advanced and 17 emerging economies from 1960 to 2014.[a] To characterize the business cycle, data on annual real GDP, real private consumption, and real gross fixed capital formation at constant 2011 prices were sourced from the Penn World Table 9.0 and divided by population to obtain per capita indicators. The housing price index was obtained from the BIS property price database and the Jordá-Schularick-Taylor Macrohistory database (Jordá, Schularick, and Taylor 2017). The stock price index was also obtained from the Jordá-Schularick-Taylor Macrohistory database and supplemented with Global Financial Database and Bloomberg.

The business cycle was extracted using the Hodrick-Prescott filter on log of GDP, consumption, and investment, with local maxima identified as peaks and minima as troughs. This yielded 147 peaks in advanced economies and 83 in emerging economies.

The depth of a slowdown was the difference between the cyclical part of log GDP per capita at the peak and the next trough.

A financial peak was distinguished from a normal peak based on the buildup of private debt as a percentage of GDP. If the speed of accumulation, defined as the average annual increase in debt over GDP, was faster than the sample median, the peak was defined as a financial peak. Otherwise, it was a normal peak. For robustness, a stricter cutoff point was applied using quartiles, such that if the speed of debt accumulation prior to the peak was lower than the top quartile of the sample, it was defined as a financial peak, and if it was smaller than the bottom quartile, as a normal peak. A household financial peak, defined as household debt buildup exceeding corporate debt buildup, was distinguished from a corporate financial peak, its opposite.

continued next page

Depth of output recessions in the full sample of economies: normal versus financial peaks

Variables	Whole Countries			
	Depth of recession (output)			
	(1)	(2)	(3)	(4)
Normal peak ($\Delta d_{priv} < median(\Delta d_{priv})$)	−4.5** [1.1]	−5.4** [1.6]	−4.3** [1.0]	−6.0** [1.3]
Financial peak ($\Delta d_{priv} < median(\Delta d_{priv})$)	−6.4** [1.1]	−7.5** [1.5]	−5.6** [1.1]	−7.2** [1.3]
Trade openness (at the peak)		3.2* [1.3]		3.4* [1.3]
Financial openness (at the peak)		−0.14 [0.10]		−0.15 [0.10]
World output growth (2-year average following the peak)		0.47 [0.48]		1.0* [0.40]
House price growth (annual, during expansion before the peak)			−7.5 [4.9]	−5.7 [4.7]
Stock price growth (annual, during expansion before the peak)			−1.4 [2.2]	−1.8 [2.5]
R^2	0.82	0.84	0.84	0.87
Observations, normal peaks	96	81	65	54
Observations, financial peaks	100	92	63	59
p-value (normal peak versus financial peak)	0.00	0.00	0.02	0.07

Notes: The dependent variable is the depth of output recession defined by the average percentage change in per capita GDP from a peak to the next trough. The constant term is not included as a regressor. Whole countries refers to all countries, either advanced economies or emerging economies referred to in the box footnote. The reported p-values test for the equality of coefficients of normal versus financial peaks. Numbers in brackets are robust standard errors. ** denotes a 1% level of significance, and * denotes 5%.

2.2.1 *Continued*

The following equation is estimated using ordinary least squares:

$$DS_{it}^{j} = b_0^{j} + b_N^{j} Peak^N + b_F^{j} Peak^F + X_{it} \cdot b^{j} + f_i^{j} + \in_{it}^{j}$$

where DS_{it}^{j} is depth of slowdown in country i at a peak occurred at time t in terms of j (either GDP, consumption, or investment); $Peak^N$ and $Peak^F$ are dummies that take the value 1 if the corresponding peak is normal and financial, respectively; f_i^{j} is country fixed effects for j variable; and $\in_{it}^{j}$ is an error term. X_{it} is a vector of control variables: trade openness, financial openness, world output growth, house price growth, and stock price growth of country i at t. Because at time t, either $Peak^N$ or $Peak^F$ is equal to 1, the constant term is excluded. World output growth is calculated as 2-year average world GDP growth after a peak. House price growth is the annual percentage change in the housing price index from a previous trough to a peak; ditto stock price growth. Trade openness is exports plus imports divided by GDP, and financial openness is total external assets plus liabilities divided by GDP.

The control variables are similar to those in Claessens, Kose, and Terrones (2011).

The results in the box table show that the difference between a financial and a normal peak in the depth of the output slowdown is 1.2–2.1 percentage points per year and statistically significant. Higher trade openness and higher world output growth mitigate the severity of recessions. The signs of the coefficient suggest that higher rises in house and stock prices before the peak deepens the slowdown, but the coefficients are not significant.

a   The advanced economies are Australia, Austria, Belgium, Canada, Denmark, Finland, France, Germany, Greece, Ireland, Italy, Japan, the Netherlands, New Zealand, Norway, Portugal, Spain, Sweden, Switzerland, the United Kingdom, and the US. Emerging economies are Argentina; Brazil; Hong Kong, China; Colombia; the Czech Republic; Hungary; Indonesia; Israel; Malaysia; Mexico; Poland; the Republic of Korea; the Russian Federation; Saudi Arabia; Singapore; Thailand; and Turkey.

Source: Park, Shin, and Tian, forthcoming.

This suggests that private debt buildups have the potential to be more damaging to economic activity in emerging market economies. The results are robust for narrower definitions of financial slowdowns. Finally, the study found that, for advanced economies, slowdowns driven by household debt tended to be deeper than those driven by corporate debt. However, when emerging economies were included, the opposite was true.

Romer and Romer (2017) argued that having policy space available can mitigate the output loss following a crisis. In this vein, Park, Shin, and Tian (forthcoming) examined whether fiscal space influences the depth of slowdowns after financial peaks. The study found that debt buildups posed bigger threats when fiscal space was relatively limited during a slowdown. In particular, an increase in the ratio of debt to GDP from a low initial value might not exacerbate a slowdown because room still existed for a fiscal policy response. If, on the other hand, a slowdown began with the ratio exceeding about 60%, then a slowdown, particularly one driven by a private debt buildup, could be more severe in emerging economies. This might have been for lack of fiscal space to permit fiscal stimulus.

Sharp increases in housing prices

Housing prices have risen sharply in some cities in Asia in recent years. The dramatic increase is causing concern that housing prices are becoming detached from fundamentals. Because residential property is an increasingly important component of personal assets in Asia, housing price fluctuations can significantly affect households' net worth and consequently their ability to consume and save. At the systemic level, housing boom-and-bust cycles pose a sizable risk to financial and macroeconomic stability. Policy makers are therefore well advised to closely monitor housing price patterns. Studies show that busts following housing booms have been especially destabilizing when they coincide with rapidly expanding credit, resulting in "twin booms." Crowe et al. (2013) found that 21 of 23 economies that experienced twin booms in housing and credit during the GFC suffered either a financial crisis or a severe drop in GDP growth.

In the housing market, rental value is thought to reflect the intrinsic value of a property. When the price starts to deviate significantly from that benchmark, explosive dynamics may be in process. Using the ratio of price to rent, Han, Pundit, and Ramayandi (forthcoming) dated episodes of sharp increases in selected Asian cities from 2000 to 2017 based on a statistical methodology suggested in Philips, Shi, and Yu (2015).[2] Data on house price and rent indexes were obtained from various national sources. Figure 2.2.7 plots in dark blue the occurrence since 2000 of sharp increases in the ratio of price to rent by quarter in capital cities where data are available. Many of the cities show multiple episodes of spikes over time. Those currently experiencing such a boom are Beijing; Hong Kong, China; Kuala Lumpur; Seoul; and Singapore. Other cities in both the PRC and the Republic of Korea show a similar trend.

In Bangkok, Jakarta, and cities in India, the analysis does not identify many periods of rapid price increases. However, the absence of alarming price escalation in the data does not necessarily mean that those housing markets are stress-free. In India, for example, the short span of quarterly data could render the estimation results unreliable and fail to reveal the evolving trend of prices over a longer period. Moreover, the common perception is that, despite severe mismatch between housing supply and demand in some Indian cities, housing prices remained unnaturally elevated, causing a buildup of unsold inventory of unaffordable housing and commercial units. As more laborers migrate into crowded Asian cities, a burning issue is housing affordability (Box 2.2.2). Where elevated housing prices have put homeownership out of reach for most segments of the population, policy makers must carefully balance the imperative of making housing accessible to more people with the need to avoid any dramatic adjustment to prices that would undermine economic stability.

2.2.7 Observed sharp increases in house prices by quarter

- ▨ Data not available
- ▨ Without sharp increase
- ▨ With sharp increase

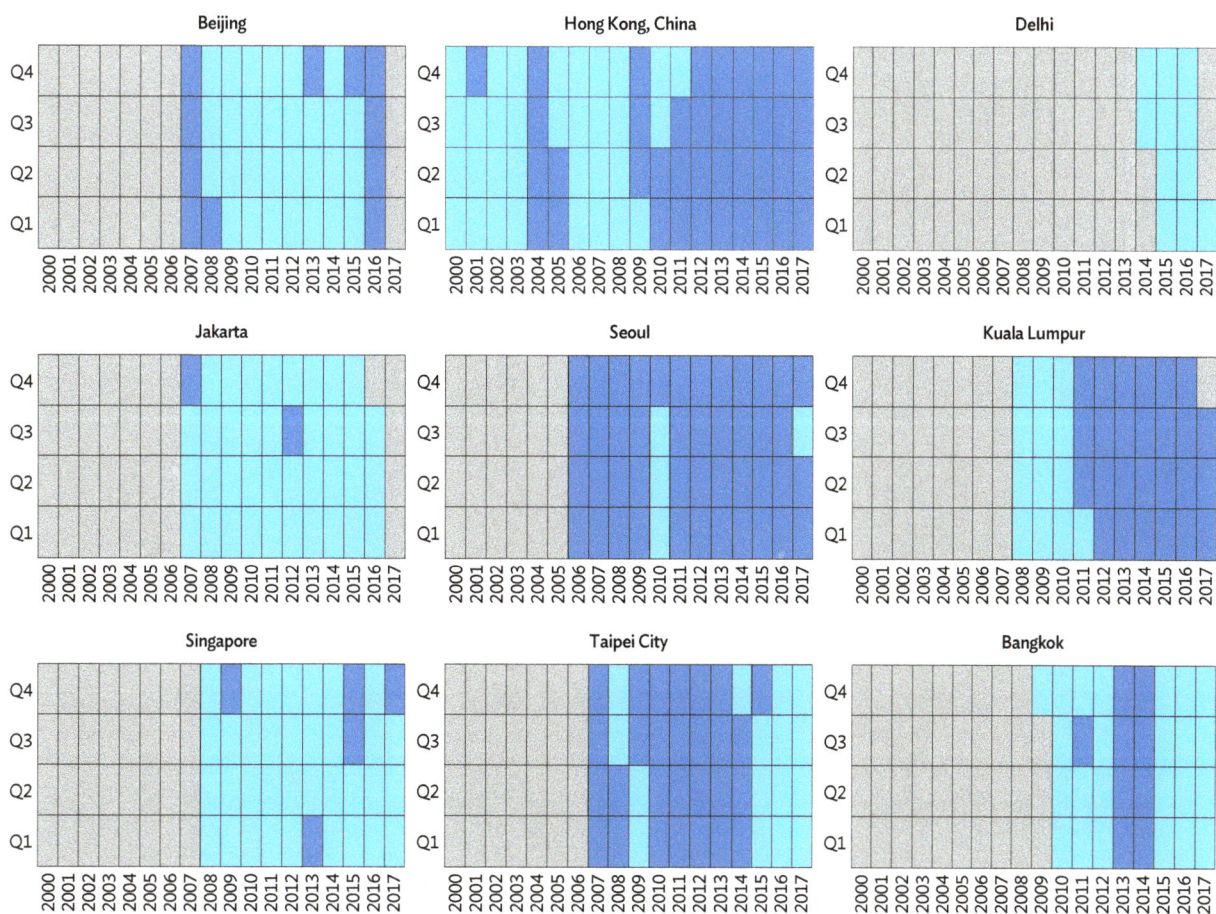

Q = quarter.
Source: Han, Pundit, and Ramayandi, forthcoming.

What drives the rapid price-to-rent ratio increases evident in many Asian cities? Han, Pundit, and Ramayandi (forthcoming) examined which macroeconomic factors may influence the likelihood of the observed spikes in eight Asian cities: Beijing; Hong Kong, China; Jakarta; Seoul; Kuala Lumpur; Singapore; Taipei City; and Bangkok. Potential drivers include aggregate demand pressures, domestic credit growth, monetary policy, exchange rate movements, capital inflow, and "growth gravity," which measures the difference in economic growth rates between the city and the larger economy.

Results from the analysis suggest that a boom in domestic aggregate demand, proxied by an increase in inflation, increases the likelihood of an explosive housing price pattern.

2.2.2 Housing affordability

The problem of unaffordable housing is pervasive in most Asian economies (Carrasco and Shah 2018). Using data and assumptions outlined in the box table, housing affordability is estimated for households in different income quintiles. Estimates compare the monthly income per household that is spent servicing the home purchase to the average monthly housing loan repayment for a residence measuring 50 square meters (m²) or else 70 m². Housing affordability is satisfied if the average monthly loan repayment does not exceed 40% of average monthly household income.

continued next page

Data and assumptions

Country	Average monthly income per capita ($)[a]	Average household size[b]		Home loan annual interest rate (%)[c]	National average cost per m² ($)[d]	Share of household expenditure on housing repayment[e]	Average home floor area (m²)[f]	Terms of repayment
India	143.3 (2014)	4.3	(2012)	8.50	464	40%	50 and 70	20 years
Indonesia	181.5 (2013)	4.3	(2012)	5.99	1,012			
Malaysia	704.8 (2014)	4.1	(2016)	5.00	1,575			
PRC	309.9 (2014)	3.1	(2016)	4.90	1,761			
Rep. of Korea	1,212.2 (2016)	2.5	(2015)	5.33	7,006			
Thailand	449.2 (2014)	3.2	(2011)	6.78	2,518			

PRC = People's Republic of China.

[a] World Bank PovcalNet. http://iresearch.worldbank.org/PovcalNet/povOnDemand.aspx (accessed 1 August 2018).

[b] CEIC data from Household Surveys and Statistics Korea. http://kostat.go.kr/portal/eng/pressReleases/1/index.board?bmode=read&aSeq=356507 (accessed 1 August 2018).

[c] HSCB housing loan interest rates in 2018. For Thailand, the average housing loan rate is from Bank of Ayudhya (Krungsri) and United Overseas Bank (Thailand) in 2018. For the Republic of Korea, the interest rate is sourced from KEB Hana Bank in 2018. http://pulsenews.co.kr/view.php?sc=30800020&year=2016&no=799333 (accessed 1 August 2018).

[d] Indian Institute of Management Bangalore working paper; Haver Analytics for the PRC; Numbeo database for Indonesia, Malaysia, the Republic of Korea, and Thailand. https://www.numbeo.com/cost-of-living/ (accessed 1 August 2018). The price in local currency is converted to US dollars using exchange rates from Haver analytics.

[e] Based on the US Bureau of Labor Statistics report on Selected Expenditure Shares of Asian and Other Families, Consumer Expenditure Interview Survey, 2003. https://www.bls.gov/opub/btn/archive/spending-by-asian-families.pdf (accessed 1 August 2018).

[f] Based on the assumption from the UN Population Division report of floor area per person (in 64% of cities, the floor area per person is 5–14 square meters). http://www.un.org/esa/population/pubsarchive/chart/14.pdf (accessed 1 August 2018).

Higher inflation may make homeowning more attractive as a store of value. Currency depreciation also increases the probability of explosive prices by increasing demand from investors who can tap sources of foreign currency. While total private credit does not significantly increase the likelihood of explosive prices, credit specifically for housing does. Further, when a city grows faster than its surroundings, it draws migrants, which raises demand for housing, thereby making sharp price increases more likely.

A larger current account deficit makes an economy a net borrower to the rest of the world, which means net capital flows into the economy. The larger the inflow, the more additional

2.2.2 Continued

Housing affordability

— 50 square meter
— 70 square meter

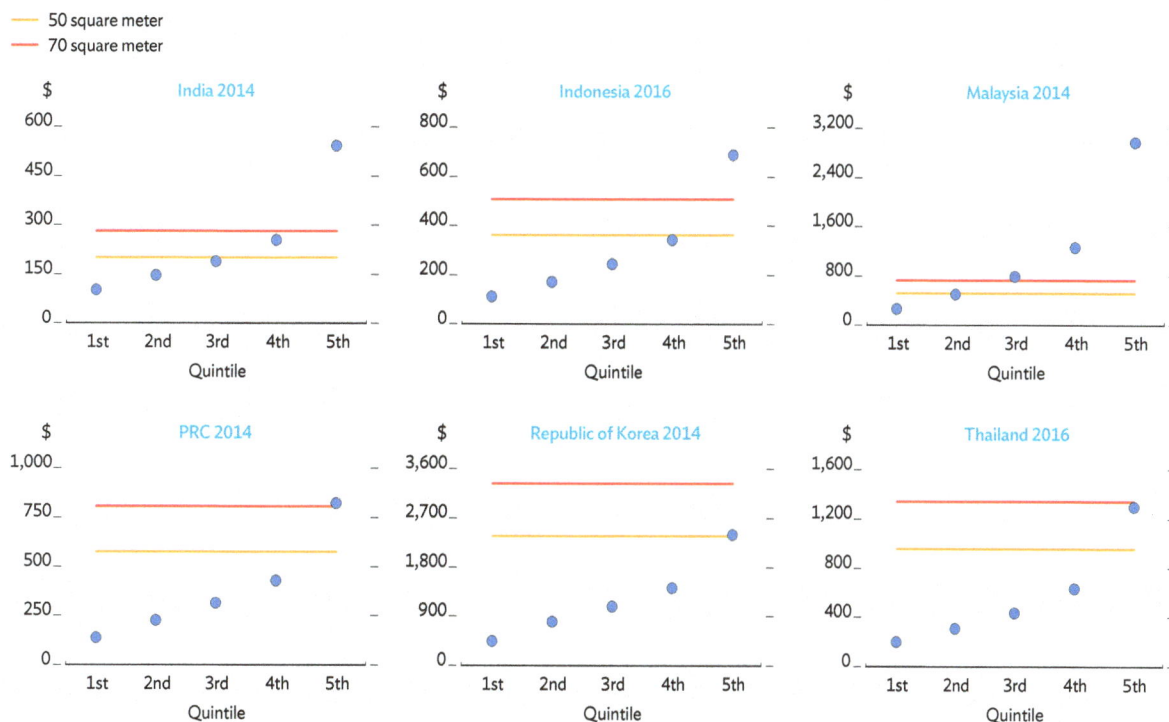

PRC = People's Republic of China.

Note: Dots show 40% of the average monthly household income for the quintile. Lines show monthly housing loan repayment, yellow for a 50 square meter home and red for 70 square meters.

Source: Han, Pundit, and Ramayandi, forthcoming.

As seen in the box figure, Malaysia seems to be the most affordable, as middle- to upper-income households can afford at least a 70 m² home. In India, the fourth and fifth quintiles can afford at least a 50 m² home.[a] The ROK is the least affordable, with even a 50 m² home unaffordable to all except the highest earners in the upper quintile. The PRC and Thailand fared slightly better, as the highest quintile household can just about afford a 70 m² home.

Indonesia features a large gap between the fourth quintile, who can barely afford a 50 m² home, and the top quintile, who can well afford a 70 m² home.

[a] These national averages of course mask detail seen in some cities. For example, in Mumbai, with a population of over 18 million, 80% of households cannot afford to a 50 m² home, while the top 20% can barely afford a 70 m² home.

liquidity comes into the economy, making more resources available to put pressure on housing prices. Interestingly, the current account position started significantly affecting pressure on housing prices only after the US introduced QE in late 2008, spurring large capital flows into emerging economies. On the other hand, tighter monetary policy, in particular higher interest rates, reduces the likelihood of explosive housing price patterns. Higher rates raise the cost of loan servicing and thus slow the credit expansion that fuels rising housing prices.

To sum up, the evidence indicates that the significant drivers of sharp housing price increases are economic booms, housing credit expansion, accommodative monetary conditions, and migration into urban centers. While capital inflow and ample global liquidity after the first QE contributed to higher housing prices, it is an open question whether prices will rise more moderately when liquidity dries up. A major concern, however, is whether or not housing prices in major Asian cities will adjust abruptly when hot money flows out in response to advanced economies tightening their monetary policies.

Cross-border spillover and contagion

The pockets of vulnerability discussed so far are specific to individual economies, but it is important to recognize that Asian economies are parts of regional and global financial systems. Asian financial markets have grown rapidly in the past 2 decades, and they have become more closely integrated with each other and with markets outside the region. While financial market expansion and integration brought many benefits to regional economies, it also created vulnerability. Shocks that arise inside or outside the region can be amplified and transmitted across borders to other economies. The shocks are transmitted through different interconnected networks, with adverse spillover effects and contagion during periods of financial stress. The GFC originated in the advanced economies but quickly spread to emerging economies through interconnected financial networks. And, of course, shocks can spread across borders within the region, as painfully illustrated by the AFC.

The figure in Box 2.2.3 shows the evolution of Asia's financial sector networks from 1996 to 2016, based on correlation of daily equity returns. The analysis employed equity rather than bank liability to take advantage of greater data availability and because equity data generally reflect market sentiment more accurately. Two key observations emerge with respect to the evolution of financial networks over time. First, markets became more interconnected during periods of stress and less interconnected during the recovery phase. The transition from pre-crisis to crisis sees a quick buildup of strong links, making markets more interconnected during a crisis. By contrast, after a crisis, many connections disappear, and these losses are not offset by the emergence of new links elsewhere. The magnitude of the linkages follows a pattern similar to the existence of linkages.

Second, there is a general deepening of market connections within Asia and between Asia and the rest of the world. For example, the number of direct connections from the PRC grew as it became more connected with economies in Southeast Asia and North America.

2.2.3 Asia's financial sector network: data, methodology, and model

The data consist of daily equity market index returns, in local currency, from 42 markets around the world, including 15 Asian markets, from 1996 to 2006. The sample period was broken down into six eras: before, during, and after the AFC and before, during, and after the GFC.

Network analysis was applied to determine the direction, relative significance, and strength of the links between equity markets, or nodes. In the box figure, the thickness of the lines indicates the average relative strength of each market or regional grouping, and the size of the node increases with the number of outward links of each respective market or regional grouping. Several aspects were assessed to examine the changes in the networks across the six periods: (i) changing density of the network; (ii) changing number of links between nodes;

(iii) changing strength of links between nodes; (iv) net and gross change in links between nodes; (v) substitutability of a node, the sum of distances to all other nodes, and proximity between nodes; and (vi) similarity of networks from one period to the next.

The analysis used a vector autoregression model to evaluate the existence and strength of links between markets. It drew on Dungey, Harvey, and Volkov (2017) to identify a network of financial linkages between nodes, proxied by equity market data for each economy. The analysis employed equity rather than bank liability because data were more available and equity data generally reflect market sentiment more accurately.

Source: ADB 2017c.

Evolution of Asia's financial sector networks, 1996–2016

a. Pre-Asian financial crisis
(1 Mar 1995–1 Jul 1997)

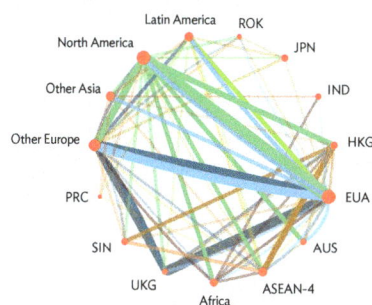

b. Asian financial crisis
(2 Jul 1997–31 Dec 1998)

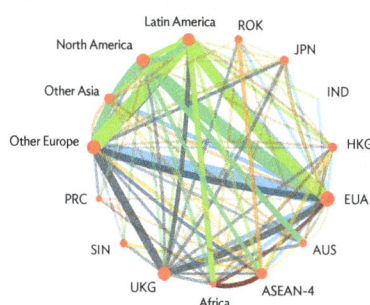

c. Post-Asian financial crisis
(1 Jan 1999–31 Dec 2002)

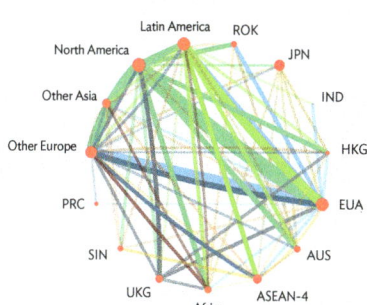

d. Pre-global financial crisis
(1 Jan 2003–14 Sep 2008)

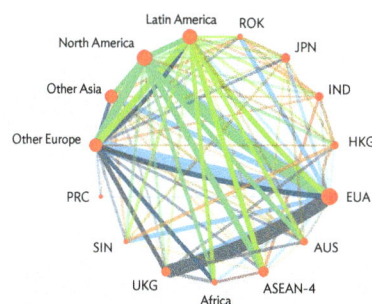

e. Global financial crisis
(15 Sep 2008–31 Mar 2010)

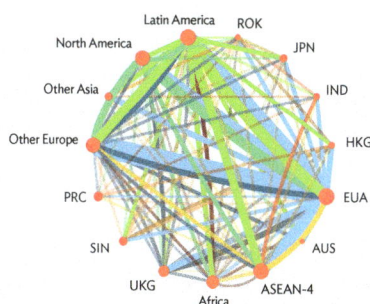

f. Post-global financial crisis
(1 Apr 2010–30 Dec 2016)

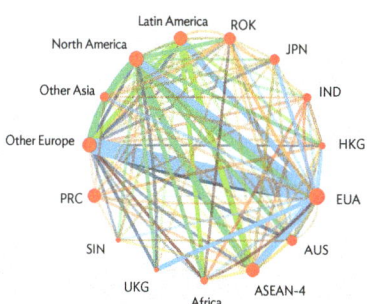

ASEAN-4 = Association of Southeast Asian Nations members Indonesia, Malaysia, the Philippines, and Thailand, AUS = Australia, EUA = euro area, HKG = Hong Kong, China, IND = India, JPN = Japan, PRC = People's Republic of China, ROK = Republic of Korea, SIN = Singapore, UKG = United Kingdom.
Notes: The figure displays the returns-based network of 15 equity markets and regional groupings from 1 March 1995 to 30 December 2016. Edges were calculated using bivariate Granger causality tests between markets at 5% level of significance. The thickness of the lines indicates the average relative strength of each market or regional grouping. The size of the nodes increases with the number of outward links of each respective market or regional grouping.
Source: ADB 2017c.

Following the AFC, Singapore and Hong Kong, China strengthened their links with other Asian economies, reinforcing their roles as regional financial hubs that connected Asian markets with the rest of the world.

These observations suggest that in times of heightened uncertainty, an adverse financial shock in one economy is likely to propagate across borders more widely and strongly to the regional and global financial system. Further, the evidence indicates that strengthened financial interconnectedness seems to be cumulative, making Asia more vulnerable to negative spillover over time.

Detecting vulnerabilities is a crucial first step in assessing the soundness of economies. The next step is to effectively keep vulnerabilities and risks from escalating into serious macroeconomic and financial crises. This calls for a thorough evaluation and possible reconfiguration of the instruments that are available to policy makers for fostering a stable and sustainable economic environment. The next section discusses stabilization policy tools that can help Asian policy makers navigate the current milieu of growing imbalances amid heightened global uncertainty.

Tools for maintaining macroeconomic stability

The pockets of vulnerability described above generate risks that can be managed with appropriate macroeconomic policies. These can be classified into two broad categories: the more conventional fiscal, monetary, and exchange rate policies, and the less conventional capital flow management and macroprudential policies. The main difference between these categories is a matter of scope, with conventional policies designed to stabilize aggregate demand directly and the other set indirectly by targeting specific segments, in particular finance, which is becoming an important source of major economic shocks.

The focus of more conventional macroeconomic management tools in the past was to stabilize output and prices, while tools that aimed to mitigate risks in the financial sector were more microprudential in nature. As the world suffered more economic crises that were induced by instability in the financial sector, the authorities became concerned about the so-called "fallacy of composition," or the folly of believing that the stability of the entire financial system could be ensured by guaranteeing the safety of all individual financial institutions. Systemic financial stability became an explicit goal of macroeconomic management, with macroprudential policies as the primary instruments. The GFC further underscored the importance of this framework. Meanwhile, the volatility of capital flow was deemed to have a significant impact on the economy, thereby making measures to manage it as an integral part of the policy makers' toolkit.

Because the real economy and the financial sector are closely intertwined, the interaction of the various macroeconomic policies has to be well understood. The efficacy of tools depends on an economy's structure, its stage of financial development, the prevailing phase in the business cycle, and the nature, size, and duration of the shock. Sometimes, too, one policy may render another policy less effective. Against the backdrop of emerging economic challenges, this section discuss a framework that can guide the implementation of policies to achieve macroeconomic stability.

Promoting countercyclical fiscal policy

A government pursues a countercyclical fiscal policy when it changes taxes and spending in ways that push the economy in the opposite direction from the business cycle. Tax cuts and higher government spending are implemented to put more money into the economy during recessions, and tax hikes and lower government spending are applied to constrain demand when the economy is at risk of overheating. In this way, countercyclical fiscal policy contributes to macroeconomic stability by moderating cyclical swings in output. By contrast, procyclical fiscal policy amplifies output swings by boosting aggregate demand when the economy is booming and dampening aggregate demand when it is on a downturn. Several empirical studies confirm that a countercyclical fiscal policy can mitigate business cycles and prevent a prolonged downturn in the aftermath of crises (Auerbach 2011, Ostry et al. 2010). Gavin et al. (1996) found that a procyclical fiscal policy, on the other hand, exacerbates the vulnerability of developing countries, deepening and lengthening slowdowns in the aftermath of shocks.

Countercyclical fiscal policy is a useful tool for stabilizing output, but only in the past 2 decades have more governments in the developing world shifted to pursuing a more countercyclical fiscal policy (Frankel, Vegh, and Vuletin 2013). Aizenman et al. (forthcoming) observed that only a small minority of 130 developing and advanced economies included in the study pursued countercyclical fiscal spending in 1960–2016. Focusing on the subregions of developing Asia, the estimated magnitude of government spending procyclicality was the highest in Central Asia at 0.92, followed by the Pacific at 0.91, East Asia at 0.50, Southeast Asia at 0.40, and South Asia at 0.35.[3] Figure 2.3.1 shows that the economies with the most procyclical government spending were, in descending order, Bangladesh, Mongolia, Vanuatu, Indonesia, Kazakhstan, Georgia, the Philippines, the Kyrgyz Republic, Papua New Guinea, Pakistan, and Azerbaijan. In these economies, estimated cyclicality exceeded 1, meaning that when GDP grew by 5%, for example, government spending grew by more than 5%.

Procyclical government spending exacerbates the business cycle and uses up valuable fiscal space needed to accommodate countercyclical policy during an economic downturn, when the economy would benefit substantially from stimulus. Yet, as the study showed, governments in many developing economies adopt procyclical policies for several reasons. When a downturn occurs, governments are confronted with financial, political, institutional, and fiscal constraints that limit their ability to undertake fiscal responses that are both timely and appropriate. Governments may also be reluctant to initiate large spending programs on infrastructure, for example, as such spending commitments are irreversible and can therefore jeopardize fiscal sustainability over the long run. Meanwhile, fiscal policy has objectives other than output stabilization, notably the efficient allocation of

2.3.1 Extent of government spending cyclicality, 1960–2016

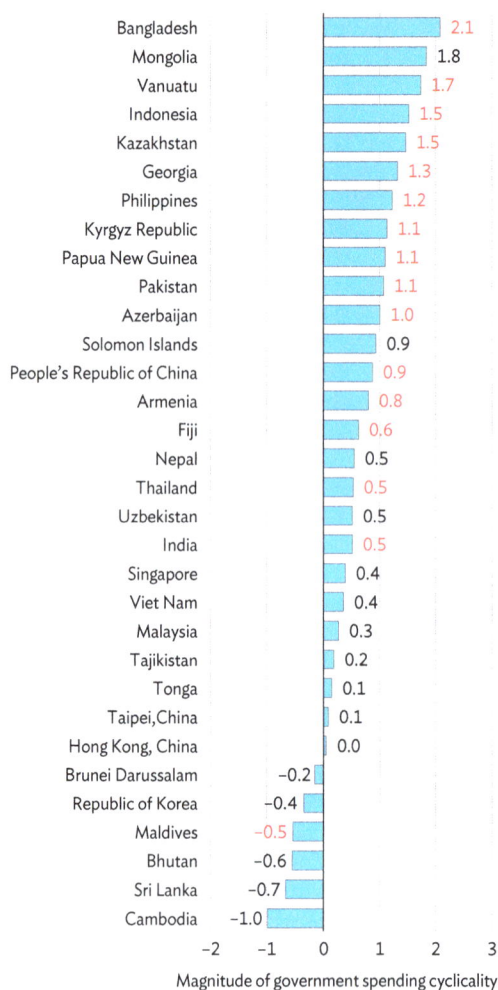

Country	Value
Bangladesh	2.1
Mongolia	1.8
Vanuatu	1.7
Indonesia	1.5
Kazakhstan	1.5
Georgia	1.3
Philippines	1.2
Kyrgyz Republic	1.1
Papua New Guinea	1.1
Pakistan	1.1
Azerbaijan	1.0
Solomon Islands	0.9
People's Republic of China	0.9
Armenia	0.8
Fiji	0.6
Nepal	0.5
Thailand	0.5
Uzbekistan	0.5
India	0.5
Singapore	0.4
Viet Nam	0.4
Malaysia	0.3
Tajikistan	0.2
Tonga	0.1
Taipei,China	0.1
Hong Kong, China	0.0
Brunei Darussalam	−0.2
Republic of Korea	−0.4
Maldives	−0.5
Bhutan	−0.6
Sri Lanka	−0.7
Cambodia	−1.0

Magnitude of government spending cyclicality

Notes: The magnitude of government spending cyclicality is estimated by country using the Prais-Winsten approach to correct for first order-autocorrelation in the residuals. A positive number means that government spending is procyclical and a negative number means that government spending is countercyclical. Red font refers to statistical significance at 5%.

Source: Aizenman et al., forthcoming.

resources, income redistribution, and structural reform. Because government priorities may shift as an economy graduates to different stages of development, it may not always be possible to pursue countercyclical fiscal policy. Nonetheless, in light of its destabilizing potential, procyclical policy should be avoided as much as possible (IMF 2017).

Available fiscal capacity, as measured by the ratio of public debt to the tax base, is a major determinant of the ability to implement countercyclical policy (Aizenman et al., forthcoming).[4] The higher the ratio, the greater the tendency towards procyclical fiscal policy.

The ratio of public debt to the tax base is a better measure of fiscal capacity than the more widely used ratio of public debt to GDP because the tax base more accurately captures the government's income stream, and hence its repayment capacity. In addition, the volatility of fiscal space is a major constraint. From 2000 to 2016, South Asia was the subregion in developing Asia that experienced the most volatility in terms of the ratio of public debt to the tax base, and it also had the most limited fiscal capacity. Meanwhile, rapid growth in public debt notwithstanding, Southeast Asia saw its fiscal capacity double during the sample period. In line with these results, simulations showed that, if fiscal space deteriorated by 10%—that is, if the ratio of public debt to the tax base increased by 10%—then procyclicality in government spending increased the most in Southeast Asia, by 13.2% followed by South Asia, by 10.2% (Figure 2.3.2).

Meanwhile, movements in interest rates also affect fiscal space. Global interest rates are rising with ongoing monetary policy normalization by the Fed. Rising interest rates push up debt repayment costs and will reduce fiscal space in Asian economies that have accumulated significant public debt. To address this challenge, governments can secure more fiscal space by paring down their debt or by broadening their tax base. In developing economies with limited fiscal revenue, investment in revenue enhancement such as through improved tax administration can expand fiscal space.

In addition to fiscal space, the analysis found, countries could benefit from countercyclical fiscal buffers that help accumulate revenue during good times and enable the mitigation of tax revenue shortfalls in bad times. The sovereign wealth funds of oil-producing countries, for example, accumulate revenue when global oil prices are high and can use them to mitigate economic downturns when global oil prices are low. Such funds are effective, however, only to the extent that they are well governed.[5]

Another countercyclical buffer is a deeper social safety net, which mitigates the adverse income effects of downturns. Because the poor tend to be the hardest hit during downturns, social safety nets such as unemployment benefits can sustain

2.3.2 Public debt to tax base ratio and government spending cyclicality

Predicted economic significance of public debt/tax base

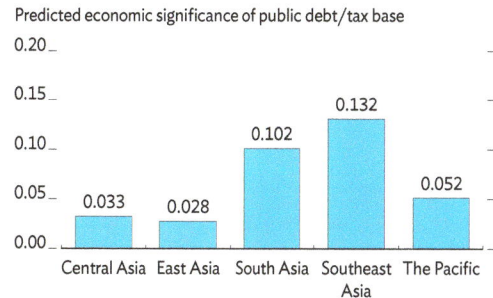

Note: This figure shows the change of government spending cyclicality by subregion in developing Asia if the subregional ratio of public debt to the tax base increases by 10%. The predicted economic significance of the ratio is calculated by 0.1*estimated coefficient of public debt/tax base*actual public debt/tax base average over 1960–2016.

Source: Aizenman et al., forthcoming.

their income and aggregate demand in the short run. Over time, they help reduce income inequality. More broadly, countercyclical policies in general can provide a social safety net for vulnerable groups.

The ability to implement discretionary countercyclical fiscal policy is affected by fundamentals, particularly the quality of governance and institutions. Political economy factors, such as the legal system and amount of corruption, may permit overspending of public revenue in good times and end up limiting access to domestic and foreign resources during downturns. This situation contributes to procyclicality in fiscal policy. Important factors that contribute to ensuring effective fiscal policy countercyclicality are a good investment climate, conducive socioeconomic conditions, and the absence of conflict.

Among macroeconomic factors, higher inflation is associated with greater fiscal procyclicality. Intuitively, inflation erodes the real value of money and thus encourages the government to spend more. Economies with larger shares of natural resources in their exports seem to be more prone to fiscal procyclicality as they tend to be less economically diversified and more susceptible to commodity price shocks. Meanwhile, economies with large shares of manufactures in their export baskets, and those that are more financially open, are less likely to pursue procyclical fiscal policy. Figure 2.3.3 shows that, while there are some differences in the magnitude of results between the full sample of economies and the developing Asia subsample, the broad patterns are similar.

Despite there being only a minority of economies that pursued countercyclical fiscal spending in 2008–2016, Aizenman et al. (forthcoming) found that government spending generally became less procyclical in the latter part of the period. This is encouraging news for macroeconomic stability. The finding is consistent with earlier studies that detected a trend toward less procyclicality in the past 2 decades.

Efficacy of monetary policy

Monetary policy is a powerful tool for macroeconomic stabilization. It has an advantage over fiscal policy in being more flexible and quickly implementable, especially if the central bank is independent. As the effect of monetary policy is transmitted through the economy's financial system by affecting the price of capital and aggregate liquidity conditions, its efficacy hinges on how smoothly the financial sector operates. This section deals with the potential for monetary policy in developing Asia to operate effectively, the cyclicality of monetary policy in the region, and the problems that could affect its implementation.

2.3.3 Economic significance of variables that can explain government spending cyclicality, 1960–2016

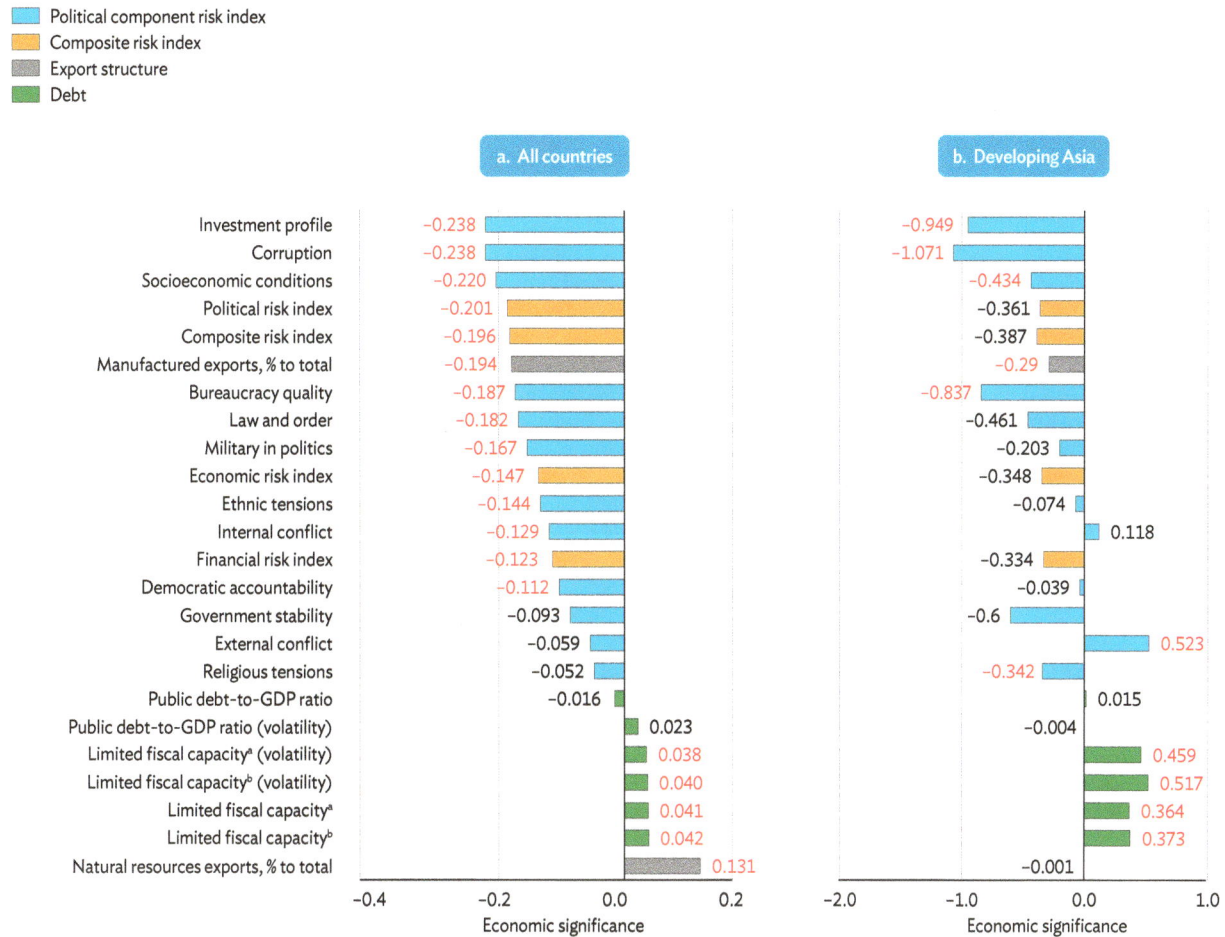

- ■ Political component risk index
- ■ Composite risk index
- ■ Export structure
- ■ Debt

a. All countries

	Economic significance
Investment profile	-0.238
Corruption	-0.238
Socioeconomic conditions	-0.220
Political risk index	-0.201
Composite risk index	-0.196
Manufactured exports, % to total	-0.194
Bureaucracy quality	-0.187
Law and order	-0.182
Military in politics	-0.167
Economic risk index	-0.147
Ethnic tensions	-0.144
Internal conflict	-0.129
Financial risk index	-0.123
Democratic accountability	-0.112
Government stability	-0.093
External conflict	-0.059
Religious tensions	-0.052
Public debt-to-GDP ratio	-0.016
Public debt-to-GDP ratio (volatility)	0.023
Limited fiscal capacity[a] (volatility)	0.038
Limited fiscal capacity[b] (volatility)	0.040
Limited fiscal capacity[a]	0.041
Limited fiscal capacity[b]	0.042
Natural resources exports, % to total	0.131

b. Developing Asia

	Economic significance
Investment profile	-0.949
Corruption	-1.071
Socioeconomic conditions	-0.434
Political risk index	-0.361
Composite risk index	-0.387
Manufactured exports, % to total	-0.29
Bureaucracy quality	-0.837
Law and order	-0.461
Military in politics	-0.203
Economic risk index	-0.348
Ethnic tensions	-0.074
Internal conflict	0.118
Financial risk index	-0.334
Democratic accountability	-0.039
Government stability	-0.6
External conflict	0.523
Religious tensions	-0.342
Public debt-to-GDP ratio	0.015
Public debt-to-GDP ratio (volatility)	-0.004
Limited fiscal capacity[a] (volatility)	0.459
Limited fiscal capacity[b] (volatility)	0.517
Limited fiscal capacity[a]	0.364
Limited fiscal capacity[b]	0.373
Natural resources exports, % to total	-0.001

GDP = gross domestic product.

[a] Public debt/tax revenue.

[b] Public debt/3-years moving average tax revenue.

Notes: The economic significance of each explanatory variable is calculated by multiplying its standard deviation with the estimated coefficient in the corresponding regression (for 137 countries and for developing member countries of the Asian Development Bank) to approximate the effect of one standard deviation increase of the variable on fiscal cyclicality. The sample period is 1960–2016. Red number font refers to statistical significance at a 20% level of significance.

Source: Aizenman et al., forthcoming.

Output cycles and inflation both reflect aggregate demand pressure in an economy. In responding to these signals, the goal of monetary policy is to limit the economy's deviation from its long-term growth trend. Monetary policy is thus expected to be countercyclical to the business cycle. The authorities in developing Asia have actively used monetary policy to navigate cyclical fluctuations of economic activity in the past decade (ADB 2017b). In Taipei,China, monetary policy was seen to actively respond to output fluctuations. In Indonesia, the Philippines, and the Republic of Korea, monitary policy seemed to be more responsive to price movements. In India, Malaysia, and Thailand, monetary policy appeared to respond to both inflation and output.

To shed light on the potential for monetary policy to operate effectively in the region, Kim (forthcoming) used a panel data set of 11 Asian economies to show that countercyclical monetary policy was effective in smoothing business and credit cycles. An increase in the interest rate as part of contractionary monetary policy caused over time a decline in real output, the inflation rate, and credit availability. When compared with macroprudential policy, which operates through similar transmission channels, the impact of monetary policy was found to be stronger on all three indicators.

While monetary policy is potentially effective in stabilizing the economy, it is not always implemented in a countercyclical manner. Monetary policy in developing Asia has generally behaved in a countercyclical manner with respect to the business cycle, but not necessarily so with respect to the credit cycle (Figure 2.3.4). The correlation coefficients between changes in the benchmark policy interest rate and the business cycle in nine economies in developing Asia since 2000 were generally positive (that is, countercyclical), but the pattern was not that uniform in the case of the credit cycle. This suggests that monetary policy in these economies tended to be tightened when the output gap was expanding, but not always so with regard to the credit gap.

When the sample is divided into episodes before and after the GFC, monetary policy is uniformly countercyclical to the business cycle after the GFC in the nine economies (Figure 2.3.5). Before the GFC, the correlation was negative in three economies. The figure therefore suggests that monetary policy in the nine economies in developing Asia has generally shifted toward a countercyclical approach.

The behavior of monetary policy with respect to the credit cycle is different. A positive correlation coefficient, indicating countercyclical policy, both before and after the GFC, is seen only in two economies (Figure 2.3.6). In two economies, the ROK and Singapore, correlation is uniformly negative, or procyclical. The figure shows that monetary policy in four other economies has recently become more procyclical with the credit cycle. This means that, in these economies, the interest rate is raised when the credit market is slowing and vice-versa.

An explanation for the differences in monetary policy is that business and credit cycles in some parts of developing Asia are not synchronized. This is illustrated in Table 2.3.1, which presents the chronology of the business and credit cycles in 10 Asian economies. For each economy, the table reports the incidences of output and credit in an upswing, above their trend (indicated with green cells), or in a downswing, below trend (orange cells). The table also marks peaks and troughs in each cycle.

2.3.4 Correlation between changes in interest rates and the business and credit cycles, Q1 2000–Q4 2017

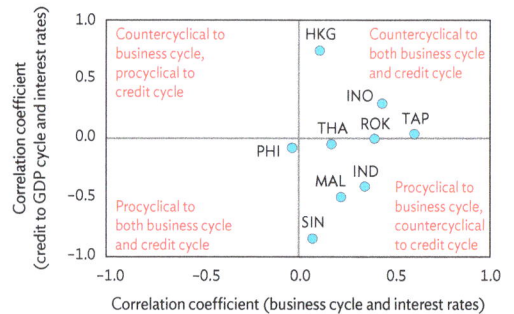

HKG = Hong Kong, China, IND = India, INO = Indonesia, MAL = Malaysia, PHI = Philippines, Q = quarter, ROK = Republic of Korea, SIN = Singapore, TAP = Taipei,China, THA = Thailand.
Source: ADB estimates.

2.3.5 Correlation between the business cycle and changes in interest rates, before versus after the global financial crisis

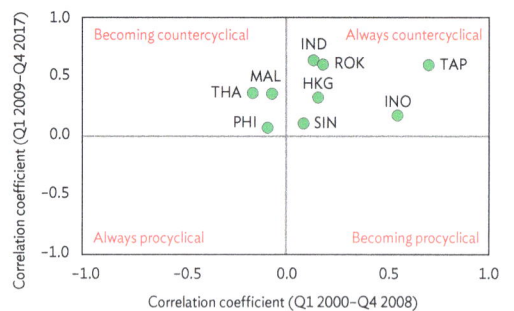

HKG = Hong Kong, China, IND = India, INO = Indonesia, MAL = Malaysia, PHI = Philippines, Q = quarter, ROK = Republic of Korea, SIN = Singapore, TAP = Taipei,China, THA = Thailand.
Source: ADB estimates.

2.3.6 Correlation between the credit cycle and changes in interest rates, before and after the global financial crisis

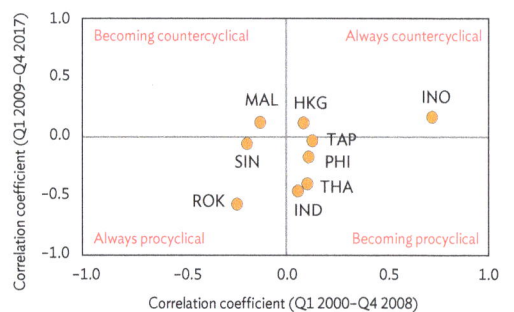

HKG = Hong Kong, China, IND = India, INO = Indonesia, MAL = Malaysia, PHI = Philippines, Q = quarter, ROK = Republic of Korea, SIN = Singapore, TAP = Taipei,China, THA = Thailand.
Source: ADB estimates.

2.3.1 Coincidence of business and credit cycles, Q1 2000–Q4 2017

Country	Indicator	2000	2001	2002	2003	2004	2005	2006	2007	2008	2009	2010	2011	2012	2013	2014	2015	2016	2017
HKG	A	P			T				P		T	P						T	
	B	T	P	T			P	T	P		T		P	T		P		T	
IND	A				T			P			T	P			T				
	B		P	T	P		T		P	T	P		T			P	T	P	
INO	A		P					T		P	T	P					T		
	B		P	T			P		T		P	T			P			T	
MAL	A	P	T			P			T	P	T	P	T	P	T	P		T	
	B		T			P		T P		T	P					T	P		
PHI	A	P			T		P		T	P		T	P	T	P			T	
	B			P				T			P	T	P	T	P	T			
ROK	A	P	T	P			T			P	T	P			T	P	T		
	B	T			P		T			P		T		P	T	P			
SIN	A	P			T				P		T	P			T	P		T	
	B	T			P		T P	T		P		T		P				T	
TAP	A	P		T			P T		P		T	P			T	P		T	
	B		P		T			P		T	P	T			P		T		
THA	A	P	T	P	T	P		T		P	T	P	T	P		T			
	B		T		P T	P				T	P	T		P	T	P		T	

2000 Dot-com bubble
2008 Global financial crisis
2010 European Union debt crisis
2013 Taper tantrum

P Peak
T Trough
▇ Cycle below trend
▇ Cycle above trend

A = output, B = private credit to GDP, GDP = gross domestic product, HKG = Hong Kong, China, IND = India, INO = Indonesia, MAL = Malaysia, PHI = Philippines, Q = quarter, ROK = Republic of Korea, SIN = Singapore, TAP = Taipei,China, THA = Thailand.
Note: Private credit to GDP data in the Philippines starts in Q4 2001.
Source: ADB estimates.

The efficacy of monetary policy for macroeconomic stabilization may be undermined when the business and credit cycles are not synchronized. Since the GFC, monetary policy in developing Asia has generally been accommodative, which is consistent with loose global liquidity. Accommodative monetary policy may have helped to promote output growth in the region but could also have pushed credit to grow too rapidly shortly after the GFC, perhaps setting a premature cap on credit growth. Table 2.3.1 suggests that some economies recently saw their output growing above trend but with credit slowing. If these economies tighten their monetary policy as a check on the widening output gap, the credit downturn will worsen and create a new set of policy problems. In other words, given the negative correlation between the credit and business cycles, if monetary policy focuses mainly on stabilizing the business cycle, it could amplify swings in the credit cycle that could induce another wave of instability in the business cycle. Thus, monetary policy might be made more effective if combined with other appropriate policies that address credit.

Sometimes, monetary policy may be dictated by external factors. Responding to an external shock like sharp currency depreciation brought about by volatile capital outflow may constrain how effectively monetary policy pursues domestic objectives, particularly where the exchange rate regime is less flexible. Again, the trick is to apply a proper mix of policies.

Flexible exchange rates can cushion external shocks

The AFC underlined the potential costs of maintaining relatively fixed exchange rate regimes. The main lesson learned is that an exchange rate arrangement that cushions the economy against external shocks is a valuable tool for macroeconomic management. Despite the evident need for greater exchange rate flexibility, a few economies retained fixed exchange rate regimes, represented by 2 in Figure 2.3.7, but the majority adopted intermediate regimes, represented by 1. Intervention in foreign exchange markets remained extensive across the region, suggesting that Asian policy makers have serious reservations about the merits of fully floating exchange rate regimes, represented by 0.

A flexible exchange rate allows an economy to adjust to adverse external shocks by letting the currency depreciate, which makes its exports more competitive. While this is a significant benefit, flexible exchange rates entail a number of costs as well, particularly when fundamentals are weak.

2.3.7 Exchange rate regime in Asian economies

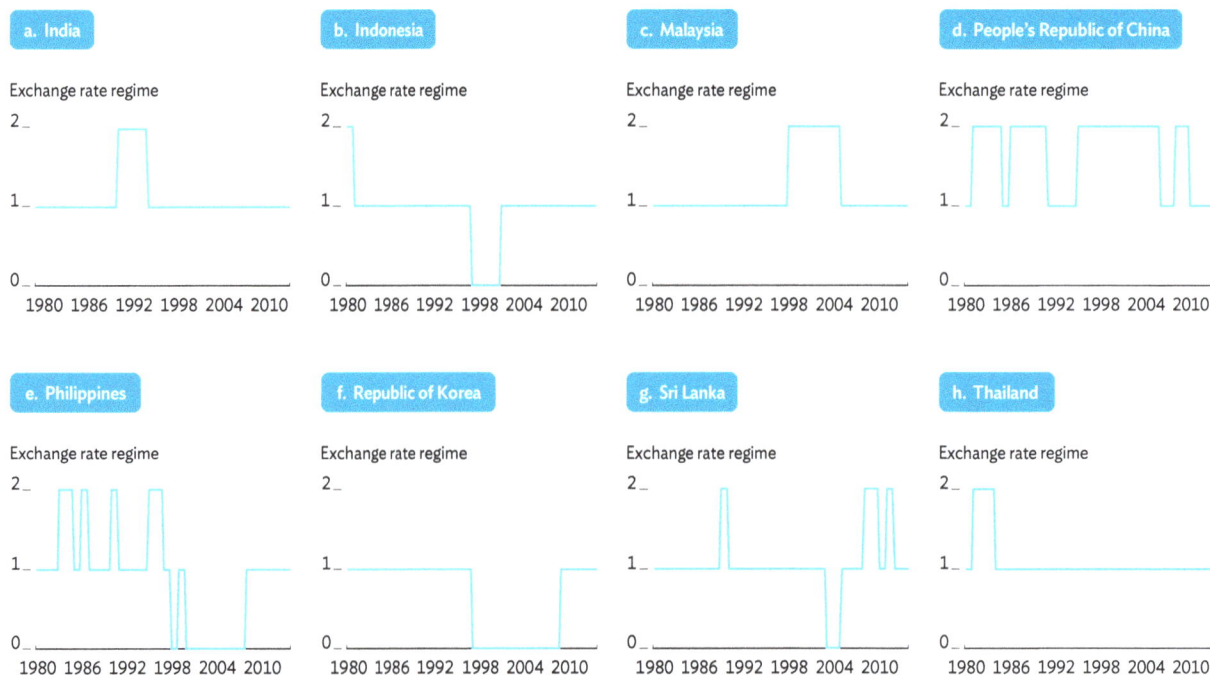

Note: Regimes for free-floating exchange rates are indicated by 0, fixed rates by 2, and intermediate controls by 1.
Source: Obstfeld, Ostry, and Qureshi 2017, based on Ghosh, Ostry, and Qureshi 2015.

These include severe volatility in financial and foreign exchange markets after a large and unexpected shock, the loss of export competitiveness if the currency appreciates too rapidly, and exacerbated currency mismatches on corporate, bank, and sovereign balance sheets from large exchange rate swings. Monetary authorities therefore act to smooth high volatility caused by external shocks and thereby manage market sentiment.

The tradeoff between exchange rate stability and insulation from foreign shocks in an environment of international capital mobility has been framed in terms of a policy "trilemma" (Mundell 1963). The trilemma is that policy makers can attain only two of three policy goals: exchange rate stability, free capital mobility, and monetary policy autonomy. For example, if policy makers opt to have a fixed exchange rate and free capital flow, they cannot have an independent monetary policy to pursue domestic objectives such as controlling inflation.

Challenging this traditional view, Rey (2015, 2016) showed that a global financial cycle constrains the monetary policy of all economies irrespective of their exchange rate regime. Similarly, Shin (2016) argued that, because dollar-denominated credit is the dominant form of funding on the international interbank market, US interest rates can have a sizable effect on financial conditions in emerging markets regardless of their exchange rate regime. Gopinath (2017a,b) emphasized the prevalence of dollar pricing in international trade and found that sticky dollar prices prevented nominal exchange rate changes from translating fully into real exchange rate changes. As what matters for trade is the real exchange rate, this situation compromises the stabilizing benefits of currency flexibility.

On the other hand, studying a group of 40 emerging markets in the period 1986–2013, Obstfeld, Ostry, and Qureshi (2017) found that economies with fixed exchange rates suffered greater economic instability caused by global financial volatility than did those that adopted fully or even partly flexible regimes. Eichengreen et al. (forthcoming) shed further light on the debate. In this analysis, drivers of risks included volatility in global and US financial markets, fluctuations in external demand, changes in the monetary policy of advanced economies, and other sources of policy uncertainty. The evidence reinforced the conclusion that economies with pegged exchange rate regimes were more likely to experience economic vulnerability in response to global financial shocks than were economies with fully floating exchange rates. More specifically, the study found that economies with pegged rates experienced sharper reductions in credit growth, prices for real estate and other risky assets, bank leverage and capital flow, and economic growth. Specifically, an increase by one standard deviation in the Londono-Wilson index, a measure of global financial volatility, implies for economies with fixed exchange rates over those with free-floating rates a reduction in quarterly domestic credit growth larger by 0.96 percentage points and a reduction in GDP growth larger by 0.29 percentage points (Box 2.3.1).

In addition, Eichengreen et al. (forthcoming) found evidence that, compared with fully flexible exchange rate regimes, intermediate regimes with limited flexibility suffered heightened sensitivity to global financial volatility in terms of GDP growth, capital flow, and domestic financial conditions. Changes in external demand caused by global growth shocks affected credit growth, banking system leverage, and capital flow in emerging economies, but there was no evidence of negative effects on output growth. Interestingly, the evidence did not support the notion that more flexible exchange rate regimes provide insulation from the Fed's ongoing monetary policy normalization (Eichengreen et al., forthcoming). This may reflect the dominant role of the US dollar in interbank credit flows and international trade, as discussed above.

In short, the exchange rate regime matters, as suggested by the greater sensitivity of domestic financial and macroeconomic conditions to global shocks in fixed and intermediate currency regimes. While rigid exchange rate regimes that use hard pegs, single currency pegs, and basket pegs provide the least insulation from external shocks, the notion that intermediate regimes, which use exchange rate bands and crawls and managed floats, can adequately cushion adverse shocks should be reconsidered.

Capital account policies for dealing with external shocks

The size and volatility of capital flow in Asia complicates macroeconomic management. Capital flow affects exchange rates, inflation, and the financial system. The destabilizing potential of capital flow is revealed in the extent and variety of measures implemented to control the capital account since the AFC. Figure 2.3.8 plots capital account legal restrictions on aggregate inflow and outflow using indexes constructed in Fernandez et al. (2016).[6] The aggregate index provides a sweeping view of the evolution of capital account regimes in the region over time. The international financial centers in Hong Kong, China and in Singapore fully liberalized their capital accounts. At the other end of the spectrum, the PRC and India maintained strict control over capital flow, though the PRC began to liberalize its capital account in 2013.

2.3.8 Capital restriction indices

— Hong Kong, China
— India
— Indonesia
— Malaysia
— People's Republic of China
— Philippines
— Rep. of Korea
— Singapore
— Thailand
— Viet Nam

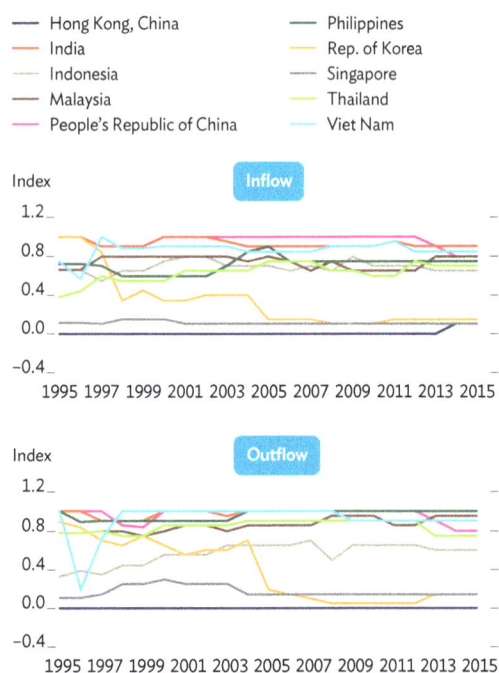

Index

Inflow

1.2
0.8
0.4
0.0
−0.4

1995 1997 1999 2001 2003 2005 2007 2009 2011 2013 2015

Index

Outflow

1.2
0.8
0.4
0.0
−0.4

1995 1997 1999 2001 2003 2005 2007 2009 2011 2013 2015

Source: Fernández et al. 2016, updated in 2017.

2.3.1 Insulating benefits of exchange rate regimes

Eichengreen et al. (forthcoming) extended the analysis by Obstfeld, Ostry, and Qureshi (2017) to estimate the impact of global shocks on different macroeconomic and financial indicators: credit availability, property prices, stock returns, loan-to-deposit ratio, a set of capital flow measures, and GDP growth. This was done by controlling for key differences between economies with managed exchange rates and those with flexible exchange rates by looking at how the different exchange rate regimes insulated the effect of an external shock to these indicators.

To measure the external shock, the study considered several different indicators, including the Londono–Wilson index (Londono and Wilson 2018), which represents global volatility conditions as implied by the computed weighted average market value of equity

options in seven countries: France, Germany, Japan, the Netherlands, Switzerland, the United Kingdom, and the US. The box table provides the estimated impact of a global volatility shock on domestic macroeconomic and financial indicators in emerging market economies.

The table reports the coefficients of intermediate and fixed exchange rate regimes, the Londono–Wilson index, and their interactions. An increase in the Londono–Wilson index had a significant negative effect on real domestic credit growth, real house price escalation, change in the loan-to-deposit ratio, net capital flows, and real GDP growth in fixed regimes. An increase in the index also had negative and significant effect on change in the loan-to-deposit ratio, asset flows, and real GDP growth in intermediate regimes.

1 The impact of the Londono–Wilson index on variables in emerging markets

DV	EV	(1)	(2)	(3)	(4)	(5)
1. Real domestic credit growth	Intermediate	0.3	2.4	2.5	2.5	3.8*
	Fixed	1.4	11.0**	10.9**	12.3**	10.6**
	LW	-1.7***	-0.6	-0.5	0.0	
	Inter × LW		-0.6	-0.7	-0.7	-1.0
	Fix × LW		-3.0**	-3.0**	-3.3**	-2.8**
2. Real house price growth	Intermediate	1.6***	-0.1	-0.3	0.2	0.1
	Fixed	1.3	23.6***	23.7***	23.5**	21.4***
	LW	-2.4***	-0.3	-0.3	-0.2	
	Inter × LW		0.6	0.7	0.5	0.7
	Fix × LW		-6.8***	-6.8***	-6.8**	-6.0**
3. Real stock returns	Intermediate Regime	2.3	-2.5	-2.9	-4.1	0.5
	Fixed Regime	0.3	5.6	4.9	7.8	5.5
	LW	-8.3***	-8.3***	-9.6***	-11.3***	
	Inter × LW		1.5	1.6	1.8	0.6
	Fix × LW		-1.7	-1.6	-2.1	-1.9
4. Change in the loan-to-deposit ratio	Intermediate	-0.2	3.7	3.7	4.9	4.3
	Fixed	1.2	6.4*	6.4*	8.0**	7.1**
	LW	-0.3	0.6	0.6	1.4**	
	Inter × LW		-1.2	-1.2	-1.5**	-1.4**
	Fix × LW		-1.6*	-1.6*	-2.0**	-1.9**
5. Net capital flows	Intermediate	1.9**	6.7*	6.3	4.7	7.4*
	Fixed	2.3	13.5**	13.4**	9.9*	13.7**
	LW	-0.7	0.8	0.9	1.4	
	Inter × LW		-1.5	-1.4	-1.2	-1.6
	Fix × LW		-3.5*	-3.4*	-2.7*	-3.4*
6. Liability flows	Intermediate	1.2	-1.6	-2.3	-6.0	0.4
	Fixed	3.5*	13.2	12.8	8.0	15.1*
	LW	-4.2***	-3.5***	-3.5***	-2.2**	
	Inter × LW		0.9	1.1	1.6	0.5
	Fix × LW		-3.0	-2.8	-2.0	-3.3
7. Asset flows	Intermediate	0.8	8.4**	8.7**	10.7***	7.0*
	Fixed	-1.0	0.4	0.6	2.0	-1.4
	LW	3.5***	4.3***	4.4***	3.6***	
	Inter × LW		-2.4**	-2.5**	-2.8***	-2.1*
	Fix × LW		-0.4	-0.6	-0.7	-0.1
8. Real GDP growth	Intermediate	0.1	1.4**	1.3**	1.7**	1.4**
	Fixed	0.2	3.1***	3.1***	2.8**	3.1***
	LW	-0.6***	-0.2	-0.3*	-0.1	
	Inter × LW		-0.4**	-0.4*	-0.5**	-0.4*
	Fix × LW		-0.9***	-0.9**	-0.8**	-0.9**

DV = dependent variables, EV = explanatory variables, GDP = gross domestic product, LW = Londono–Wilson index, Inter = intermediate.

Note: The table reports only the coefficients of intermediate and fixed exchange rate regimes, the Londono–Wilson index, and their interactions. The dependent variables are as per the first column of Tables 1.1–1.7 and 1.9 in Eichengreen et al. (forthcoming). *** indicates statistical significance at the 1% level, ** at the 5% level, and * at the 10% level, based on clustered standard errors by country.

Source: ADB estimates.

In the early 2000s, when capital flowed into Asia, many economies tightened their inflow restrictions while loosening outflow restrictions. Some Asian economies tightened restrictions to control a surge of capital inflow that came with the expansion of global liquidity after the GFC. Then, after 2013, concerns about rising global interest rates nudged policy makers toward introducing restrictions on outflow.

Although many economies manage capital flow, the evidence is mixed on how effectively various measures control the volume and composition of cross-border flows (Magud, Reinhart, and Rogoff 2011). The evidence is that efficacy tends to be stronger for control over the composition of flow (You, Kim, and Ren 2014, Kim and Yang 2012) than over volume (Jittrapanun and Prasartset 2009, Edwards 2007) and for inflow over outflow (Van der Laan, Cunha, and Lélis 2017). Moreover, measures imposed on a particular type of capital flow can influence other types through substitution and complementary effects, both within an economy and across borders (Forbes et al. 2016).

Controls on capital flow have multiple objectives, notably to change the flow volume, alter inflow composition toward direct investment, alleviate pressure on the real exchange rate, and foster monetary policy independence. Using data on a set of 10 economies in developing Asia (India; Indonesia; Hong Kong, China; Malaysia; the PRC; the Philippines; the ROK; Singapore; Thailand; and Viet Nam) from 2000 to 2015, Jongwanich (forthcoming) evaluated whether capital flow restrictions were effective in achieving these objectives. The analysis further divided capital flow into direct investment, equity investment, debt securities, and "other investment," which includes trade credits, loans, currency and deposits, and other accounts receivable and payable through banks. The following discussion summarizes the findings (Box 2.3.2).

One finding was that, while not all capital account policies were effective in influencing the volume of their targeted flow, restrictions on direct investment and equity inflow seemed to be effective. Among capital outflow restrictions, only those on "other investment" had an effect on the intended flow. The study also found that tightening and loosening capital controls had effects that were not necessarily symmetrical. Easing controls on equity inflow, especially for nonresidents, had a stronger effect than tightening controls. This observed pattern can be attributed to many Asian authorities subjecting nonresident enterprises and investors that issue equities to more stringent requirements than it imposes on residents. Also, equity inflow restrictions seemed to reduce equity outflow, and liberalization increased them, as buying and selling shares tended to be easier than transacting other types of assets, making equity flows flexible.

2.3.2 The efficacy of capital controls

Jongwanich (forthcoming) examined the effect of legal restrictions on the volume of capital flow both in and out by estimating the regression equations below using data from 10 economies in developing Asia (Hong Kong, China; India; Indonesia; Malaysia; the PRC; the Philippines; the Republic of Korea; Singapore; Thailand; and Viet Nam) during the period 2000–2015. The equations estimated are

$$\left(\frac{CFI_k}{GDP}\right)_{it} = \alpha_{0,it} + \alpha_{1,it}CRI_{k,it} + X_{it}\theta + \eta_i + \varepsilon_{it}$$

$$\left(\frac{CFO_k}{GDP}\right)_{it} = \alpha_{0,it} + \alpha_{1,it}CRO_{k,it} + X_{it}\theta + \eta_i + \varepsilon_{it}$$

where $(CFI_k/GDP)_{it}$ is capital inflow type k (direct investment, equity, debt, other investment) as a share of GDP into country i at time t and $(CFO_k/GDP)_{it}$ is capital outflow type k as a share of GDP from country i at time k. $CRI_{k,it}$ is the capital inflow restriction index for type k capital in country I at time t, and $CRO_{k,it}$ is the outflow restriction index for type k capital in country i at time t. X_{it} is a vector of control variables that represent push and pull factors affecting flows. η_i is the unobserved country specific effect and ε_{it} is the error term.

Jongwanich (forthcoming) extended the above specifications to test as well for the possibility of asymmetric effects from tightening ($D^{tighten}$) versus loosening (D^{loosen}) restrictions, differential effects from resident ($CRN_{k,it}$) versus nonresident ($CRR_{k,it}$) restrictions, the effects of outflow restrictions on inflow ($CRO_{k,it}$) and inflow restriction on outflow ($CRI_{k,it}$), the substitution effects of restrictions on one type of flow on all other types of flow (CRI_k or CRO_k), and the effects of capital account policies imposed by other economies ($CRI_{k,j\neq it}$ or $CRO_{k,j\neq it}$).

The estimation was done using a system generalized method of moments approach for the panel of economies, following Arellano and Bond (1991) and Blundell and Bond (1998).

A summary of results is presented in box table 1 for inflow and box table 2 for outflow. The negative and significant coefficients for the first effect show that restrictions on direct investment and equity inflows, and on other investment outflow, are effective in reducing the volume of their targeted flows. The negative sign on the dummy variable indicates that for the second effect, loosening restrictions on equity inflow (a drop in the index) more effectively controls inflow than does tightening. The third effect shows that equity inflow restrictions on nonresidents is effective, and the fourth shows that equity inflow restrictions seem to reduce equity outflows, and that easing increases them. Substitution and complementary effects exist between most types of flow for inflow and outflow restrictions.

1 Summary of estimated coefficients of interests: inflow

Effect	Direct investment	Equity	Debt	Other investment
1. Individual: $CRI_{k,it}$	–1.089***	–2.851**	–0.105	–2.278
2. Asymmetric: $D^{tighten}$	0.892	–0.033	1	1
D^{loosen}	0.236	–2.585*	1	1
3. Resident versus nonresident: $CRNI_{k,it}$	2	–1.650**	–0.448	3
$CRRI_{k,it}$	2	–0.934	0.927	3
4. Outflow controls: $CRO_{k,it}$	–0.074	2.028	0.407	–2.540
5. Substitution/complementary effects within an economy:				
CRI_{direct}	n.a.	–1.739**	–0.781*	–1.034
CRI_{equity}	–3.695**	n.a.	–1.760	–8.214
CRI_{debt}	–0.076	–1.414*	n.a.	–6.811
CRI_{other}	–1.288	–1.219	–0.123	n.a.
6. Substitution/complementary effects across economies: $CRI_{k,j\neq it}$	18.426*	–18.007**	–38.425**	–85.784**

*** = statistical significance at 1%, ** = statistical significance at 5%, * = statistical significance at 10%, n.a. = not applicable.

[1] Test on asymmetric effects is not carried out because the control on its own inflow is not statistically significant.

[2] Estimations are not carried out because controls on inflow are mostly on nonresidents.

[3] Controls on other investment inflow do not distinguish between residents and nonresidents.

continued next page

2.3.2 Continued

2 Summary of estimated coefficients of interests: outflow

Effect	Direct investment	Equity	Debt	Other investment
1. Individual: $CRO_{k,it}$	-8.966	1.747	2.276	-3.203***
2. Asymmetric: $D^{tighten}$	1	1	1	0.243
D^{loosen}	1	1	1	-3.520
3. Resident versus nonresident: $CRNO_{k,it}$	2	-0.755	1.571	3
$CRRO_{k,it}$	2	1.409	0.926	3
4. Inflow controls: $CRI_{k,it}$	-0.932	-2.145***	2.470	1.913
5. Substitution/complementary within an economy:				
CRO_{direct}	n.a.	-2.355***	1.063	1.138
CRO_{equity}	-0.114	n.a.	2.504**	11.568
CRO_{debt}	-4.677	0.136	n.a.	-5.336
CRO_{other}	1.397	-6.386	0.030	n.a.
6. Substitution/complementary across economies: $CRO_{k,j \neq it}$	12.221	30.799*	-36.806	-166.183***

*** = statistical significance at 1%, ** = statistical significance at 5%, * = statistical significance at 10%, n.a. = not applicable.

[1] Test on asymmetric effects is not carried out because the control on its own inflow (the preceding result) is not statistically significant.

[2] Estimations are not carried out because controls on outflow are mostly on residents.

[3] Controls on other investment outflow do not distinguish between residents and nonresidents.

There were complementary effects between equity, debt, and direct inflows, such that restrictions on one type of flow might constrict others, possibly by influencing market sentiment (Gochoco-Bautista, Jongwanich, and Lee 2012). With regard to outflow, allowing residents to engage in more direct investment abroad by reducing restrictions on their capital flow encouraged more equity outflow. In another example, a substitution effect was found between equity and debt outflow, in that restrictions on equity outflow increased debt security outflow. There were cross-border effects as well. Restrictions on direct investments in one economy redirected such investments to its neighbors. On the other hand, restrictions on other types of assets reduced inflow in all economies. A similar complementary effect was seen for outflow restrictions on equity and debt securities.

A second finding is that capital flow restrictions had only limited effect on increasing the share of more stable direct investment in total capital inflow. The evidence suggests that only restrictions on inflow of debt securities, which may reduce both debt and equity inflows, could help increase the share of direct investment in total capital flow. On the other hand, direct investment inflow responded significantly and positively to high economic growth and other strong macroeconomic fundamentals such as financial development and good governance.

A third point is that capital flow restrictions can be useful if selectively considered for mitigating currency appreciation in real terms when it is caused by capital inflow.

Finally, under a managed exchange rate regime, monetary authorities have more autonomy in setting interest rates if they impose restrictions on total capital inflow. Besides restrictions, the study found that changes in the exchange rate could cushion shocks caused by volatile capital flows and foster monetary policy autonomy.

As long as emerging economies face sudden large surges and reversals in capital flow, contributing to the buildup of financial vulnerability, restrictions and other capital flow management measures will remain integral to the toolkit for fashioning macroeconomic stabilization policy. In sum, the evidence suggests that measures do influence capital flow, but policy makers must recognize that they may not always achieve their intended objectives and that the indiscriminate use of interventions can be costly. Because both restriction and liberalization are effective in achieving specific policy objectives, depending critically on circumstances, they must be designed and implemented prudently.

Macroprudential policies

Macroprudential policy aims to mitigate risks to the financial system using different measures that address credit, liquidity, and capital flow to protect the health of banks and influence domestic lending, exchange rates, foreign capital flow, and housing prices.

To examine how prevalent these measures are, Khan, Ramayandi, and Schröder (forthcoming) compiled a dataset on the use of macroprudential actions in 61 economies, 21 of them advanced and 40 emerging, from 2000 to 2016 that uniquely matched each macroprudential action to a specific target variable that it was meant to influence (Table 2.3.2).[7]

To summarize, the study identified 1,386 macroprudential interventions from 2000 to 2016. Most interventions—1,151 of them, or 83%—were in emerging market economies, while the remaining 228, or 17%, were in advanced economies. By type, a minimum reserve requirement for commercial banks was, at 486 interventions, the most commonly used, followed by regulatory controls on capital to be held by banks or other financial institutions on their balance sheets (189), limits on credit or credit growth (149), and caps on the loan-to-value ratio (132). The least-used interventions, at fewer than 21 instances each, were exposure limits, maturity mismatch limits, caps on the loan-to-deposit ratio, and other restrictions on lending. Overall, tightening restrictions were more common than easing restrictions.

2.3.2 Macroprudential measures by instrument type, 2000–2016

Policy instruments	Banking[a]	Domestic loans[b]	Exchange rate[c]	Foreign capital movement[d]	House prices	Total
Total	190	733	75	120	259	1,386
Capital requirements	65	106	0	6	12	189
Caps on foreign currency lending	0	12	24	27	2	65
Debt-to-income or debt service-to-income ratio	1	23	0	1	33	58
Exposure limits	7	11	0	1	2	21
Levies or taxes on financial institutions and activities	7	38	9	1	64	119
Limits on credit or credit growth	6	87	5	14	37	149
Limits on maturity mismatch	0	1	0	3	0	4
Limits on net open positions or currency mismatch	0	4	24	19	0	47
Liquidity requirements	10	34	3	4	0	51
Loan-to-value ratio	0	47	0	2	83	132
Loan-to-deposit limits	3	5	0	0	0	8
Other restrictions on lending standards	0	6	0	0	0	6
Provisioning requirements	7	36	0	2	6	51
Reserve requirements	89	323	11	43	20	486

[a] Banking includes measures on bank assets, bank capital, bank reserves, capital adequacy ratio, credit card purchases, deposits, liquid assets ratio, loan-to-deposit ratio, nonperforming loans, and rural and thrift bank profits.

[b] Domestic loans include vehicle loans, consumer loans, credit-to-GDP ratio, domestic credit, household debt, housing loans, mortgage loans, real estate loans, total credit, and total loans.

[c] Exchange rate is local currency per US dollar.

[d] Foreign capital movement includes measures on external debt, foreign direct investment, foreign currency deposits, foreign currency liabilities, foreign currency loans, foreign exchange reserves, foreign portfolio investment, net foreign assets, net open positions to regulatory capital, and net open position in foreign exchange.

Notes: The total number of interventions is 1,379, but 7 interventions were dual instrument types (e.g., one intervention was considered both a cap on foreign currency and a limit on credit growth).

Source: Khan, Ramayandi, and Schroder, forthcoming.

In terms of target objectives, many of the interventions (733 of them, or 52.8%) aimed to influence domestic lending, followed by housing prices (259) and risk-taking by banks (190). Exchange rates and foreign capital movements were targeted by limits on net open position, but there were few of these. Some measures aimed to influence a narrow set of targets, for example, leverage limits on banks and financial institutions' targeted provision of domestic loans in general or mortgage loans in particular. Other measures like reserve requirements had wider influence.

Almost half of world-wide macroprudential interventions took place in the 18 Asian economies in the sample, underscoring the popularity of these measures in the macro management toolkits of regional policy makers. The use of these instruments in Asia, as well as globally, increased after the GFC and peaked during crises years (Akinci and Olmstead-Rumsey 2018). Asian economies have tended to rely more heavily on measures other than those related to reserve requirements, and this trend has intensified in recent years. The nature of shocks that affected asset and credit market segments of the economy post-GFC seems to have prompted the authorities in the region to rely on finely targeted policy instruments to stabilize their economies. As can be seen in Figure 2.3.9, the focus of such measures was most heavily on influencing domestic lending and housing prices.

Macroprudential policies have been analysed for their efficacy, particularly with regard to variables related to financial stability such as credit growth and housing prices. But it is also useful to understand the enabling conditions that may improve the likelihood of macroprudential policies being effective. Khan, Ramayandi, and Schröder (forthcoming) explored the issue by counting a macroprudential measure as effective when it brought down the variability of its target indicator below a certain threshold (the 6-month average of the indicator's rolling standard deviation declining after the intervention by at least 20% from the 6-month average before the intervention). Conversely, it was ineffective if there was no similar decline. The analysis showed that conditions varied under which macroprudential policies were effective.

Macroprudential policy matters. Implementing multiple policy interventions simultaneously improves their chances of being effective, regardless of their objectives. Policy makers often implemented two or more macroprudential policy measures at the same time. Singapore, for example, implemented five macroprudential policy measures simultaneously in the first quarter of 2013, mostly to address housing imbalances that were getting worse. On the other hand, the cumulative tightening of a measure introduced earlier makes it less effective, possibly because its credibility erodes.

Another observation is the importance of timing policy interventions correctly in macroeconomic cycles. The likelihood of an intervention being effective is higher if it is implemented when the economy is on a downswing. Addressing stability concerns is more difficult in an overheated economy. During an expansion phase in the credit cycle, there is more scope for macroprudential measures to have impact on the targeted variable than when demand for credit is low, irrespective of whether the measures tighten or ease restrictions (Cerutti et al. 2017).

Meanwhile, policy interventions tend to be more effective in economies with more rapid increases in the ratio of external debt to GDP. Macroprudential policy tends to be more effective when indebtedness is expanding, regardless of whether it is sourced domestically or internationally. However, this effect may be limited by extreme degrees of foreign dependence.

2.3.9 Macroprudential policy interventions in Asia

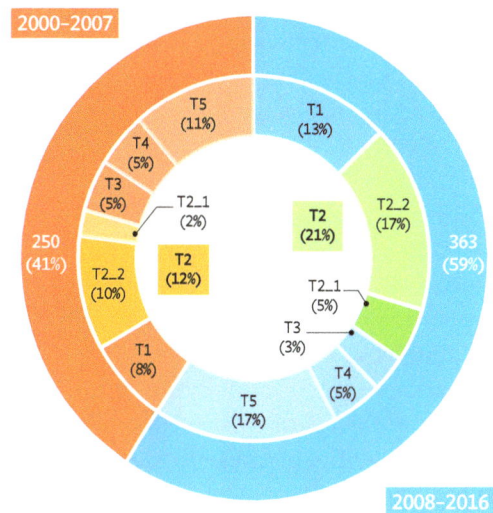

Target indicators:

T1 = Bank health measure
T2 = Domestic lending
T2_1 = Housing related lending
T2_2 = Non-housing related lending
T3 = Exchange rate
T4 = Foreign capital movement
T5 = House price

Note: Asia includes Australia; Georgia; Hong Kong, China; India; Indonesia; Kazakhstan; Malaysia; Mongolia; New Zealand; Pakistan; the People's Republic of China; the Philippines; the Republic of Korea; Singapore; Sri Lanka; Taipei,China; Thailand; and Viet Nam.

Source: Khan, Ramayandi, and Schröder, forthcoming.

When an economy is a large net borrower from international markets, its macroprudential policy measures are less likely to be effective because greater external dependence limits domestic policy independence.

In addition, changes in global conditions have an impact on the efficacy of macroprudential policies. In an increasingly integrated world, heightened global financial risk, as captured by a faster increase in the Chicago Board Option Exchange S&P 100 Volatility Index, can readily spread to the domestic economy. This makes macroprudential policy less effective by generating more uncertainty that erodes investors' confidence.

Finally, monetary policy significantly affects the efficacy of macroprudential measures, but fiscal policy and the type of exchange rate regime do not. Analysis shows that macroprudential policies are undermined when combined with monetary tightening. As argued in Malovaná and Frait (2017), making monetary policy more accommodative tends to boost credit availability, thereby providing better scope for effective macroprudential interventions. Conversely, monetary tightening seems to create a less conducive environment for macroprudential interventions by crowding out their influence.

Safeguarding Asia against heightened uncertainty

Ample policy tools exist to protect developing Asia's macroeconomic stability. The tools include countercyclical fiscal policy, flexible exchange rates, measures to manage capital flow, macroprudential policies, and the discretionary use of monetary policy. However, maximizing the efficacy of these policies requires policy makers to continuously monitor pockets of vulnerability, closely coordinate economic policy, and be alert to cross-border spillover effects, either received or transmitted, from the implementation of economic policy.

Continuous monitoring of vulnerability

The dynamics of interaction in the modern economy have become stronger and more complex, entwining the financial sector, the real economy, domestic policy, and the external sector including export industries, when viewed either from a domestic perspective or considering the economy's role in global value chains. An economic slowdown may be accompanied by a credit boom that, if it goes bust, can worsen the slowdown. Policies to buoy real economic activity during a slowdown can fuel faster growth in credit, which heightens the risk of the credit boom going bust. On the other hand, if a policy intervention restrains the boom in credit, it may end up depressing the real economy even further.

Such conundrums can worsen with spillover from a negative external shock, which modern global interconnectedness in trade and investment makes a distinct possibility. The correlation of business cycles in Asia and in the G7 economies has increased from 0.60 before the GFC to 0.82 since the crisis. The correlation of Asia's business cycle with that of Latin America has more than doubled, from 0.36 before the GFC to 0.78 after. Such jumps in correlation highlight tighter connection between economic cycles in Asia and elsewhere, suggesting a higher probability of shock spillover and contagion.

Viewed optimistically, stronger and more complex interactions, both internal and external, enhance opportunities for economic growth and development. However, economies become vulnerable to potential policy conflicts and spillover from negative shocks. To respond to these challenges, economies in developing Asia have to maintain sound fundamentals and navigate economic currents carefully.

Successful navigation entails avoiding potentially negative consequences from policy intervention while keeping macroeconomic indicators steady.

Challenges that emanate from current global economic dynamics expose pockets of vulnerability, as discussed in the second section of this chapter. These pockets are not independent of each other. When capital is flowing massively into Asia, for example, Asian currencies tend to strengthen, private debt tends to mount at a faster rate, and housing prices tend to increase sharply. Volatility in capital flows thereby render pressure on the exchange rate, private credit, and housing prices. Any consequent exchange rate movements affect balance sheets and by extension the amount of debt. Another factor is how a strong and stable exchange rate often indicates positive confidence in an economy. When a currency suffers massive downward pressure on its exchange rate, its depreciation may stall or even reverse capital inflow, or push up the cost of credit through a higher risk premium, or accelerate the escalation of housing prices.

Interdependence linking these vulnerabilities compounds the complexity of achieving macroeconomic stability, as handling one vulnerability may inadvertently worsen another. Consequently, maintaining macroeconomic stability requires close and continuous monitoring of vulnerability. Such vigilance should enable the authorities to identify problems early on and impose corrective measures in a timely way to mitigate existing imbalances and even preemptively head off emerging ones.

Economic policy coordination

As noted above, developing Asia has the policy tools it needs to deal with the consequences of interactions among pockets of vulnerability, but policy makers have to be wary of conflicts and tradeoffs that can arise in the complex intricacies of a modern economy. This requires policy coordination to optimize the chances of maintaining macroeconomic stability.

Actions to coordinate stabilization policies can be divided into two categories based on their scope: domestic coordination and cross-border cooperation. The former entails coordinating domestic government agencies to maximize policy efficacy and minimize potentially conflicting objectives. Meanwhile, cross-border cooperation is necessarily intergovernmental in nature and covers activities ranging from information exchange to actual coordination of interventions. The objective is usually to minimize unwanted cross-border spillover.

Domestic policy coordination

The objective of domestic policy coordination is to enable policy makers to make their policies more effective while at the same time avoid conflicts wherein different macroeconomic stabilization policies undermine each other. Coordinated implementation of different stabilization policies can either enhance efficacy when they work in the same direction or destroy it when they push in opposite directions. A countercyclical fiscal policy in a downturn may benefit from being complemented by an accommodative monetary policy to promote private activity, as both will work to revive economic growth. On the other hand, dire fiscal straits may enfeeble the monetary authority and keep it from pursuing appropriate policy, in which case fiscal dominance prevails, and fiscal policy effectively dictates monetary policy.

Consider an economy running a current account deficit because it has an overvalued currency under a fixed exchange rate regime. This currency is thus under pressure to depreciate. To stabilize the currency, policy makers can adopt a sterilization strategy of selling the country's foreign exchange reserves to buy their own currency and thereby boost its value. However, this option is limited by the amount of foreign exchange available.

A more effective way to mitigate this downward pressure on the currency is to raise domestic interest rates by a sufficient margin. This will attract foreign capital inflow, and the local currency will then be boosted without the monetary authority having to sell its foreign exchange reserves.

Unfortunately, this will be problematic if the government has been borrowing heavily to finance a fiscal deficit. The higher interest rate makes it more costly for the government to roll over its debt or acquire new financing. If the public debt overhang is large and the available fiscal space is limited, the higher interest rate immediately adds to the deficit and undermines investors' confidence in the economy, which may initiate capital outflow. As a result of this outflow, demand for the local currency likely falls, frustrating the attempt to use the interest rate to boost demand for it and thus mitigate depreciation pressure.

In the example above, the capacity of the monetary authority to increase the interest rate toward stabilizing the currency is overwhelmed by heavy debt and limited fiscal space. An increase in the interest rate could intensify pressure on the currency to depreciate, rather than providing relief. The efficacy of monetary policy intervention is thus undermined by a difficult fiscal situation, dubbed "fiscal dominance." Proper coordination between fiscal and monetary authorities, such as through institutionalizing a framework for the two to coordinate their plans, may reduce the likelihood of fiscal dominance emerging.

Such coordination would have improved the chances of appropriate stabilization policy tools being effective.

The proper calibrating of monetary and macroprudential policies to manage business and credit cycles is another arena for possible conflicts and tradeoffs. When the credit and business cycles are synchronized with each other, the monetary authority has the option to use either policy, or both, to simultaneously stabilize both cycles. The impact of monetary policy on output and credit, however, is often found to be much larger than that of macroprudential policy. Consequently, under these circumstances, the degree of success achieved by macroprudential policy may be undermined by monetary policy if it is applied simultaneously.

Policy makers face a dilemma when credit and business cycles are not synchronized—when, for example, economic growth is in a downturn but credit is undergoing excessive expansion. Tightening macroprudential policy by imposing a ceiling on credit growth would address the problem of excessive credit expansion. However, it would depress momentum in the real economy even further, worsening the downturn. On the other hand, loosening monetary policy to stimulate the economy would expand access to credit and worsen the rate of loan default. In such a situation, a better result may be achieved by properly coordinating the two policies such that, despite monetary expansion, the tightening of some macroprudential policies applies the brakes to excessive credit expansion.

Stabilization policy should take into account as well possible distributive effects. For example, even if macroprudential policy can succeed in reducing credit growth, it may cause small borrowers to lose access to credit and dash their hopes of starting or expanding a small business.

A case in point is the implementation of macroprudential policy to address a rapid increase in housing prices, such as caps on the ratio of loan size to home value. Such a policy can readily stabilize the housing market and quell a rapid increase in housing prices. However, the impact of tighter credit is not felt equally across all income groups. Affordability becomes an important issue (Box 2.2.2 on page 72). Those in lower-income groups are more adversely affected by credit rationing. Reducing access for lower-income earners to credit undermines their already low prospects of owning their own home. Effective policy coordination among government agencies can help mitigate this problem. Complementing the housing market stabilization policy with, for example, a policy that provides housing subsidies targeted to lower-income groups both restrains housing prices and makes housing more affordable for the poor.

Financial deepening objectives may also be adversely affected by policies to promote financial stability.

Ayyagari, Beck, and Martinez Peria (2017) suggested that the implementation of macroprudential policy can, depending on its intensity, dampen firms' hopes of funding their growth, and this is particularly so of smaller and younger firms. Among such firms, those with the weakest balance sheets—with high leverage, low profitability, and low interest-coverage ratios— are the ones that get their credit curtailed by macroprudential policies. This suggests that, although the macroprudential policy reduced, as intended, credit to firms pretty much across the board, it is still the most fragile firms that end up being the worst affected. Effective policy coordination within the economy can provide special credit schemes exclusively for smaller and younger firms with potential, thereby advancing the development objective of financial deepening even as macroprudential measures are applied to stabilize the financial sector.

Cross-border cooperation

The main objective of cross-border policy cooperation is to avoid unwanted spillover from policy changes in one economy onto other economies, and to minimize contagion from negative shocks. The activities covered by cross-border cooperation range from merely exchanging information on economic conditions to active policy cooperation by, for example, establishing a currency union.

Exchanging data and information is the minimum requirement to increase awareness about potential spillover from and to other economies. Policies to manage capital flow, for example, may produce either complementary or substitution effects between different types of international capital flow. Analysis suggests that, in the case of foreign direct investment, inflow into one economy often increases after restrictions are applied by the authorities in other economies that, because they have comparable production bases, compete for investment.

The substitution effect in capital inflows is evident, however, only in the case of foreign direct investment. Short-term inflow such as for portfolio investment and other flows that are channeled mostly through the banking system tend to decline after the imposition of restrictions in neighboring economies. This negative association reflects complementarity among these short-term inflows to emerging economies in Asia. A change in market sentiment in one country is often mirrored in other economies in the region, moving in the same direction. When the authorities in one economy in the region impose controls on short-term inflow, investors tend to get more cautious about investment prospects throughout the region.

With regard to outflow, controls on equity and other investment flows appear to be the only ones that have significant cross-border spillover effects. In terms of the behavior of the equity outflow, economies in the region seem to substitute for each other. That is, when one country imposes restrictions on equity outflow, these types of outflow from other countries in the region tend to increase. At other times economies are complementary. That is, restrictions imposed in one country or a few may affect investor sentiment and provoke equity outflow from other nearby or similar countries as well, even though they have not imposed the restrictions. In short, cross-border spillover from controls on capital inflow and outflow— whether the spillover is characterized by substitution or complementation—suggests that cooperation needs to be instituted across economies, particularly those with comparable production bases and within a single region.

The conduct of cross-border policy cooperation is often challenged, however, by differing incentives in different economies. A study on cross-border spillover and contagion in the financial market, which looked in particular at how asset returns among markets were related, shed some light on the issue (Dungey, Kangogo, and Volkov, forthcoming). The issue of cross-border policy cooperation is complicated by the role played by developed core economies in an interconnected world, which tend to absorb positive shocks from emerging markets on the periphery and to transmit dampening effects back to the periphery (Box 2.4.1).

Spillover is not always bad, as it can have either an amplifying or a dampening effect on markets. However, the differing nature of spillover depending on whether it is received or transmitted across markets appears to be closely associated with the size of the economy. As economies get larger, they progressively receive more spillover that amplifies returns, and they progressively transmit more dampening effects on other economies. Such asymmetrical distribution of benefits and costs from spillover is one reason why economies need to reach genuinely workable agreements for cross-border policy cooperation. Further, developing common incentives for forging successful cross-border cooperation can lay the foundation for better regional cooperation in the future.

Difficult as it may be to define an effective platform for cross-border policy cooperation, the need is obvious given the impact of cross-border spillover, in particular from policy pursued in more influential economies. By considering the cross-border effects on others of policy pursued at home, and by working to minimize the risk of contagion, policy makers can position themselves better to promote global stability. While monetary policy is generally understood to be oriented towards domestic objectives such as price stability and a sound financial system, the authorities in larger economies in particular should pay heed to cross-border spillover and contagion.

2.4.1 Examining spillover and contagion

Dungey, Kangogo, and Volkov (forthcoming) considered the roles of spillover and contagion in affecting financial stability, arguing that it is important to understand the distinction between spillover and contagion when designing policy for stability. Spillover reflects the usual, expected relationship between markets in terms of how a shock in one market may transmit to another, through either balance sheets, trade, or the movement of portfolio investment. In general, spillover is relatively stable, and any changes are likely to come slowly. Contagion, on the other hand, is abrupt and unexpected. It generally has a negative connotation, referring to a case in which a shock in one market causes an unexpected decline in the performance of another. Another phenomenon is decoupling, whereby a shock in one market causes an unexpectedly small change in the performance of another. When markets respond to a shock in a way typical of neither decoupling nor contagion, then interdependence is likely. That is, the spillover effects from the previous relationship are maintained, but now sparking higher or lower market volatility.

Box figure 1 illustrates how spillover can have either amplifying and dampening effects. The top panel shows a market's estimated receipt of shocks, and the bottom panel shows the transmission of shocks from another market. The spillover effect for each market during each historical phase is given in separate columns. In the pre-GFC period, the average spillover effect that markets transmitted to others was similar in size, the exceptions being Sri Lanka and the US, which were almost neutral. Relative to the later phases, the shocks received before the GFC were small, though with more heterogeneity than the transmissions sent in the same period. Some countries, such as Australia and India, received on average negative, or dampening, effects from spillover. In contrast, positive or amplifying spillover was received in Hong Kong, China; Indonesia; and Thailand.

Since the pre-GFC period, the transmission of shocks from source markets has generally declined, but during the GFC the magnitude of received spillover tended to be larger.

continued next page

1 Average receiving and transmitting effects by period and market

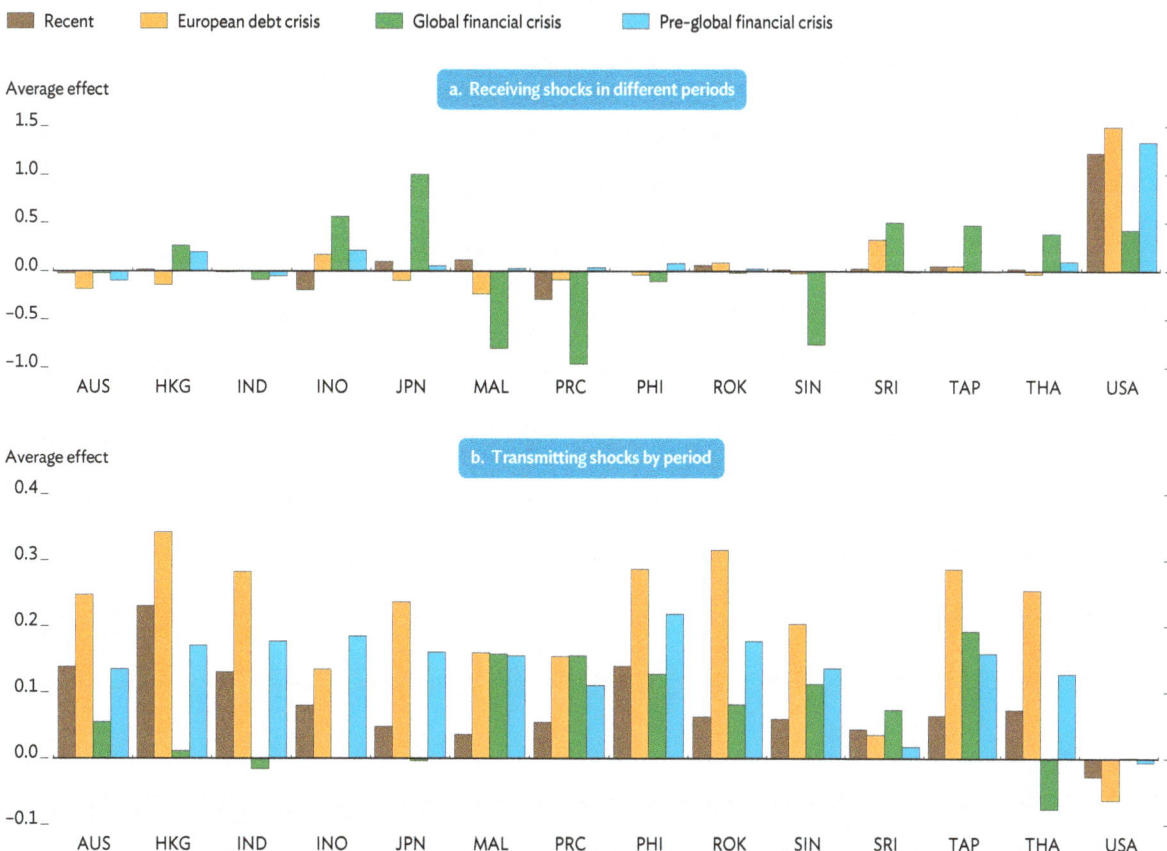

Legend: ■ Recent ■ European debt crisis ■ Global financial crisis ■ Pre-global financial crisis

AUS = Australia, HKG = Hong Kong, China, IND = India, INO = Indonesia, JPN = Japan, MAL = Malaysia, PHI = Philippines, PRC = People's Republic of China, ROK = Republic of Korea, SIN = Singapore, SRI = Sri Lanka, TAP = Taipei,China, THA = Thailand, USA = United States of America.

Source: Dungey, Kangogo, and Volkov, forthcoming.

2.4.1 Continued

Unlike some other markets, Malaysia, the PRC, and Singapore received dampening effects. Japan received large amplifying effects as a flight to quality attracted skittish investors into its market. The most recent episode shows a return to conditions more similar to pre-GFC in terms of transmission effects. The effects may be slightly smaller but still mostly positive in Asian markets. The exception again is the US, where its transmitted spillover tends to dampen other markets on average, while it receives positive spillover from elsewhere.

Turning to contagion, box figure 2 suggests that equity returns in most markets closely mimic those in the US during the pre-GFC period and tend to do so less in later periods. In most of the markets, contagion parameters dropped markedly from the pre-GFC period to the GFC, increased again slightly during the European debt crisis of 2010–2013, and then dropped further in the most recent period. Consequently, the prognosis is mostly decoupling and therefore less contagion in these markets transmitted from the US market over the period of the sample. During the period from the GFC to the European debt crisis, there is some evidence of recoupling, and hence higher contagion, but it is more limited than in the pre-GFC era.

Notably different patterns are observed in the PRC and Japan. The contagion effect from the US to the PRC market is strongest in the current period and, unlike for the other markets, the relationship between the PRC and the US has tended to strengthen over time. That is, the PRC became more sensitive to shocks emanating from the US in the later part of the sample.

In Japan, the market has recoupled with the US in the most recent period, though with somewhat lower transmission parameters than pre-GFC. Except for these two markets, contagion from the US to Asia has recently tended to weaken.

To investigate possible incentives for national authorities to pursue coordinated policy action across borders, the results on spillover in Dungey, Kangogo, and Volkov (forthcoming) were analyzed in light of the size of the economy, using GDP, adjusted for purchasing power parity, from an International Monetary Fund database. The extent of incoming spillover was found to be positively associated with the country size, while the extent of outgoing spillover was negatively associated with the size. That is, as an economy increases in size, it progressively receives from other markets more spillover that amplifies its returns, and it transmits more dampening effects to other markets. This aligns with center-and-periphery analysis, whereby larger core markets receive more positive shocks than those on the periphery (Kaminsky and Reinhart 2002). The evidence also supports the hypothesis that spillover relates to the size of the economy (Agenor et al. 2017). This poses problems for cross-border policy cooperation because national interests connected with spillover do not cleanly align with economic size. A developed core financial market commonly tends to absorb more positive shocks from periphery markets, which are often emerging markets, and transmit dampening effects back to the periphery. Such asymmetry poses challenges to finding a mutually satisfactory cross-border agreement for coordinating policy actions.

2 Structural transmission parameters from the US market by period

■ Recent   ■ European debt crisis   ■ Global financial crisis   ■ Pre-global financial crisis

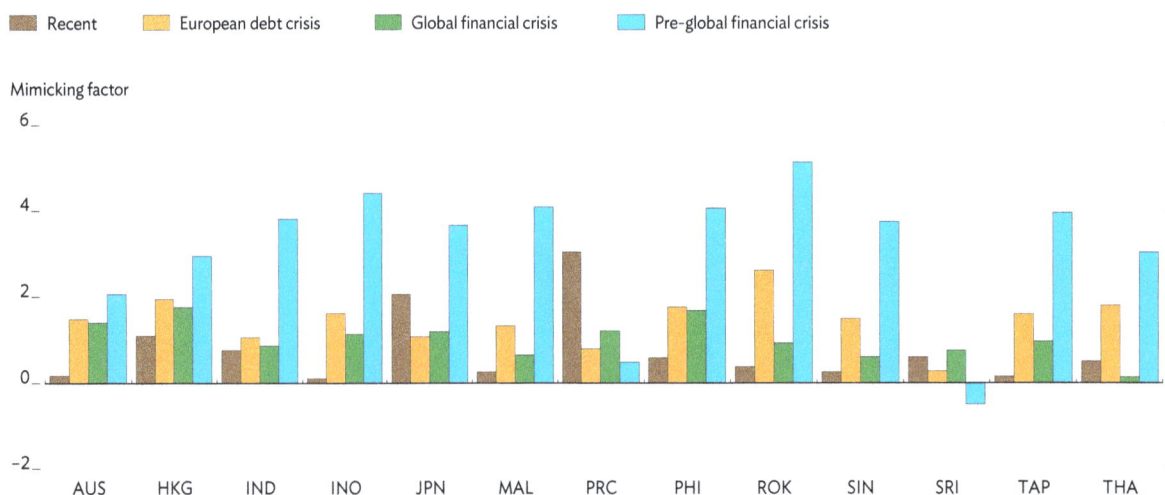

AUS = Australia, HKG = Hong Kong, China, IND = India, INO = Indonesia, JPN = Japan, MAL = Malaysia, PHI = Philippines, PRC = People's Republic of China, ROK = Republic of Korea, SIN = Singapore, SRI = Sri Lanka, TAP = Taipei,China, THA = Thailand.
Source: Dungey, Kangogo, and Volkov, forthcoming.

Stabilization policies work best when fundamentals are strong

To maintain stability under the current environment of heightened uncertainty, Asia may need to deploy the full range of policy tools at its disposal. These policies work best when fundamentals that support economic, social, and political stability are strong. Examples of strong fundamentals include low and stable inflation, healthy fiscal and external balances, and sound financial systems. Further, robust fundamentals such as relatively low public debt are conducive to countercyclical fiscal policy able to smooth business cycles and prevent deep recessions.

On the other hand, when a highly indebted government applies fiscal stimulus to fight recessions, it may end up harming business confidence and discouraging investment. Similarly, monetary policy is more credible and effective if the central bank has a history of being committed to price stability. When, by contrast, central banks with poor records of fighting inflation cut interest rates to boost growth, the lower interest rates often cause only higher inflation and currency depreciation.

Yet Asia's enviable track record of maintaining strong fundamentals built up over decades through sensible and disciplined policies does not guarantee strong fundamentals in the future. This requires continued efforts to pursue sound fiscal policies, independence for central banks, strong financial sectors, market-oriented structural reform, and adequate social safety nets.

Endnotes

1   The empirical literature provides several indicators that can influence exchange market pressure. Recent studies include Lim, Mohapatra, and Stocker (2014), Ahmed and Zlate (2014), Frankel and Saravelos (2012), Aizenman and Binici (2016), Aizenman and Hutchison (2012), Eichengreen and Gupta (2015), and Dabrowski, Smiech, and Papiez (2015).

2   The Backward Sup Augmented Dickey-Fuller approach suggested in Philips et al. (2015) is used to detect the start and end dates of explosive ratios of housing price to rent. Unlike a traditional random walk test, this approach is a right-tailed test to check whether explosive patterns are in process, using a specially constructed test statistic.

3   Cyclicality of fiscal policy is estimated by regressing the change in log of real government final expenditure on change in log of real GDP. A positive and significant relation indicates fiscal procyclicality, a negative and significant relation indicates fiscal countercyclicality, and a statistically insignificant relation indicates fiscal acyclicality. The results reported here are for the sample of Asian economies. Results for the full set of economies are available in Aizenman et al. (forthcoming).

4   The results here use general government tax including social contributions, though robustness checks with value-added tax, personal income tax, and corporate income tax are available in Aizenman et al. (forthcoming).

5   See, for example, Alesina, Campante, and Tabellini (2008) which argued that procyclical government spending is driven by voters who seek to reduce the large but hidden political rents appropriated by corrupt governments during boom times.

6   The capital control indexes in Fernández et al. (2016) are constructed by first coding how restrictive controls are at the level of individual transactions and then aggregating subindexes to obtain more finely gradated indexes specific to assets, inflow, and outflow.

7   The dataset was constructed by building on existing databases in Lim et al. (2013), Shim et al. (2013), Cerutti et al. (2017), Lee, Asuncion, and Kim (2016), and Budnik and Kleibl (2018), as well as by extending the sample based on information sourced from International Monetary Fund Article IV consultations and its *Annual Report on Exchange Arrangements and Exchange Restrictions*, and from national authorities.

Background Papers

Aizenman, J., Y. Jinjarak, H. Nguyen, and D. Park. Forthcoming. *Fiscal Revenue, Fiscal Space, and Expenditure Cyclicality Patterns: A Comparison of Asia, Latin America, and OECD Countries.* Asian Development Bank.

Beck, T. Forthcoming. *The Micro Impact of Macroprudential Policies: Firm-level Evidence.* Asian Development Bank.

Dungey, M., M. Kangogo, and V. Volkov. Forthcoming. *Changing Vulnerability in Asia: Contagion and Systemic Risk.* Asian Development Bank.

Eichengreen, B., D. Park, A. Ramayandi, and K. Shin. Forthcoming. *Exchange Rates and Insulation: Asia and Beyond.* Asian Development Bank.

Han, X., M. Pundit, and A. Ramayandi. Forthcoming. *Detecting Explosive Housing Prices for Cities in Selected Asian Economies.* Asian Development Bank.

Jongwanich, J. Forthcoming. *Effectiveness of Capital Account Policies: Evidence from Emerging Asian Countries.* Asian Development Bank.

Khan, F., A. Ramayandi, and M. Schröder. Forthcoming. *Conditions for Effective Macroprudential Policy Interventions.* Asian Development Bank.

Kim. S. Forthcoming. *Macroprudential Policy in the Asian Economies.* Asian Development Bank.

Patnaik, I. and M. Pundit. Forthcoming. *Financial Shocks and Exchange Market Pressure.* Asian Development Bank.

Park, D., K. Shin, and S. Tian. Forthcoming. *Debts and Depth of Recessions.* Asian Development Bank.

References

ADB. 2017a. *Asian Development Outlook: Transcending the Middle-Income Challenge.* Asian Development Bank.

——. 2017b. *Asian Development Outlook: Sustaining Development Through Public–Private Partnership.* Asian Development Bank.

——. 2017c. *Asian Economic Integration Report 2017: The Era of Financial Interconnectedness, How Can Asia Strengthen Financial Resilience?* Asian Development Bank.

Agénor, P. R., E. Kharroubi, L. Gambacorta, G. Lombardo, and L. P. da Silva. 2017. The International Dimensions of Macroprudential Policies. *BIS Working Papers* 643. Bank for International Settlements.

Ahmed, S. and A. Zlate. 2014. Capital Flows to Emerging Market Economies: A Brave New World? *Journal of International Money and Finance* 48.

Aizenman, J. and M. Binici. 2016. Exchange Market Pressure in OECD and Emerging Economies: Domestic vs. External Factors and Capital Flows in the Old and New Normal. *Journal of International Money and Finance* 66.

Aizenman, J. and M. M. Hutchison. 2012. Exchange Market Pressure and Absorption by International Reserves: Emerging Markets and Fear of Reserve Loss during the 2008–2009 Crisis. *Journal of International Money and Finance* 31(5).

Akinci, O. and J. Olmstead-Rumsey. 2018. How Effective are Macroprudential Policies? An Empirical Investigation. *Journal of Financial Intermediation* 2018(33).

Alesina, A., F. Campante, and G. Tabellini. 2008. Why Is Fiscal Policy Often Procyclical? *Journal of the European Economic Association* 6(5).

Arellano, M. and S. Bond. 1991. Some Tests for Specification of Panel Data: Monte Carlo Evidence and An Application to Employment Equations. *Review of Economic Studies* 58(2).

Auerbach, A. J. 2011. Long-term Fiscal Sustainability in Major Economies. *BIS Working Paper* 361.

Ayyagari, M., T. Beck, and M. S. Martinez Peria. 2017. Credit Growth and Macroprudential Policies: Preliminary Evidence on the Firm Level. *Bank of International Settlements Papers* No. 91.

Blundell, R. and S. Bond. 1998. Initial Conditions and Moment Restrictions in Dynamic Panel Data Models. *Journal of Econometrics* 87(1).

Budina, N., T. Kinda, A. Schaechter, and A. Weber. 2012. Fiscal Rules at a Glance: Country Details from a New Dataset. *IMF Working Papers* 12/273. International Monetary Fund.

Budnik, K. and J. Kleibl. 2018. Macroprudential Regulation in the European Union in 1995–2014: Introducing a New Data Set on Policy Actions of a Macroprudential Nature. *ECB Working Paper* 2123.

Carrasco, B. and S. A. H. Shah. 2018. How to Address the Lack of Affordable Housing in Asia. *Asian Development Blog*. Asian Development Bank. https://blogs.adb.org/blog/how-address-lack-affordable-housing-asia.

Cerutti, E., R. Correa, E. Fiorentino, and E. Segalla. 2017. Changes in Prudential Policy Instruments—A New Cross-Country Database. *International Journal of Central Banking* 13(2).

Claessens, S., A. Kose, and M. Terrones. 2011. How Do Business and Financial Cycles Interact? *IMF Working Paper* No. 11/88. International Monetary Fund.

Crowe, C., G. Dell'Ariccia, D. Igan, and P. Rabanal. 2013. How to Deal with Real Estate Booms: Lessons from Country Experiences. *Journal of Financial Stability* 9(3).

Dabrowski, M. A., S. Smiech, and M. Papiez. 2015. Monetary Policy Options for Mitigating the Impact of the Global Financial Crisis on Emerging Market Economies. *Journal of International Money and Finance* 51.

Dungey, M. H., D. J. Harvey, and V. Volkov. 2017. The Changing International Network of Sovereign Debt and Financial Institutions. *Discussion Paper Series* 2017-04. University of Tasmania.

Edwards, S. 2007. Capital Controls, Capital Flow Contractions, and Macroeconomic Vulnerability. *NBER Working Paper* 12852. National Bureau of Economic Research.

Eichengreen, B. and P. Gupta. 2015. Tapering Talk: The Impact of Expectations of Reduced Federal Reserve Security Purchases on Emerging Markets. *Emerging Markets Review* 25.

Fernandez, A., M. Klein, A. Rebucci, and M. Uribe. 2016. Capital Control Measures: A New Dataset. *IMF Economic Review* 64(3). International Monetary Fund. 10.1057/imfer.2016.11.

Frankel, J. and G. Saravelos. 2012. Can Leading Indicators Assess Country Vulnerability? Evidence from 2008–09 Global Financial Crisis. *Journal of International Economics* 87(2).

Frankel, J. A., C. A. Vegh, and G. Vuletin. 2013. On Graduation From Fiscal Procyclicality. *Journal of Development Economics* 100(1). doi: 10.1016/j.jdeveco.2012.07.001.

Forbes, K., M. Fratzscher, T. Kostka, and R. Straub. 2016. Bubble Thy Neighbor: Portfolio Effects and Externalities from Capital Controls. *Journal of International Economics* 99(C).

Garriga, A.C. 2016. Central Bank Independence in the World: A New Dataset. *International Interactions* 42(5). doi: 10.1080/03050629.2016.1188813.

Gavin, M., R. Hausmann, R. Perotti, and E. Talvi. 1996. Managing Fiscal Policy in Latin America and the Caribbean: Volatility, Procyclicality, and Limited Creditworthiness. *IDB Working Paper* 326. Inter-American Development Bank.

Ghosh, A., J. Ostry, and M. Qureshi. 2015. Exchange Rate Management and Crisis Susceptibility: A Reassessment. *IMF Economic Review* 63.

Girton, L. and D. Roper. 1977. A Monetary Model of Exchange Market Pressure Applied to the Postwar Canadian Experience. *American Economic Review* 67(4).

Gochoco-Bautista, M. S., J. Jongwanich, and J. W. Lee. 2012. How Effective Are Capital Controls in Asia? *Asian Economic Papers* 11(2).

Gopinath, G. 2017a. The International Price System, *Proceedings of the Jackson Hole Symposium* (Federal Reserve Bank of Kansas City).

——. 2017b. Rethinking International Macroeconomic Policy. Unpublished manuscript, Harvard University.

Ilzetzki, E., C. M. Reinhart, and K. S. Rogoff. 2017. Exchange Arrangements Entering the 21st Century: Which Anchor Will Hold? *NBER Working Paper* 23134. National Bureau of Economic Research.

IMF. 2017. How to Select Fiscal Rules: A Primer. *IMF How-To-Note*. International Monetary Fund. Fiscal Affairs Department.

Jittrapanun, T. and S. Prasartset. 2009. Hot Money and Capital Controls in Thailand. *TWN Global Economy Series* 15. Third World Network.

Jordà, O., M. Schularick, and A. M. Taylor. 2017.
    Macrofinancial History and the New Business Cycle Facts.
    In *NBER Macroeconomics Annual 2016*, 31. University of
    Chicago Press.

Kaminsky, G. L. and C. M. Reinhart. 2002. Financial Markets
    In Times of Stress, *Journal of Development Economics*, 69(2).

Kim, S. and D. Y. Yang. 2012. Are Capital Controls Effective?
    The Case of the Republic of Korea. *Asian Development
    Review* 29(2). https://ssrn.com/abstract=2204266.

Lee, M., R. C. Asuncion, and J. Kim. 2016. Effectiveness of
    Macroprudential Policies in Developing Asia: An Empirical
    Analysis. *Emerging Markets Finance and Trade Journal* 52(4).

Lim, C. H., I. Krznar, F. Lipinsky, A. Otani, and X. Wu. 2013.
    The Macroprudential Framework; Policy Responsiveness,
    and Institutional Arrangements. *IMF Working Papers*
    13(166). International Monetary Fund.

Lim, J. J., S. Mohapatra, and M. Stocker. 2014. Tinker, Taper, QE,
    Bye? The Effect of Quantitative Easing on Financial Flows to
    Developing Countries. *Policy Research Working Paper* 6820.

Londono, J. and B. A. Wilson. 2018. Understanding Global
    Volatility. IFDP Note. Washington, DC: Board of
    Governors of the Federal Reserve System.
    https://doi.org/10.17016/2573-2129.40.

Magud, N. E., C. M. Reinhart, and K. S. Rogoff. 2011. Capital
    Controls: Myth and Reality—A Portfolio Balance Approach.
    NBER Working Paper 16805. National Bureau of Economic
    Research.

Malovaná, S. and J. Frait. 2017. Monetary Policy and
    Macroprudential Policy: Rivals or Teammates?, *Journal of
    Financial Stability* 32(C).

Mundell, R. 1963. Capital Mobility and Stabilization Policy under
    Fixed and Flexible Exchange Rates. *Canadian Journal of
    Economics and Political Science* 29.

Obstfeld, M., J. Ostry, and M. Qureshi. 2017. A Tie That Binds:
    Revisiting the Trilemma in Emerging Market Economies.
    IMF Working Paper WP/17/130. International Monetary
    Fund.

Ostry, J., A. Ghosh, J. Kim, and M. Qureshi. 2010. Fiscal Space.
    IMF Staff Position Note SPN/10/11. International Monetary
    Fund.

Park, D., A. Ramayandi, and K. Shin. 2014. Capital Flows
    During Quantitative Easing and Aftermath: Experiences of
    Asian Countries. *ADB Economics Working Paper Series* 409.
    Asian Development Bank.

Patnaik, I., J. Felman, and A. Shah. 2017. An Exchange Market
    Pressure Measure for Cross Country Analysis. *Journal of
    International Money and Finance* 73.

Philips, P., S. Shi, and J. Yu. 2015. Testing for Multiple Bubbles:
    Historical Episodes of Exuberance and Collapse in the
    S&P 500. *International Economic Review* 56(4).

Rey, H. 2015. Dilemma not Trilemma: The Global Financial Cycle and Monetary Policy Independence. *NBER Working Paper* 21162. National Bureau of Economic Research.

———. 2016. International Channels of Transmission of Monetary Policy and the Mundellian Trilemma. *IMF Economic Review* 6. International Monetary Fund.

Romer, C. and D. Romer. 2017. New Evidence on the Aftermath of Financial Crises in Advanced Countries. *American Economic Review* 107(10).

Shim, I., B. Bogdanova, J. Shek, and A. Subelyte. 2013. Database for Policy Actions on Housing Markets. *BIS Quarterly Review*. September.

Shin, H. 2016. The Bank/Capital Markets Nexus Goes Global. Remarks made at the London School of Economics and Political Science. http://www.bis.org/speeches/sp161115.pdf.

Van der Laan, C. R., A. M. Cunha, and M. T. C. Lélis. 2017. On the Effectiveness of Capital Controls during the Great Recession: The Brazilian Experience (2007–2013). *Journal of Post Keynesian Economics* 40(2). DOI: 10.1080/01603477.2016.1262744.

You, Y., Y. Kim, and X. Ren. 2014. Do Capital Controls Enhance Monetary Independence? *Review of Development Economics* 18(3).

3

ECONOMIC TRENDS AND PROSPECTS IN DEVELOPING ASIA

Central Asia

Higher oil prices and remittances improve the subregional outlook. The growth projection for 2018 is revised up from 4.0% to 4.1%, with stronger growth in Kazakhstan, but unchanged at 4.2% for 2019. The inflation forecast is trimmed from 8.5% to 8.4% for 2018 and from 7.9% to 7.7% for 2019, reflecting slower inflation in most economies in the first half of 2018. Reassessed prospects for Azerbaijan, Kazakhstan, and Turkmenistan prompt narrower forecasts for the subregional current account deficit in both years.

Subregional assessment and prospects

Growth accelerated in the first half of 2018 in several Central Asian economies. With projected growth now higher for Armenia, Georgia, and Kazakhstan, this *Update* raises the subregional growth forecast for 2018 from 4.0% in *Asian Development Outlook 2018 (ADO 2018)* to 4.1% while maintaining the earlier April forecast of 4.2% for 2019 (Figure 3.1.1).

Global oil prices higher than envisaged in April boosted growth in Kazakhstan in the first half, albeit slightly less than a year earlier. Oil and natural gas production rose, as did first quarter exports and investment. Anticipating more buoyant global oil prices, this *Update* raises Kazakhstan's growth forecasts from 3.2% to 3.7% for 2018 and from 3.5% to 3.9% for 2019. Growth in other petroleum exporters varied. With oil production rising marginally, Azerbaijan reversed contraction in the first half of 2017 to grow by 1.3% despite a decline in oil-related investment. Growth in Turkmenistan, driven by public investment, was marginally less than a year earlier. In Uzbekistan, insufficient precipitation and the lingering impact of last year's currency devaluation prompt downward revision of growth projections from 5.5% to 4.9% for 2018 and from 5.6% to 5.0% for 2019.

Among subregional petroleum importers, Armenia saw expansion accelerate on sharply higher investment in the first half of 2018, raising its growth prospects. Growth accelerated as well in Georgia thanks to gains in remittance-backed

3.1.1 GDP growth, Central Asia

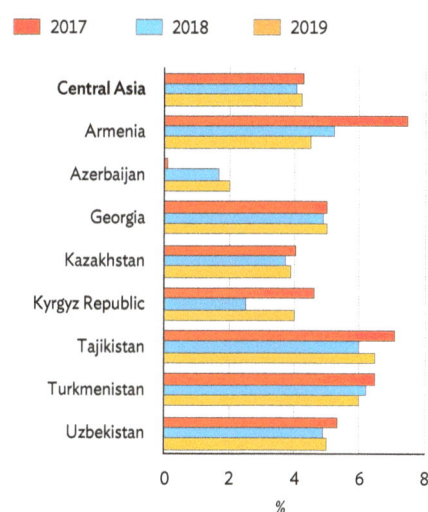

Source: *Asian Development Outlook* database.

The subregional assessment and prospects were written by Kenji Takamiya. The section on Kazakhstan was written by Manshuk Nurseitova, consultant, and the other economies by Muhammadi Boboev, Grigor Gyurjyan, Jennet Hojanazarova, George Luarsabishvili, Gulkayr Tentieva, Nail Valiyev, and Begzod Djalilov, consultant. All authors are in the Central and West Asia Department of ADB.

private consumption and higher capital investment. Sustained growth in the Russian Federation and improved relations with Uzbekistan helped boost growth in Tajikistan. However, declines in mining and manufacturing slashed growth in the Kyrgyz Republic.

Average annual inflation in the first half of 2018 slowed in most of the subregion compared with a year earlier. With forecast inflation in Azerbaijan reduced from 7.0% to 4.5% for 2018 and from 8.0% to 5.0% for 2019—and with smaller reductions for Georgia, the Kyrgyz Republic, and Tajikistan for 2018—this *Update* trims projected subregional inflation in 2018 from 8.5% to 8.4% and in 2019 from 7.9% to 7.7%, despite higher forecasts for Armenia, Kazakhstan, and Turkmenistan.

A more stable exchange rate subdued inflation in Azerbaijan to 3.0% in the first half of 2018 from 13.9% a year earlier. Inflation in Kazakhstan slowed from 7.7% to 6.3%, partly reflecting currency appreciation in early 2018. In the Kyrgyz Republic, currency appreciation and slower growth helped trim inflation from 2.7% to 2.3%. As the impact in Georgia of earlier excise tax hikes receded, inflation in the first 7 months fell by more than half to 2.8%. Prudent monetary policy and a jump in inexpensive food imports from Uzbekistan slashed inflation in Tajikistan from 9.0% in the first half of 2017 to 1.6%. In Uzbekistan, continued tight monetary policy and exchange rate interventions slowed inflation from 14.7% to 12.7% in the first half of 2018. By contrast, cuts in subsidies, higher import prices, and expansionary credit policy call for raising inflation projections for Turkmenistan from 8.0% to 9.4% in 2018 and from 8.0% to 8.2% in 2019. The inflation forecast for Armenia in 2019 is slightly raised as a significant cut in the income tax should boost demand (Figure 3.1.2).

Higher projections for global oil prices prompt revised forecasts for a wider current account surplus in Azerbaijan and narrower deficits in Kazakhstan and Turkmenistan. Despite larger deficits now forecast for Armenia and, in 2018, Tajikistan, this *Update* narrows the projected subregional current account deficit, as a share of combined GDP, from 2.1% to 1.3% in 2018 and from 2.2% to 1.2% in 2019. Azerbaijan's current account surpluses are now projected at 7.9% in 2018 and 10.9% in 2019, and Kazakhstan's deficits at 1.5% in 2018 and 2.5% in 2019. In Turkmenistan, strengthening natural gas prices and slowing growth in public investment allow deficit forecasts to be trimmed to 8.5% in 2018 and 7.8% in 2019. Higher growth calls for wider deficit forecasts for Armenia, now 4.5% in 2018 and 4.0% in 2019. Faster import growth reverses Tajikistan's current account balance projection for 2018 from a 1.1% surplus to a 2.5% deficit (Figure 3.1.3).

3.1.2 Inflation, Central Asia

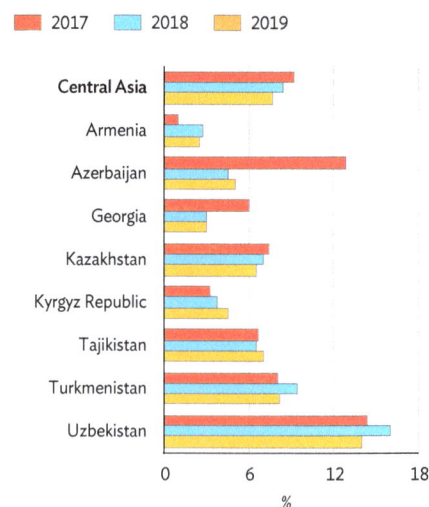

Source: *Asian Development Outlook* database.

3.1.3 Current account balance, Central Asia

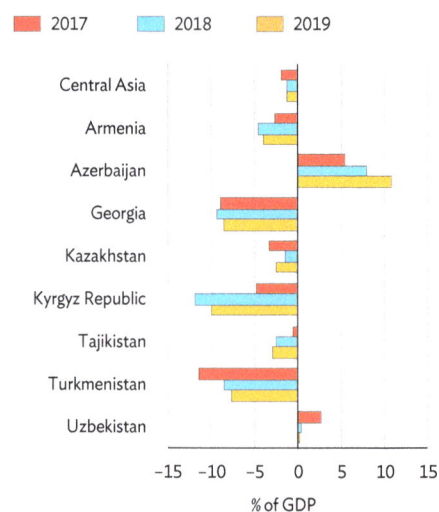

Source: *Asian Development Outlook* database.

Kazakhstan

The economy grew by 4.1% in the first half of 2018, reflecting broad gains in industry, services, and agriculture. Inflation was 6.4%. With expansion greater than expected in private consumption, investment, and exports, stimulated in part by higher petroleum prices, growth forecasts are raised to 3.7% for 2018 and 3.9% for 2019, while faster growth and higher fuel prices prompt higher projections for inflation, at 7.0% in 2018 and 6.5% in 2019. Current account deficits are now forecast narrower, at 1.5% in 2018 and 2.5% in 2019, thanks to higher petroleum prices.

Updated assessment

The economy grew at an annual pace of 4.1% in the first half of 2018, near the 4.3% rate recorded in the same period of 2017 (Figure 3.1.4). Industry expanded by 5.2% on a 5.5% gain in mining and 5.2% growth in manufacturing driven by a government industrialization program. Higher petroleum prices prompted production increases of 6.2% for oil and 6.4% for gas. Agriculture expanded by 4.0% on higher livestock production. Construction growth slowed to 3.8% from 5.9% in the first half of 2017 partly because some pipelines and industrial projects reached completion. Services grew by 3.7%, led by gains of 4.9% in transportation, 5.9% in trade, and 5.9% in communication.

Demand-side data are available for only the first quarter of 2018. In this period, consumption rose by 0.1% as a 3.9% increase in private consumption barely offset a 16.4% fall in public consumption (Figure 3.1.5). Investment expanded by 2.7%, reflecting a 3.2% rise in fixed investment including oil and gas projects and the modernization of a major petrochemical plant. The expansion also reflected higher purchases of equipment and machinery. Despite higher imports of such capital goods, net exports rose on increased exports of oil, gas, and grain.

Average annual inflation in the first half of 2018 slowed to 6.4% from 7.7% in the same period of 2017 as food price inflation fell by half to 5.2%, though prices rose by 8.5% for other goods and by 5.8% for services (Figure 3.1.6). Appreciation of the Kazakhstan tenge from T332 to T319 per US dollar in the first quarter helped moderate inflation. However, depreciation resumed in April, and the exchange rate reached T355 per dollar in early August.

Budget revenue rose by 4.6% in the first half of 2018, to the equivalent of 15.3% of estimated GDP, as taxes rose by 15.4% and despite decreases in nontax payments and transfers from the National Fund of the Republic of Kazakhstan (NFRK). Improved tax administration helped boost revenue collection. Expenditure rose by 6.2% to equal 15.9% of estimated GDP, with increases of 26.5% for defense, 20.4% for social programs,

3.1.4 Supply-side contributions to growth

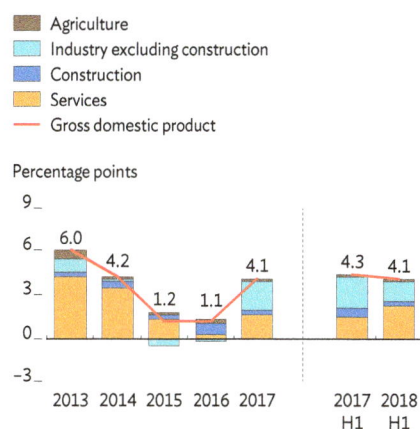

Source: Republic of Kazakhstan. Ministry of National Economy. Committee on Statistics.

H = half.

3.1.5 Demand-side contributions to growth

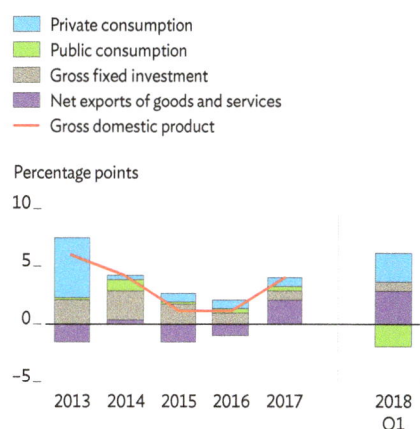

Q = quarter.

Source: Republic of Kazakhstan. Ministry of National Economy. Committee on Statistics.

and 13.0% for debt service contributing to an overall budget deficit equal to 0.6% of GDP. Net receipts into the NFRK were, at nearly $1.9 billion, more than double those in the first half of 2017 as tax revenue from oil firms increased by 34.0%, outward transfers decreased by 11.5%, and revenue from product-sharing agreements more than tripled to provide 21.0% of total NFRK inflows.

The National Bank of Kazakhstan, the central bank, gradually reduced its policy rate from 10.25% at the end of 2017 to 9.0% on 5 June 2018 (Figure 3.1.7) as inflation slowed to the 2018 target range of 5%–7%. Broad money grew by 2.3% in the first half of the year, reversing a decline of 0.8% a year earlier. The banking industry is recovering, with new loans issued in the first half of this year 27.0% higher than in the same period of 2017. Nonperforming loans declined to 8.8% of the total from 9.3% a year earlier, while interest income rose by 1.7%.

The current account deficit narrowed by half to $1.4 billion, or 1.6% of GDP, in the first half of 2018 as the trade surplus rose by 46.2% to $12.5 billion and the deficit in services narrowed by 7.4%. Foreign direct investment rose by 53.8% to $4.8 billion. Central bank foreign exchange reserves declined by 2.1% to an estimated $30.1 billion, or cover for 8 months of imports of goods and services, while NFRK assets reached $58.1 billion (Figure 3.1.8). External debt at the end of the first quarter of 2018 was $166.6 billion (102.2% of estimated GDP), of which $104.5 billion (64.1% of GDP) was intercompany debt incurred by oil and gas projects implemented by subsidiaries of foreign companies operating in Kazakhstan. Public and publicly guaranteed external debt reached $14.4 billion to equal 8.6% of GDP, with $1.6 billion due in 2018 and $1.7 billion in 2019.

The official unemployment rate remained at 4.9% at the end of July 2018. With more than 23% of the labor force recorded as self-employed, the government plans to introduce in 2019 a modest tax on self-employment to bring such workers into the tax net and enable their participation in the compulsory medical insurance system.

Prospects

Along with industry, the service sector is a main driver of the economy, supplying more than 57% of GDP. With economic recovery and increased income mainly from higher oil prices, services are now forecast to grow by 3.2% in both 2018 and 2019, up from *ADO 2018* projections of 2.5% for 2018 and 3.0% for 2019. On the demand side, private consumption and total investment are both projected to grow faster than forecast in *ADO 2018*, with investment growing by 1.0 percentage point more in 2018 than earlier projected and higher oil prices raising projected net exports. Accordingly, this *Update* raises the growth projections for both 2018 and 2019 by about half a percentage point.

3.1.6 Monthly inflation

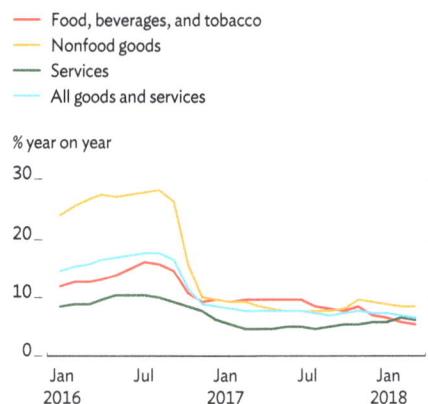

— Food, beverages, and tobacco
— Nonfood goods
— Services
— All goods and services

Source: Haver Analytics (accessed 4 September 2018).

3.1.7 Interest rate and broad money

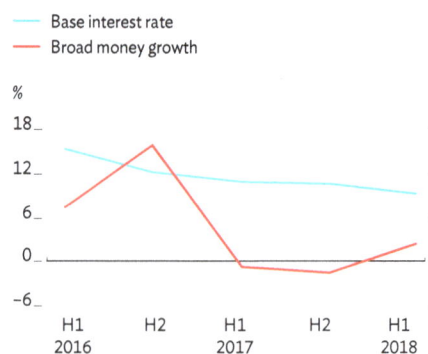

— Base interest rate
— Broad money growth

H = half.
Note: Broad money growth refers to percent changes from December of the previous year.
Source: National Bank of the Republic of Kazakhstan.

With higher fuel prices, faster growth, and a broad-based increase in real income, this *Update* projects somewhat higher inflation in 2018 and 2019 than forecast in *ADO 2018*. Progress in modernizing agriculture and food processing may help limit food price inflation to 6.2%. However, prices for other goods are projected to rise by 8.0%–8.5% in 2018 and 2019, with inflation in services reaching 6.4% in 2018 before subsiding to 5.8% in 2019. The value-added tax in the Russian Federation, the source of up to 40% of Kazakhstan's imports, will rise from 18% to 20% in 2019, contributing to inflation next year. As the central bank calculates that the current policy rate can keep inflation within a range of 5%–7% in 2018 and somewhat less in 2019, no changes in the policy rate are anticipated.

The budget was amended in April 2018 using an oil price of $55 per barrel, or $10 above the price used in the budget approved in November 2017, and the GDP forecast was updated. Under these revisions, and assuming higher direct tax payments from oil companies, projected revenue rose to equal 15.1% of GDP. Planned expenditure, boosted by 4.5% to fund new social initiatives described below, now equals 16.6% of GDP, yielding a forecast budget deficit equal to 1.5% of GDP. The 2019 budget plans revenue at 14.6% of GDP and expenditure at 15.6%, narrowing the deficit to 1.0%. Guaranteed transfers from the NFRK are to decline from T2.6 trillion in 2018 to T2.3 trillion in 2019, with no additional transfers permitted. The projected non-oil deficit in the budget expands to 7.6% of GDP in 2018 from 7.1%, as approved in the November 2017 budget, and narrows to 6.2% in 2019. Year-end public debt is now forecast to equal 25.1% of GDP in 2018 and 24.1% in 2019.

The President announced in March 2018 the adoption of the Five Social Initiatives program, which includes an income tax cut for low wage earners from 10% to 1% effective in January 2019 and new mortgage loan subsidies to help families purchase property. In addition, a new public pension scheme launched in July 2018 raised pensions by 15%–20%.

With crude oil prices now forecast to average more than $70 per barrel in 2018 and 2019, the trade surplus is projected at $24.8 billion in 2018 and $25.4 billion in 2019, both higher than anticipated in *ADO 2018*. Accordingly, this *Update* narrows current account deficit forecasts for 2018 and 2019, assuming that deficits in services and primary income persist and that crude oil and natural gas output stabilizes at current levels (Figure 3.1.9). International reserves are projected to reach at year-end $31.0 billion in 2018 and $31.5 billion in 2019. NFRK receipts are projected to fall from $6.1 billion in 2017 to $5.9 billion this year and next; more than 76% of receipts will be taxes on oil companies. NFRK assets are projected to decline to $56.6 billion at the end of 2018 and to $55.7 billion a year later as transfers to the budget exceed receipts.

3.1.8 Reserves and assets

NFKR = National Fund of the Republic of Kazakhstan.
Source: Haver Analytics (accessed 4 September 2018).

3.1.9 Current account balance

Source: *Asian Development Outlook* database.

External debt, including intercompany debt, is now forecast at 102% of GDP at the end of 2018, falling to 96% at the end of 2019.

Looking further ahead, a large privatization program from this year until 2020 is designed to lower state participation in the economy to 15% of GDP, thereby enhancing the role of the private sector and making it the main driver of economic growth. In providing budget investments to support economic diversification, upgrade infrastructure, and modernize traditional industries and the agro-industrial complex, the government will prioritize projects that boost productivity and create public goods, in particular those enhancing physical and social infrastructure, knowledge and skills, and innovation. Public–private partnerships (PPPs) will be further established and developed for use in such projects, with PPP legislation streamlined and rationalized. In addition, commercial banks will be instructed to recognize PPP contracts in which the state provides payments as collateral for loans.

The financial landscape is newly augmented by the Astana International Financial Centre, inaugurated on 5 July 2018 to become a financial hub for Central Asia and eventually further afield, while developing the market in Kazakhstan for insurance and banking services, in particular Islamic financing. Finance activity is expected to increase in 2018, spurred by initial public offerings planned for Kazakhstan's largest state-owned enterprises.

As the economy remains dependent on exports of oil, gas, metals, and grain, the main risks to the outlook stem from uncertainty regarding commodity prices.

3.1.1 Selected economic indicators, Kazakhstan (%)

	2018		2019	
	ADO 2018	Update	ADO 2018	Update
GDP growth	3.2	3.7	3.5	3.9
Inflation	6.8	7.0	6.2	6.5
Current acct. bal. (share of GDP)	–3.3	–1.5	–3.4	–2.5

Source: ADB estimates.

Other economies

Armenia

Growth accelerated to 8.3% in the first half of 2018 from 6.9% in the same period of 2017, reflecting higher demand. Industry excluding construction expanded by 6.8% with strong growth in machinery, food, beverages, pharmaceuticals, textiles, basic metals, and mineral products. Construction grew by 8.8%, reflecting higher investment. Services rose by 9.5% with gains in all subsectors, while agriculture grew by 5.7% following a 5.3% decline in 2017.

On the demand side, private consumption grew by 4.4% in the first half of 2018 on higher consumer lending, moderate inflation, and positive consumer sentiment. Fiscal consolidation cut public consumption by 9.1%. Total investment increased by 76%, reflecting a sharp rise in inventories, increased government capital spending, and higher private and foreign direct investment. Net exports declined as imports outgrew exports. With these developments, this *Update* raises GDP growth projections for both 2018 and 2019.

Monetary policy remained accommodative through July 2018 as the Central Bank of Armenia reduced its policy rate by 25 basis points to 6.0% in February 2017. A stable external environment, a fairly steady exchange rate, and favorable weather helped contain inflationary pressures in the first 7 months of 2018. Month-on-month inflation was 2.3% in July 2018, below the central bank target band of 2.5%–5.5%. Average annual inflation rose to 2.4% in January–July 2018 from 0.5% in January–July 2017. Accordingly, this *Update* retains the inflation forecast for 2018 but raises the forecast for 2019 as a significant cut in the income tax should boost demand.

The current account deficit expanded considerably to 9.0% of GDP in the first quarter of 2018 from 4.9% a year earlier as the trade balance worsened and investment income and employee earnings from abroad declined. Exports grew at an annual rate of 38.5% and imports by 44.4%, widening the trade deficit to the equivalent of 14.9% of GDP in the first quarter of 2018 from 11.3% a year earlier. Services remained in surplus as receipts from tourism, information technology, and construction services grew further. Net remittances through banks fell by 10.7% to $252.0 million in first half of 2018, though inward remittances from the Russian Federation rose by 15.6%, partly because of ruble appreciation. With the trade deficit expanding faster than anticipated, this *Update* revises current account forecasts for deeper deficits in 2018 and 2019.

3.1.2 Selected economic indicators, Armenia (%)

	2018		2019	
	ADO 2018	Update	ADO 2018	Update
GDP growth	4.0	5.3	4.2	4.5
Inflation	2.7	2.7	2.2	2.5
Current acct. bal. (share of GDP)	-3.2	-4.5	-2.8	-4.0

Source: ADB estimates.

Azerbaijan

The economy expanded by 1.3% in the first half of 2018, reversing 1.3% contraction in the same period of 2017. The large petroleum sector expanded by 0.1%, with marginally higher oil production, while the rest of the economy grew by 2.0%. Industry expanded by 1.2% as manufacturing rose by 10.3% while construction shrank by 10.5%. Growth in agriculture accelerated to 7.6% from 2.2% in the same period in 2017 thanks to a campaign to expand cotton cultivation that raised crop production by 14.6%. Growth in services at 3.1% included expansion by 7.4% in tourism, 7.1% in transportation, and 4.9% in information and communication technology. Even as a stable exchange rate and faster growth boosted private consumption, higher oil revenue lifted net exports. Investment fell by 14.1% as outlays ebbed in the oil sector.

Fiscal policy remained expansionary in the first half of 2018 as a higher-than-expected 27.1% rise in tax revenue allowed expenditure 16.2% above the budget plan. With oil prices staying high, the authorities have proposed a further 9.7% increase in outlays, funded by an 18.9% rise in transfers from the sovereign wealth fund, to support growth in the rest of 2018. On balance, this *Update* maintains *ADO 2018* growth forecasts for 2018 and 2019.

Average annual inflation plunged to 3.0% in the first half of 2018 from 13.9% a year earlier. Food rose by 3.0%, other goods by 3.8%, and services by 2.4%. The exchange rate has remained unchanged since the beginning of 2018, limiting price rises for imports. Responding to lower inflation, the Central Bank of Azerbaijan lowered its policy rate in three steps from 15.0% in January 2018, where it had been for more than a year, to 10.0% in June 2018. With exchange rate stability and utility tariff increases now unlikely before the fourth quarter of 2018, this *Update* sharply reduces forecasts for inflation in 2018 and 2019.

The trade surplus widened to $4.3 billion in first half of 2018 from $3.2 billion a year earlier. Merchandise exports grew by 34.7%, partly reflecting oil prices above expectations but also non-oil exports rising by 20.1%. Imports grew by 36.8% on higher imports of machinery, automobiles, and metal ore. With higher oil prices likely, this *Update* raises the projection for the current account surplus in 2018 and, by a much larger margin, in 2019.

Georgia

Growth accelerated from 5.0% in 2017 to an estimated 5.7% in the first half of 2018, supported mainly by industry and services. Industry expanded at an annual rate of 7.1%, reflecting gains of 6.6% in manufacturing and 8.7% in construction. Services grew by 5.1%, driven by increases of 10.9% in tourism, 5.1% in wholesale and retail trade, and 13.4% in real estate and business services. Small firms in particular benefited from

3.1.3 Selected economic indicators, Azerbaijan (%)

	2018		2019	
	ADO 2018	Update	ADO 2018	Update
GDP growth	1.7	1.7	2.0	2.0
Inflation	7.0	4.5	8.0	5.0
Current acct. bal. (share of GDP)	6.9	7.9	6.2	10.9

Source: ADB estimates.

3.1.4 Selected economic indicators, Georgia (%)

	2018		2019	
	ADO 2018	Update	ADO 2018	Update
GDP growth	4.5	4.9	4.7	5.0
Inflation	3.5	3.0	3.0	3.0
Current acct. bal. (share of GDP)	−9.5	−9.5	−8.5	−8.5

Source: ADB estimates.

a new concessional tax regime featuring lower rates, easier compliance, and automatic refunds for excess payment of value-added tax, as well as a tax liability write-off for defunct firms. On the demand side, higher capital investment fueled growth, as did private consumption that benefitted from an 18.3% rise in remittances in the first half of 2018 over a year earlier.

Despite tight credit, this *Update* raises the growth forecast for 2018, assuming that tourism remains strong and that business and investor confidence keeps investment vibrant, and for 2019, assuming continued strength in domestic and external demand.

Inflation slowed by half from 6.0% in 2017 to 2.8% year on year in July 2018, which was also the average annual rate in the year to date. Core inflation fell below 2.0%. The slowdown reflected inflation easing to 2.3% for food and 4.4% for tobacco and alcoholic beverages, along with an 8.3% price decline for clothing and footwear and a 1.4% decline for communication services. Further, credit growth moderated to 4.2% in the first half of 2018, prompting the National Bank of Georgia, the central bank, to cut its policy rate to 7.0% in July. This *Update* trims the inflation forecast for 2018 to match the forecast for 2019, which is unchanged.

The current account deficit widened to equal 11.6% of GDP in the first quarter of 2018 as growth in exports trailed that of imports in absolute terms. Exports of goods and services expanded by 23.4% in the quarter, thanks to strengthening external demand and government support for the export sector; in the first half, exports of goods rose by 28.5%. Meanwhile, rising domestic demand, strong growth, and improved business and consumer confidence boosted imports by 22.9% in the first half, notably for consumer and investment goods. Despite oil prices higher than expected and robust public investment, this *Update* maintains earlier projections for the current account deficit.

Kyrgyz Republic

Growth slowed to 0.1% in the first half of 2018 from 5.6% in the same period of 2017. Outside the large gold sector, growth was 2.1%. By sector, industry fell by 6.0%, reversing 31.9% growth a year earlier with declines of 23.3% in mining (including lower gold output) and 6.1% in manufacturing but gains of 70.0% in textiles and apparel, 24.8% in nonmetal products, and 3.0% in electricity. Construction expanded by 6.3%, reflecting a 5.0% rise in investment. Agriculture increased by 1.6% with higher livestock production. On the demand side, private consumption is estimated to have grown slightly as an 11.7% rise in remittances boosted retail trade by 5.4%.

In view of the declines in mining and processing, this *Update* trims projected growth in 2018. However, it maintains the growth projection for 2019 with the expectation of some improvement in the domestic economy and higher growth in Kazakhstan and the Russian Federation, the country's main regional partners.

Average annual inflation in the first half of 2018 slowed to 2.3% from 2.7% a year earlier, reflecting a 2.7% decline for food thanks to a good harvest and a 0.6% decline for other goods despite a 3.5% rise in prices for services. The 12-month inflation rate at the end of June was 0.8%. A slight appreciation of the Kyrgyz som helped contain inflation. In view of these developments, this *Update* reduces the inflation forecast for 2018. However, it maintains the 2019 forecast because the som may weaken in tandem with the currencies of regional partners if they depreciate against the US dollar.

Trade expanded in the first 6 months of 2018 by 17.1%. Gains in textiles, food, and cotton raised exports by 4.9%, while higher imports of oil products, construction materials, and consumer goods boosted imports by 22.8%. The trade deficit consequently rose to $1.6 billion from $1.2 billion in the first half of 2017. However, with remittances also higher, this *Update* maintains the projected current account deficits for 2018 and 2019, especially as poor compliance with Eurasian Economic Union veterinary and agricultural standards constrains Kyrgyz exports to other members.

Tajikistan

Growth accelerated in the first half of 2018 to 7.2% from 6.0% in the same period of 2017. This improvement reflected recovery in the Russian Federation and better relations with Uzbekistan, which boosted exports and remittances, as well as sustained robust public investment. Private investment, however, continued to languish. Industry expanded by 16.7% from a high base (albeit down from 24.3% in the same period of 2017) as mining grew by 19.7%, manufacturing by 22.2%, and electricity generation by 3.0%. Agriculture rose by 8.5% in the first half, up slightly from 8.4% a year earlier, thanks to favorable weather and wider area under cultivation. With a 7.0% increase in remittances boosting disposable income, retail trade expanded by 14.6%, raising services growth to 7.9% from 5.1% in the same period of 2017.

With remittances and thus retail trade and services projected to rise further in the rest of 2018, this *Update* retains the earlier growth forecast for 2018. It similarly retains the forecast for higher growth 2019 in anticipation of expected gains in manufacturing and mining, remittances, and the production of domestic alternatives to imports.

3.1.5 Selected economic indicators, Kyrgyz Republic (%)

	2018		2019	
	ADO 2018	Update 2018	ADO 2018	Update 2018
GDP growth	3.5	2.5	4.0	4.0
Inflation	4.0	3.8	4.5	4.5
Current acct. bal. (share of GDP)	–12.0	–12.0	–10.0	–10.0

Source: ADB estimates.

3.1.6 Selected economic indicators, Tajikistan (%)

	2018		2019	
	ADO 2018	Update 2018	ADO 2018	Update 2018
GDP growth	6.0	6.0	6.5	6.5
Inflation	7.5	6.5	7.0	7.0
Current acct. bal. (share of GDP)	1.1	–2.5	–3.0	–3.0

Source: ADB estimates.

Average inflation slowed to 1.6% in the first half of 2018 from 9.0% a year earlier, reflecting prudent monetary policy and a surge in inexpensive food imports from Uzbekistan that trimmed food prices by 0.5%. Also limiting inflation were moderate depreciation of the Tajik somoni at 3.7%, flat global food prices, and slow credit growth. Prices rose by 1.7% for goods other than food and by 2.1% for services. With credit growth held low by stricter procedures for screening borrowers, and with continuing problems at two large banks, this *Update* revises down the inflation forecast for 2018. Meanwhile, it maintains the inflation forecast for 2019 in view of expected liquidity growth from potential bank recapitalization, public salary hikes, higher electricity tariffs, and further somoni depreciation.

The trade deficit expanded by 23.3% to $1 billion in the first half of 2018 as imports rose in response to higher disposable income and construction on the Rogun hydropower plant. With work on the Rogun plant continuing and anticipated gains in domestic demand, this *Update* now projects a current account deficit for 2018, not the surplus earlier forecast. The forecast deficit for 2019 is unchanged.

Turkmenistan

The government reported growth at 6.2% in first half of 2018, down slightly from 6.5% in the same period of last year. On the supply side, expansion came mainly from industry, reflecting gains in hydrocarbons, and from services, reflecting double-digit growth in transport and trade, with growth in construction and agriculture more modest. On the demand side, public investment continued to support growth but expanded more gradually than before to address external imbalances. Gross investment is estimated to equal 37% of GDP in 2018, down from 41% last year. Further fiscal tightening may occur this year and next to mitigate macroeconomic risk. In view of these developments, this *Update* reduces growth projected for both 2018 and 2019.

The government further reported that state revenue in the first half of the year exceeded the budget plan by 3% thanks to higher energy exports and income from the economy outside the large hydrocarbon sector. Expenditure was reported 15% below budget because of slower investment spending and subsidy cuts, bringing the state budget close to balance.

These subsidy cuts, along with rising import prices and expansionary credit policy, have spurred inflation even with broad money growth projected to slow to 8.0% this year from 11.0% in 2017. The government continues to maintain price controls for basic goods, services, and utilities while supporting efforts to replace imports with locally produced food and household goods. Nevertheless, the International Monetary Fund projects average annual inflation to reach 9.4% in 2018

3.1.7 Selected economic indicators, Turkmenistan (%)

	2018		2019	
	ADO 2018	Update	ADO 2018	Update
GDP growth	6.5	6.2	6.7	6.0
Inflation	8.0	9.4	8.0	8.2
Current acct. bal. (share of GDP)	−9.0	−8.5	−8.0	−7.8

Source: ADB estimates.

from 8.0% last year. The exchange rate remains fixed, but the Turkmen manat has appreciated strongly in real terms since devaluation in 2015. Meanwhile, the central bank continues to ration foreign exchange and promote noncash payments domestically. This *Update* raises inflation projections for both 2018 and 2019.

Export performance is expected to improve in 2018 and 2019 with increased gas exports to the People's Republic of China and higher energy prices. The government reported exports up by 41.0% year on year in the first half of 2018 and imports down by 43.0%. This *Update* therefore trims the current account deficits projected for 2018 and 2019. Foreign direct investment, estimated to equal 5.0% of GDP in 2018, will continue to support expansion in hydrocarbons. External public debt is projected to increase further to 31.2% of GDP in 2018 and 33.6% in 2019. Sound debt monitoring and management are therefore required to ensure that external borrowing remains sustainable.

Uzbekistan

According to government sources, GDP expanded by 4.9% in the first half of 2018, down from 7.0% in the same period of 2017. Growth came mainly from industry (excluding construction) and services. Industry expanded by 10.7%, propelled from 7.6% growth a year earlier by gains of 7.3% in manufacturing and 32.8% in mining. Services grew by 7.6%, slowing from 11.6% with sluggish expansion in transport at 2.3% and retail trade at 0.9%. Construction expanded by 9.7%, accelerating from 8.7% a year earlier with growth at 11.6% in both housing and commercial buildings. Growth in agriculture slowed to 2.7% from 5.8% as crop diversification and a water deficit held growth in crop output to 1.1%. In view of these developments, and of the protracted economic impact of a new exchange rate regime introduced in 2017, this *Update* trims projected growth in 2018 and 2019, with some improvement expected in 2019 if water shortages ease.

On the demand side, growth came mainly from investment. Gross fixed capital investment expanded by 13.4%, up from 8.3% a year earlier as modernization and infrastructure programs boosted outlays in manufacturing, housing, and mining—despite foreign direct investment declining by 8.3%. Private consumption stagnated, as reflected in lower retail trade growth, for lack of inflation adjustments to wages and pensions.

The consumer price index reportedly rose in the first half of 2018 at an annual rate of 12.7%, down from 14.7% in the same period a year earlier and near the center of the target range of 11.5%–13.5% set by the Central Bank of the Republic of Uzbekistan. While food prices rose by 9.5%, higher utility tariffs raised prices for services at an annual rate of 16.6% and

3.1.8 Selected economic indicators, Uzbekistan (%)

	2018		2019	
	ADO 2018	*Update*	ADO 2018	*Update*
GDP growth	5.5	4.9	5.6	5.0
Inflation	16.0	16.0	14.0	14.0
Current acct. bal. (share of GDP)	0.5	0.5	0.1	0.1

Source: ADB estimates.

for goods other than food by 13.8%. To contain inflation, the central bank maintained tight monetary policy by keeping the refinancing rate at 14.0%. This *Update* retains earlier projections for inflation.

Exports of goods and services reportedly grew by 31.1% in the first half of 2018, up from 13.1% a year earlier with sharp increases in services and energy. Streamlined export procedures raised exports of food by 58.9% and textiles by 16.7%. Industrial modernization and infrastructure development programs contributed to a 62.2% rise in imports, a sharp rise from 9.2% a year earlier that widened the trade deficit to $2.1 billion from $0.1 billion a year earlier. Meanwhile, inward remittances by individuals rose by 14.0% to $2.3 billion. With positive income flows and net transfers forecast to outweigh deficits in goods and services, this *Update* retains earlier projections for small current account surpluses in 2018 and 2019.

East Asia

Growth was resilient in the first half of 2018, moderating only slightly as both domestic and external demand remained robust. Inflation edged up, and the subregional current account surplus weakened. The growth forecast is unchanged for 2018, but a dip in 2019 is now projected a little deeper as trade tensions take their toll. Inflation will be lower than previously expected in both years with moderating increases for food, and the current account surplus will be narrower than forecast earlier.

Subregional assessment and prospects

Growth in East Asia moderated in the first half of 2018 relative to *ADO 2018* projections in April. In the People's Republic of China (PRC), growth decelerated to 6.8% as expansion moderated in all sectors. Consumption rose faster than expected, but investment growth weakened as local governments trimmed infrastructure spending. Growth was lower than earlier forecast in Hong Kong, China but higher in other economies on robust private consumption and exports, as well as supportive monetary and fiscal policies.

Subregional inflation remained tame but rose slightly in the first half of 2018 in all economies except the Republic of Korea (ROK), where wage hikes and oil price increases had only modest impact. Food price increases raised PRC inflation to 2.3% in August and pushed up rates in Mongolia and Taipei,China, where currency depreciation also played a part, and in Hong Kong, China, where rents also climbed.

East Asia's current account surplus narrowed in the first half of 2018 as growth in imports outpaced exports. In the PRC, the current account registered a deficit equal to 0.4% of GDP, bringing a small decline in gross official reserves. In Mongolia, the deficit widened as mining-related imports surged. Current account surpluses narrowed in the ROK and Taipei,China but widened in Hong Kong, China on increased income from inbound tourism.

3.2.1 GDP growth, East Asia

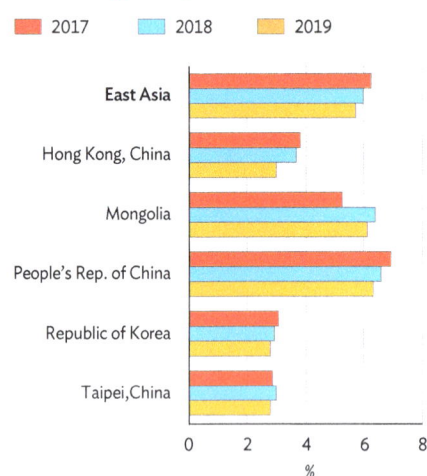

Source: *Asian Development Outlook* database.

The section on the PRC was written by Dominik Peschel and Jian Zhuang, and the part on other economies by Cindy Castillejos-Petalcorin, Benno Ferrarini, Amar Lkhagvasuren, Declan Magee, Nedelyn Magtibay-Ramos, Donghyun Park, and Michael Timbang, consultant. Authors are in the East Asia and Economic Research and Regional Cooperation departments of ADB. Subregional assessment and prospects were written by Reza Vaez-Zadeh, consultant, Economic Research and Regional Cooperation Department.

The trend in exports and domestic demand will largely buoy if not lift 2018 GDP growth rates in all East Asian economies, though combined GDP growth will slip from 6.3% in 2017 to 6.0% in 2018, as forecast in April, and to 5.7% in 2019, slightly lower than projected earlier. Growth in the PRC will follow a similar pattern, with expansionary fiscal policy holding the growth slowdown from 6.9% in 2017 to 6.6% in 2018, unchanged from the previous forecast, and to 6.3% in 2019, revised down from 6.4%. In Hong Kong, China and in Taipei,China, growth will be higher in 2018 than projected in April, but forecasts are unchanged for 2019, with accommodative policies and domestic demand supporting growth. Mongolia will see growth accelerate sharply this year as private consumption and exports increase, with the forecast for 2019 revised up as well, but growth forecasts are revised slightly down for the ROK as trade partners' higher tariffs threaten to hurt exports (Figure 3.2.1).

Inflation in East Asia is forecast at 2.1% in 2018 and 2019, lower than the April projections (Figure 3.2.2). The PRC will see prices rise by 2.2% in both 2018 and 2019, less than previously forecast, as prices rose slower than anticipated in the first 8 months of 2018 and inflation in 2019 will be lower than projected in April. The inflation forecast is pared down as well for the ROK with slower growth, and for Mongolia in 2018 with excises on fuel eliminated, but raised for Hong Kong, China with rising rents and import prices, and for Taipei,China with currency depreciation and higher oil prices.

The combined current account surplus will shrink from the equivalent of 2.4% of subregional GDP in 2017 to 1.6% in 2018 and 1.1% in 2019, both below previous forecasts (Figure 3.2.3). With export growth expected to be tamped down by trade tensions, the current account surplus of the PRC will shrink relative to GDP substantially more than previously forecast, especially in 2019. The surpluses of the ROK and Hong Kong, China will also narrow more than projected earlier, and Mongolia's deficits will be markedly higher than forecast (though down from 2017) as imports rise to supply mining investment. In Taipei,China, currency depreciation will attenuate import demand, propping up current account surpluses in both years more than previously forecast.

Rising trade tensions harbor downside risks to growth forecasts for East Asia, especially if they escalate enough to depress consumer and investor confidence, disrupt supply chains, impede foreign direct investment, or, in the PRC, derail structural reform and prudent macroeconomic management. Volatile food prices, commodity price swings, and any unexpectedly abrupt monetary tightening in the US constitute further downside risks to the outlook.

3.2.2 Inflation, East Asia

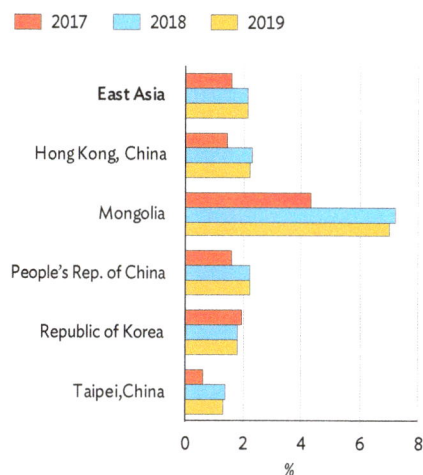

Source: *Asian Development Outlook* database.

3.2.3 Current account balance, East Asia

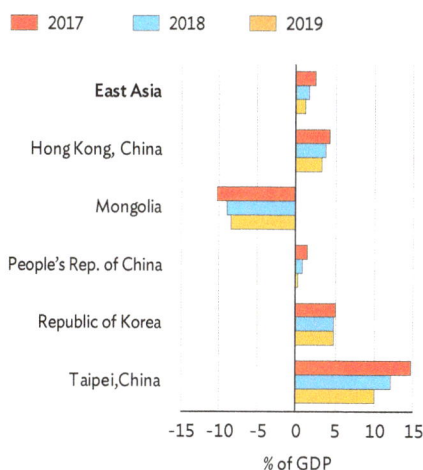

Source: *Asian Development Outlook* database.

People's Republic of China

The growth forecast is unchanged at 6.6% for 2018 as economic performance remained strong in the first half of the year despite moderation starting in the second quarter. The forecast for 2019 is revised down to 6.3%, reflecting slower demand growth and trade conflict with the US. Supply-side reform, strong service sector growth, and monetary and fiscal support will keep the economy on track. In both years, inflation will moderate and the current account surplus will narrow more than previously anticipated.

Updated assessment

GDP growth decelerated slightly to 6.8% year on year in the first half of 2018 from 6.9% in the same period of 2017, with growth in the second quarter slowing to 6.7% (Figure 3.2.4). On the supply side, the economy continued to be restructured away from industry and toward services. The service sector was again the main growth driver with 7.6% growth year on year in the first half, though marginally down from 7.7% a year earlier. Trade, catering, transport, and information technology services maintained high growth, while financial and real estate services weakened. Growth in secondary industry (mining, manufacturing, construction, and utility production and supply) slipped to 6.1% from 6.4% in the first half of 2017. Strong increases in consumer and high-tech manufacturing, and in manufacturing for export, partly offset deceleration in mining and raw materials, where production was subject to retrenchment targets. Agriculture grew by 3.2%, down from 3.5% in the same period of 2017 mainly because of adverse weather. Its contribution to GDP growth in the first half remained unchanged from a year earlier at 0.2 percentage points as the contribution of industry edged down from 2.6 points to 2.5 and that of services was unchanged at 4.1 points (Figure 3.2.5).

Robust service sector growth helped keep the labor market healthy in the first half of 2018, with the unemployment rate in cities declining from 5.0% in January 2018 to 4.8% in June, according to surveys published only since the beginning of 2018. However, unemployment bounced back to 5.0% in August 2018 as economic momentum weakened and new college graduates entered the labor market.

On the demand side, consumption remained, in line with *ADO 2018* projections, the major driver of growth in the first half of 2018 as growth in household consumption rose to 6.7% from 6.1% a year earlier. Consumer confidence held up well in the first quarter but fell significantly in June and remained subdued in July as the economy lost momentum in the second quarter. Accordingly, retail sales were up by only 6.5% year on year in real terms in August 2018, decelerating from 8.9% a year earlier. Moreover, real household disposable income grew

3.2.4 Economic growth

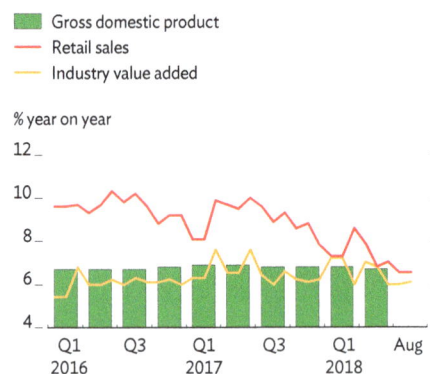

■ Gross domestic product
— Retail sales
— Industry value added

% year on year

Q = quarter.
Source: National Bureau of Statistics.

3.2.5 Supply-side contributions to growth

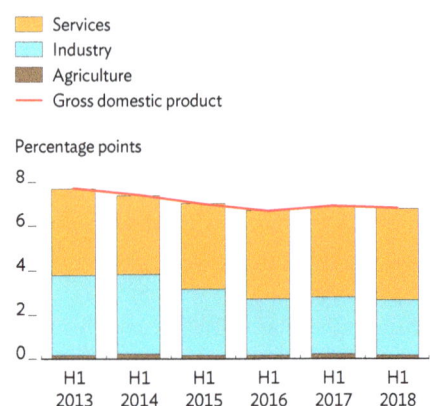

■ Services
■ Industry
■ Agriculture
— Gross domestic product

Percentage points

H = half.
Source: National Bureau of Statistics.

by only 6.6% in the first half of 2018—lagging GDP growth and down from 7.3% a year earlier—having been tamped down by a 20.3% increase in personal income tax collection, which exceeded the 14.4% increase in total tax revenue. Consumption nevertheless contributed 5.3 percentage points to GDP growth in the first half, up from 4.4 points in the same period of 2017 (Figure 3.2.6).

As anticipated in *ADO 2018*, investment growth weakened further in the first half of 2018, contributing 2.1 percentage points to growth, or 0.3 points less than in the same period in 2017. As local governments streamlined infrastructure spending both on and off budget to contain growth in local government debt, growth in infrastructure investment dropped sharply to 4.2% in the first 8 months of 2018 from 19.8% a year earlier (Figure 3.2.7). In the same period, real estate investment growth accelerated from 7.9% in 2017 to 10.1%, but this was mostly from land purchases while investment in housing construction declined. Encouraged by solid growth in profits from manufacturing, investment growth in the subsector in the first 8 months of 2018 accelerated to 7.5% from 4.5% in the year-earlier period.

As the foreign trade surplus shrank significantly, net exports dragged on growth again, subtracting 0.7 percentage points in the first half of 2018, compared with positive contributions of 0.1 points in the first half of 2017 and 0.6 points in the whole year. Strong import growth, both in US dollar terms and by volume, reflected consumption driving growth, while exports grew at a slightly lower rate than a year earlier.

Consumer price inflation averaged 2.1% in the first 8 months of 2018, up from 1.5% in the same period of 2017 as food prices recovered from a decline in 2017 and inflation for other goods and services remained at 2.3% (Figure 3.2.8). Producer price inflation softened to 4.0% in the period from 6.4% a year earlier, reflecting base effects after supply-side reform induced a spike in the index in 2017. In July 2018, prices for newly constructed homes in the top 70 cities were on average 6.6% higher than a year earlier, driven by durable growth in sales and slow progress in making new floor space available (Figure 3.2.9).

After a cut of 100 basis points in the required reserve ratio in April 2018, mainly to manage liquidity, the People's Bank of China, the central bank, cut the ratio by another 50 basis points for most banks in late June 2018, triggering a decline in interbank rates. The central bank designated the resulting additional liquidity mostly for bank financing of debt restructuring for state-owned enterprises. In late July, it injected CNY502 billion into the banking system through a 1-year medium-term lending facility, which lowered interbank rates further (Figure 3.2.10). The benchmark deposit and lending rates have remained unchanged.

3.2.6 Demand-side contributions to growth

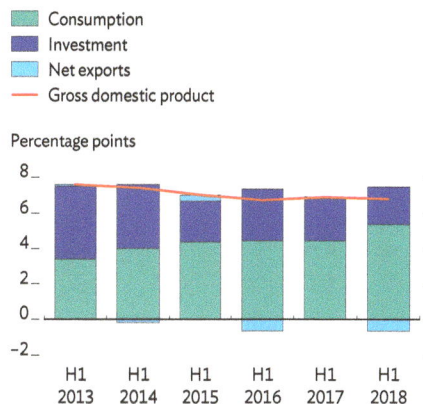

H = half.
Source: National Bureau of Statistics.

3.2.7 Growth in fixed asset investment

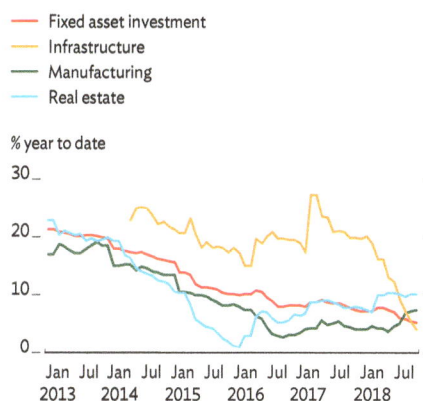

Source: National Bureau of Statistics.

3.2.8 Monthly inflation

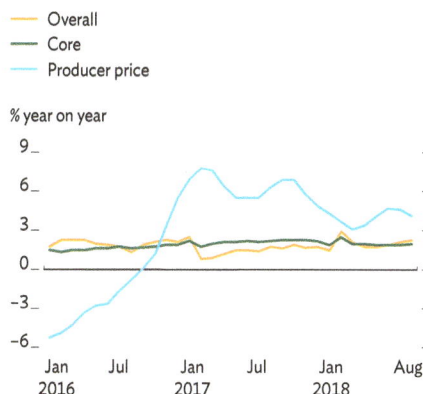

Source: National Bureau of Statistics.

Broad money (M2) was 8.2% higher at the end of August 2018 than a year earlier. Total social financing, a broader credit aggregate that includes elements of shadow banking, was up by 10.1%, outstanding bank loans up by 12.6%, and outstanding shadow bank financing down by 3.8% (Figure 3.2.11). The reduction in shadow bank financing was a consequence of regulatory tightening to keep financial institutions from using asset and wealth management products as ways to avoid recording activities on the balance sheet. This put banks back in the driver's seat of credit growth. In the first 8 months of 2018, growth in outstanding corporate bond financing rebounded from its low in late 2017, while growth in corporate equity financing decelerated.

Fiscal policy was tight in the first 8 months of 2018. Fiscal revenue grew by 9.4% year on year, slightly down from 10.2% a year earlier, while fiscal expenditure growth slowed by half to 6.9% from 13.4% a year earlier. The deficit of the general budget, combining the center and local governments, equaled 1.7% of GDP in the first half of 2018, down from 2.4% in the same period of 2017 and 3.7% in the year as a whole. To reduce the tax burden on low- and middle-income earners, the Ministry of Finance proposed in June 2018 an amendment to the personal income tax law. With tax brackets adjusted upward, a higher standard personal allowance, and additional specific deductions, the proposed amendment aims to encourage private consumption in the short run and help alleviate income inequality in the longer run—at the cost, though, of likely reducing the share of direct taxes in revenue. The new tax brackets and standard allowance becomes effective on 1 October 2018, followed by the remaining changes on 1 January 2019.

The current account registered a deficit equal to 0.4% of GDP in the first half of 2018. This followed a 1.1% deficit in the first quarter, the first time a quarterly deficit has been recorded since 2001. Exports grew by 10.3% in US dollar terms as demand from the advanced economies and Southeast Asia remained high, while imports increased by 17.6%, driven by resilient domestic demand. As a result, the merchandise trade surplus narrowed by a quarter to $155.9 billion from $214.4 billion a year earlier and the deficit in services widened. Net direct investment increased to $84.9 billion in the first half of 2018, up sharply from $13.9 billion a year earlier, in line with a surge of foreign direct investment (FDI) inflow that started in the last quarter of 2017 (Figure 3.2.12). Quarterly data suggest that FDI inflow peaked in the first quarter of 2018, which is consistent with expectations that worsening trade tensions will dampen FDI into the PRC. In line with an expected reversal in capital flow in the second quarter, estimates that exclude net FDI flow show moderate net outflow in the first half of 2018. Official reserves decreased slightly by $29.8 billion to stand at $3.2 trillion at the end of June and have remained broadly stable since.

3.2.9 Residential property prices

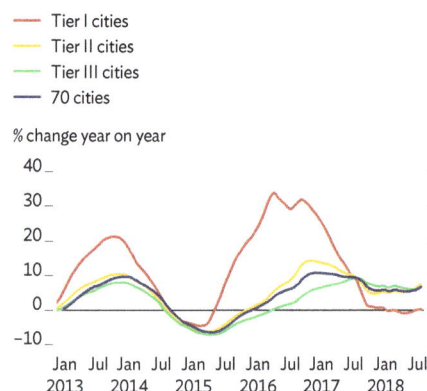

Note: Tier I includes 4 cities: Beijing, Shanghai, Guangzhou, and Shenzhen; Tier II includes 31 provincial capital cities, municipalities, and sub-provincial cities; Tier III includes 35 other cities.

Sources: National Bureau of Statistics; ADB estimates.

3.2.10 Policy and interbank market interest rates

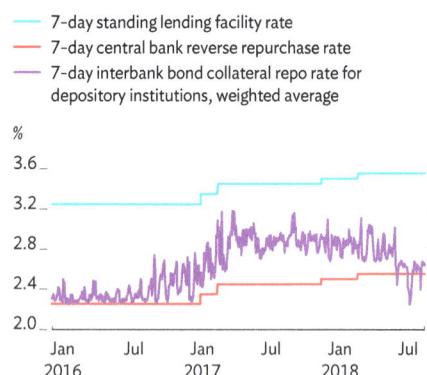

Sources: People's Bank of China; National Interbank Funding Center.

3.2.11 Growth of broad money and total social financing

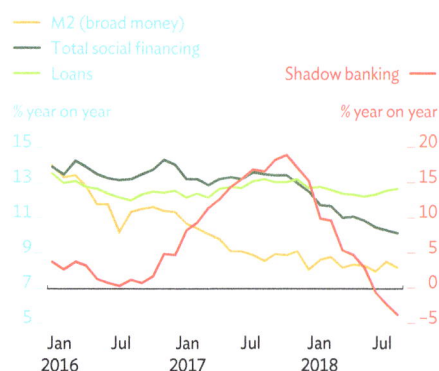

Note: Shadow banking = entrusted loans + trust loans + banker's acceptance bills.

Sources: People's Bank of China; ADB estimates.

The renminbi strengthened in the first 7 months of 2018 by 1.1% in real effective terms (taking inflation into account) and in the first 8 months by 0.9% in nominal effective terms (against a trade-weighted basket of currencies), when it weakened by 4.4% against the US dollar, having come under pressure in mid-June (Figure 3.2.13). This rapid depreciation had multiple causes: the domestic economy losing momentum, the current account deficit, falling domestic interest rates, and worsening uncertainty about external trade. The central bank did not follow the US Federal Reserve's interest rate hike in June 2018 because the PRC had a weaker domestic growth outlook. Alongside monetary easing, government bond yields softened, narrowing the spread over US treasuries (Figure 3.2.14) and thereby reinforcing incentives for capital flight and putting pressure on the renminbi. Although capital outflows seem to have stayed moderate, the central bank reintroduced in August 2018 a 20% reserve requirement on foreign exchange forward sales, to take pressure off the renminbi. It then reintroduced the "counter-cyclical factor," which augments central bank discretion in the daily fixing of the exchange rate. This allows it to slow renminbi depreciation, but greater intervention by the central bank distorts market determination of the exchange rate and drains official foreign exchange reserves.

Prospects

The softening GDP growth trend in the second quarter of 2018 is expected to continue in the second half of 2018, given a downtrend in the housing market, ongoing tight conditions for nonbank lending, and lower export growth relative to imports. However, supportive monetary and fiscal policies are likely to soften the impact of these factors. Monetary policy has recently become more accommodative with increased liquidity supplied to banks, and fiscal policy is expected to become more supportive, which will boost infrastructure investment and bolster consumption. Services will likely continue to be a driver of growth, and agriculture will contribute steadily, but industry will face headwinds and thus contribute less. Fiscal and monetary loosening, combined with the strong momentum in the first half of 2018, will likely keep GDP growth on track to reach the *ADO 2018* forecast of 6.6% in 2018. Growth is now forecast to slow in 2019 slightly more than expected earlier to 6.3%, given slowing growth in industry, continued restrictions on nonbank financing, and adverse effects from the trade conflict with the US—these factors partly offset by higher fiscal expenditure and an expected pickup in the housing market (Figure 3.2.15).

Consumption will remain the main driver of growth in 2018 and 2019. Support will again come from continued solid wage growth in a tight market for skilled blue-collar workers,

3.2.12 Balance of payments components

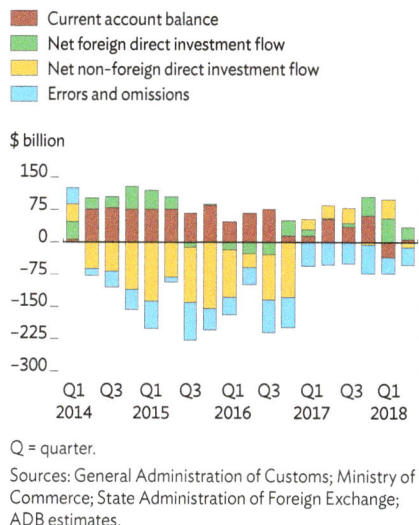

Q = quarter.
Sources: General Administration of Customs; Ministry of Commerce; State Administration of Foreign Exchange; ADB estimates.

3.2.13 Exchange rates

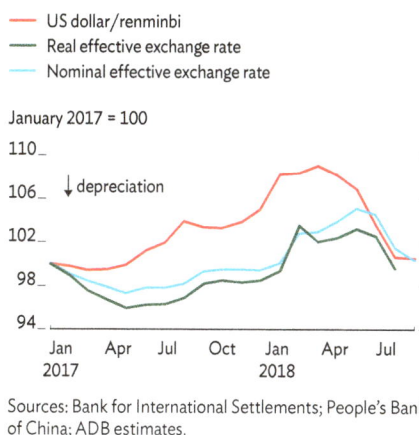

Sources: Bank for International Settlements; People's Bank of China; ADB estimates.

3.2.14 Interest rate spread

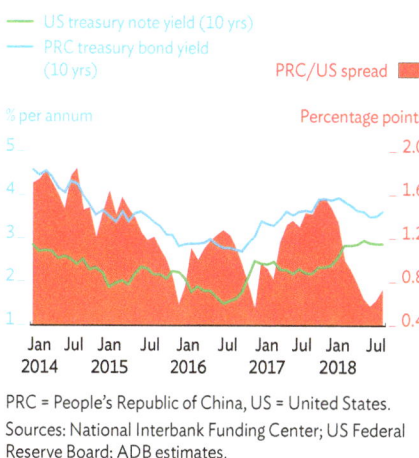

PRC = People's Republic of China, US = United States.
Sources: National Interbank Funding Center; US Federal Reserve Board; ADB estimates.

resilient consumer confidence reinforced by a reduced personal income tax burden, and higher government spending on social priorities as the government strives to ensure that its growth target is achieved.

Supported by more expansionary fiscal policy, investment growth will pick up in the remainder of 2018 and stay solid through 2019. While construction growth will remain weak this year, owing to restrictions on the residential market in many cities, it will likely pick up in 2019 in response to continued demand and lower housing stocks in large cities. In heavy industry, excess capacity and high debt will continue to limit investment, while investment in services and in emerging and consumer-oriented industries is expected to persist. While government investment in infrastructure slowed to a surprising extent in the first 8 months of 2018, recovery is assured by the government having stepped up in August the issuance of special bonds for shanty town renovation and other local government infrastructure projects. In addition, the government aims to accelerate urban infrastructure spending and ease restrictions on public–private partnership.

Net exports are now forecast to drag on GDP growth in both 2018 and 2019, given that the trade conflict with the US and worsening impediments to global trade and investment dim the outlook for PRC exports. However, the adverse impact of US tariffs on PRC exports will likely be mitigated by a weaker renminbi and/or lower profit margins for producers and exporters. With merchandise imports outgrowing exports, the current account surplus will likely narrow to the equivalent of 0.7% of GDP in 2018 and 0.2% in 2019, lower than projected in *ADO 2018*.

Consumer prices are forecast to rise on average by only 2.2% in 2018 and in 2019, both projections slightly down from *ADO 2018* forecasts (Figure 3.2.16). From the moderate increase in the first 8 months of 2018, consumer prices in general will likely edge up in the remainder of 2018. Inflation drivers include higher oil prices, resilient consumer demand, and a weaker renminbi that will mean price increases for imported consumer and intermediary goods in the rest of the year. In addition, the government announced in June 2018 plans to gradually adjust prices for water and electricity supply and wastewater and garbage removal, toward enhancing environmental protection by 2025, but these reforms should have only limited impact on inflation in the short term. Housing prices are expected to continue rising given low construction activity in the first 7 months of 2018 and shrinking inventories.

The downward revision for inflation in 2019 is predicated on weaker GDP growth and moderate pass-through of renminbi depreciation. New PRC tariffs on imports from the US should have only limited effects on domestic consumer

3.2.15 GDP growth

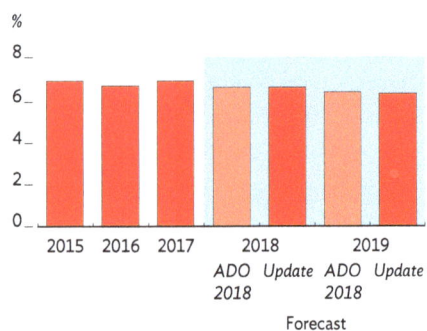

Source: *Asian Development Outlook* database.

3.2.16 Inflation

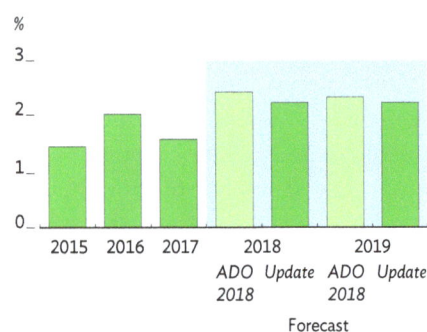

Source: *Asian Development Outlook* database.

prices as most such products are not counted in the consumer price basket and most agricultural commodities heretofore imported from the US can be sourced from other countries, produced domestically, or replaced with functionally equivalent products. In the important case of soybeans, applying these strategies can perhaps ease the impact of tariffs but not eliminate them, and the resulting increase in animal feed costs is expected to translate into higher meat prices.

Amid the economic slowdown and the trade conflict with the US, the government announced in July 2018 fiscal measures including the speeding up of special bond issuance, as mentioned above, and a reduction in taxes and fees for businesses. This development and the reduced personal tax burden indicate that fiscal policy will be more expansionary in the remainder of 2018, with constraint in fiscal spending in the first 8 months of 2018 giving way to higher infrastructure spending in the rest of the year and into 2019, but not to large-scale fiscal stimulus. Ample room exists to increase expenditure, as the general budget deficit, which amounted to CNY781 billion in the first 8 months of 2018, can increase by a further CNY1.6 trillion in the remaining 4 months before exceeding this year's fiscal deficit target of 2.6% of GDP. Moreover, this deficit ceiling does not apply to infrastructure expenditure financed through the issuance of new special bonds, the majority of which remain to be issued to reach the targeted CNY1.35 trillion increase in 2018.

The more accommodative monetary policy that began at the end of June 2018 is expected to continue. While cuts to benchmark deposit and lending rates are not expected in 2018 because they could cause capital outflow, the central bank will likely provide additional liquidity to banks throughout 2018 and 2019 in measured steps—by further cutting the required reserve ratio and offering additional credit through medium-term lending facilities—to ensure adequate credit supply while limiting the risk of financial instability and capital outflow. Under current conditions, a broadly looser monetary policy harbors the risk of banks extending more credit to troubled entities in need of debt restructuring, thereby exacerbating the risk of default. Already, many "special mention" loans, a category one notch above nonperforming loans, have accumulated on the balance sheets of local banks, especially in economically weaker regions (Figure 3.2.17). At the same time, regulatory tightening on shadow banking is expected to continue, making it difficult for weaker corporate clients to get nonbank financing.

Pressures on the exchange rate may intensify over the forecast period with domestic growth losing momentum, uncertainty over the future course of the trade conflict with the US, and the narrowing of both the current account surplus and the interest rate spread over US rates. Further significant

3.2.1 Selected economic indicators, People's Republic of China (%)

| | 2018 | | 2019 | |
	ADO 2018	Update	ADO 2018	Update
GDP growth	6.6	6.6	6.4	6.3
Inflation	2.4	2.2	2.3	2.2
Current acct. bal. (share of GDP)	1.3	0.7	1.2	0.2

Source: ADB estimates.

3.2.17 Problematic bank loans by category

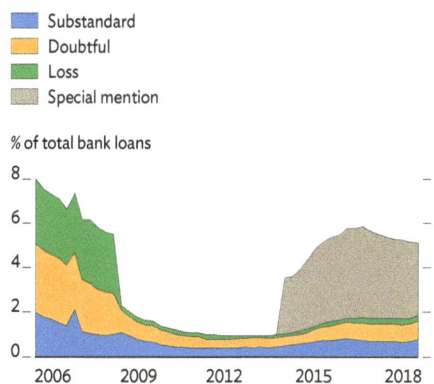

■ Substandard
■ Doubtful
■ Loss
■ Special mention

Note: "Special mention" loans data started in 2014.
Source: China Banking and Insurance Regulatory Commission.

weakening of the renminbi could reprise both the exchange rate as a bone of contention with the US and the large capital outflow seen in 2015–2016 (Figure 3.2.18). As the authorities aim to prevent either eventuality, the central bank may be forced to stabilize the exchange rate during the forecast period.

External uncertainties have mounted since the publication of *ADO 2018* in April. The trade conflict between the US and the PRC continues, and the scope and level of tariffs on US imports from the PRC could increase further. A downside risk to the forecast would be trade frictions escalating to the extent that they depress consumer and investor confidence, severely disrupt supply chains, impede technology transfer and FDI, and hit export-oriented industries.

A domestic risk would be a perceived need to counter external headwinds by delaying structural reform, especially of state-owned enterprises, and derailing economic policy-making that aims to head off financial risk. While a more expansionary fiscal policy with higher infrastructure spending helps to sustain economic growth in the short run, over the longer term it increases the financial burden on local governments, necessitating expedited reform of intergovernmental fiscal relations. Such reform needs to carefully consider differences among local governments in terms of their economic endowment and management ability.

3.2.18 Official reserves and net capital flows

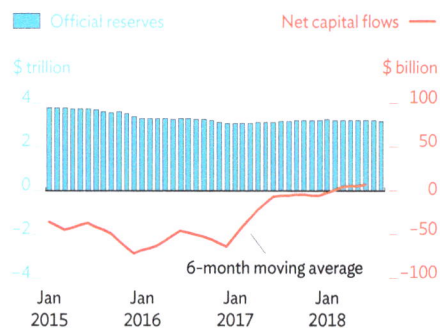

Note: Capital flows include foreign direct investments, and errors and omissions.

Sources: People's Bank of China; State Administration of Foreign Exchange; ADB estimates.

Other economies

Hong Kong, China

After hitting a growth rate of 4.6% year on year in the first quarter of 2018—the highest rate since the third quarter of 2011—the economy slowed in the second quarter to yield 4.0% growth in the first half of the year, marginally down from 4.1% a year earlier. The softening reflected a broad decline in domestic demand and moderating external demand. Growth in gross fixed capital formation plummeted to 2.2% in the first half of 2018 from 6.7% a year earlier, mainly as investment in building and construction contracted in the second quarter after 1.9% expansion in the first. Private consumption remained robust, however, rising by 7.4% in the first half and outpacing 4.8% growth a year earlier as consumer sentiment was underpinned by favorable labor market conditions. Unemployment fell to a seasonally adjusted 2.8%, the lowest in more than 20 years.

With deepening uncertainty surrounding trade friction between the US and the PRC, export growth slowed to 4.9% year on year in the first half. Trade in services followed the same pattern, rising faster in the first quarter than in the second. On the supply side, agriculture, fishing, mining, and quarrying declined by 4.8% in the first quarter, but manufacturing grew by 1.1% and services by 4.4%. Retail sales expanded by a vibrant 13.4% in the first half, helped by strong domestic demand.

The growth forecast is revised up for 2018, to accommodate exceptionally strong growth in the first quarter, but unchanged for 2019, when growth is expected to slow as global trade tensions mount and US interest rates continue to rise. Domestic demand should remain supportive of growth in both years, buttressed by high government spending, the buoyant property market, and high wage growth in the tight labor market. Meanwhile, rising inbound tourism should benefit services exports.

Consumer prices rose by an average of 2.3% in the first half of 2018, driven mainly by higher prices for tourism services and private housing rentals, and are expected to rise similarly in the second half and in 2019, led by higher global prices and continued feed-through of earlier rises in residential rents. The inflation forecast is thus marginally raised for both years.

The current account surplus equaled 2.4% of GDP in the first quarter of 2018, higher than the 2.2% recorded in the previous quarter as exports rebounded strongly. However, in light of intensifying trade headwinds, current account surpluses are now expected to be narrower in both 2018 and 2019 than previously forecast. Worsening global tensions and slower demand growth from the People's Republic of China are the main downside risks.

3.2.2 Selected economic indicators, Hong Kong, China (%)

	2018		2019	
	ADO 2018	Update 2018	ADO 2018	Update 2018
GDP growth	3.2	3.7	3.0	3.0
Inflation	2.2	2.3	2.1	2.2
Current acct. bal. (share of GDP)	3.9	3.7	3.5	3.3

Source: ADB estimates.

Mongolia

Having revived in 2017, growth remained strong at 6.3% in the first half of 2018, propelled by domestic demand. Investment, predominantly in one mining project, remained the main source of growth, contributing 12.6 percentage points. Consumption contributed 3.9 points as a surge in credit to households fueled private expenditure. Net exports subtracted 10.3 points as imports rose to supply busier mines, outpacing export growth. On the supply side, industry, supported by recovery in mining and expansion in manufacturing, lifted GDP growth by 2.1 points, and services added another 3.7 points, but agriculture's contribution to growth fell to 0.5 points as drought brought livestock losses. Inflation accelerated to average 6.5% in the first half of 2018, mainly because food prices rose with drought and reduced domestic supply of meat because of higher exports, but also reflecting higher prices for petroleum products.

The budget recorded a surplus equal to 2.8% of GDP in the first half of the year as revenue substantially outgrew expenditure. A cumulative 3 percentage point reduction in the central bank policy rate in 2017 and 2018 pushed up credit growth by 19.4% year on year and the broad money supply by 28.7%. Concerned about risk posed by mounting consumer loans, the central bank set a cap in July on the ratio of household debt service to income. Nonperforming loans grew by 16.3% but remained relatively stable at 8.5% of the total.

The current account deficit widened to 10.7% of GDP in the first half of 2018 as a 32.7% rise in imports dwarfed 15.7% growth in exports. A consequence of this and of capital outflow mainly to repay commercial debt was a 0.6% decline in gross reserves, now covering 4.6 months of imports. The Mongolian togrog depreciated by 1.5% against the US dollar in the first 8 months of 2018 but rose against the currencies of trade partners in both trade-weighted and inflation-adjusted terms.

Growth forecasts for 2018 and 2019 are revised up to reflect unexpected strength in private consumption and coal exports, as well as assumed recovery in agriculture in 2019. Slower growth in mining and related investments will, however, likely slow growth a bit in 2019. The inflation forecast for 2018 is revised down as pass-through from currency depreciation in 2016 fades, and with the government expected to follow its annulment of excise taxes on fuel with further interventions to stabilize fuel prices. A higher current account deficit is now projected for both years as stronger economic growth pushes up imports and as mining profits are repatriated, though most profits are then reinvested. Risks to the outlook would include disrupted implementation of an International Monetary Fund program, major changes in the flows of foreign direct investment in 2019, and large fluctuations in meat or export prices.

3.2.3 Selected economic indicators, Mongolia (%)

	2018		2019	
	ADO 2018	Update	ADO 2018	Update
GDP growth	3.8	6.4	4.3	6.1
Inflation	8.0	7.2	7.0	7.0
Current acct. bal. (share of GDP)	−6.3	−8.9	−7.0	−8.5

Source: ADB estimates.

Republic of Korea

GDP expanded by 2.8% year on year in the first half of 2018, the same rate of expansion as in the first half of 2017, propelled by buoyant consumption and external demand. Net exports improved in real terms as higher exports of services pushed all exports up by 3.2%, outpacing import growth. Private consumption surged by 3.2%, up from 2.2% growth a year earlier on higher incomes from wage hikes and a rebound in spending by tourists from the PRC. Growth in government consumption more than doubled to 5.3% from 2.6% a year earlier with the implementation of programs to create jobs and boost other social spending. Consumption growth cushioned drag from a slowdown in investment growth, which plunged to 1.2% from 12.0% as government investment declined, major infrastructure projects reached completion, new construction investments tapered, and capital improvements in manufacturing and information technology slowed.

On the supply side, services led the expansion with growth by 3.1% in January–June, up from 1.8% in the same period of last year. Growth in manufacturing eased from 4.2% to 3.0% as higher input costs squeezed production. Agriculture rebounded from contraction a year earlier to grow by 2.5%.

Consumer price inflation slowed to 1.4% in the first 8 months of 2018 from 2.1% a year earlier. This was comfortably below the revised target of 1.6% for the year, allowing the Bank of Korea, the central bank, to keep its policy interest rate at 1.5%, unchanged since November 2017. Similarly, fiscal policy remained expansionary as a $3.8 billion supplementary budget boosted business subsidies and aimed to reduce youth unemployment. The current account surplus fell from the equivalent of 4.8% of GDP in the first half of 2017 to 3.7% in the same period of this year, with both exports and imports posting lower growth.

Growth forecasts for 2018 and 2019 are downgraded slightly because exports will likely suffer under tariffs levied by both the PRC and the US, two of the Republic of Korea's largest trade partners. Supportive fiscal policy to prop up consumption is expected to continue but is unlikely to boost growth; consumer sentiment dipped in July in response to worsening unemployment despite government job creation programs.

Inflation is forecast to trend slightly lower than previously forecast as oil price recovery and wage hikes exert less impact than expected. So is the current account surplus as PRC–US trade tensions threaten exports. More generally, these tensions pose downside risks to the growth forecasts, as does possible financial market instability prompted by rising US interest rates and high household debt.

3.2.4 Selected economic indicators, Republic of Korea (%)

	2018		2019	
	ADO 2018	*Update*	ADO 2018	*Update*
GDP growth	3.0	2.9	2.9	2.8
Inflation	1.9	1.8	2.0	1.8
Current acct. bal. (share of GDP)	4.9	4.8	4.8	4.7

Source: ADB estimates.

Taipei,China

GDP grew by 3.2% year on year in the first half of 2018, up from 2.5% in the same period of 2017. Private consumption was the largest contributor to growth, adding 1.5 percentage points as it rose by 2.7% on the strength of higher incomes and a steady decline in the unemployment rate to 3.7% by the end of June 2018. Government consumption expanded by 6.2%, a notable reversal from 2.0% contraction in the first half of 2017 as the implementation since September 2017 of the Forward-looking Infrastructure Development Program lifted infrastructure spending. Overall investment nevertheless declined. Merchandise export growth remained robust at 10.9%, albeit down from 12.5% a year earlier.

Momentum is likely to continue for the rest of the year, spurred by strong demand in Asia and the US. The GDP growth forecast for 2018 is revised upward on expectations of continued growth in government expenditure on infrastructure, its likely stimulation of private investment, continuing strength in exports, the maintenance of an accommodating monetary policy, and the steady tightening of the labor market, which bodes well for household spending. The growth forecast for 2019 is unchanged, however, in anticipation of marginally lower global growth next year.

Average annual consumer price inflation doubled to 1.6% in the first 6 months of 2018 from 0.7% a year earlier on higher prices for vegetables, cigarettes, and imports. Core prices, excluding food and energy, rose by 1.2%. The local currency depreciated by 2.7% against the US dollar in the same period because interest rate differentials with the US widened as the central bank kept its policy rate unchanged. The inflation forecast is revised up to accommodate rising international oil prices and continued weakening of the local currency against the US dollar.

The current account surplus remained high at the equivalent of 12.7% of GDP in the first half of 2018, though a tad lower than a year earlier as the trade surplus expanded by 5.1% but the combined surplus in the service and income accounts narrowed. Considering robust export growth in the first half of this year, continuing global growth, and the dampening effect of a weaker currency on import demand, the forecast for the current account surplus is raised for both 2018 and 2019.

A major downside risk to the outlook is any escalation of the trade dispute between the US and the People's Republic of China, the two major destinations for exports from Taipei,China. Exports of machinery and electrical equipment, which represent more than half of the total, are especially vulnerable. As manufacturing accounts for over 30% of GDP, a sharp decline in such exports would reverberate throughout the economy.

3.2.5 Selected economic indicators, Taipei,China (%)

	2018		2019	
	ADO 2018	Update	ADO 2018	Update
GDP growth	2.9	3.0	2.8	2.8
Inflation	1.1	1.4	1.1	1.3
Current acct. bal. (share of GDP)	10.0	12.0	9.0	10.0

Source: ADB estimates.

South Asia

With robust growth continuing, *ADO 2018* forecasts are retained at 7.0% for 2018, picking up to 7.2% in 2019. Growth projections for India are unchanged despite notable quickening in the April–June quarter. Subregional inflation projections are raised to 4.9% for 2018 and 5.2% for 2019, mainly because of higher inflation in India and Pakistan. The current account deficit is forecast to widen to 2.9% of subregional GDP in both 2018 and 2019 as output gaps close and currencies weaken.

Subregional assessment and prospects

Forecast growth in South Asia remains as projected in *ADO 2018* at 7.0% in 2018 and 7.2% in 2019 (Figure 3.3.1). The weighted subregional forecast reflects the dominance of the Indian economy, at about 80%. While India grew by 8.2% in the first quarter of fiscal year 2018 (FY2018, ending 31 March 2019), much faster than expected, the modest widening of fiscal and current account deficits left it vulnerable to portfolio capital outflow and currency depreciation despite its large buffer of foreign exchange reserves. Robust growth in the first quarter of FY2018 spanned the economy, aided by a favorable base effect as growth in the first quarter of FY2017 hit a 3-year low following demonetization in late 2016 and the introduction of a goods and services tax in mid-2017. Yet the Indian rupee depreciated against the dollar by more than 12% from 1 January 2018 to mid-September, highlighting the vagaries of global capital markets unsettled first by the beginning of monetary tightening in the US and then by a global trade war and worsening political tensions. In response to headline inflation rising above the medium-term monetary policy target of 4%, elevated core inflation, and a closing output gap, the Reserve Bank of India, the central bank, raised the policy interest rate in two rate hikes of 25 basis points each in June and August 2018. Growth in FY2018 is nevertheless expected to accelerate to 7.3% on stronger domestic demand

3.3.1 GDP growth, South Asia

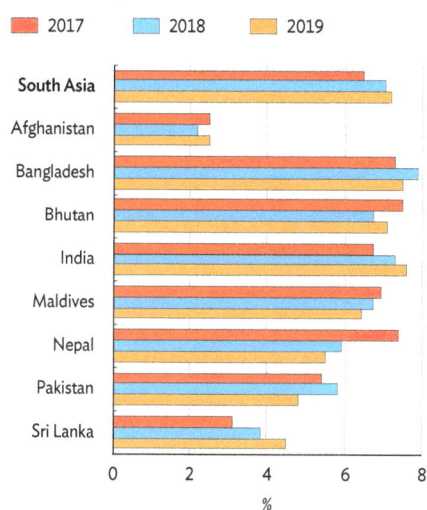

Source: *Asian Development Outlook* database.

The subregional assessment and prospects were written by Lei Lei Song. The section on Bangladesh was written by Jyotsana Varma, Soon Chan Hong, Md. Golam Mortaza, and Barun K. Dey; India by Abhijit Sen Gupta; Pakistan by Guntur Sugiyarto, Farzana Noshab, and Ali Khadija; and other economies by Abdul Hares Halimi, Savindi Jayakody, Manbar Singh Khadka, Utsav Kumar, Kanokpan Lao-Araya, Masato Nakane, Tshewang Norbu, David Oldfield, Lei Lei Song, and Hasitha Wickremasinghe, as well as consultants Abdulla Ali, Remedios Baes-Espineda, Macrina Mallari, and Danileen Parrel. Authors are in the Central and West Asia and South Asia departments of ADB.

following adjustment to a modernized tax regime and with banks focusing on new lending while resolving problem loans. Growth is seen to edge up to 7.6% in FY2019 as investment further improves in response to higher capacity utilization.

Growth rates in the other seven South Asian economies require revision. In FY2018 (ending mid-2018), growth in Bangladesh, Nepal, and Pakistan exceeded *ADO 2018* projections. Bangladesh achieved its highest GDP growth rate in more than 4 decades on strong consumption and public investment. Nepal performed better than expected with sustained consumption and more fixed investment. Growth in Pakistan was driven by robustly higher agricultural output, an uptick in industry, and sustained expansion in services. Growth forecasts vary for these three economies in FY2019, with growth in Bangladesh sustaining at 7.5%, the forecast for Nepal retained, and the projection for Pakistan downgraded as it deals with fiscal and external imbalances. Growth in Bhutan in FY2018 is now estimated below the *ADO 2018* projection as industry and tourism underperformed forecasts, and the growth forecast for FY2019 is revised down as construction on hydropower plants continues to lag earlier expectations. The growth forecast for Maldives is retained for 2018 but reduced for 2019 with tourism expected to weaken. Drought lowers the projection for growth in Afghanistan in 2018, but the forecast for 2019 is unchanged. For Sri Lanka, this *Update* lowers growth projections for both 2018 and 2019 as the government implements structural adjustment, supported by the International Monetary Fund, to lift fiscal performance toward sustaining higher growth.

Inflationary pressures in South Asia are rising, largely because output gaps are closing and currencies weakening (Figure 3.3.2). The projection for average inflation in 2018 is revised up slightly from 4.7% in *ADO 2018* to 4.9% in line with a higher inflation forecast of 5.0% for India on higher oil prices and currency depreciation. Elsewhere, inflation is as projected or lower than projected in *ADO 2018*, with most benefitting from a good monsoon. The forecast for average inflation in 2019 is revised slightly higher, from 5.1% to 5.2%, because of projected acceleration in Pakistan with revised energy prices, currency depreciation, and some tax increases intended to alleviate fiscal and external imbalances.

The combined current account deficit is now forecast to equal 2.9% of subregional GDP in both years, revised up from 2.5% in 2018 and 2.6% in 2019 as almost every economy in South Asia is now expected to have a wider current account deficit than forecast in *ADO 2018* because of high oil prices, import dependence, slowing external demand, and robust domestic demand (Figure 3.3.3). Externally financed investment drives especially large deficits in Bhutan and Maldives.

3.3.2 Inflation, South Asia

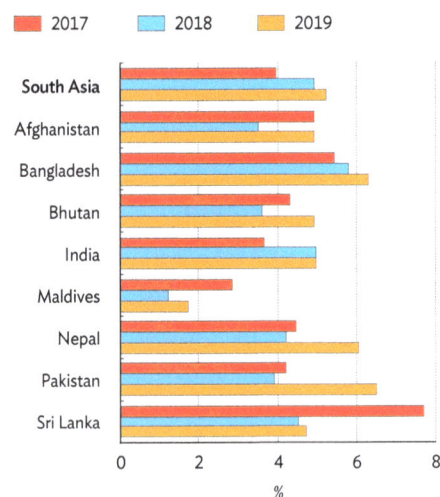

Source: *Asian Development Outlook* database.

3.3.3 Current account balance, South Asia

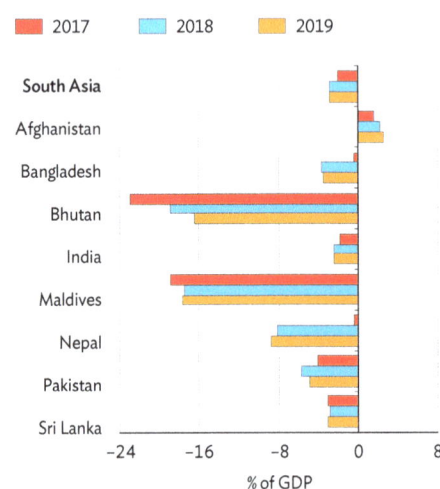

Source: *Asian Development Outlook* database.

Bangladesh

Growth in fiscal year 2018 (FY2018, ended 30 June 2018) expanded robustly on stronger consumption and public investment spending coupled with a revival in exports. Inflation nevertheless remained in check. A surge in imports widened the current account deficit by more than anticipated despite a strong rebound in remittances. For FY2019, this *Update* projects continued high growth, moderately higher inflation, and a slight narrowing of the current account deficit.

Updated assessment

Bangladesh achieved in FY2018 its fastest economic expansion since 1974 as GDP growth reached 7.9%, a marked improvement from a year earlier (Figure 3.3.4). Growth was led by a steep rise in private consumption as remittances recovered and by higher public investment, which increased to the equivalent of 8.0% of GDP from 7.4% a year earlier. This outcome reflected strong progress in implementing large public sector projects, notably the Padma Bridge and Dhaka Metro Rail. Even as exports revived from a weak performance, a surge in imports made net exports a larger drag on growth than a year earlier.

On the supply side, growth was driven by faster-than-expected 12.1% expansion in industry, mainly in construction and manufacturing, with output from large and small manufacturers alike growing more briskly. Construction benefited from markedly higher investment, including housing. Agriculture growth was, at 4.2%, higher than a year earlier as the authorities quickly moved to offset flood-induced losses to the summer and monsoon rice crops by supplying seedlings and extending other support services to farmers. The result was a bountiful winter crop. At 6.4%, growth in services was lower than a year earlier with slowing in transport, financial, education, and health services.

Inflation edged up to average 5.8% in FY2018 from 5.4% in the previous year. Price pressure came from higher domestic rice prices following crop losses, rising global oil prices, upward adjustments to administered domestic prices for natural gas and electricity, and depreciation of the Bangladesh taka. Inflation declined to 5.5% year on year in June 2018 as food inflation, which had exceeded 7.0% for many months, fell to 6.0% with the benefit of large rice imports in the second half of the year and the arrival to market of a good winter rice crop. Nonfood inflation rose to 4.9%, mainly reflecting currency depreciation (Figure 3.3.5).

Broad money growth slowed to 9.2% in FY2018 from 10.9% a year earlier, well below the monetary program target of 13.3% as net foreign assets declined (Figure 3.3.6). Private credit growth accelerated to 16.9% from 15.7% a year earlier, slightly exceeding the target. With sales of national savings certificates financing much of the budget deficit, net bank credit to the government declined by 2.5%, holding expansion in domestic

3.3.4 Demand-side contributions to growth

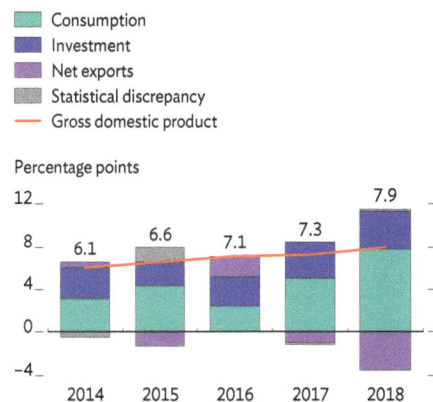

- Consumption
- Investment
- Net exports
- Statistical discrepancy
- Gross domestic product

Percentage points

Note: Years are fiscal years ending on 30 June of that year.
Sources: Bangladesh Bureau of Statistics. http://www.bbs
.gov.bd; ADB estimates.

3.3.5 Monthly inflation

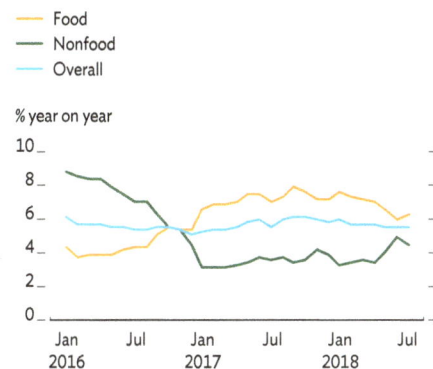

- Food
- Nonfood
- Overall

% year on year

Source: Bangladesh Bank. 2018. *Monthly Economic Trends.*
August. https://www.bb.org.bd.

3.3.6 Contributions to broad money growth

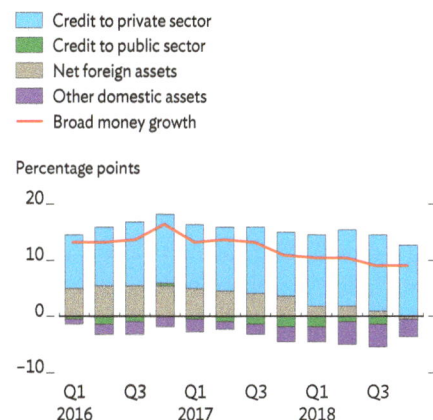

- Credit to private sector
- Credit to public sector
- Net foreign assets
- Other domestic assets
- Broad money growth

Percentage points

Q = quarter.
Sources: Bangladesh Bank. 2018. *Major Economic
Indicators, Monthly Update.* August. https://www.bb.org.bd;
ADB estimates.

credit slightly below target. Rapid import growth during the year, despite currency deprecation, reduced net foreign assets, slowing growth in reserve money and putting pressure on bank liquidity. In response, Bangladesh Bank, the central bank, reduced in April the required cash reserve ratio by 1.0 percentage point to 5.5% and lowered the repo rate by 75 basis points to 6.00% to support growth in the private sector and forestall any marked increase in bank lending rates (Figure 3.3.7).

Budget revenue in FY2018 was again less than planned as collections of income and value-added taxes fell short of budget targets. Nevertheless, revenue increased to equal 11.5% of GDP from 10.2% in FY2017. Spending climbed to 16.5% of GDP from 13.6%, mainly reflecting a sharp 76% increase in spending on the Annual Development Program, which rose to equal 6.6% of GDP from 4.3% in FY2017. The shortfall in revenue was offset by economies in spending that held the budget deficit under 5.0% of GDP, as planned, successfully keeping the ratio of public debt to GDP broadly stable. Domestic sources financed 58% of the deficit.

Of Bangladesh's 47 nonfinancial state-owned enterprises, 34 earned a combined profit of $1.6 billion in the first 10 months of FY2018, and the remainder incurred a combined loss of $472 million, yielding a net profit of $1.1 billion, compared with a net profit of $1.2 billion in the whole of FY2017 (Figure 3.3.8). The net profit of the Bangladesh Petroleum Corporation fell to $487 million from $1.1 billion in FY2017 with the rise in global oil prices. Notably, domestic fuel prices had not been lowered earlier in line with global oil prices to allow the corporation to earn profits to put toward offsetting losses on sales and repaying debt incurred when global oil prices had been very high. The net profit of the Bangladesh Telecommunications Regulatory Commission rose to $753 million from $504 million on 4G spectrum auctions. That of the Bangladesh Oil, Gas, and Mineral Resources Corporation increased only slightly to $118 million from $116 million because revenue from a 22.7% increase in domestic gas prices for all users went mostly to higher production costs. The Bangladesh Power Development Board was able to cut its net loss sharply to $152 million from $560 million in FY2017, mainly thanks to retail electricity tariffs 6.7% higher.

Government spending on subsidies rose in FY2018 to $2.7 billion, equal to 1.0% of GDP, from $2.0 billion or 0.8% a year earlier (Figure 3.3.9). No subsidy was paid to the Bangladesh Petroleum Corporation for a third consecutive year as pricing policy allowed profits. The Bangladesh Power Development Board received a subsidy of $438 million, down from $527 million in the previous year. Agriculture continued to receive the largest subsidy, the allocation to support farmers' fertilizer, diesel, and electricity inputs having been increased to $731 million from $456 million.

3.3.7 Interest rates

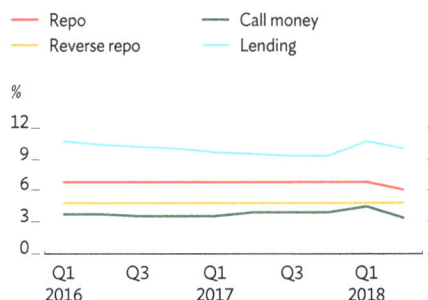

Q = quarter.
Sources: Bangladesh Bank. 2018. *Major Economic Indicators, Monthly Update*. August. https://www.bb.org.bd; ADB estimates.

3.3.8 Profits and losses of state-owned enterprises

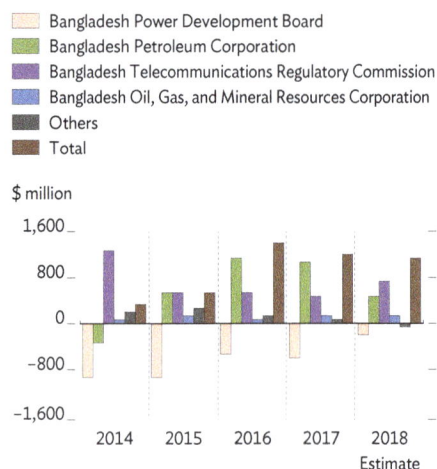

Note: Years are fiscal years ending on 30 June of that year.
Sources: Ministry of Finance. *Bangladesh Economic Review 2018*. https://www.mof.gov.bd; ADB estimates.

3.3.9 Government subsidies

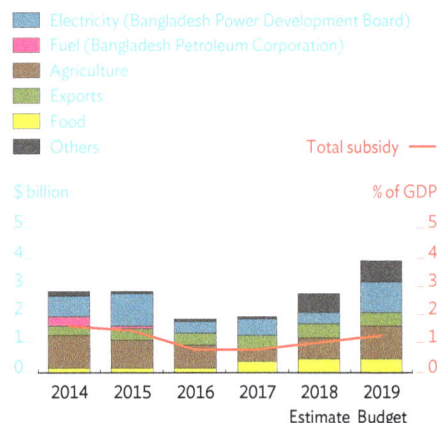

Note: Years are fiscal years ending on 30 June of that year.
Sources: Ministry of Finance. *Medium Term Macroeconomic Policy Statement from 2018–19 to 2020–21*. https://www.mof.gov.bd; ADB estimates.

Exports grew by 6.4% in FY2018, recovering from 1.7% growth a year earlier (Figure 3.3.10). Growth in garment exports—which accounted last year for about 80% of all exports—rebounded from nil to 8.8% mainly on stronger demand from the European Union as sales to the US increased by only 2.3%. Other exports declined by 7.0% with lower demand abroad for engineering products, petroleum byproducts, and leather goods.

Import growth surged to 25.2% in FY2018 from 9.0% a year earlier. The sharp expansion reflected higher demand for capital goods, export-related intermediate goods, and food grains to offset large crop losses, together accounting for 88% of the rise (Figure 3.3.11). The pickup in imports of capital goods reflected the authorities' medium-term priority on infrastructure that facilitates rapid economic growth.

Remittances grew robustly by 17.3% to reach $15.0 billion in FY2018, after declining in the previous 2 years, the rebound underpinned by an increase in the number of workers going abroad in the past few years, taka depreciation, and measures to foster money transfer through official channels.

The surge in import demand doubled the trade deficit to $18.3 billion in FY2018, with net deficits in services and primary income also increasing. Despite higher remittances, the current account deficit thus ballooned to $9.8 billion, equal to 3.6% of GDP, from just $1.3 billion or 0.5% a year earlier (Figure 3.3.12).

Net capital and financial inflows increased to $9.4 billion in FY2018. While net foreign direct investment was unchanged from a year earlier at $1.6 billion, the bulk of financing came from $4.8 billion in medium- and long-term loans, plus $1.6 billion from commercial banks and a $0.7 billion net increase in trade credit and other short-term financing. Nevertheless, the larger current account deficit drained $600 million from central bank foreign exchange reserves, leaving $32.9 billion at the end of June 2018, or cover for 5.6 months of imports of goods and services projected for FY2019 (Figure 3.3.13).

The taka depreciated by 3.7% against the US dollar in FY2018 with the surge in import payments in conjunction with a central bank decision to leave rate determination more to the market (Figure 3.3.14).

Prospects

GDP growth in FY2019 is forecast at 7.5%. Private consumption is likely to remain buoyant as remittances continue to recover. Growth in public investment is expected to ease but remain another key growth driver, and private investment may step up slightly as the central bank reaches out to small enterprises and agriculture. Finally, exports are expected to expand at a steady pace despite somewhat slower growth in Bangladesh's main trade partners.

3.3.10 Exports

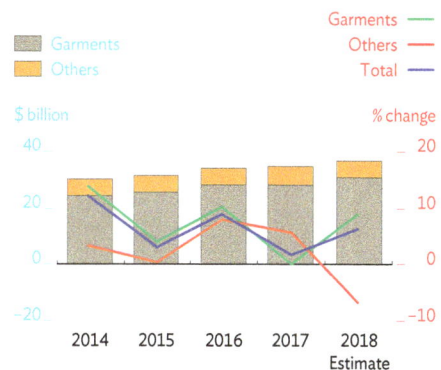

Note: Years are fiscal years ending on 30 June of that year.
Sources: Export Promotion Bureau; Bangladesh Bank. http://www.bb.org.bd; ADB estimates.

3.3.11 Imports

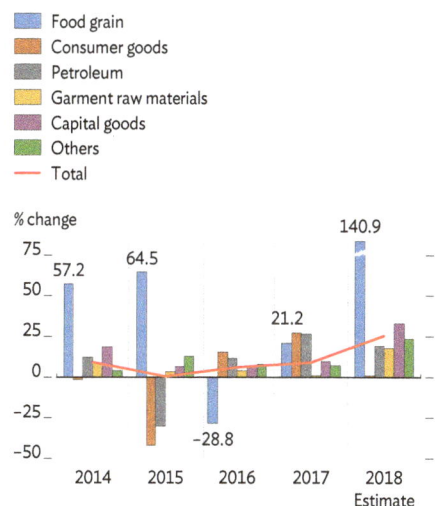

Note: Years are fiscal years ending on 30 June of that year.
Source: Bangladesh Bank. https://www.bb.org.bd.

3.3.12 Current account components

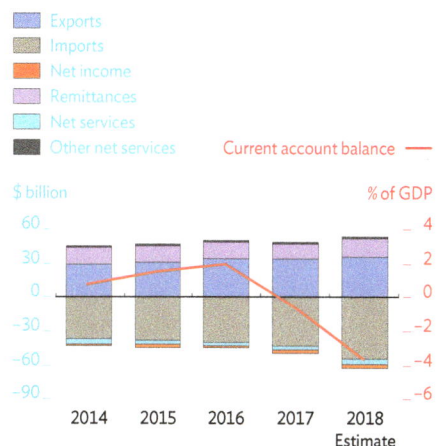

Note: Years are fiscal years ending on 30 June of that year.
Sources: Bangladesh Bank. https://www.bb.org.bd; ADB estimates.

Agriculture growth in FY2019 is expected at 2.9%, taking into account the high base set in FY2018 (Figure 3.3.15). Industry growth is projected at 11.5% as private consumption remains strong and exports expand. Expansion in services, at 6.2%, will mirror trends in agriculture and industry.

Inflation is expected at 6.3% in FY2019, unchanged from the *ADO 2018* projection, with higher global fuel prices, currency depreciation, and upward adjustments to natural gas and electricity prices.

The central bank monetary policy statement for the first half of FY2019 prioritized balancing inflation and output risks and promoting financial and external stability. It kept the main policy repo rate unchanged at 6.0%, while the monetary program set private sector credit expansion at 16.8%, essentially unchanged from a year earlier. The central bank aims to provide adequate credit to agriculture, manufacturing, and small and medium-sized enterprises, using intensive and intrusive supervision to ensure that credit flows are for productive use. To improve the monetary transmission mechanism and financial stability, it will continue its efforts to move toward a pricing system for national savings certificates linked to market rates. The central bank will also help banks reduce their nonperforming loans.

The FY2019 budget targets revenue equal to 13.4% of GDP, up from 11.5% a year earlier (Figure 3.3.16). Revenue is projected to grow by 30.8% and spending by 25.1%, with current spending 29.8% higher mostly to pay higher interest, subsidies, incentives, and current transfers. The Annual Development Program is envisaged growing by 16.6%, down from a year earlier with the higher base effect. Total expenditure is slated to equal 18.3% of GDP, up from 16.5% a year earlier. The deficit is targeted at 4.9% of GDP.

Few major revenue-enhancing tax measures are proposed. Increased revenue is seen coming largely from better compliance thanks to systems automation and the simplification and clarification of the tax code and regulations. Attaining the revenue target will be a challenge, however, without implementing the new value-added tax. As in the past, expenditure control will compensate for any revenue shortfall to meet the targeted deficit.

The government's subsidy bill in FY2019 is expected to increase to $3.9 billion, or 1.3% of GDP, from $2.7 billion, or 1.0% of GDP in FY2018, mainly to allocate more to electric power and agriculture (Figure 3.3.9). Power subsidies are increased to $1.1 billion toward buying natural gas. The agriculture subsidy is raised to $1.1 billion from $731 million, and the food subsidy to $482 million from $474 million, while the export subsidy is unchanged at $482 million.

3.3.13 Foreign exchange reserves

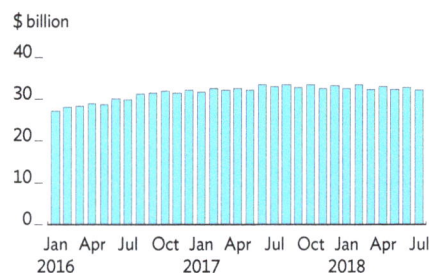

Source: Bangladesh Bank. 2018. *Major Economic Indicators, Monthly Update.* August. https://www.bb.org.bd.

3.3.14 Exchange rates

Source: Bangladesh Bank. 2018. *Monthly Economic Trends.* August. https://www.bb.org.bd.

3.3.15 GDP growth

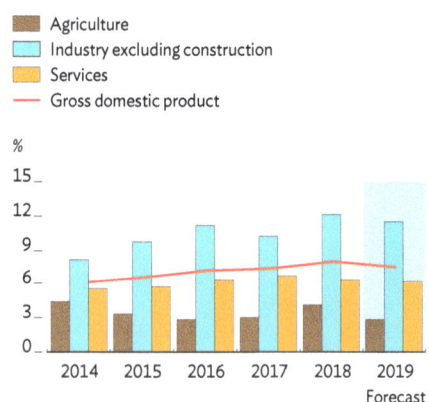

Note: Years are fiscal years ending on 30 June of that year.
Sources: Bangladesh Bureau of Statistics. http://www.bbs.gov.bd; ADB estimates.

Export growth is projected to ease to 6.0% in FY2019 from 6.4% in the previous year as growth moderates in the major industrial countries, especially in the important European and US markets for garment exports, and as global uncertainty and trade tensions mount. Central bank flexibility on the exchange rate should make the forecast attainable.

Growth in imports is projected to slow to 12.0% in FY2019 with the higher base effect. Growth in imports of intermediate goods is expected to moderate after last year's substantial inventory building, but import payments will rise on higher global oil prices and real demand, and with the leasing of two floating storage and regasification units for liquefied natural gas. Capital goods imports are projected to grow moderately in tandem with budgeted allocations to the Annual Development Program. Food grain imports are likely to slow because prospects for domestic crops are good and the import duty on rice is being revived.

Sharply slowing import growth will moderate the widening of the trade deficit to 23.8% in FY2019 from 92.8% a year earlier. Remittances are forecast to strengthen by 16.0% to $17.4 billion on top of the large improvement in FY2018. Against continued sizeable deficits in services and primary income, larger remittances are expected to shrink the current account deficit slightly to $10.8 billion, or 3.5% of GDP. While the current account deficit relative to GDP is expected to decline slightly in FY2019, its absolute size of over $10 billion is new to Bangladesh.

The outlook is subject to downside risks, notably from inability to rein in import demand as projected, failure to mobilize appropriate financing to cover the large projected current account deficit, an unexpectedly large increase in global oil prices, or unfavorable weather.

3.3.1 Selected economic indicators, Bangladesh (%)

	2018		2019	
	ADO 2018	Update	ADO 2018	Update
GDP growth	7.0	7.9	7.2	7.5
Inflation	6.1	5.8	6.3	6.3
Current acct. bal. (share of GDP)	−2.2	−3.6	−1.9	−3.5

Note: Years are fiscal years ending on 30 June of that year.

Sources: Bangladesh Bureau of Statistics. http://www.bbs.gov.bd; ADB estimates.

3.3.16 Fiscal indicators

- Capital spending and net lending
- Current spending
- Development spending
- Domestic financing
- Foreign financing
- Tax revenue
- Nontax revenue

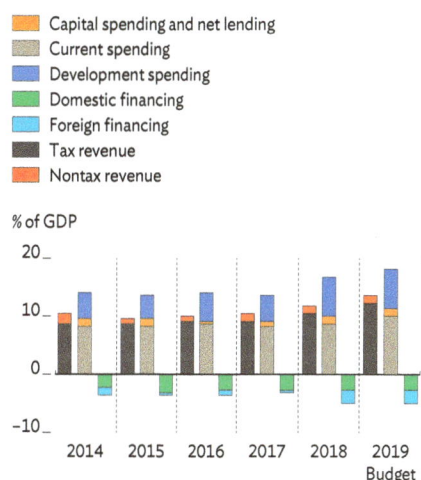

Note: Years are fiscal years ending on 30 June of that year.
Sources: Ministry of Finance. *Annual Budget 2018–19, Budget in Brief*. https://www.mof.gov.bd; ADB estimates.

India

Growth in the first quarter of fiscal year 2018 (FY2018, ending 31 March 2019) strengthened sharply from a year earlier and is on track to meet the *ADO 2018* forecast. An uptick in oil prices motivates a marginal increase to the inflation forecast even as monetary policy tightens. The forecast for the current account deficit is revised up on higher oil prices. Growth and inflation forecasts for FY2019 are maintained, but the current account deficit is now forecast a bit wider to accommodate higher domestic demand and oil prices.

Updated assessment

GDP grew by a strong 8.2% year on year in the first quarter of FY2018 after recording healthy 7.7% expansion in the fourth quarter of FY2017 (Figure 3.3.17). Robust growth was aided by a favorable base effect as economic growth in the first quarter of FY2017 had decelerated to a 3-year low in response to demonetization in late 2016 of large bills and with production rescheduling ahead of the introduction in July 2017 of a goods and services tax (GST). The upward trend in growth reflected improved domestic demand, reduced drag from net exports, and a steady revival in industry (Figure 3.3.18).

Private consumption expanded by 8.6% in the first quarter of FY2018, likely supported by recovery in rural demand as the effects of demonetization waned and as the government hiked procurement prices for crops by an unusually high margin to bolster rural incomes and provided an impetus to rural housing. Growth in public consumption remained healthy at 7.6%.

Investment grew by 10%, recording a second consecutive quarter of double-digit growth. This probably stemmed primarily from heightened government capital expenditure on new infrastructure. Also aiding investment growth is improved business environment reflected in India having climbed 30 positions in a ranking on the ease of doing business.

Aided by robust winter crop production, agriculture grew by 5.3%. Livestock, forestry, and fisheries, which contribute nearly 45% of agricultural output, grew by 8.1%. A low base and the resolution of GST teething problems helped manufacturing grow by 13.5% in the first quarter of FY2018, its highest rate in more than 2 years. Production of food, motor vehicles, and metal products remained buoyant. The government's push for affordable housing and new infrastructure saw construction grow by 8.7%.

Growth in services moderated a bit from the fourth quarter of FY2017 to 7.3%. Growth in trade, transport, and communication services remained tepid at 6.7% as these activities continued to adjust to the GST and the formalization it brought. Financial services received a fillip as more credit was extended to business, though deposit growth remained subdued. Robust growth in corporate business

3.3.17 Demand-side contributions to growth

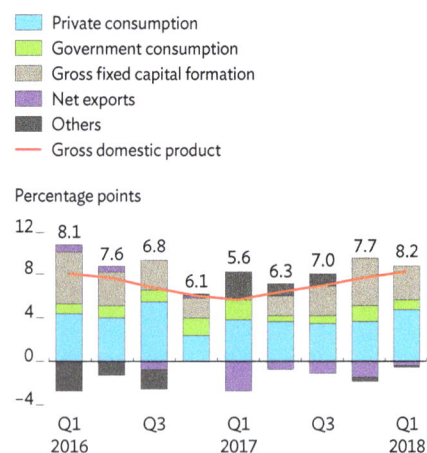

- Private consumption
- Government consumption
- Gross fixed capital formation
- Net exports
- Others
- Gross domestic product

Percentage points

Q = quarter.

Note: Years are fiscal years ending on 31 March of the next year.

Sources: Ministry of Statistics and Programme Implementation. http://www.mospi.nic.in; CEIC Data Company (accessed 1 September 2018).

3.3.18 Supply-side contributions to growth

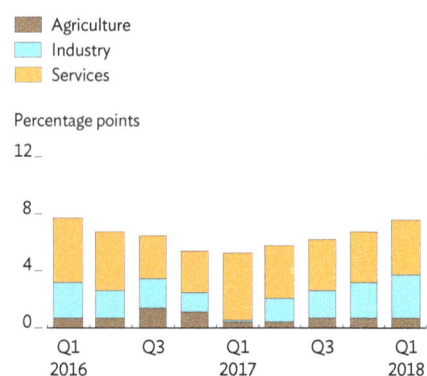

- Agriculture
- Industry
- Services

Percentage points

Q = quarter.

Notes: Years are fiscal years ending on 31 March of the next year. Sectoral output valued at basic prices.

Sources: Ministry of Statistics and Programme Implementation. http://www.mospi.nic.in; CEIC Data Company (accessed 1 September 2018).

services is likely to have aided growth in professional services. Public expenditure on services recorded 9.9% growth, helped by strong growth in current expenditure.

Inflation averaged 3.6% in FY2017, steadily inching up during the year (Figure 3.3.19). This trend continued in FY2018 with inflation averaging 4.5% in the first 5 months. Food inflation remained benign in this period as prices rose only moderately for vegetables and meat and fell for pulses, which suffered a glut. Core inflation rose considerably on base effects and steadily rising prices for non-tradeable services like health care, education, and recreation, likely indicating supply bottlenecks.

The Reserve Bank of India, the central bank, responded to elevated core inflation, headline inflation above the medium-term target of 4%, and a closing output gap with two rate hikes of 25 basis points each in June and August 2018, bringing the repo rate to 6.50% (Figure 3.3.20).

Bank health continues to be a concern as the percentage of stressed loans, both nonperforming and restructured, remained elevated at 12.1% in March 2018 (Figure 3.3.21). The quality of loans for infrastructure, engineering goods, and gems and jewelry continued to deteriorate while sectors such as food processing and textiles improved. The government is pursuing initiatives to improve bank health. Many companies have entered insolvency resolution, and several are heading for liquidation, thereby improving the culture of corporate repayment. The central bank introduced a corrective action framework in 2017, under which 11 public banks are subjected to remedial action plans to prevent further capital erosion.

Nonfood credit growth improved from less than 7.0% in FY2017 to 12.6% in April–August 2018 (Figure 3.3.22). This largely reflected a revival in credit to services like transport operators, traders, and nonbank financial companies, even as credit to industry and infrastructure remained muted. Credit for housing grew by 15.7% as the government focused on affordable housing.

The schedule for medium-term fiscal consolidation was lengthened by a year such that the central government now targets a budget deficit narrowed to the equivalent of 3.3% of GDP in the current fiscal year (Figure 3.3.23). This revision was intended to avoid endangering recovery and reprising depressed growth experienced a year earlier. The deficit in April–July 2018 stood at 86.5% of the full-year target, improving on last year, when it was 92.4%.

Personal income tax collection grew by a healthy 11.4%, signaling improved compliance. Corporate tax collection remained anemic, however, possibly reflecting reduced tax rates for small and medium-sized companies. Growth in indirect tax revenue was buoyant with robust collection of GST revenue. Monthly GST revenue has picked up since early 2018 but remains short of achieving budgeted targets.

3.3.19 Monthly inflation

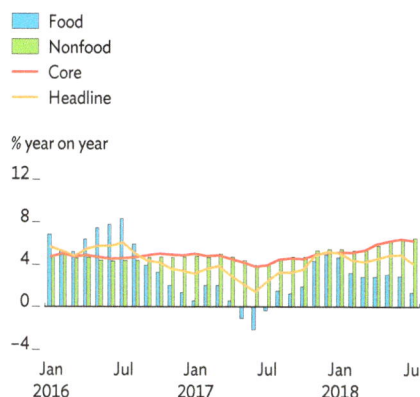

Sources: CEIC data company (accessed 7 September 2018); ADB estimates.

3.3.20 Policy interest rates

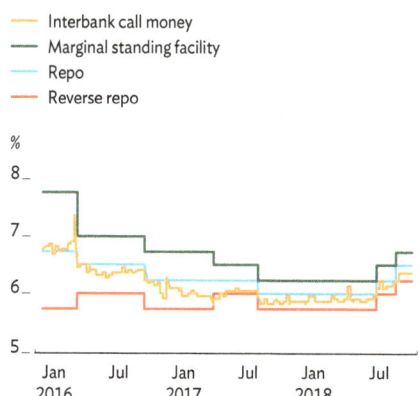

Sources: Bloomberg; CEIC Data Company (accessed 7 September 2018).

3.3.21 Stressed advances ratio

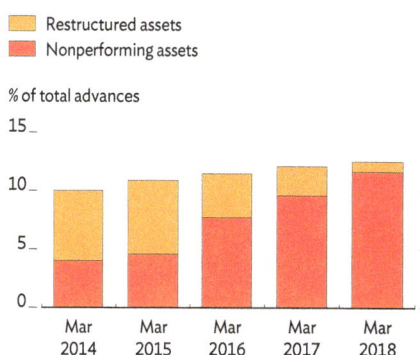

Note: March 2018 disaggregated data is based on June 2018 Financial Stability Report.
Source: Reserve Bank of India. http://www.rbi.org.in.

The central government's focus on building infrastructure pushed capital expenditure growth to 17.4% in April–July 2018 while current expenditure grew by only 9.1%. Capital expenditure increases were notably large for roads and railways.

The trade deficit widened to $80.4 billion in April–August 2018, with the July deficit the highest in 5 years (Figure 3.3.24). Imports grew by 17.3% to $216.4 billion, with high global oil prices and a modest uptick in volume pushing oil imports 53.6% higher than in April–August 2017. Gold imports contracted by 1.4%, possibly because rising interest rates generated attractive alternatives for parking wealth. Imports other than oil or gold grew by 8.9%, buoyed by engineering goods, electronic goods, chemicals, and textiles. Robust growth in imports of capital goods could indicate improved growth momentum.

Exports grew by 16.1% to $136.1 billion. Despite a decline in volume, the value of petroleum exports increased, benefitting from higher oil prices. Exports other than oil grew by 9.5% with healthy growth in textiles, pharmaceuticals, aluminum products, and computer hardware. Exports of gems and jewelry contracted with subdued demand.

The surplus in services grew by 2.1% in the first quarter of FY2018. Strong growth in transport and travel service imports pushed overall imports of services up by 6.8%. Exports of services grew at a tamer 4.9%, though export growth in telecommunication, travel, and software services remained strong, as did remittance inflows. A significant widening of the trade deficit brought the current account deficit to the equivalent of 2.4% of GDP in the first quarter of FY2018, up from 1.9% in the fourth quarter of FY2017.

Foreign direct investment inflows grew by a strong 8.0% to $16.0 billion in the first 4 months of FY2018 as guidelines were liberalized and the ease of doing business improved. Portfolio investment witnessed a net outflow of $7.5 billion, by contrast, with yields rising in the advanced economies and concerns about the impact of high oil prices on India's macroeconomic fundamentals (Figure 3.3.25). As a result, the Indian rupee depreciated by more than 10% against the US dollar from the beginning of FY2018 to mid-September 2018 (Figure 3.3.26), even as reserve holdings declined by $25 billion to $400 billion (Figure 3.3.27). Several measures were introduced in mid-September to encourage external borrowings by corporations and portfolio inflows to stabilize the Indian rupee. Despite portfolio outflows, the Sensex index recorded stock market gains by 15.4% from April to August 2018, primarily driven by domestic investors (Figure 3.3.28). However, the Sensex weakened by 3.5% in the first half of September.

3.3.22 Bank credit

— Industry
— Services
— Personal loans
— Housing
— Nonfood

% year on year

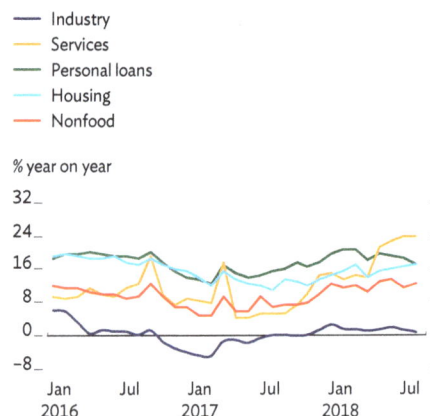

Sources: Bloomberg (accessed 7 September 2018); Centre for Monitoring Indian Economy.

3.3.23 Federal budget indicators

■ Tax revenue
■ Nontax revenue
■ Other revenue
■ Current expenditure
■ Capital expenditure
■ Deficit financing

% of GDP

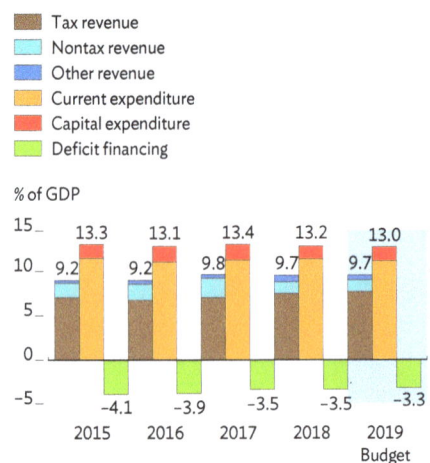

Note: Years are fiscal years ending on 31 March of the next year.
Source: Ministry of Finance Union Budget 2016–2018. http://indiabudget.nic.in.

Prospects

Forecasts in *ADO 2018* assumed healthy growth in the advanced economies, strong domestic consumption, some revival in private investment, and moderately higher oil prices. This *Update* considers a rebound that was stronger than expected in recent quarters, oil prices above forecasts, a weakening rupee, and rising trade protectionism globally.

Domestic demand will continue to drive growth in FY2018. Rural consumption will be aided by a normal monsoon and higher procurement prices. The rural economy aside from agriculture benefitted from higher budget allocations to a rural employment scheme, strengthened support for rural housing, and work on roads and irrigation projects. An index of rural consumer sentiment recorded in June 2018 its highest score since November 2017, reflecting improved income. Urban consumption is expected to be lackluster, however, as interest rates and oil prices rise and job prospects dampen.

Private investment revived with announcements of new private sector projects, inching up in the first half of 2018 (Figure 3.3.29). Improved demand has steadily tightened industry capacity utilization in recent quarters, which is likely to further spur investment. Progress on resolving corporate insolvency and bankruptcy cases is likely to improve credit flows and bolster investment. The central government has budgeted 10.1% growth in public investment for FY2018, and state governments 14.3%. However, strict fiscal constraints could force governments to cut back capital expenditure if fiscal pressures intensify. Net exports are expected to drag on growth somewhat, with imports likely to expand more than exports.

A normal monsoon with improved spatial distribution foreshadows strong growth in agriculture. Manufacturing growth is expected to rebound from disruption caused by GST implementation last year. The Nikkei purchasing managers' index for manufacturing trended higher in April–August 2018 than in FY2017, boosted by domestic and export orders (Figure 3.3.30). Moreover, the central bank's business expectation index has registered positive annual growth for 6 consecutive quarters, indicating a healthy outlook for manufacturing. Construction is expected to benefit from the government's emphasis on affordable housing and other public works.

The purchasing managers' index for services has been positive for 6 months, reaching a recent peak in July. Leading indicators like sales of commercial vehicles and bank credit indicate some strengthening in transportation and financial services. Healthy growth prospects in the advanced economies augur well for tradeable services.

Little scope exists to stimulate growth with monetary policy—which is likely to remain tight with inflation averaging above the midpoint of the target band, inflation

3.3.2 Selected economic indicators, India (%)

	2018		2019	
	ADO 2018	Update	ADO 2018	Update
GDP growth	7.3	7.3	7.6	7.6
Inflation	4.6	5.0	5.0	5.0
Current acct. bal. (share of GDP)	−2.2	−2.4	−2.4	−2.5

Note: Years are fiscal year ending on 31 March of the next year.
Source: ADB estimates.

3.3.24 Trade indicators

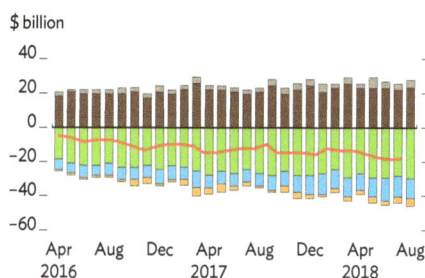

- Gold imports
- Oil imports
- Other imports
- Oil exports
- Other exports
- — Trade balance

Sources: CEIC Data Company (accessed 7 September 2018); ADB estimates.

expectations high, and the output gap closing—or with fiscal policy, given the government's commitment to fiscal consolidation and the headwinds developing from higher oil prices, weaker currency, and the impact of rising bond yields on India's debt burden.

On balance, GDP growth is expected to be 7.3% in FY2018, in line with the *ADO 2018* forecast, as strong growth in recent quarters is balanced in the coming quarters by higher oil prices and policy rates and anticipated spillover from global trade turmoil and slower global capital flows. Growth is expected to accelerate to 7.6% in FY2019, again in line with *ADO 2018*, with investment likely to improve in tandem with the balance sheets of banks and corporations as insolvency and bankruptcy cases are resolved. The successful implementation of GST is expected to provide additional revenue, enable more public investment, and bolster corporate productivity by removing internal obstacles to business.

Higher inflationary pressures since the middle of FY2017 will continue into FY2018. Rising global oil prices and a weaker currency will mean higher retail prices for petroleum products in FY2018 with little government intervention to control them. Core inflation is expected to continue to trend slightly higher as growth narrows the output gap and improved demand allows higher input costs to be increasingly passed on to consumers. Subdued food inflation in the first quarter of FY2018 notwithstanding, markedly higher procurement prices will likely push up retail prices, though by how much depends on the extent of procurement at the higher prices. Agricultural input costs inflated by higher fuel prices could also push up food inflation in FY2018. The forecast for average inflation is raised to 5.0% in FY2018 from 4.6% in *ADO 2018*.

The impact on inflation from the increase in procurement prices will likely fade in the second half of FY2019. Core inflation pressures are similarly seen abating as some recent reform initiatives reap growth dividends and improve potential GDP. A recent hike in policy rates by 50 basis points should help keep core inflation in check. Average inflation is forecast at 5.0% in FY2019, as in *ADO 2018*.

As pressure on inflation builds, the central bank is expected to maintain a tight policy to rein in inflation expectations. Having raised policy rates by a cumulative 50 basis points in the first half of FY2018, as noted above, the central bank is likely to wait and watch the effects of these hikes over the next few quarters. However, stress on the exchange rate and the resulting impact on inflation could warrant additional hikes in rest of FY2018.

The central government's fiscal deficit is expected to decline to the equivalent of 3.3% of GDP in FY2018, while the aggregate of state government deficits is targeted to ease to 2.6% of GDP. The smaller central government budget deficit comes mainly from slower growth in current expenditure,

3.3.25 Portfolio capital flows

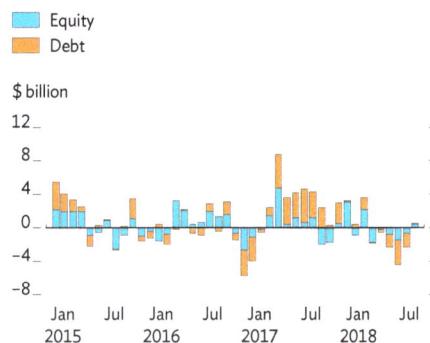

Source: Security and Exchange Board of India.

3.3.26 Exchange rates

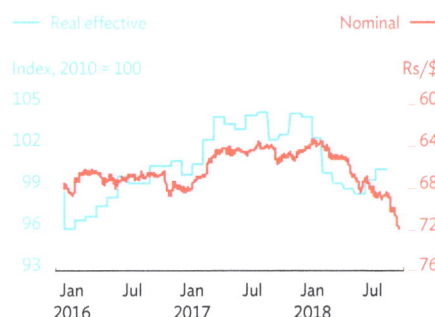

Source: Bloomberg (accessed 7 September 2018).

3.3.27 International reserves

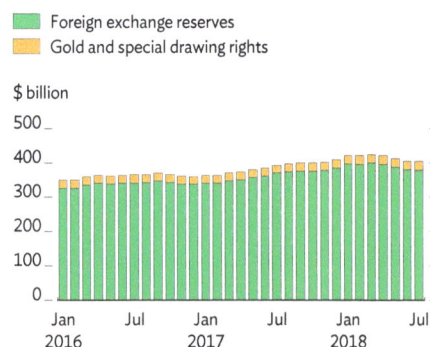

Source: CEIC Data Company (accessed 7 September 2018).

down to 10% in FY2018 from 15% in FY2017. Developing headwinds from high oil prices, currency depreciation, and a sluggish start to disinvestment could pose challenges to meeting the fiscal consolidation target. The fuel subsidy budgeted for FY2018 is only 1.9% higher than in FY2017 and may end up being exceeded, considering that the average price for imported oil in April–August 2018 was 29.2% higher than a year earlier. The increase in crop procurement prices is unlikely to have major fiscal implications because the budget envisaged a generous increase in the food subsidy. A recent reduction of GST tax rates for some commodities in the highest bracket at 28% could, while boosting aggregate demand, adversely affect GST revenue collection. Some of these impacts will be offset as compliance improves with the introduction of digital measures to facilitate interstate transactions.

Export growth is expected to remain strong in the first half of FY2018, benefitting from the low base following GST implementation in 2017, when exporting firms received input tax credits only after delays, causing shortages of working capital and weakening export performance. The increase in oil prices should help exports of refined petroleum grow at a healthy rate. Export competitiveness will likely be boosted by recent currency depreciation and successful measures to improve the ease of doing business. Exports are forecast to grow by 11% in FY2018, though any intensification of global trade conflict would pose a major downside risk. Import growth is expected to pick up as well, primarily on higher oil prices and domestic consumption. Gold imports may increase with revival in the rural economy. Higher domestic demand would similarly push up imports of electronics and capital goods, even as some commodity imports like ores and minerals may experience slower growth as price increases moderate. Imports are expected to grow by 12% in FY2018.

While robust growth in the advanced economies bodes well for exports of tradeable services, any significant raising of trade barriers in these markets would hit exports. Remittances from the advanced economies could be affected as well by trade turmoil, but remittances from oil-exporting countries will likely stay buoyant as oil prices remain high. The current account deficit is now expected to widen in FY2018 to the equivalent of 2.4% of GDP, beyond the 2.2% forecast in *ADO 2018*.

Healthy growth in the advanced economies, a more competitive exchange rate, and measures to make manufacturing more competitive are expected to boost exports by 10% in FY2019. At the same time, high oil prices and rising demand for imports as domestic demand picks up will push import growth to the same rate. The current account deficit is nevertheless forecast to widen a bit in FY2019 to 2.5% of GDP. Current account deficits should be financed comfortably with healthy capital flows, though some drawdown in reserves may be warranted.

3.3.28 Stock price indices

- Emerging markets excluding Asia
- MSCI AC AP excluding Japan
- Sensex

Index, 2017 = 100

Source: Bloomberg (accessed 7 September 2018).

3.3.29 New investment projects

Rs trillion

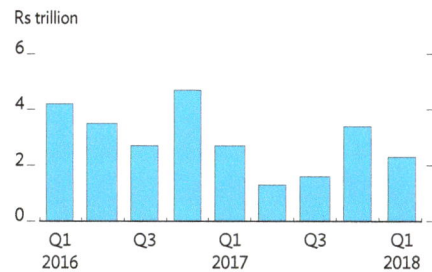

Q = quarter.
Note: Years are fiscal years ending on 31 March of the next year.
Source: Centre for Monitoring Indian Economy.

3.3.30 Purchasing managers' index

- Manufacturing
- Services

Index

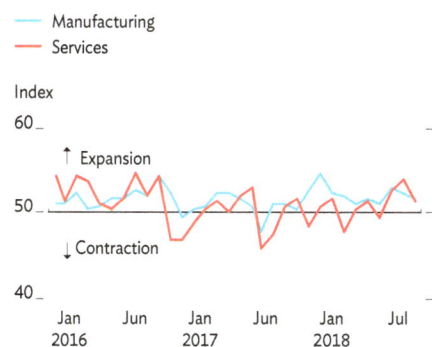

Note: Nikkei, Markit.
Source: Bloomberg (accessed 7 September 2018).

Pakistan

Growth accelerated in fiscal year 2018 (FY2018, ended 30 June 2018), and inflation remained moderate. However, expansionary fiscal policy widened budget and current account deficits, draining foreign exchange reserves. A newly elected government that took office on 18 August is formulating policies to deal with the twin deficits and implement its economic and social welfare agenda.

Updated assessment

Economic growth in FY2018 accelerated to 5.8%, the highest in 13 years, on robust agriculture, an uptick in industry, and sustained expansion in services (Figure 3.3.31). Agriculture growth at 3.8% nearly doubled that of a year earlier with marked increases in the major food crops, cotton, and livestock, which were made possible by government policy that improved the availability of inputs and credit. Industry growth climbed from 5.4% to 5.8% on faster expansion in manufacturing and mining, with construction sustaining its growth above 9%. Services, by far the largest sector, maintained growth at 6.4%, underpinned by strong expansion in wholesale and retail trade and a pickup in general government services.

Growth in private consumption in FY2018 slowed slightly from a year earlier to 6.3% but, with an 81.1% share of GDP, remained the largest contributor to growth (Figure 3.3.32). Government consumption picked up, bringing total consumption expenditure to 93.2% of GDP. Public sector fixed investment grew by 17.1% on top of 27.5% expansion in FY2017, reflecting higher spending on energy and infrastructure in connection with the China–Pakistan Economic Corridor (CPEC). This growth was, however, from a low base as public investment still provides only 5.4% of GDP.

Growth in private investment fell markedly to only 1.1% in FY2018 despite improved security and energy supply. The drop reflected business caution in light of worsening problems with the balance of payments and in anticipation of national elections in July 2018. Private investment is usually only about 10% of GDP, held down by inadequate infrastructure, a weak business environment, and concerns over macroeconomic instability. Public and private fixed investment, equaling 15.1% of GDP, hardly increased from a year earlier. While exports of goods and services increased markedly by volume, the contribution of net exports to growth remained negative.

Consumer price inflation averaged 3.9% in FY2018, slightly down from 4.2% a year earlier as agricultural output improved substantially and drove food inflation down to only 1.8%, or 2 percentage points lower than a year earlier. Nonfood inflation rose to average 5.4% on strong domestic demand, higher global commodity prices, and currency depreciation in the second half of the year. While headline and food inflation year on year

3.3.31 Supply-side contributions to growth

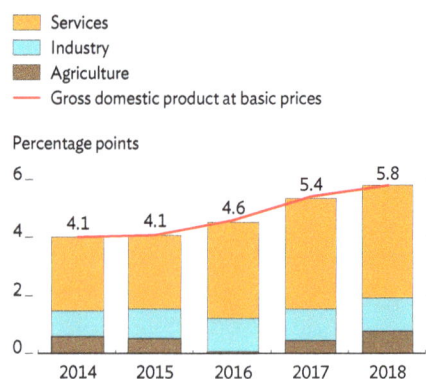

Note: Years are fiscal years ending on 30 June of that year.
Source: Ministry of Finance. *Pakistan Economic Survey 2017–18*. http://www.finance.gov.pk.

3.3.32 Demand-side contributions to growth

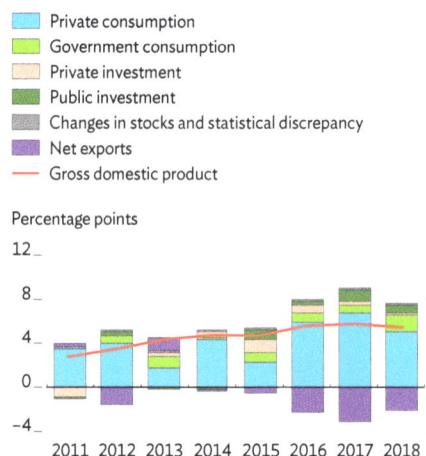

Note: Years are fiscal years ending on 30 June of that year.
Source: Ministry of Finance. *Pakistan Economic Survey 2017–18*. http://www.finance.gov.pk.

trended higher during the year, core inflation, which excludes food and energy, rose to 7.1% in June 2018 (Figure 3.3.33).

In response to continued strong import demand and a large decline in net foreign assets, the State Bank of Pakistan, the central bank, allowed greater market determination of the Pakistan rupee–US dollar exchange rate from December 2017 (Figure 3.3.34) and raised the policy rate by a cumulative 75 basis points to 6.50% in two steps by the end of FY2018, the first in January and the second in May (Figure 3.3.35).

The rupee depreciated by 15.3% against the US dollar in the 8 months to July 2018, and the average rate on new lending to the private sector increased by only 41 basis points to 7.83% by June. While the very large decline in net foreign assets held by the central bank in itself should have sharply reduced bank reserves and curtailed commercial bank lending, the central bank needed to provide PRs1.1 trillion of budgetary support to the government, which expanded reserve money by 14%. This expansion enabled commercial banks to meet credit demand with increased lending to the private sector by 15% and to state-owned enterprises by 30% (Figure 3.3.36).

The deficit in the general government budget, which consolidates federal and provincial accounts, surged to PRs2.3 trillion, which was equal to 6.6% of GDP in FY2018, up from 5.8% a year earlier and significantly higher than the budget target of 4.1% (Figure 3.3.37). Revenue grew by only 5.9% but fell as a percentage of GDP to 15.2% from 15.5% a year earlier. Tax revenue increased by 12.5% to equal 13.0% of GDP. However, nontax revenue declined sharply by 0.8 percentage points to 2.2% of GDP with marked declines in profit transfers from most sources but a modest increase from the central bank. Expenditure increased by 10.1% to equal 21.8% of GDP, up by 0.5 percentage points from FY2017. Current expenditure rose by 0.7 percentage points to 17.0% of GDP on higher interest payments, defense spending, and federal government subsidies. Development expenditure fell to 4.7% of GDP from 5.3% as current spending exceeded the budget and revenue fell short.

About two-thirds of the deficit was financed by domestic sources, and the remainder came from net external sources. Among the domestic sources, borrowing from the central bank amounted to the equivalent of 3.3% of GDP, while nonbank sources provided the equivalent of 1.0% of GDP. Net external financing increased from 1.7% of GDP to 2.3% as gross foreign borrowing rose by 14%. Public external debt and liabilities increased by $9.3 billion to $75.4 billion in FY2018, equal to 22.4% of GDP.

The current account deficit swelled to $18 billion, or 5.8% of GDP, significantly up from 4.1% in FY2017 (Figure 3.3.38). Exports revived to grow by 12.6% to $25 billion with increases in such traditional standbys as textiles, chemicals, leather, and food, but imports increased by 14.7% to $56 billion. This

3.3.33 Monthly inflation

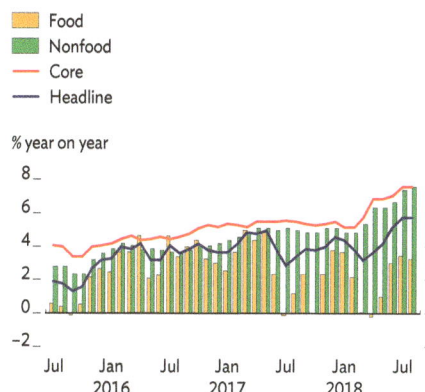

Source: State Bank of Pakistan. *Economic Data.* http://www.sbp.org.pk (accessed 11 September 2018).

3.3.34 Exchange rates

Source: State Bank of Pakistan. *Economic Data.* http://www.sbp.org.pk (accessed 11 September 2018).

3.3.35 Interest rates

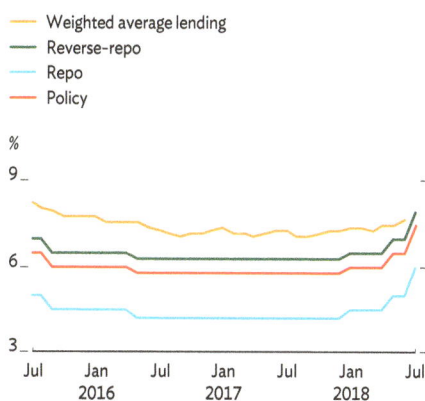

Sources: State Bank of Pakistan. *Economic Data.* http://www.sbp.org.pk (accessed 15 August 2018); *Monetary Policy Information Compendium July 2018.*

was partly purchases of machinery and transport equipment for the CPEC and other investments but also of intermediate goods for agriculture and the textile and metal industries—and of petroleum, which has accounted for just over a third of the increase in imports as the current account deficit escalated over the past 2 years. The deficit in services and primary income also increased substantially, by 19.0% to $11.2 billion. Workers remittances grew by a modest 1.4% but remained large at $19.6 billion (Figure 3.3.39).

Net inflows to the financial account grew by only $2 billion in FY2018 to reach $12 billion (Figure 3.3.40). As they were insufficient to finance the growing current account deficit, $6.3 billion in official foreign exchange reserves needed to be drawn down. By the end of FY2018, reserves had fallen to $9.9 billion, or only 2 months of import cover (Figure 3.3.41). Under greater market influence, the rupee depreciated by 16% to PRs121 per US dollar at the end of FY2018. After national elections in late July the rate stabilized at about PRs124 per dollar.

Worsening macroeconomic imbalances brought credit rating downgrades from *stable* to *negative* from Fitch Ratings in January 2018 and Moody's Investors Service in June.

Prospects

A newly elected government urgently needs to address the large budget and current account deficits, rising debt obligations, and falling foreign exchange reserves. This requires mobilizing substantial external financing to buy time for orderly reform to reduce the large external and domestic imbalances. Such resources may be acquired from bilateral and multilateral sources, the diaspora, and international capital markets. The key challenges are to adopt the right reforms and achieve good outcomes to sustain public support.

Assuming government success in obtaining financing, Pakistan has reasonable growth prospects for FY2019 on the strength of improved security and energy supply, continued investment in the CPEC and other initiatives, and recognition of the need to rein in deficits. Challenges to maintaining growth momentum are tighter monetary and fiscal policies to contain domestic demand, currency depreciation, and tension in the global trade environment. On balance, this *Update* projects GDP growth in FY2019 at 4.8%, down by 1.0 percentage point from last year.

On the supply side, water shortages in some areas are likely to restrain agricultural production. Growth in manufacturing and services will likely be affected by fiscal and monetary tightening. On top of dealing with macroeconomic imbalances, the new government has to undertake tariff reform to contain rapidly rising and potentially disruptive intercompany arrears in the energy sector—so called "circular debt" that exceeds

3.3.36 Credit to nongovernment entities

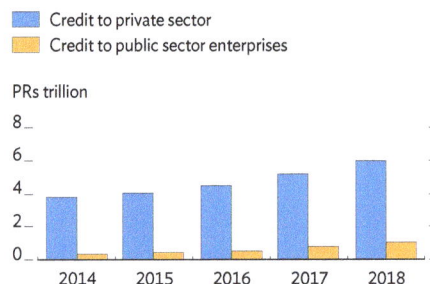

■ Credit to private sector
■ Credit to public sector enterprises

PRs trillion

Note: Years are fiscal years ending on 30 June of that year.
Sources: State Bank of Pakistan. *Monetary Policy Compendium July 2018; Monthly Statistical Bulletin August 2018.*

3.3.37 Government budget indicators

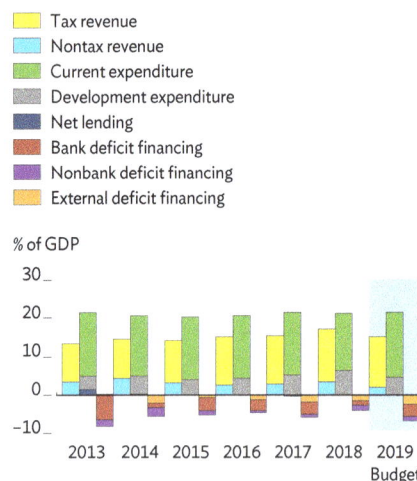

■ Tax revenue
■ Nontax revenue
■ Current expenditure
■ Development expenditure
■ Net lending
■ Bank deficit financing
■ Nonbank deficit financing
■ External deficit financing

% of GDP

Note: Years are fiscal years ending on 30 June of that year.
Sources: Ministry of Finance. *Budget in Brief FY2018–2019; Summary of Consolidated Federal & Provincial Budgetary Operations, July–June 2017–2018.*

3.3.38 Current account components

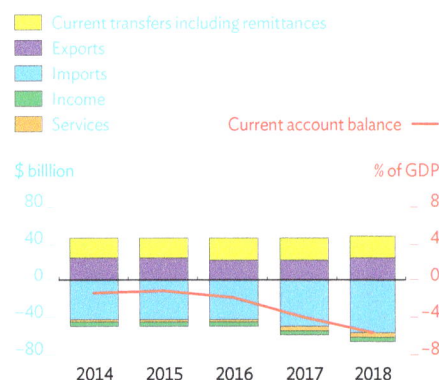

■ Current transfers including remittances
■ Exports
■ Imports
■ Income
■ Services
— Current account balance

$ billion   % of GDP

Note: Years are fiscal years ending on 30 June of that year.
Source: State Bank of Pakistan. *Economic Data.* http://www.sbp.org.pk (accessed 15 August 2018).

PRs1.4 trillion, or 5% of GDP. Gas prices were already raised by as much as 143% in September.

Average annual inflation is projected to reach 6.5% in FY2019 because of currency depreciation and elevated international oil prices. Inflation accelerated sharply for both food and other purchases in the first 2 months of FY2019, to 5.8% from 3.2% a year earlier. The central bank increased the policy rate by 100 basis points to reach to 7.50% in July 2018 in an effort to contain inflation. It is likely to raise the rate further as part of its monetary tightening.

The federal government budget for FY2019, written by the outgoing government and administered by it until the new government took office in August 2018, set a deficit target equal to 4.9% of GDP, much lower than the FY2018 outturn of 6.6% of GDP. Revenue was targeted at 16.3% of GDP, including a 17.7% increase in tax collection to be achieved mainly by improving tax administration. However, the budget reduced tax rates without any rationalization on the expenditure side. Expenditure was set at 21.2% of GDP. The budget called for 82% of deficit financing to come from domestic sources.

A revenue target equal to 16.3% of GDP in a slowing economy would be a tall order, considering that the revenue ratio has averaged 14.9% in the past 5 years. For FY2019, the new government presented supplementary budget proposals for parliamentary approval with the objectives of reducing development expenditure, introducing regulatory duties on selected luxury items to generate additional revenue, and reversing earlier tax cuts, while also withdrawing the petroleum development levy to ease the burden on the general public. The focus over the medium term must be to further enhance the revenue base to enable durable expansion in funding for social welfare and infrastructure that is necessary to lift growth.

The current account deficit is now expected to moderate from the equivalent of 5.8% GDP in FY2018 to 5.0% in FY2019 but exceed the *ADO 2018* projection of 4.5%. Exports are likely to continue to expand with the benefit of currency depreciation, fiscal incentives, and improved electricity supply and connectivity. However, slower growth in some advanced economies poses a risk to the forecast, as do rising trade tension and protectionism. Growth in import demand will be contained by some scaling back of budgeted expenditure, additional import duties and taxes under discussion in the government, tighter monetary policy, and a freer exchange rate. The current account balance will benefit as well from more stable prices for oil and other imported commodities. Import growth already slowed in the first 2 months of FY2019. Worker remittances will continue to cushion the current account, but any significant increase will depend on more effort to tap diaspora resources.

3.3.39 Remittances

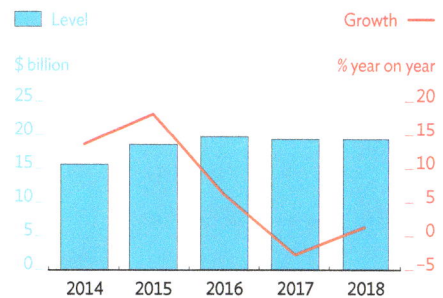

Note: Years are fiscal years ending on 30 June of that year.
Source: State Bank of Pakistan. *Economic Data.*
http://www.sbp.org.pk (accessed 15 August 2018).

3.3.40 Capital and financial account balance

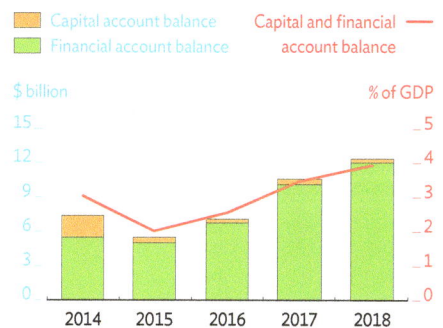

Note: Years are fiscal years ending on 30 June of that year.
Source: State Bank of Pakistan. *Economic Data.*
http://www.sbp.org.pk (accessed 15 August 2018).

3.3.41 Gross international reserves

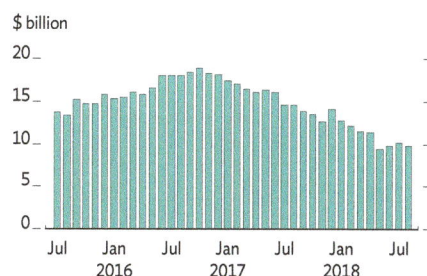

Source: State Bank of Pakistan. *Economic Data.*
http://www.sbp.org.pk (accessed 11 September 2018).

Growth sustainability will depend on how effectively the government manages the fiscal and current account deficits, and on its consistent implementation of policy to arrest the widening of imbalances and preserve macroeconomic stability. Recent actions to tighten monetary policy and allow exchange rate flexibility are costly but necessary. Further monetary tightening, stronger fiscal discipline, and decisive efforts to contain losses incurred by public sector enterprises would help address external imbalances and fiscal risks. Moreover, macroeconomic resilience and higher growth that is more sustainable and inclusive critically depends on vigilance in assuring that new external liabilities are phased in responsibly, fiscal consolidation is resumed over the medium term, and reform is accelerated to enhance the tax base, address distortionary tax incentives, and resolve the structural issues that undermine export competitiveness.

3.3.3 Selected economic indicators, Pakistan (%)

	2018		2019	
	ADO 2018	Update	ADO 2018	Update
GDP growth	5.6	5.8	5.1	4.8
Inflation	4.5	3.9	4.8	6.5
Current acct. bal. (share of GDP)	−4.9	−5.8	−4.5	−5.0

Note: Years are fiscal year ending on 30 June of that year.

Source: ADB estimates.

Other economies

Afghanistan

The forecast for GDP growth in 2018 is revised down from *ADO 2018* after drought in the first half of the year, the worst in decades, hit the wheat crop in the north and west. Production losses are estimated at 70% in the large rainfed area and 7% in irrigated fields. Reliable indicators for manufacturing and services are unavailable, but growth in both sectors is thought to have slowed because of political uncertainty before parliamentary elections in October 2018. Large attacks by the Taliban and the Islamic State in August and September seemed to counter earlier indications of progress in negotiating a peace settlement. A ministerial conference on 27–28 November 2018 in Geneva is expected to renew international commitment to Afghanistan's return to peace, development, and self-reliance.

The growth projection for 2019 is retained but with risks clearly on the downside. Both Iran and Pakistan, Afghanistan's main trade partners, are expected to experience slower growth in 2019, and business investors are likely to stay on the sidelines before a presidential election expected in April next year.

Average annual inflation in the first half of 2018 braked to only 0.8% from 6.1% a year earlier. Food prices were 0.5% lower, reversing unusually high food inflation in the first half of 2017, when border closings with Pakistan limited imports. With trade normalized and food inflation moderating in the second half of 2017, this base effect will fade, lifting inflation in the second half of 2018 to broadly align with price developments in Afghanistan's trade partners. On balance, inflation in 2018 is now expected lower than forecast in *ADO 2018*. The 2019 inflation projection is retained.

The afghani depreciated against the US dollar by 7.9% from January 2018 to mid-September. Gross foreign exchange reserves are little changed at almost $8.1 billion. Exports reportedly increased in the first half of the year, benefitting from expanded air connections with India for high-value goods such as fruit. Nevertheless, the current account surplus is forecast to narrow in 2018 because imports, which are 10 times exports, will grow faster than expected partly to bring in more food. The current account is now forecast to slip into deficit in 2019 with rising imports and declining grants. Cereal imports, mostly wheat flour, are expected to be 25% higher in 2018 and 2019 than the 5-year average. New US sanctions on Iran threaten to stymie Indian investment and work on Chabahar port, a strategic transit point for developing Afghanistan's global trade.

3.3.4 Selected economic indicators, Afghanistan (%)

	2018		2019	
	ADO 2018	Update	ADO 2018	Update
GDP growth	2.5	2.2	2.5	2.5
Inflation	5.0	3.5	5.0	5.0
Current acct. bal. (share of GDP)	3.3	0.4	2.6	−0.5

Source: ADB estimates.

Bhutan

GDP growth in fiscal year 2018 (FY2018, ended 30 June 2018) is estimated to have moderated slightly more than projected in *ADO 2018* in April. Official GDP data are not available, but indicators show industry and tourism performing below expectations. Hydropower production declined slightly by 2.9% because late monsoon rains meant weaker water flows. Hydropower plant construction slowed somewhat more than expected as two large projects approached completion and two others experienced delays because of contract and financial liquidity issues. International tourist arrivals fell from a high base set a year earlier, but foreign exchange earnings grew by 5.0%.

Credit to the private sector expanded by 16.9% in FY2018, mainly for housing construction and services, demonstrating buoyant domestic demand. Lending to priority sectors gained momentum as exhibited by 17.1% expansion in agriculture and 13.1% in manufacturing.

Higher growth is expected in FY2019 with electricity from the newly commissioned Mangdechhu Hydropower Plant, a rebound in generation from other plants, some improvement in tourism, and continued momentum in the private sector. The *ADO 2018* forecast for the year is slightly lower because an interim budget for the first half of FY2019, adopted because of a change in government, focused on wrapping up projects under the Eleventh Five-Year Plan, 2013–2018 rather than initiating new ones.

Inflation trended downward throughout FY2018 to average well below the April forecast, reflecting low wholesale price inflation in India averaging 3.5% and India's adoption in July 2017 of a value-added tax that markedly lowered prices for over 80% of Bhutan's imports. While food inflation remained at about 6%, nonfood inflation, which makes up 60% of the consumer price index, fell by half to 1.8%, substantially moderating overall inflation. Inflation is still projected to accelerate in FY2019 as the impact of Indian tax reform fades and domestic prices align with wholesale prices in India, but less than forecast in April.

Imports fell by 0.6% in the first 3 quarters of FY2018 from the year-earlier period on easing construction demand, while exports increased by 2.8%, markedly narrowing the trade deficit by 5.3%. Remittance inflows increased sharply by 51.3% in FY2018, as RemitBhutan, an online platform for foreign-currency accounts launched in September 2016, formalized fund transfers from abroad. With a smaller trade deficit and improved secondary income, the current account deficit is estimated to have narrowed in FY2018 well below the *ADO 2018* forecast. In anticipation of higher hydropower exports and continued slowing in hydropower plant construction, the current account deficit forecast for FY2019 is adjusted downward.

3.3.5 Selected economic indicators, Bhutan (%)

	2018		2019	
	ADO 2018	Update	ADO 2018	Update
GDP growth	7.1	6.7	7.4	7.1
Inflation	4.6	3.6	5.4	4.9
Current acct. bal. (share of GDP)	–22.2	–19.0	–18.8	–16.5

Note: Years are fiscal years ending on 30 June of that year.

Source: ADB estimates.

Maldives

Tourism and construction are poised to drive GDP growth as projected for 2018, despite rising political tensions and delays affecting some projects. Tourist arrivals grew by 10.5% in the first half of the year, up from 6.1% in the first half of 2017. Europe provided 51% of arrivals and 75% of the increase, reflecting higher flight frequency and new carriers from that region. Visitors from the People's Republic of China continue to trend lower from their 2014 peak but still made up 18% of arrivals. Growth in bed-nights, a proxy for tourism earnings, accelerated to 13.5% from 8.3%. Construction was also buoyant, evidenced by 52.2% higher imports of construction materials and 30.7% expansion in bank loans for construction and real estate.

The projection for growth in 2019 is trimmed, however, in light of tourism prospects tempered by slowing growth in the main markets and heightened uncertainty from global trade tensions. Risks to the outlook are tourism earnings further crimped by possible deterioration in the political environment, a low and weakening stock of usable foreign reserves, and issues regarding fiscal and public debt sustainability.

Average consumer prices fell by 0.4% in the first half of 2018 from a large 3.8% increase a year earlier. This mainly reflected government actions starting in mid-2017 to contain food prices, which created a very high base effect, and to stabilize electricity and transportation prices by reducing import duties on fuel as global oil prices rose. Moreover, the harmonization of utility rates across the country since April 2018 lowered water-supply and electricity prices in the atolls, and the reversal of the 2016 decision to remove blanket subsidies reduced prices for rice, flour, and sugar. Given these developments, inflation forecasts are lowered sharply for both 2018 and 2019.

Imports rose in the first half of 2018 by 22.9% year on year to $1,441 million, largely to supply strong construction, while exports, mainly fish, slipped from $171 million to $159 million, pushing the trade deficit to $1,282 million, or 28.0% higher than a year earlier. Gross foreign reserves grew by $187 million to $773 million at the end of June, mainly reflecting a $106 million increase in commercial bank deposits to $485 million, which suggests that buoyant tourism earnings in the second half will keep the current account deficit close to the forecast. The $82 million increase in usable reserves to $288 million was buoyed by $100 million from the private placement of a government bond issue in May, but usable reserves still provide cover for only 1.3 months of estimated 2018 imports. This *Update* widens projections for the current account deficit, especially for 2019 as tourism weakens.

3.3.6 Selected economic indicators, Maldives (%)

	2018		2019	
	ADO 2018	Update	ADO 2018	Update
GDP growth	6.7	6.7	6.8	6.4
Inflation	3.1	1.2	3.0	1.7
Current acct. bal. (share of GDP)	−17.3	−17.5	−17.1	−17.7

Source: ADB estimates.

Nepal

GDP growth in fiscal year 2018 (FY2018, ended 16 July 2018) exceeded the *ADO 2018* projection because government expenditure, especially capital expenditure, expanded beyond expectations. This catalyzed a marked pickup in industry, which grew by 8.8% mainly on strong manufacturing and construction, and broad growth in services at 6.6%. Growth in agriculture, by contrast, slowed to 2.8% as expected after floods in August 2017 caused rice output to fall.

On the demand side, growth in consumption was, at 3.4%, little changed from a year earlier. Fixed investment grew by 15.7% to provide 30.8% of GDP, up from 28.3% in FY2017. Private investment advanced by 15.9% with increases for energy, manufacturing, and tourism that reflected a favorable sociopolitical environment after successful elections in 2017. Public investment rose by 14.9%, raising its share to 5.2% of GDP.

Inflation slowed to average 4.2% in FY2018, below the *ADO 2018* forecast. Despite a spike in domestic oil prices, inflation moderated from a year earlier owing to subdued inflation in India and improved management of domestic supply. While average food inflation rose to 2.8% from 2.0% a year earlier, nonfood inflation eased to 5.3% from 6.5%.

Import growth was much higher than anticipated at 27.8%, with large increases for construction materials and capital goods, but a 15.6% increase in exports beat expectations to limit the widening of the trade deficit to $10.9 billion, equal to 37.7% of GDP. Although growth in worker remittances and travel receipts remained strong, a marked fall in grants helped keep net invisible earnings at $8.5 billion, little changed from a year earlier. As a result, the current account deficit expanded to $2.4 billion, or more than double the *ADO 2018* projection as a share of GDP. Strong financial inflows nevertheless increased gross foreign exchange reserves marginally to $10.1 billion, providing 9.4 months of cover for imports of goods and services.

The growth forecast for FY2019 is retained, assuming a normal monsoon and moderation in investment and budget expenditure in line with constraints on economic capacity. The inflation forecast is also retained in light of higher inflation now expected in India. The current account deficit is expected to exceed the *ADO 2018* projection despite somewhat slower growth in imports of capital and consumer goods than in FY2018 and a forecast stabilizing of global oil prices. The main risk to the outlook is that growth in remittances— and in invisible income in general—may fall substantially behind trade deficit expansion. The government aims to narrow the deficit over the medium term by promoting exports of competitive products and services and boosting their supply.

3.3.7 Selected economic indicators, Nepal (%)

	2018		2019	
	ADO 2018	Update	ADO 2018	Update
GDP growth	4.9	5.9	5.5	5.5
Inflation	5.5	4.2	6.0	6.0
Current acct. bal. (share of GDP)	–3.5	–8.2	–5.8	–8.7

Notes: Years are fiscal years ending 16 July of that year. GDP growth at basic prices.

Source: ADB estimates.

Sri Lanka

Bad weather and policy tightening held GDP growth to 3.3% in 2017. The government is implementing wide-ranging structural reform supported by the International Monetary Fund. Fiscal performance improved with tax revenue rising as a share of GDP and a small primary surplus in 2017. Heavy debt repayment coming due in the next few years underscores the need for continued structural reform.

GDP growth stayed subdued in the first quarter of 2018 at 3.5% year on year. Agriculture recovered with better weather to grow by 5.3% as rice production increased by 53.3%, partly reversing contraction in the first quarter of 2017. Services advanced by 4.8%, but industry expanded by only 1.1%, held back by a 4.7% decline in construction and only modest growth in manufacturing. The first quarter saw private consumption revive, continued tightening in government consumption spending, stagnant fixed investment, and lower net exports. With external demand coming off a high base in the second half of 2017 and little change expected in investment and government expenditure, projections for growth in 2018 and 2019 are marked down from *ADO 2018*. A downside risk stems from approaching elections.

Normalizing agriculture in 2018 and a high base last year brought headline inflation down to 1.6% year on year in April. It picked up to 3.4% in July on higher food prices, currency depreciation, rising global oil prices, and the government's adoption in May of automatic fuel pricing. These pressures and the scheduled introduction of automatic pricing for electricity later this year will see inflation trend higher to average 4.5% in 2018, which is below the *ADO 2018* forecast. With growth lower than anticipated in 2019, the inflation forecast for 2019 is also lowered. Weakening inflation and growth led the Central Bank of Sri Lanka to ease monetary policy in April by cutting the standing lending facility rate by 25 basis points.

Exports grew by 6.2% in the first half of 2018, as expected, with garments and textiles growing by 5.7%. Imports expanded by 12.7%, which was more than expected and came mainly from higher fuel prices, as well as gold for jewelry and personal vehicles. A 0.6% decline in imports of investment goods underscores the lackluster investment environment. The trade deficit widened by 20.2%. Earnings from tourism and remittances, the main offsets to trade deficits, increased by 5.8%. With higher oil prices, high dependence on imports, and only a marginal recovery in remittances, projections for the current account deficit are raised for both 2018 and 2019. The Sri Lankan rupee has depreciated against the dollar all year, ending 5% lower at the end of August. Gross official foreign exchange reserves peaked at $9.9 billion in April 2018 with sizable capital inflows but fell to $8.4 billion in July.

3.3.8 Selected economic indicators, Sri Lanka (%)

	2018		2019	
	ADO 2018	Update	ADO 2018	Update
GDP growth	4.2	3.8	4.8	4.5
Inflation	5.2	4.5	5.0	4.7
Current acct. bal. (share of GDP)	-2.7	-2.9	-2.5	-3.1

Source: ADB estimates.

Southeast Asia

Growth in the subregion is now expected to be slightly slower in 2018 than the *ADO 2018* forecast in April, with lower inflation and a smaller current account surplus. Macroeconomic performance in 2019, on the other hand, will likely to be largely in line with April forecasts. Risks to this outlook increasingly tilt downward as trade tensions escalate around the world and international financial markets become subject to heightened volatility. For individual economies, prospects and risks vary widely.

Subregional assessment and prospects

As growth moderates in major global markets apart from the US, weighted average GDP growth in Southeast Asia is now forecast at 5.1% this year, marginally lower than earlier forecast (Figure 3.4.1). Growth should pick up in 2019 with the combined subregional GDP forecast to grow by 5.2%, as earlier envisaged.

Many factors—including moderation in export growth, softer domestic demand, subdued agriculture, higher inflation, net capital outflow and a worsening balance of payments—dim the growth outlook in 6 of the 10 economies in the subregion: Indonesia, the Lao People's Democratic Republic (Lao PDR), Malaysia, Myanmar, the Philippines, and Viet Nam. Brunei Darussalam and Thailand, by contrast, look set to outperform *ADO 2018* forecasts. In Thailand, strong export growth, buoyant domestic demand, and a major turnaround in agriculture underpin faster growth, while in Brunei Darussalam, a hefty increase in domestic investment into oil and gas extraction is nudging up growth more than earlier foreseen. Meanwhile, growth in Cambodia and Singapore is holding up well, in line with the April projections, as both economies experience strong export growth and domestic demand.

3.4.1 GDP growth, Southeast Asia

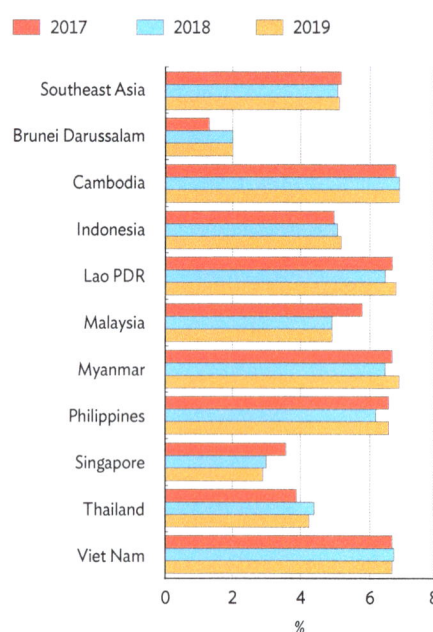

Lao PDR = Lao People's Democratic Republic.
Source: *Asian Development Outlook* database.

The subregional assessment and prospects were written by Kwang Jo Jeong and Dulce Zara. The section on Indonesia was written by Emma Allen and Priasto Aji; Malaysia by Valerie Mercer-Blackman and Shiela Camingue-Romance; the Philippines by Aekapol Chongvilaivan and Teresa Mendoza; Thailand by Thiam Hee Ng; Viet Nam by Cuong Minh Nguyen, Nguyen Luu Thuc Phuong, and Chu Hong Minh; and other economies by Poullang Doung, Jan Hansen, Soulinthone Leuangkhamsing, Rattanatay Luanglatbandith, Chaw Su Nwe, Pilipinas Quising, Yumiko Tamura, Shu Tian, and Mai Lin Villaruel. Authors are in the Southeast Asia and Economic Research and Regional Cooperation departments of ADB.

The Philippines faces the largest downward revision to its growth forecast for this year, by 0.4 percentage points, followed by Malaysia by 0.3 points, the Lao PDR, Myanmar, and Viet Nam by 0.2 points, and Indonesia by 0.1 points. Although the Philippines should post strong growth both this year and next, the economy has softened since *ADO 2018* was published in April with agriculture sluggish, export prospects moderating, inflation exceeding expectations, and monetary policy in a tightening mode. The slowdown in Malaysia comes as export growth moderates and investment suffers a setback with the new government deciding to reexamine several large infrastructure projects approved by its predecessor. Indonesia is likely to post slightly slower but still robust growth this year as continued monetary tightening to ease pressure on the balance of payments dampens aggregate demand. Viet Nam is slowing slightly in 2018 as export growth plateaus, agriculture and construction growth slows, and mining continues to contract. Economic prospects in the Lao PDR and Myanmar are similarly somewhat dimmer than foreseen earlier.

Despite higher international petroleum prices, subregional inflation is now projected lower in 2018 and 2019 than forecast in *ADO 2018* (Figure 3.4.2). This year, higher government subsidies for fuel are expected to hold inflation down in Indonesia, the largest economy in Southeast Asia, and in Malaysia. US dollar appreciation will do the same in highly dollarized Cambodia, as will softening housing and public transportation costs in Singapore. In five of the remaining six Southeast Asian economies, inflation is now seen higher than earlier forecast as rising international oil prices and depreciating local currencies build up more inflationary pressure than foreseen in Brunei Darussalam (where inflation remains very low), the Lao PDR, the Philippines, Thailand, and Viet Nam. Other inflationary factors are, in the Philippines, stagnant agriculture and rice supply bottlenecks and, in Viet Nam, continued upward adjustment of government-administered fees for medical services, education, and transportation.

The subregional current account surplus is expected to narrow as export growth moderates more than expected and import bills rise faster than foreseen because of higher international oil prices (Figure 3.4.3). The surplus is now expected to fall to the equivalent of 2.5% of subregional GDP this year, slightly more steeply than projected earlier. The forecast marginal narrowing of next year's surplus is in line with *ADO 2018* projection. Individually, deficits this year in Cambodia, Indonesia, and the Philippines are now seen wider, and surpluses in Malaysia and Viet Nam narrower. The Lao PDR and Myanmar are now likely to see smaller current account deficits. There is no change in the 2018 current account forecasts for Brunei Darussalam, Singapore, and Thailand.

3.4.2 Inflation, Southeast Asia

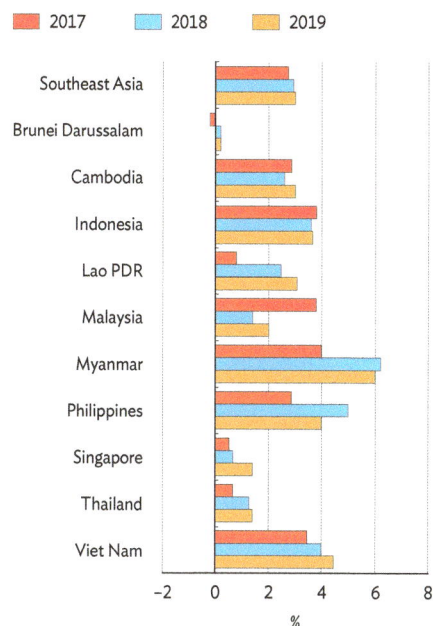

Lao PDR = Lao People's Democratic Republic.
Source: *Asian Development Outlook* database.

3.4.3 Current account balance, Southeast Asia

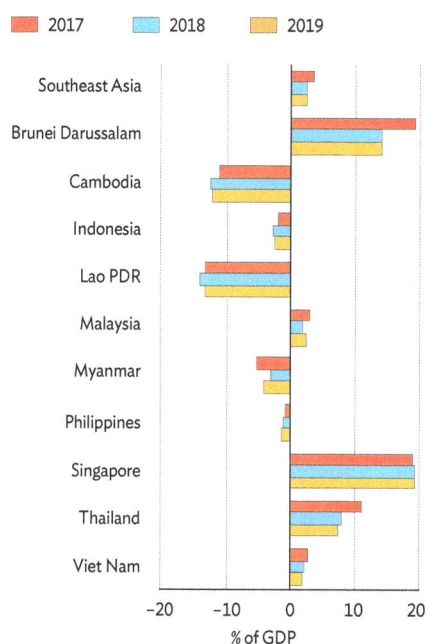

Lao PDR = Lao People's Democratic Republic.
Source: *Asian Development Outlook* database.

Indonesia

Strong domestic demand enabled the economy to post 5.2% GDP growth in the first half of 2018. Growth is forecast at 5.2% for the whole year, while inflation is likely to be contained at 3.4%. Both forecasts are revised down from *ADO 2018* in April. As pressures on the balance of payments and the Indonesian rupiah is unlikely to abate in the near term, the current account deficits this year and next are now projected higher than forecast in April.

Updated assessment

GDP growth edged up to 5.2% in the first half 2018 from 5.0% in the same period of last year (Figure 3.4.4). In the first half of the year, growth improved from 5.1% in the first quarter to 5.3% in the second, partly reflecting a spike in domestic demand in June as Eid al-Fitr celebrations, marking the end of Ramadan, were earlier than in the previous year.

Boosted by rising incomes, the disbursement of civil servant bonuses and government social transfers, and expenditures tied to regional elections in June, private consumption grew by 5.1% in the first half of the year. A pickup in government consumption, in contrast with stagnation in the first half of last year, added impetus to domestic consumption. Supported by higher government infrastructure investment and a substantial increase in inventories, domestic investment grew by 8.4% in the first half of this year, the highest rate of expansion since 2012. Meanwhile, exports of goods and services rose in real terms by 6.9%, up from 5.6% growth in the first half of 2017, helping to sustain higher GDP growth.

By sector, a slowdown in agriculture was more than offset by higher growth in industry and services. A delayed harvest slowed agriculture growth to 4.1% in the first half of the year from 5.1% in the same period of 2017. Growth in manufacturing picked up to 4.3% in the first 6 months of 2018 from 3.9% a year earlier. Industries within manufacturing that performed well were food and beverages, machinery and equipment, and the highly export-oriented footwear and apparel business. The government's push to build more infrastructure helped construction to maintain growth at 6.5%, as in the first half of last year. Meanwhile, policy shifts in favor of metal ore exports saw improvements in mining. Helped by buoyancy in exports as well as in domestic demand, services expanded by 5.9% and generated almost half of GDP growth (Figure 3.4.5). Stronger consumption boosted business in hotels and restaurants, wholesale and retail trade, and transportation and storage.

In the first 8 months of 2018, inflation averaged 3.2%, comfortably in the lower half of the 2.5%–4.5% inflation target range set by Bank Indonesia, the central bank (Figure 3.4.6). Despite the delayed harvest, food prices were well contained

3.4.4 Demand-side contributions to growth

- Gross fixed capital formation
- Government consumption
- Private consumption
- Net exports
- Stocks
- Statistical discrepancy
- Gross domestic product

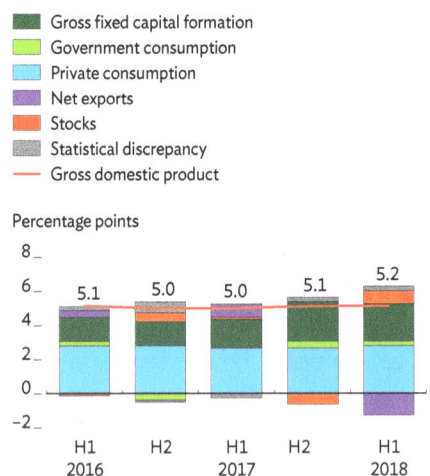

H = half.
Source: CEIC Data Company (accessed 30 August 2018).

3.4.5 Supply-side contributions to growth

- Agriculture
- Industry
- Services
- Gross domestic product

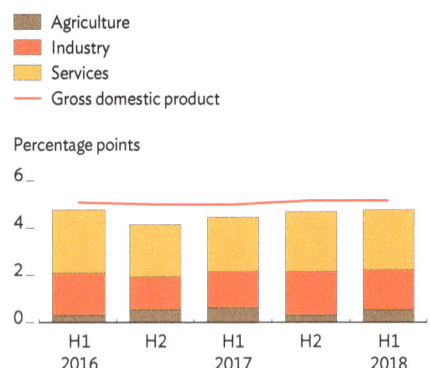

H = half.
Source: CEIC Data Company (accessed 30 August 2018).

3.4.6 Monthly inflation

- Headline
- Core
- Administered
- Volatile

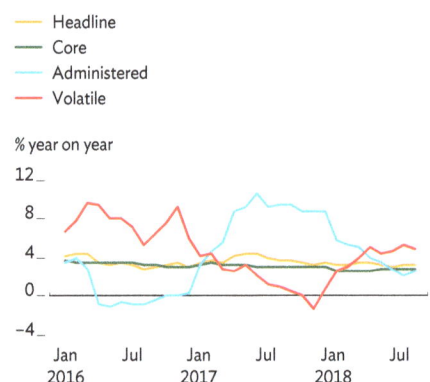

Source: CEIC Data Company (accessed 30 August 2018).

by timely food imports and continued deft supply management. Energy prices remained stable under the government's policy to keep domestic fuel prices unchanged.

Even as inflation remained within the official target range, the balance of payments came under stress in the first half of the year, with the current and financial accounts both posting deficits. The overall balance of payments fell into a deficit of $8.2 billion in the first half of the year, reversing a surplus of $5.3 billion a year earlier (Figure 3.4.7). Gross international reserves dropped to $117.9 billion at the end of August after climbing to a high of $132.0 billion in January of this year. Reserves still provide cover for 6.6 months of imports of goods and services and payments on the government's external debt.

The dollar value of merchandise exports rose by 10.3% in the first 6 months of the year, slowing from 15.3% growth in the first half of 2017 (Figure 3.4.8). Meanwhile, the import bill ballooned by 23.1%, twice the growth rate in the corresponding period of last year, as international oil prices rose and imports of capital goods increased for energy and transport infrastructure projects. Consequently, the trade surplus narrowed sharply to $2.6 billion from $10.5 billion a year earlier. Coupled with a continuing structural deficit in trade in services and primary income flows, the narrowing trade surplus caused the current account deficit to double from a year earlier to $13.7 billion, or the equivalent of 2.6% of GDP (Figure 3.4.9).

On the financial account, inflows of both foreign direct investment and portfolio capital declined substantially, further worsening the external payments position. Net foreign direct investment declined by 24.3% from a year earlier, sliding to $5.4 billion in the first 6 months of the year as multinational companies operating in Indonesia stepped up their repatriation of profits and investment abroad. The first half of the year also saw net outflow of portfolio investment amounting to $1.1 billion, a sharp reversal from net inflow of $14.7 billion a year earlier. Reflecting the capital outflow, from January to August this year, the Jakarta composite index fell by 5.3% as foreigners sold $3.4 billion in Indonesian stocks. Foreign holdings of rupiah-denominated government bonds still increased by $815 million but at a cost of much higher yields. Total external debt held by the public and private sectors rose by $18.4 billion in the 12 months to the end of June 2018 to reach $355.7 billion, equal to 34.3% of GDP. However, the share of short-term debt, in terms of its remaining maturity, declined to 15.1% in June 2018 from 17.2% a year earlier.

As the balance of payments deteriorated and the US dollar strengthened against the currencies of emerging markets following interest rate hikes by the US Federal Reserve, the Indonesian rupiah depreciated by nearly 8.0% in the first 8

3.4.7 Balance of payments

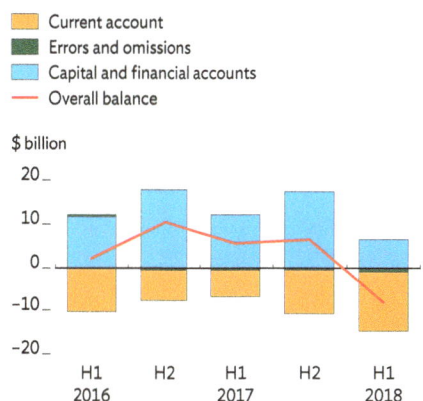

- Current account
- Errors and omissions
- Capital and financial accounts
- Overall balance

Source: CEIC Data Company (accessed 30 August 2018).

3.4.8 Merchandise trade

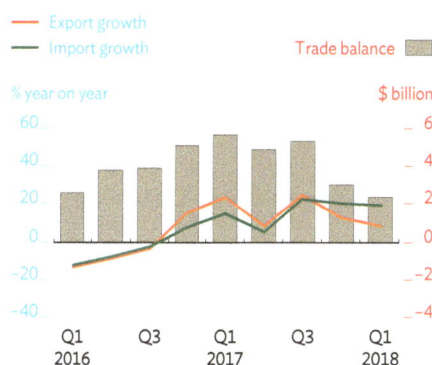

- Export growth
- Import growth
- Trade balance

Q = quarter.
Source: CEIC Data Company (accessed 30 August 2018).

3.4.9 Current account components

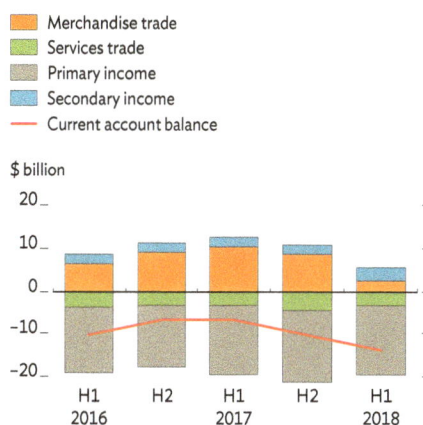

- Merchandise trade
- Services trade
- Primary income
- Secondary income
- Current account balance

H = half.
Source: CEIC Data Company (accessed 30 August 2018).

months of 2018, reaching a low of Rp14,711 to the dollar on 31 August (Figure 3.4.10). In response to heightened external vulnerability, the central bank raised its policy 7-day reverse repo rate four times by a total of 125 basis points, from 4.25% to 5.50%, from May to August (Figure 3.4.11). The rate increases were consistent with the central bank strategy to stay ahead of the curve and thereby keep domestic financial markets competitive amid uncertainty in global financial markets, as well as better manage the balance of payments. The rate increases have been complemented by interventions in the foreign exchange market to support the weakening rupiah.

Meanwhile, fiscal consolidation proceeded apace. The fiscal deficit in the first half was equal to only 1.5% of GDP, much lower than 2.7% in the corresponding period of last year. The government continued to move ahead with revenue reform that included amending some regulations on nontax revenue. Improvements in both tax and nontax revenue brought a 16.5% revenue increase year on year in July, with cumulative revenue collection reaching 52.5% of the annual budget target. Meanwhile, making public expenditure more efficient continued to be a policy priority, with emphasis placed on the timely realization of capital spending and the more efficient management of social assistance programs. Government expenditure in July was 7.7% higher than in the same period of last year, with cumulative spending reaching 51.6% of the budget target for the year. Rising international oil prices increased oil and gas revenue in January–July by 36.0% over the same period of 2017, while expenditure on energy subsidies rose by 61.0% year on year.

Prospects

While export growth may moderate, domestic demand should hold up, even with continued monetary tightening to mitigate pressure on the balance of payments. Accordingly, GDP growth is forecast at a robust 5.2% this year, up from 5.1% in 2017 and only marginally lower than the 5.3% forecast in *ADO 2018*. Growth is expected to edge up to 5.3% in 2019, as forecast in April.

Steady growth is projected for private consumption in the near term. Rising incomes and minimum wages in the formal economy should support consumption, as should the 2018 Asian Games in Jakarta and Palembang in the second half of August and election-related spending on the approach to national elections in April 2019. Private investment will continue to benefit from policy reform pursued since 2015 that, among other things, simplified business regulations and improved logistics. However, some private investors may adopt a wait-and-see stance as national elections near.

3.4.10 Gross international reserves and exchange rate

Source: CEIC Data Company (accessed 17 September 2018).

3.4.11 Policy rates

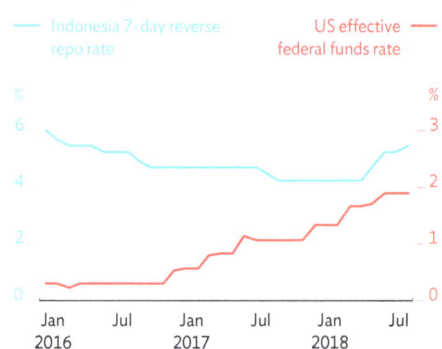

Source: CEIC Data Company (accessed 17 September 2018).

3.4.1 Selected economic indicators, Indonesia (%)

	2018		2019	
	ADO 2018	Update	ADO 2018	Update
GDP growth	5.3	5.2	5.3	5.3
Inflation	3.8	3.4	4.0	3.5
Current acct. bal. (share of GDP)	-2.2	-2.6	-2.2	-2.6

Source: ADB estimates.

Public spending on infrastructure should hold up in the second half of 2018 with the scheduled completion of several large projects in the coming months. Credit growth accelerated to 10.7% in June, its highest rate since 2015, boosted by loans to support public infrastructure projects (Figure 3.4.12). Performance has been strong in road construction and maintenance, irrigation system expansion, and the procurement of equipment and machinery, though challenges remain in infrastructure planning and project preparation and implementation.

By sector, a moderate pickup is expected for industry growth, with construction remaining robust and the manufacturing purchasing managers' index showing a positive result in most recent months (Figure 3.4.13). With domestic demand holding up well, the service sector should carry its first-half growth rate into the second half. Service sector activities, particularly in hotels and restaurants, should get some support from the upcoming International Monetary Fund–World Bank annual meetings in Bali. Earnings from agricultural commodities are expected to remain moderate, however, as prices for palm oil and rubber stay soft.

For the rest of this year and into next year, domestic inflation is expected to remain muted. Food inflation should stay moderate with improved monitoring of domestic prices and better food distribution channels. Inflationary pressure from higher global oil prices is not expected as long as the government keeps fuel prices unchanged. With recent rupiah depreciation, imported products may see some upward price adjustments this year and next. Inflation is expected to increase from 3.2% in the first 8 months of 2018 to an average of 3.4% in 2018 and 3.5% in 2019, both projections lower than *ADO 2018* forecasts of 3.8% for 2018 and 4.0% for 2019.

Import growth is likely to outpace that of exports, especially as capital goods imports will be strong to support the pickup in domestic investment. The current account deficit is thus expected to widen to equal 2.6% of GDP both this year and next, wider than the 2.2% deficit forecast in April. Among government measures to contain the current account deficit is a review of various import policies. In addition, rupiah depreciation against the US dollar may provide some relief by shrinking the deficit in the primary income account. As pressure on the balance of payments and the rupiah is unlikely to abate in the near term, policy makers are well advised to continue to closely monitor vulnerabilities and consider measures to boost exports and foreign investment. The central bank is likely to continue to use monetary policy this year and next to support the balance of payments and stabilize the exchange rate. At the same time, it is further strengthening macroprudential controls on banks to ensure the financial stability that is critical to sustaining strong economic growth over the medium term.

3.4.12 Bank loans

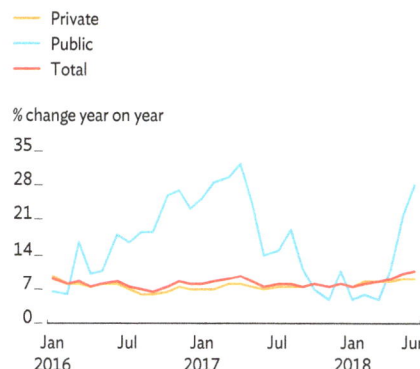

Notes: Total loans are commercial and rural bank loans to public and private entities. Public loans are to publicly owned other financial corporations, state and local governments, and public nonfinancial corporations. Private loans are to privately owned other financial corporations, private nonfinancial corporations, and other private entities.
Source: CEIC Data Company (accessed 7 September 2018).

3.4.13 Manufacturing purchasing managers' index

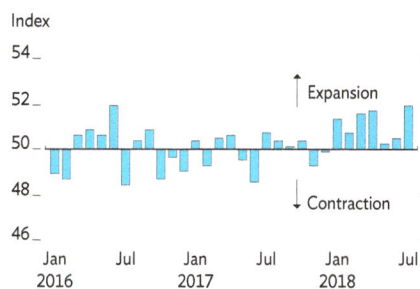

Source: Bloomberg (accessed 30 August 2018).

On the fiscal front, the government is unlikely to revise the 2018 budget because tax receipts are on target and the fiscal deficit is likely to be on target too (Figure 3.4.14). The proposed budget for 2019 is conservative in that it targets a fiscal deficit equal to only 1.8% of GDP. To maintain development momentum, public investment spending will increase modestly, while state-owned enterprises will receive capital injections equal to 0.1% of GDP. Public social spending will likely rise to finance village funds for the poor and vulnerable groups, as well as other conditional cash transfers.

Domestic risks to the outlook include import policies on capital goods that could adversely affect much-needed infrastructure projects, slowing growth in the short and medium term. External risks similarly tilt downward. Continued capital outflow could worsen the external payments position, further weaken the rupiah, stoke higher inflation, and hamper growth. Any escalation of global trade tensions would exacerbate many above-mentioned risks for Indonesia, both directly and secondhand through their effects on Indonesia's neighbors and trade partners.

3.4.14 2018 Fiscal performance

····· Revenue target
—— Actual revenue
····· Expenditure target
—— Actual expenditure

Source: CEIC Data Company (accessed 7 September 2018).

Malaysia

The economy recorded moderating growth, declining inflation, and a shrinking current account surplus in the first half of the year. Sluggish domestic investment and exports more than offset stronger private consumption. GDP growth is now seen to be lower this year and next than forecast in April in *ADO 2018*. Meanwhile, both inflation and the current account surplus are likely to be lower than earlier forecast in 2018 but higher in 2019. Risks to the outlook are tilted to the downside more than in April.

Updated assessment

GDP grew by 4.9% in the first half of 2018, slowing from 5.7% in the same period of 2017 (Figure 3.4.15). On the demand side, stronger domestic consumption supported growth but not enough to keep weaker investment and exports from pulling it down. Private consumption in the first half rose by 7.4%, up from 6.9% in the same period a year earlier, driven by a steady rise in employment and wages. Job growth pushed the unemployment rate down to 3.3% in the second quarter from 3.4% a year earlier. The reinstatement of fuel subsidies in March 2018 and the elimination in June of the goods and services tax (GST) also seemed to help private consumption. Meanwhile, growth in government consumption was 1.8%, down two-thirds from a year earlier as public outlays on emoluments, pensions, and gratuities fell.

Domestic investment contracted by 5.1% in the first half of the year, reversing a 7.2% increase in the corresponding period of 2017. Growth in private investment slowed to 3.4% in the first half from 10.0% a year earlier as firms reduced spending on construction and drew down inventories to frontload exports ahead of the escalating trade conflict between the US and the People's Republic of China. Meanwhile, public investment contracted by 5.2% in the first half, after a decline by nearly 1.0% in the first half of 2017.

Despite higher growth in the value of exports, especially petroleum and manufactures, growth in the volume of exports of goods and services slowed to 2.9% in the first 6 months of 2018 from 9.2% in the same period of last year, acting as another drag on GDP growth in the first half.

Most major sectors slowed in the first half of the year. Output from agriculture stagnated following impressive 7.1% growth in the same period of 2017. Bad weather was to blame, but so were low international palm oil prices, which hovered around $660 per ton in May, the lowest price since July 2016, amid rising global inventories.

Growth in industry decelerated to 3.6% in the first half from 4.8% a year earlier. Within industry, subdued export demand dampened manufacturing growth to 5.1% from 5.8%, mining contracted with disruption from maintenance

3.4.15 Demand-side contributions to growth

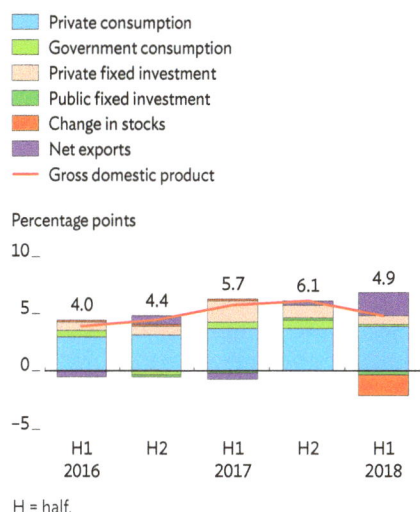

- Private consumption
- Government consumption
- Private fixed investment
- Public fixed investment
- Change in stocks
- Net exports
- Gross domestic product

H = half.
Sources: Haver Analytics; Bank Negara Malaysia. 2018. *Monthly Statistical Bulletin.* September. http://www.bnm .gov.my (accessed 12 September 2018).

and repair on liquefied natural gas (LNG) pipelines, and
construction growth slowed sharply to 4.8% from 7.5%, partly
reflecting a rising number of unsold residential properties and
oversupply of office space and shopping complexes. Meanwhile,
strong domestic consumption helped make services the only
major sector to accelerate growth, from an already high 6.1%
in the first half of last year to 6.5%. Within the service sector,
wholesale and retail trade continued to be buoyant, as did
information and communications.

Slower growth was accompanied by lower inflation in
the first half of the year. Inflation fell to 1.5% in the first 7
months of 2018 from 3.9% in the same period of last year.
Transportation prices, which have a weight of 13.7% on the
consumer price index, rose by an annual average of only 2.8%
in January–July 2018, sharply down from 13.9% a year earlier.
Meanwhile, food prices rose by an average of 2.3% year on year
in the first 7 months of 2018, slowing from 4.0% in the same
period of 2017 (Figure 3.4.16). The abolition of the 6.0% GST
from 1 June, as the new government transitioned toward
reintroducing a narrower sales and services tax on 1 September,
may have softened domestic prices, but inflation is expected to
pick up in the remaining months of 2018.

The value of merchandise exports rose by 16.0% in the
first 6 months of the year, up from 12.3% growth in the same
period of 2017 despite growth moderation by volume. At the
same time, the value of merchandise imports expanded by
13.2%, accelerating slightly from 12.6% growth in the first
half of 2017. Growth in imports of capital and intermediate
goods moderated, but imports of consumer goods grew by
double digits to support stronger domestic consumption.
As exports rose faster than imports, the trade surplus swelled
to $15.7 billion in the first half of this year from $11.6 billion
a year earlier. Part of the larger trade surplus was offset
by deepening deficits in services and the income account.
The current account surplus therefore widened by less than
the trade surplus, reaching $4.8 billion in the first half or
the equivalent of 2.7% of GDP, up from 2.1% a year earlier
(Figure 3.4.17).

Net capital inflow remained positive in the first half of
the year despite huge portfolio outflow in the second quarter.
This helped create in the first half of the year a capital account
surplus of $7 billion and an overall balance of payments
surplus of $4.4 billion, equal to 2.5% of GDP and up from
1.3% in the first half of 2017. The balance of payments surplus
pushed international reserves to $104.5 billion in July 2018,
which exceeds Malaysia's short-term external debt and covers
7.5 months of retained imports. Meanwhile, the Malaysian
ringgit depreciated by 4.5% against the US dollar from
1 January to mid-September this year, largely reflecting the
strength of the dollar.

3.4.16 Monthly inflation

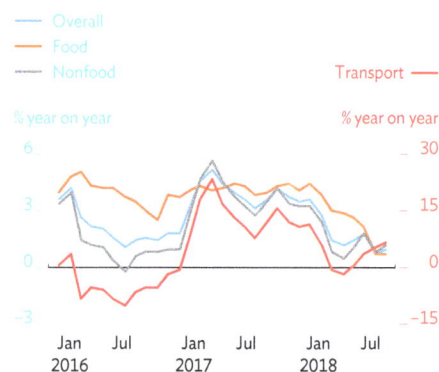

Source: Haver Analytics (accessed 12 September 2018).

3.4.17 External balances

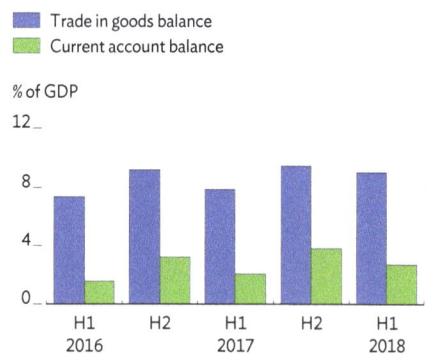

H = half.
Source: Haver Analytics (accessed 12 September 2018).

Lower inflation and the swelling current account surplus enabled Bank Negara, the central bank, to keep its policy interest rate unchanged since it raised it by 25 basis points to 3.25% in January 2018. The central bank has hinted at allowing more exchange rate flexibility, and in mid-August it eased its currency-conversion rules for exporters, notably relaxing the requirement that they convert all their export proceeds into ringgit. Meanwhile, claims on the private sector grew by 7.0% year on year to the end of July 2018, and the money supply grew by 6.6%.

The fiscal deficit narrowed, despite higher expenditure under the new government, as the continued rise in oil prices significantly boosted oil revenue in the first half of 2018, lifting total revenue by 10.0% (Figure 3.4.18). Buoyant tax collection from individuals and corporations helped to push fiscal revenue above projections.

At the same time, government expenditure grew by 5.1% on huge increases in mandated transfers to statutory bodies and state governments, as well as on subsidies with the notable reintroduction of the fuel subsidy. The net result was a budget deficit equal to 4.5% of GDP in the first half of 2018, down from 5.2% a year earlier but much higher than the original budget target of 2.8% for the whole year.

Prospects

Domestic private consumption is seen continuing to support economic growth in the near term. However, current moderation in exports is likely to persist for a while and domestic investment to remain more subdued than expected in *ADO 2018*. Forecasts for GDP growth are therefore revised down from *ADO 2018*, from 5.3% to 5.0% for 2018 and from 5.0% to 4.8% for 2019 (Figure 3.4.19).

Private consumption is expected to remain buoyant in the near term, as indicated by a rise in the consumer sentiment index to a 21-year high of 133 in the second quarter of this year from below 100 in the first quarter. Although manufacturing wages have softened since their peak in June 2018, household purchasing power should hold up well as inflation remains low. The 3-month GST holiday from June to August should further boost private consumption. The government will need to lower expenditure to make up for lost GST revenue and meet its fiscal targets over the medium term.

Although the index on business conditions rose to a 6-year high of 116 in the second quarter, and bank credit for manufacturing and construction rose robustly in the same period, domestic investment will likely continue to be subdued (Figure 3.4.20). The new government's decision to suspend quite a few large infrastructure projects put some investors on the sidelines for the time being. The postponement and possible cancellation of some key infrastructure projects—such as the

3.4.18 Fiscal performance

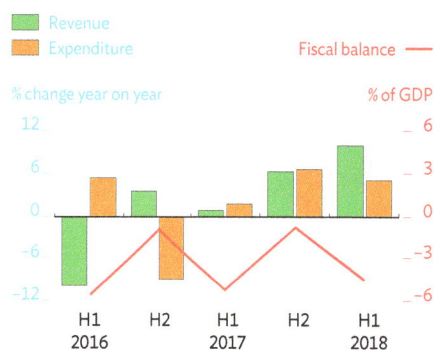

H = half.
Sources: Haver Analytics; CEIC Data Company (both accessed 12 September 2018).

3.4.19 GDP growth

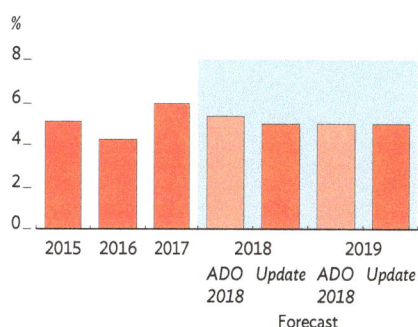

Source: *Asian Development Outlook* database.

3.4.2 Selected economic indicators, Malaysia (%)

	2018		2019	
	ADO 2018	Update	ADO 2018	Update
GDP growth	5.3	5.0	5.0	4.8
Inflation	2.6	1.4	1.8	2.0
Current acct. bal. (share of GDP)	2.4	2.0	2.1	2.4

Source: ADB estimates.

East Coast Rail Link, the Light Rail Transit Line 3, the Kuala Lumpur–Singapore high-speed rail link, and two oil pipelines in Sabah—are likely to cut public investments next year.

Having contributed significantly to growth last year in Malaysia's highly trade-dependent economy, exports are likely to soften growth prospects this year. The disruption of LNG exports from pipeline repairs will keep exports subdued this year. Meanwhile, palm oil exports face downward pressure from acute labor shortages in agriculture and cost pressures as the minimum wage rises, but cuts in the tax rate on exports of crude palm oil in September 2018 could help keep palm oil exports steady in the near term.

By sector, agriculture is expected to improve in the near term, assuming normal weather. Mining and quarrying are forecast to remain modest this year as LNG operations resume following repairs. Growth in manufacturing will be supported by strong gains from rising oil prices and demand for electronics exceeding expectations (Figure 3.4.21). Services should see steady expansion in line with rising domestic consumption and with growth in insurance and other business-related services.

Meanwhile, inflation will likely stay contained with the continuation of domestic fuel subsidies and the replacement of the broad GST with a narrower sales and services tax. The inflation forecast for 2018 is therefore revised down to 1.4% from 2.6% in April, rising to 2.0% in 2019, above the April forecast of 1.8%, as the impact on prices from the recent one-off fiscal measures fades (Figure 3.4.22).

The value of merchandise exports should hold up well despite subdued volume growth, as in the first half of the year, partly thanks to higher international energy prices. At the same time, imports are likely to swell largely on buoyant demand for imported consumer goods. This *Update* projects a current account surplus equal to 2.0% of GDP in 2018, only slightly lower than earlier foreseen.

Lower inflation and a continuing current account surplus should allow the central bank to maintain an accommodative monetary policy. The policy interest rate is likely to hold in the near term unless capital outflow accelerates in response to higher US interest rates. With the removal of the GST, the government may face a budget deficit this year higher than the original target of 2.8% of GDP. A persistent deficit will be a challenge for the government in the next few years unless it finds new sources of revenue over the medium term (Box 3.4.1).

Risks to the outlook tilt to the downside. Any escalation of the global trade tensions or heightened volatility in international financial markets would be the main external risks, while continued policy reversals and widening fiscal deficit would be domestic risks.

3.4.20 Confidence indexes

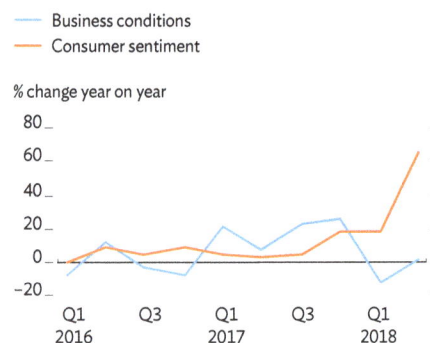

Q = quarter.
Source: Haver Analytics (accessed 12 September 2018).

3.4.21 Electrical and electronics exports

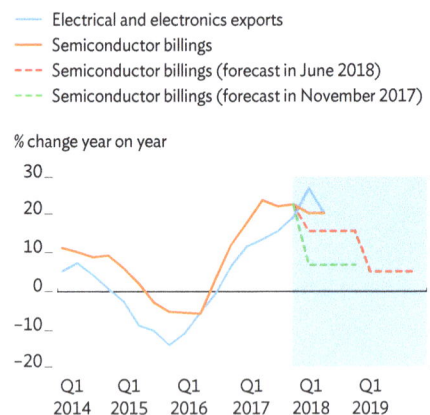

Q = quarter.
Sources: Haver Analytics; World Semiconductor Trade Statistics, https://www.wsts.org (both accessed on 12 September 2018).

3.4.22 Inflation

Source: *Asian Development Outlook* database.

3.4.1 A new sales tax and its fiscal implications

The newly elected government abolished the 6.0% GST from 1 June 2018 and reinstated the sales and services tax (SST) from 1 September with the objective of lowering consumer prices and reducing the cost of living for the poor and the middle class.

As the GST was collected at every stage of a supply chain, it had a broader base than the SST that replaces it. The SST has two components. The sales tax is a single-stage tax applied selectively on importers and manufacturers of certain goods, and the service tax applies to certain categories of services. Although the newly reinstated SST covers more items than the SST that was withdrawn in 2015, when it was replaced by the GST, it still covers only 38% of goods and services, compared with 60% coverage under the now abolished GST. The lower coverage of the SST is likely to reduce government tax revenue and widen the fiscal deficit (box table).

Projected revenue from the SST this year is only RM21 billion, equal to 1.5% of GDP, or less than half the 2018 budget projection of GST revenue at RM43.8 billion, or 3.0% of GDP. Lower tax revenue could set back the government's fiscal consolidation program of recent years, endangering its fiscal deficit target over the short to medium term. However, as the 2018 budget assumed a crude oil price of $52 per barrel and oil prices have picked up to average in 2018 more than $75 per barrel as of mid-September, higher oil revenues could partly cover the shortfall in 2018 created by the tax switch.

Assuming that oil prices average $74 per barrel in the whole of 2018, then 2019 petroleum revenue should rise to an estimated 1.4% of GDP, well up from the original target of 0.8%. This should cushion the adverse effect of the new tax regime on the fiscal deficit, but the government will need to seek new sources of revenue to meet its medium-term target of closing the fiscal gap by 2020. The goal of relying less on oil revenue to finance public spending would appear to suffer a major setback with the tax switch, exposing fiscal health to the volatility of international commodity prices.

Fiscal implications of the switch from GST to SST

Item	Goods and services tax	Sales and services tax
Rate	6% from 1 April 2015 0% from 1 June 2018 to 31 August 2018	5% and 10% for sales tax 6% for services tax
Annual revenue	2017 (actual): RM44.3 billion 2018 (est.): RM43.8 billion	2018 (est.): RM21 billion
Annual revenue as share of GDP	2017 (actual): 3.2% 2018 (est.): 3.0%	2018 (est.): 1.5%
Coverage	472,000 companies 60% of goods and services	Estimated <100,000 companies 38% of goods and services
Threshold for business registration and taxation	Annual revenue of RM500,000	Value of taxable goods and services provided in 12 months exceeding MR500,000

Note: The 2018 budget assumed oil prices at $52 per barrel.

Sources: Maybank Research, 20 July 2018; Official Website, Malaysia Goods and Services Tax, http://gst.customs.gov.my/en/Pages/default.aspx; Ministry of Finance, http://www.treasury.gov.my/index.php/en/gallery-activities/press-release.html; ADB estimates.

Philippines

With GDP growth softening unexpectedly in the first half of 2018, growth forecasts are revised down to 6.4% this year and 6.7% in 2019, when public investment in infrastructure and social sectors is slated to accelerate. The recent buildup of inflationary pressure should moderate next year as tighter monetary policy reins in inflation expectations. The current account will continue to post deficits on the back of moderation in exports and acceleration in imports of capital goods needed for the infrastructure development program.

Updated assessment

Growth in domestic investment helped the economy to grow by 6.3% in the first half of 2018, easing from 6.6% in the same period of last year on lower export growth and private consumption and, after last year's rebound, a plateauing of agriculture (Figure 3.4.23). Domestic investment rose by 16.4% in the first half of the year on brisk construction and a 17.1% expansion in outlays for industrial machinery and equipment. Public construction growth quickened to 22.1%, more than double 9.3% expansion in the first half of 2017, while private construction rose by a robust 7.3%. With domestic investment climbing steadily by an annual average approaching 17.0% in the past 5 years, the country's ratio of fixed investment to GDP reached 27.2% in the first half of 2018, its highest in over two decades, laying the foundation for sustained growth over the medium term (Figure 3.4.24).

Growth in merchandise exports moderated in real terms after a rebound in 2017, while household consumption eased slightly from its brisk pace last year. Growth in exports of goods and services slowed to 9.8% year on year in the first half of the year from 19.5% in the same period of last year. Growth in merchandise exports fell by more than half from a hefty 22.7% in the first 6 months of 2017 to 8.9% in the first half of this year. Growth in electronics exports, which account for half of all exports, eased, while shipments of agricultural products contracted. Service exports held up well, rising by 12.8% despite a temporary closure of Boracay island, a major tourist destination.

Household consumption, comprising two-thirds of GDP, rose by 5.7% in the first half of 2018, a bit lower than the 5.9% rise a year earlier. Unexpectedly higher inflation softened demand, even as support from remittances continued. Meanwhile, helped by a rise in expenditure on social priorities such as education, health care, and conditional cash transfers to poor families, as well as government salaries, growth in government consumption almost tripled to 12.6% from 4.3% in the first half of 2017.

3.4.23 Demand-side contributions to growth

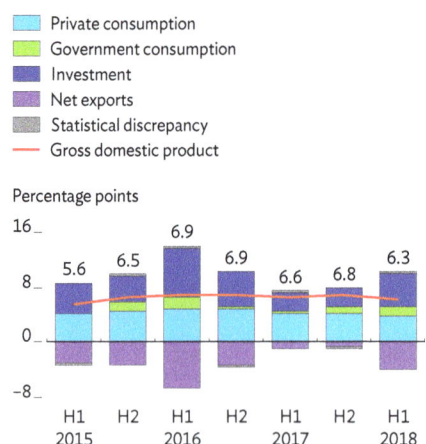

- Private consumption
- Government consumption
- Investment
- Net exports
- Statistical discrepancy
- Gross domestic product

H = half.
Source: CEIC Data Company (accessed 25 August 2018).

3.4.24 Fixed investment

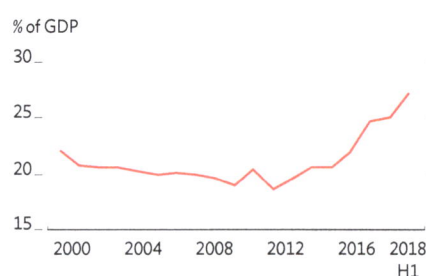

H = half.
Source: CEIC Data Company (accessed 3 September 2018).

By sector, continued strength in industry and services partly mitigated stagnation in agricultural output, which rose by only 0.7% in the first half of the year after growing by 5.6% in the same period of last year with recovery from a dry spell in 2016 attributed to El Niño (Figure 3.4.25). The major crops rice, maize, and sugarcane posted declines in the second quarter. In the first half, output from fisheries declined by 1.7%, deepening a 0.8% contraction in the same period of 2017.

Industry grew by 7.0% in the first half of the year, almost the same pace in the same period in 2017. Manufacturing contributed two-thirds of industry growth despite slowing from 7.8% growth in the first half of last year to 6.6% this year in response to softer export demand (Figure 3.4.26). Meanwhile, construction posted strong 11.5% expansion and contributed to quickening growth in construction-related manufactures such as cement and metals. Growth in services accelerated to 6.7% from 6.5% in first half of 2017. With robust retail trade, transportation, communications, and finance, the service sector was the biggest contributor to GDP growth.

Even as economic growth moderated, headline inflation rose to average 4.8% in the first 8 months of 2018, significantly up from 2.8% in the same period of last year. It accelerated on supply-side factors such as poor crop production, higher international prices for oil, and additional excise taxes on fuel, sugar-sweetened beverages, and cigarettes implemented since last January 2018, as well as with depreciation of the Philippine peso. Recent fare increases for public transportation and minimum wage increases in some regions kept up the pressure. Annual inflation reached 6.4% in August, up from 3.4% in January (Figure 3.4.27). Meanwhile, core inflation, excluding volatile food and energy prices, edged up to average 3.7% in the first 8 months of the year from 2.5% a year earlier, suggesting that demand has also stoked inflation.

Sluggish exports and accelerating growth in imports, especially of machinery and equipment and of intermediate products to meet surging domestic investment needs, widened the trade deficit to an equivalent of 14.7% of GDP in the first half of the year from 12.1% in the same period last year. Strong remittances and earnings from service exports, particularly business process outsourcing and tourism, partly offset the rising trade deficit. Nevertheless, the current account deficit widened to the equivalent of 1.9% of GDP in the first half from 0.1% in the same period of 2017 (Figure 3.4.28).

In the financial account, foreign direct investment rose, amounting in the first half of the year to $5.8 billion, 42.4% higher than in the same period in 2017 (Figure 3.4.29). Portfolio investment registered a higher net outflow, however, partly in response to the higher US interest rates as monetary policy there normalizes. The overall balance of payments therefore recorded a deficit equal to 2.1% of GDP in the first half of the

3.4.25 Supply-side contributions to growth

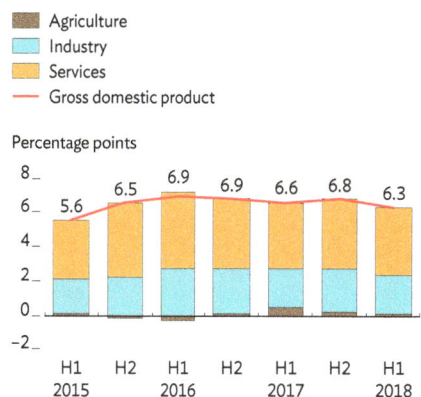

- Agriculture
- Industry
- Services
- Gross domestic product

Percentage points

H = half.
Source: CEIC Data Company (accessed 25 August 2018).

3.4.26 Contributions to industry growth

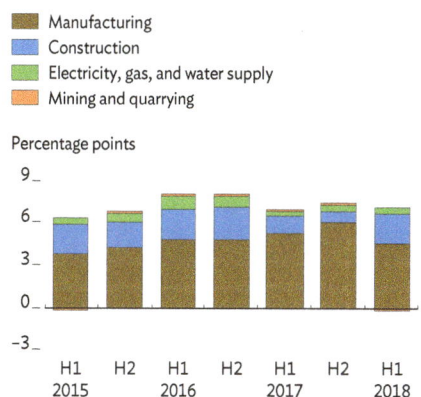

- Manufacturing
- Construction
- Electricity, gas, and water supply
- Mining and quarrying

Percentage points

H = half.
Source: CEIC Data Company (accessed 25 August 2018).

3.4.27 Contributions to inflation

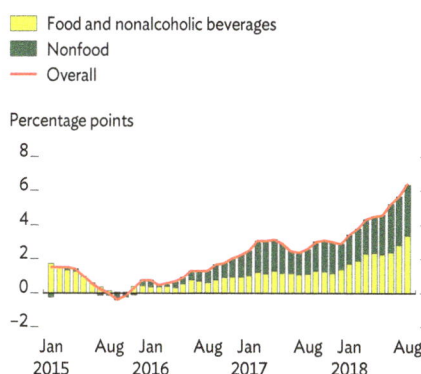

- Food and nonalcoholic beverages
- Nonfood
- Overall

Percentage points

Source: CEIC Data Company (accessed 7 September 2018).

year, wider than the 0.5% deficit in the first half of 2017 and pushing the peso down by 8.0% against the US dollar since the beginning of 2018. Nevertheless, gross international reserves stood in August at $77.8 billion, or cover for 7.5 months of imports of goods and payments on services and primary income.

The buildup of inflationary pressures and peso depreciation prompted Bangko Sentral ng Pilipinas, the central bank, to raise its policy interest rate three times so far in 2018 by a cumulative 100 basis points. From January to August this year, the overnight reverse repurchase rate rose from 3.0% to 4.0%. Even as it hiked the policy rate, the central bank cut the reserve ratio requirement for banks twice this year, bringing it down to 18.0% in June. These realignments in monetary policy were done toward gradually relying more on interest rates to manage domestic liquidity and less on reserve requirements.

Trends in fiscal policy suggest that public spending was on track in the first half of 2018. Disbursements excluding interest payments rose by 22.0% year on year, outpacing programmed disbursements by 3.0%, with infrastructure spending a significant contributor (Figure 3.4.30). Infrastructure spending was above program by 4.3%. Revenue rose by nearly 20.0% and exceeded the budget target by more than 8.0%. Tax collections, which provide 90% of all revenue, were 17.4% higher, boosted by additional revenue collected under the Tax Reform for Acceleration and Inclusion Law (Figure 3.4.31). The ratio of tax to GDP thus rose to 15.2% of GDP from 14.2% a year earlier. With a fiscal deficit equal to only 2.3% of GDP in the first half, the government is likely to keep the deficit under the 3.0% ceiling for the full year.

Prospects

The growth outlook has softened somewhat since *ADO 2018* was published in April as agriculture became sluggish, export prospects moderated, inflation exceeded expectations, and concomitant monetary tightening occurred. GDP growth forecasts are revised down from 6.8% to 6.4% for 2018 and from 6.9% to 6.7% for 2019 (Figure 3.4.32). While growth from agriculture and allied activities is likely to be only barely positive this year, industry and services look set to maintain solid growth trajectories.

Export growth is expected to be moderate because prospects for major external markets are uneven. The firming up of US growth is tempered by growth moderation in Japan, the destination for about 15% of Philippine exports. Although Philippine exports to the PRC, Southeast Asia, and the US increased in the first half of 2018, exports to Japan declined by a steep 17.7%. Meanwhile, trade tensions between the US and other major economies including the PRC may slow growth globally and weigh on external demand. On the other hand,

3.4.28 Current account components

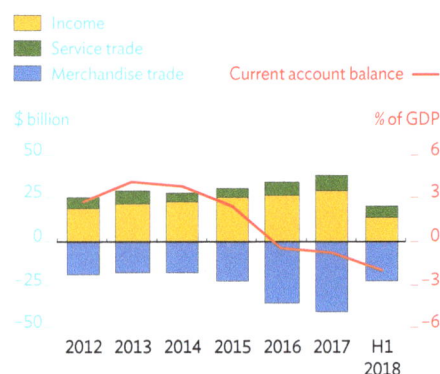

H = half.
Source: CEIC Data Company (accessed 17 September 2018).

3.4.29 Foreign direct investment

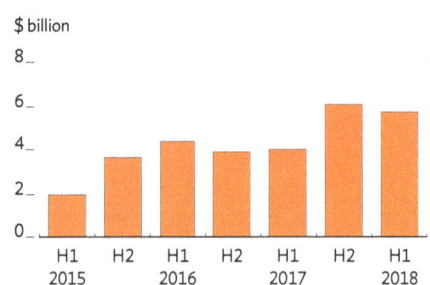

H = half.
Source: CEIC Data Company (accessed 25 August 2018).

3.4.30 Government expenditure

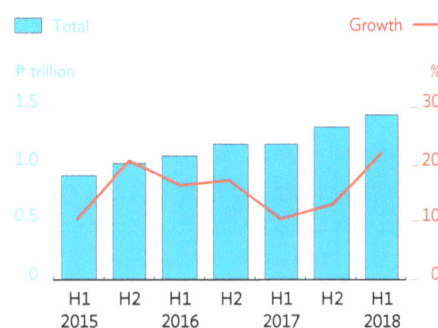

H = half.
Note: Government expenditure excludes interest payments.
Source: CEIC Data Company (accessed 10 September 2018).

some manufacturers in the PRC who now face higher US tariffs may relocate production to Southeast Asia, possibly the Philippines.

Private consumption, while easing from last year's rapid growth, should continue to grow briskly in the near term on continued growth in remittances from overseas Filipinos, solid job creation including under the public infrastructure program, and a resulting decline in unemployment. The unemployment rate fell to 5.4% in July 2018 from 5.6% in July 2017 with more jobs in services and industry. The reduction in income taxes for most workers should further boost consumption.

The outlook for investment continues to be positive both this year and next. Imports of capital goods rose by 16.7% in the first 7 months of the year, while bank credit to businesses increased by 19.7% year on year in July with higher lending for trade, manufacturing, construction, and real estate. The government's infrastructure program gathered momentum as infrastructure spending rose by 47.0% year on year in the first 7 months of 2018. Of the 75 projects proposed under the government's infrastructure development program, 44 were under implementation in August.

Earlier this year, the government approved the Ease of Doing Business Act, which streamlines and shortens procedures for government transactions all the way down to local government. Additional initiatives aim to simplify export and import procedures and streamline customs clearance. The effective implementation of reform promises to boost private investment.

With the recent buildup of inflationary pressures, inflation is expected to average 5.0% in 2018, higher than the earlier forecast of 4.0% and exceeding the government's target range of 2.0%–4.0% (Figure 3.4.33). Rising global commodity prices should maintain inflationary pressures. As monetary tightening begins to kick in, inflation will likely moderate in 2019 to 4.0%, the forecast revised up marginally from 3.9%. The removal of administrative constraints and nontariff barriers on food imports, and the implementation of programs to enhance productivity in agriculture, should alleviate over time constraints on the delivery of affordable rice.

The current account deficit is expected to widen to equal 1.8% of GDP in 2018 and 2.0% in 2019, exceeding *ADO 2018* forecasts. Higher international prices for oil and other commodities will apply further pressure on the current account. Merchandise exports may recover in 2019, but growth in imports will continue to outpace them, the imbalance eased by continued growth in remittances and earnings from tourism and business process outsourcing.

With inflation exceeding the official target in 2018 and continuing uncertainty about portfolio capital flows, monetary policy is likely to remain on a tightening trend in the near

3.4.31 Government revenues

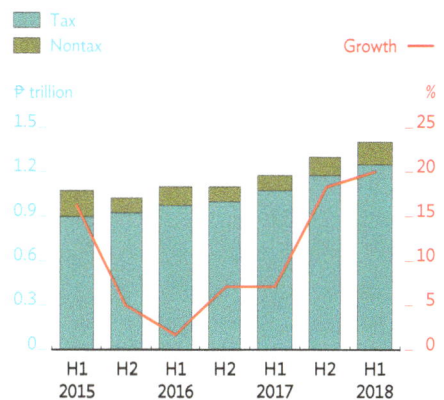

H = half.
Source: CEIC Data Company (accessed 7 September 2018).

3.4.32 GDP growth

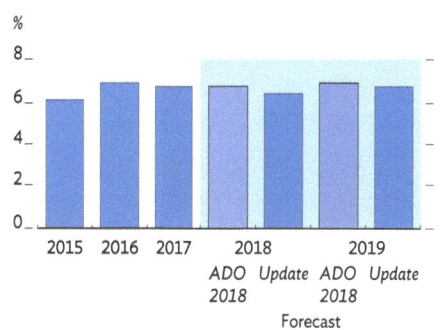

Source: *Asian Development Outlook* database.

3.4.33 Inflation

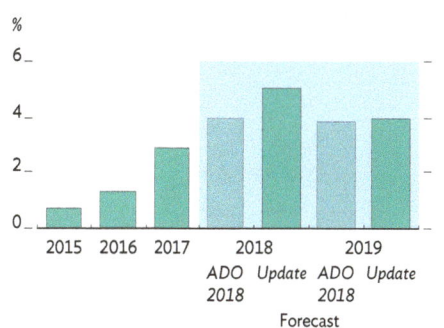

Source: *Asian Development Outlook* database.

term. Indeed, the central bank has made its intentions clear by announcing that it stands ready to follow through with additional monetary tightening if necessary to stem further inflation—and to counter in foreign exchange markets the effects of portfolio outflows caused by the normalization of monetary policy in the advanced economies.

Fiscal policy is on track to achieve the original budget targets for this year. Budget proposals for 2019 call for a fiscal deficit equal to 3.2% of GDP. Government spending will equal 19.7% of GDP in 2019, up from the 19.2% budget target for this year, while revenues are targeted at 16.5%, up from the 16.2% budget target this year. Within this budgetary envelope, larger outlays are planned for infrastructure development and social programs including national health insurance, free tertiary education in state colleges and universities, free irrigation for smallholder farmers, and social protection for the poor affected by transitory price increases arising from tax reform. On the revenue side, succeeding phases of the comprehensive tax reform include the rationalization of fiscal incentives to investors and further tax hikes on alcohol and tobacco. These measures are seen as vital to providing a stable revenue base to support the large public investment program and, at the same time, meet the fiscal deficit ceiling of 3.0% of GDP by 2022.

External risks to the outlook include unexpectedly swift interest rate tightening in the US, heightened volatility in international financial markets, and uncertain trade policy in the advanced economies. However, the economy seems to have the resilience to adjust to these risks, as external debt equaled only 22.5% of GDP at the end of June 2018 and national government debt, most of it domestic, was at the end of 2017 down to the equivalent of 42.1% of GDP.

3.4.3 Selected economic indicators, Philippines (%)

	2018		2019	
	ADO 2018	Update	ADO 2018	Update
GDP growth	6.8	6.4	6.9	6.7
Inflation	4.0	5.0	3.9	4.0
Current acct. bal. (share of GDP)	–1.0	–1.8	–1.4	–2.0

Source: ADB estimates.

Thailand

Helped by strong export growth, buoyant domestic demand, and a major turnaround in agriculture, the economy grew by 4.8% in the first half of the year, outperforming the *ADO 2018* forecast in April. GDP growth is now revised up to 4.5% for 2018 and 4.3% for 2019. In line with stronger growth, inflation forecasts are also revised up but only marginally as inflationary pressures remain muted. A pickup in investment should narrow current account surpluses both this year and next.

Updated assessment

Expansion in demand at home and abroad enabled GDP growth at 4.8% in the first half of 2018, much higher than 3.7% in the same period of 2017 (Figure 3.4.34). Merchandise exports continued to perform well, growing by 11.1% in US dollar terms, up from 7.3% a year earlier. Exports of automobiles rose by a strong 15.1%, while electronics posted a 12.4% increase. Exports of other manufactures such as petroleum, chemicals, and petrochemicals also grew rapidly, while agricultural exports posted only modest growth, with a decline in rubber shipments offsetting increased exports of rice and tapioca.

On the domestic demand side, consumer confidence improved in the first half of 2018 as incomes rose, farm production rebounded, and public welfare spending increased. Private consumption grew in turn by 4.1%, much faster than 3.0% recorded a year earlier. Domestic investment gathered pace as the government pursued an ambitious infrastructure plan, thereby pushing up public investment and buoying business sentiment. Public investment rebounded strongly by 4.5% with construction on housing development projects, electric power plants and distribution systems, and railways (Figure 3.4.35). Meanwhile, private investment grew by 3.2%, and manufacturing capacity utilization climbed to 70.1% in June 2018, the highest since October 2012. Private construction expanded well, mostly in and around Bangkok.

By sector, agriculture expanded by 8.3% in the first half of the year. Helped partly by favorable weather, most major crops such as rice, pineapple, and maize saw higher yields. Manufacturing rebounded with 3.5% growth, a much higher gain than the anemic 1.5% expansion a year earlier. Meanwhile, a 12.5% rise in international tourist arrivals helped the service sector turn in a solid performance, with impressive expansion in hotels and restaurants, transport and communication, and wholesale and retail trade (Figure 3.4.36).

In line with strong economic growth, the unemployment rate remained low at 1.2% in the first half of the year. The number of workers employed rose by 0.4% year on year as bumper harvests pushed employment in agriculture up by 4.5% and the rebound in manufacturing fueled a 1.3% increase in factory jobs.

3.4.34 Supply-side constributions to growth

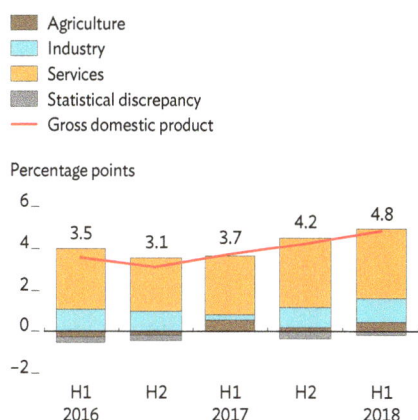

Legend:
- Agriculture
- Industry
- Services
- Statistical discrepancy
- Gross domestic product

Percentage points

H = half.

Source: Office of the National Economic and Social Development Board, http://www.nesdb.go.th (accessed 29 August 2018.)

3.4.35 Fixed investment growth

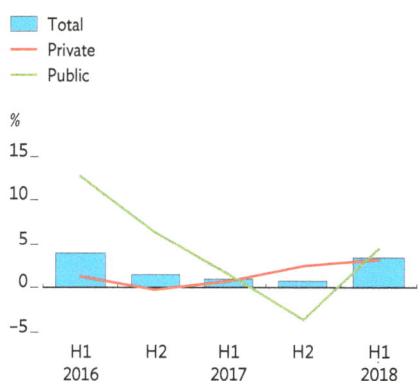

Legend:
- Total
- Private
- Public

%

H = half.

Source: Office of the National Economic and Social Development Board, http://www.nesdb.go.th (accessed 29 August 2018.)

3.4.36 Tourist arrivals

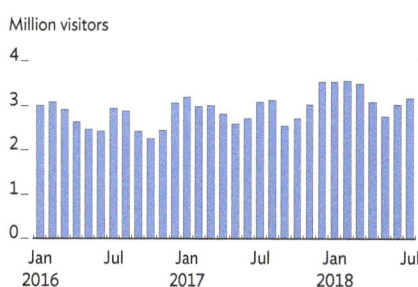

Million visitors

Source: CEIC Data Company (accessed 4 September 2018).

Stronger growth and a tighter labor market created some inflationary pressure, as did higher international oil prices. In the first 8 months of 2018, headline inflation year on year averaged 1.1% and core inflation 0.7%, both up from 0.6% in the same period of last year (Figure 3.4.37). Inflation remains close to the bottom end of the target range of 1.0%–4.0% set by the Bank of Thailand, the central bank.

The balance of payments surplus shrank as the strong rise in export earnings was accompanied by higher imports. Much of the hefty 17.3% increase in merchandise imports in the first half of the year was in raw materials, intermediate goods, and machinery and equipment needed to supply the pickup in investment, but imports of consumer goods picked up as well in line with higher consumer spending. The merchandise trade surplus thus narrowed by a quarter to $12.4 billion in the first half of the year from $16.6 billion a year earlier (Figure 3.4.38). At the same time, the net service balance, including primary and secondary income, rose to $8.9 billion from $7.7 billion, partly compensating for the narrower surplus in goods. The current account surplus was $21.4 billion, equal to 8.4% of GDP. This was lower than the $24.2 billion surplus posted in the same period of last year.

The combined capital and financial accounts in the balance of payments witnessed a net outflow of $10.5 billion in the first half of the year. This was caused by net outflows of portfolio capital and other investments as yields began rising in the advanced economies. It caused the Thai baht to depreciate by 0.2% against the dollar in the first 8 months of 2018. The overall balance of payments yielded a surplus of $7.6 billion in the first half, smaller than the $10.2 billion surplus in the same period of last year. Nevertheless, the surplus in the balance of payments helped the country add to its official foreign currency reserves, which at the end of July 2018 stood at a very healthy $205.5 billion, or cover for 9.1 months of imports. These international reserves provide an ample cushion 3.4 times the country's short-term external debt.

With inflationary pressures edging up but firmly under control, and with the balance of payments still comfortable despite capital outflow and baht depreciation, the central bank kept its policy interest rate unchanged at a low 1.50% to support the economy and firm up the current economic rebound. Bank credit to the private sector accelerated, with annual growth at 5.4% in the second quarter, higher than 4.7% growth in the first quarter and 4.3% growth in the last quarter of 2018.

Like monetary policy, fiscal policy is supportive of growth, with the budget continuing in deficit though somewhat less than last year. The fiscal deficit in the first 9 months of FY2018 (ending 30 September 2018) amounted to B493.9 billion, equal to 4.1% of GDP and higher than the deficit of 3.8% in

3.4.37 Inflation and policy interest rate

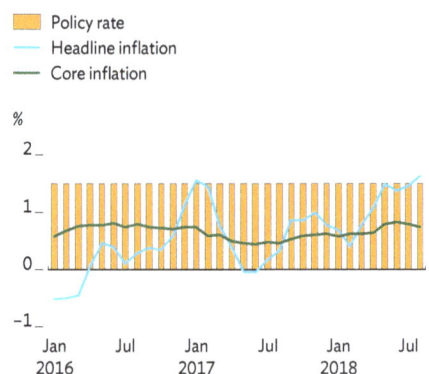

Source: CEIC Data Company (accessed 4 September 2018).

3.4.38 Trade indicators

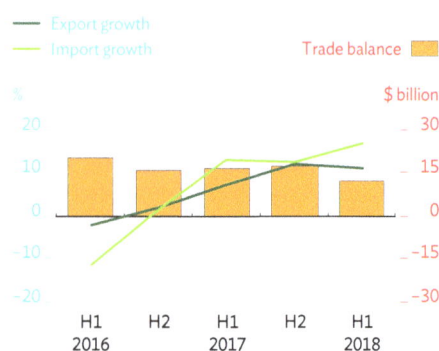

H = half.
Source: Bank of Thailand. http://www.bot.or.th (accessed 4 September 2018).

the same period a year earlier. Government revenue in the period increased by 5.4% year on year. In the first 9 months, revenue was 3.5% above the official target. Meanwhile, expenditure increased by 3.2% in the first 9 months of FY2018 to reach 82.2% of the FY2018 annual budget. This put the government on track to achieve its budget projections. Although rising in recent years, public debt remains manageable, equal to 40.9% of GDP at the end of July 2018. Moreover, almost all public debt is domestic.

Prospects

Although GDP growth will likely moderate somewhat from the large rebound in the first half of the year, it is now expected to grow by 4.5% in 2018 and 4.3% in 2019, both forecasts higher than in April (Figure 3.4.39). The revision reflects strong external and domestic demand underpinned by upbeat consumer sentiment and the public infrastructure development program.

Having performed well in the first half, exports should continue to contribute to growth both this year and next. The dollar value of merchandise exports is forecast to continue to expand at an annual rate of 10.0% both this year and next. While manufacturing will be the main source of exports, agricultural exports should also hold up well.

Private consumption is forecast to continue to grow at an annual rate of 4.0%–4.5% both this year and next, supported by rising incomes and employment. The consumer confidence index has been climbing steadily in recent months, reaching in July its highest since May 2013 (Figure 3.4.40). Government efforts to support low-income families should help sustain consumption growth, with more than 11 million people who earn less than B100,000 per year now qualified for a newly introduced card that entitles them to B200 per month for buying household goods (B300 for those earning less than B30,000 per year) and up to B1,500 per month for public transportation fares. However, high household debt, equal to 77% of GDP at the end of first quarter of 2018, may constrain household spending.

Investment is foreseen building on the pickup in the first half, with public investment expected to accelerate in the near term on a big jump in the government's capital budget and faster disbursement on large infrastructure projects nearing their construction phase. Private investment is expected to improve upon its performance in the first half. As manufacturing capacity utilization is already at its highest in more than 5 years and business sentiment is improving, companies are likely to invest in capital equipment. A leading indicator of this is a significant rise in the value of investments for which applications have been approved in recent months.

3.4.39 GDP growth

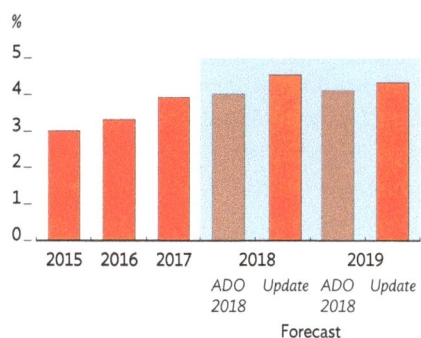

Source: Asian Development Outlook database.

3.4.4 Selected economic indicators, Thailand (%)

	2018		2019	
	ADO 2018	Update	ADO 2018	Update
GDP growth	4.0	4.5	4.1	4.3
Inflation	1.2	1.3	1.3	1.4
Current acct. bal. (share of GDP)	8.0	8.0	7.5	7.5

Source: ADB estimates.

3.4.40 Consumer confidence and business sentiment indexes

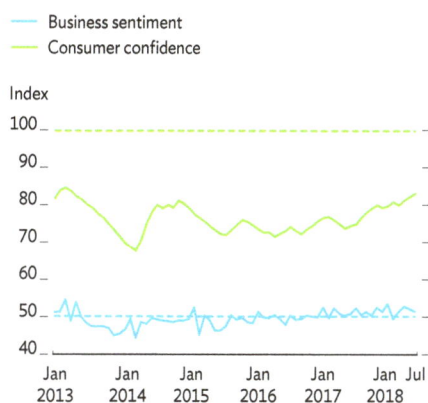

Note: A reading <50 denotes deteriorating business sentiment, while a reading <100 denotes deteriorating consumer confidence.

Sources: CEIC Data Company; Bank of Thailand. http://www.bot.or.th (accessed 4 September 2018).

By sector, agriculture is unlikely to sustain its first half growth pace in the second half. While agricultural production will continue to grow, supported by ample irrigation, some farm areas were flooded by heavy rains in August. Manufacturing is expected to post robust growth, supported by domestic and external demand alike. Export-oriented industries are seen to continue to do well as global demand remains robust (Figure 3.4.41). The service sector will continue to contribute strongly to growth, with services tied to tourism poised to benefit as growth in tourism remains buoyant.

As the economy sustains higher growth, inflation will continue to edge up but will still be well within the central bank target range. Inflation is forecast at 1.3% this year and 1.4% next year, only marginally higher than *ADO 2018* forecasts (Figure 3.4.42).

The trade surplus is likely to continue to narrow as merchandise import growth outpaces export growth. Imports of raw materials, intermediate goods, parts and components, and capital goods are all seen to rise strongly to support domestic investment and growth. In tandem with the narrowing trade surplus, the current account surplus is expected to narrow to the equivalent of 8.0% of GDP this year and 7.5% next year, as forecast in *ADO 2018* (Figure 3.4.43). Foreign direct investment may start to rise in 2019, as foreign investors are reported to be showing strong interest in the Eastern Economic Corridor now under development. Portfolio flows may reverse, drawn back to Thailand by its stronger economic performance. In any case, the overall balance of payments is expected to continue in surplus. International reserves will remain more than sufficient to cover import needs.

In light of strengthening growth, rising but low inflation, a comfortable balance of payments, and abundant international reserves, monetary policy is unlikely to change in the near term. Similarly, fiscal policy is expected to remain accommodative as spending on public infrastructure continues to accelerate and project implementation brings rapid disbursement. The fiscal deficit for the whole of 2018 is expected to be close to the government target of 3.5% of GDP.

Risks to the outlook arise from any further escalation of global trade tensions. Having imposed new tariffs on each other's products this year, the US and the PRC have contingency plans for widening the range of goods on which the tariffs are imposed. As Thailand is an open economy, it could be adversely affected by any slowdown in global trade that may result. A second risk to the outlook would be sudden and substantial capital flight out of Thailand. Higher global interest rates, especially in the US, have already prompted net capital outflow from Thailand this year. However, the country's comfortable external payments position leaves it well placed to weather such external risks.

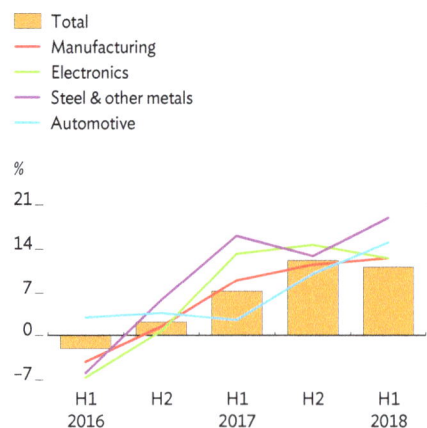

3.4.41 Exports growth by product group

H = half.

Source: Bank of Thailand. http://www.bot.or.th (accessed 4 September 2018).

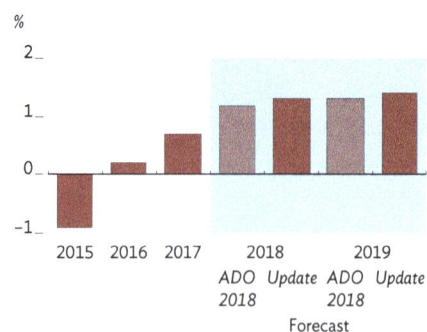

3.4.42 Inflation

Source: *Asian Development Outlook* database.

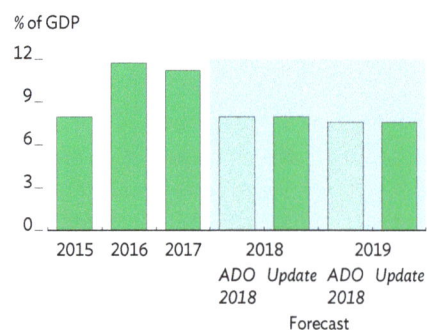

3.4.43 Current account balance

Source: *Asian Development Outlook* database.

Viet Nam

The economy maintained 7.1% growth in the first half of 2018, in line with the *ADO 2018* forecast in April. With growth moderation likely in the second half of the year for exports, agriculture, and construction—and with continued contraction in mining—GDP growth for the whole year is now seen slightly lower than earlier forecast. As inflation is on an upward trend and unlikely to change course in the near term, inflation forecasts for this year and next are revised up. The current account surplus is forecast to narrow more than foreseen in April.

Updated assessment

Vietnam posted 7.1% GDP growth in the first half of 2018, up from 5.8% in the same period in 2017 (Figure 3.4.44). On the demand side, rising income lifted private consumption growth to 7.2% from 7.0% a year earlier. Private investment remained robust, supported by high credit growth and strong foreign direct investment (FDI). Exports of goods and services rose by 15.7% by volume in the first half of the year from 14.4% a year earlier. Strength in exports, domestic private consumption, and investment more than offset deceleration in government consumption and public investment that resulted from fiscal consolidation.

Most major sectors continued to perform solidly. Output from agriculture and allied activities grew by 3.9% in the first half of this year, up from 2.7% in the first half of 2017. Thanks to favorable weather and strong export demand, farm output increased by 3.3%, up from 2.1% growth in the first half of 2017, while forestry and fisheries also remained buoyant.

Industrial production expanded by 9.3% in first half of the year, sharply higher than 5.4% expansion in the same months of last year. A 13.0% rise in manufacturing output was driven by impressive increases in export-oriented industries such as in telecommunications, electronics, and textiles. Acceleration in industry more than offset moderation in construction from 8.5% growth in the first half of last year to 7.9% this year as measures took hold to curb bank lending to real estate. Driven partly by a hefty rise in international tourist arrivals, the service sector posted nearly 7.0% growth in the first half of the year, the same pace as in the first 6 months of last year. As tourist arrivals rose by 27.2% in the first half, hotels and restaurants, transportation and communications, and wholesale and retail trade continued to be buoyant (Figure 3.4.45).

Strong growth put upward pressure on inflation, as did a hike in government-administered fees and higher international oil prices. Headline inflation inched up to 4.7% year on year in June 2018 from the low of 2.5% in June 2017, and average annual inflation in the first 6 months of the year reached 3.3% (Figure 3.4.46). Driven by hikes in several administered fees,

3.4.44 Supply-side contributions to growth

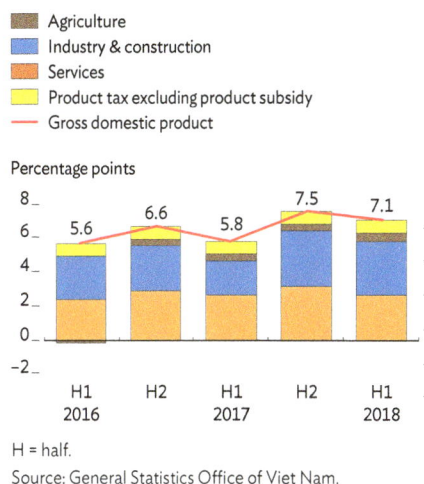

Agriculture
Industry & construction
Services
Product tax excluding product subsidy
Gross domestic product

Percentage points

H = half.
Source: General Statistics Office of Viet Nam.

3.4.45 Visitor arrivals

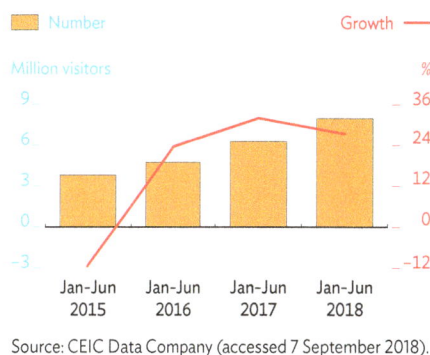

Number   Growth

Source: CEIC Data Company (accessed 7 September 2018).

3.4.46 Monthly inflation

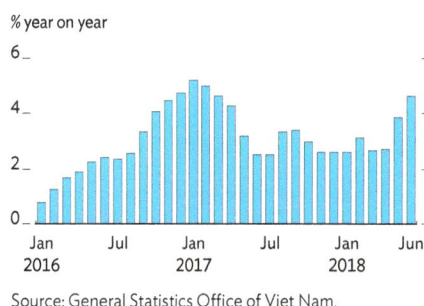

% year on year

Source: General Statistics Office of Viet Nam.

prices for medical services surged by 16.7% in the first half of the year while tuition for public education increased by 6.8%. Meanwhile, transportation costs went up by 9.7%, largely because of higher gasoline prices.

The balance of payments posted an estimated surplus equal to 8.4% of GDP in the first half of the year, with the current and capital accounts both registering surpluses. Helped by a merchandise trade surplus in the first half, the current account yielded a surplus estimated to equal 5.0% of GDP, reversing a deficit of 1.1% in the same period a year earlier (Figure 3.4.47). The trade surplus was made possible by 17.0% growth in merchandise exports that far outstripped 10.5% growth in imports. The main items experiencing export growth were mobile phones and other electronic products, which now account for 31.6% of all exports, up from 11.5% in 2011.

Bolstered by strong FDI and rising portfolio capital inflows, the capital account recorded a surplus equal to an estimated 7.9% of GDP in the first half of 2018. FDI commitments reached $16.2 billion in the first 6 months, and disbursements an estimated $8.4 billion, up by 8.4% year on year. A major part of FDI flowed into export-oriented manufacturing of mobile phones and other electronics. Meanwhile, net portfolio capital inflow was an estimated $2.3 billion in the first half of the year, further helping the capital account to post a surplus. Official foreign exchange reserves thus rose from the equivalent of 2.7 months of imports at the end of 2017 to 3 months of import cover by June. Meanwhile, the Viet Nam dong, having remained stable against the US dollar in the first 6 months of the year, depreciated by about 1% in June, partly in response to rising US interest rates (Figure 3.4.48).

The stock market was volatile in the first half of the year, rising to an 11-year high of 1,200 at the beginning of April, slumping below 1,000 in May–July as interest rates and returns on capital rose in other capital markets, and then gradually recovering (Figure 3.4.49).

Despite upwardly creeping inflation, State Bank of Viet Nam, the central bank, maintained its policy interest rate unchanged since a cut in July 2017, in an attempt to keep monetary and credit growth in line with its official targets. At the end of June 2018, growth in the money supply (M2) was an estimated 16.2% year on year, and growth in bank credit was 15.0%, largely in line with the central bank's annual targets (Figure 3.4.50).

The government's fiscal consolidation program progressed in the first half of the year. Budget revenue increased by 15.7% in the first 6 months, reaching the equivalent of 28.7% of GDP. Meanwhile, expenditure increased by a more modest 11.4%, thanks partly to rationalized spending, still slower than originally planned. The budget posted a small surplus equal to 0.1% of GDP in the first half of the year, reversing a deficit

3.4.47 Current account balance

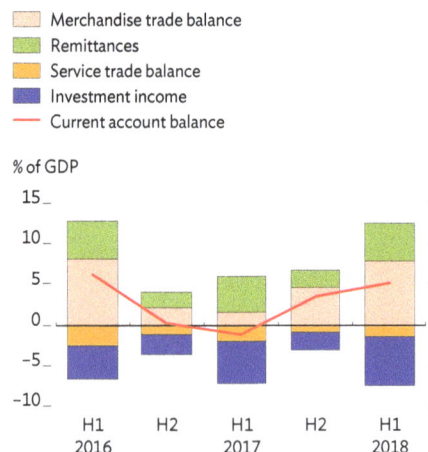

H = half.
Source: General Statistics Office of Viet Nam.

3.4.48 Exchange rates

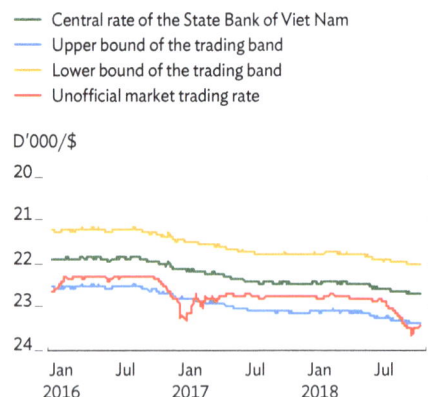

Sources: State Bank of Viet Nam; ADB observations.

3.4.49 Ho Chi Minh stock exchange index

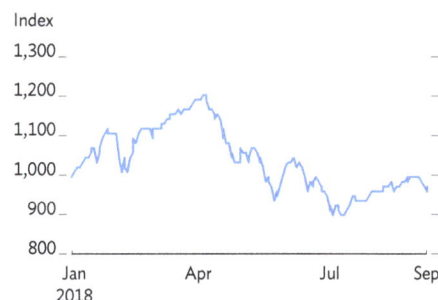

Source: Bloomberg (accessed 8 September 2018).

of nearly 1.0% a year earlier. Efforts to rein in the fiscal deficit helped to lower the ratio of public debt to GDP to an estimated 58.5% at the end of June 2018 from 63.7% at the beginning of 2017.

Structural reform of state-owned enterprises (SOEs) and the banking system continued in the first half of 2018, though at a lackluster pace for SOEs. Although the selling of government stakes in 16 SOEs and divestment of state capital added about D28 trillion to the budget, it was only one-fifth of last year's figure. Meanwhile, equitization plans were approved for only 19 SOEs in the first half of the year, way behind the government's target of equitizing at least 85 SOEs before year-end.

The share of nonperforming loans (NPLs) in the banking system fell to 2.1% in June 2018, down from 2.5% at the beginning of 2017 as banks stepped up NPL resolution through debt collection and the sale of collateral. Meanwhile, all NPLs on bank balance sheets and warehoused with the state-owned Viet Nam Asset Management Company, combined with bank loans deemed at high risk of becoming NPLs in the near term, were estimated by the government at 6.9% of all outstanding loans in mid-2018, down from the 10.1% in December 2016. NPL resolution has received fresh impetus from legal reform effected in 2017 that facilitated the disposal of collateral and the restructuring of bad assets.

Prospects

Economic growth will likely hold up fairly well in the near term thanks to continued strength in domestic demand. However, growth moderation in the European Union, Japan, and the People's Republic of China could dent export opportunities for Viet Nam, as could escalating trade friction around the world that threatens to disrupt global value chains and production networks in which Viet Nam is tightly integrated. Severe floods in July and August could undermine agriculture, while aging mines will likely drive down mining output. The growth forecast for this year is therefore revised down from 7.1% in *ADO 2018* to 6.9%, while the forecast for 2019 is retained (Figure 3.4.51). Meanwhile, inflation forecasts are adjusted upward from 3.7% to 4.0% for 2018 and from 4.0% to 4.5% for 2019.

Prospects for private consumption continue to be bright, while the outlook for private investment remains stable under the government's continuing efforts to improve the business environment and facilitate the opening of new businesses. Acceleration in public capital expenditure in the second half of the year is expected to boost growth in investment.

Growth in merchandise exports is likely to moderate in the near term although Viet Nam's participation in various free trade agreements should support continued access to foreign markets for major exports.

3.4.50 Credit and money supply growth

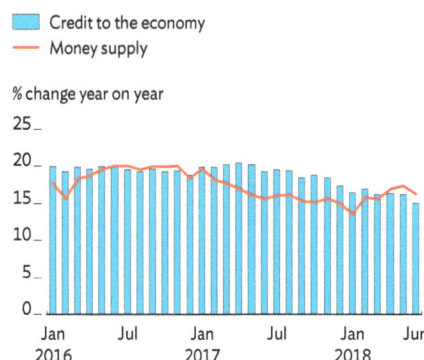

Sources: State Bank of Viet Nam; ADB estimates.

3.4.51 GDP growth

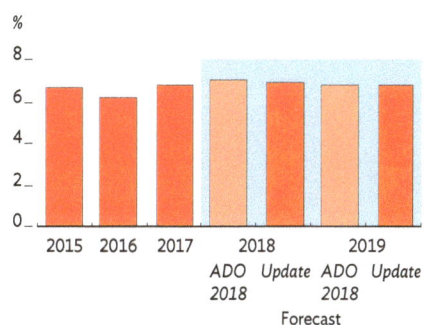

Source: *Asian Development Outlook* database.

3.4.5 Selected economic indicators, Viet Nam (%)

	2018		2019	
	ADO 2018	Update 2018	ADO 2018	Update 2018
GDP growth	7.1	6.9	6.8	6.8
Inflation	3.7	4.0	4.0	4.5
Current acct. bal. (share of GDP)	2.5	2.3	2.0	2.0

Source: ADB estimates.

By sector, agriculture should post slower growth at 2.5% this year, below the earlier forecast and the government target of 3.0%, following severe floods in recent months. Mining output, which contracted by 1.3% in the first half of the year, continues to be handicapped by aging mines and oil fields and unfavorable weather. Growth in construction will moderate in the rest of the year as the government seeks to prevent a real estate bubble. The manufacturing purchasing managers' index reached a record high of 55.7 in June, indicating continued improvement in business conditions, but some softening in industry growth cannot be ruled out as exports moderate in the coming months (Figure 3.4.52). Meanwhile, services are likely to hold up well thanks to rising private consumption and buoyant tourism.

Despite the downward revision for growth this year, inflationary pressures are likely to persist over the near term. The dong has exhibited more weakness since July and could come under continued pressure as US interest rates rise and the dollar strengthens. If the renminbi of the People's Republic of China continues to depreciate against the US dollar, the dong could further weaken as well, adding to inflation. Moreover, inflation could be fueled by rising international oil prices or an upsurge in food prices—which, accounting for about a third of the consumer price index, rose by 2.3% in the first 8 months of 2018, reversing a declining trend in the same period of last year. Average annual inflation is therefore forecast to edge up to 4.0% in 2018 and further to 4.5% in 2019, both projections higher than in April (Figure 3.4.53).

The emergence of a trade deficit in July and August signaled that growth in merchandise imports is likely to outpace that of exports. The current account surplus will likely narrow even if net service exports remain steady. Forecasts for the current account surplus are therefore revised down to the equivalent of 2.3% of GDP this year and maintained at 2.0% next year. On the capital account, FDI continues to be a major source of strength. However, if trade tensions escalate, foreign investors may consider adjusting their business strategies, dampening FDI inflows to Viet Nam. Although FDI remained strong in the first half of this year, it has been less buoyant since then (Figure 3.4.54).

Amid the complexities of the emerging macroeconomic environment, Viet Nam is cautiously deploying fiscal and monetary policies to maintain stability while supporting growth. Fiscal policy continues to focus on broadening the tax base and strengthening tax administration. Although the central bank has kept its policy interest rate unchanged, it has taken other measures to stabilize the exchange rate, notably selling US dollars to commercial banks in July and August. Interest rates for central bank bills issued since late July have also been adjusted upward, pushing up the interbank money

3.4.52 Purchasing managers' index

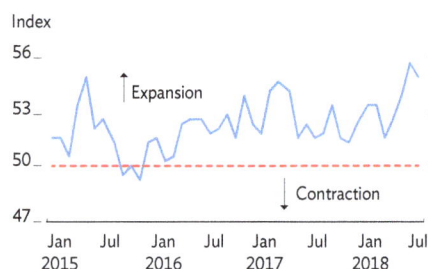

Note: Nikkei, Markit.
Source: Bloomberg (accessed 5 September 2018).

3.4.53 Inflation

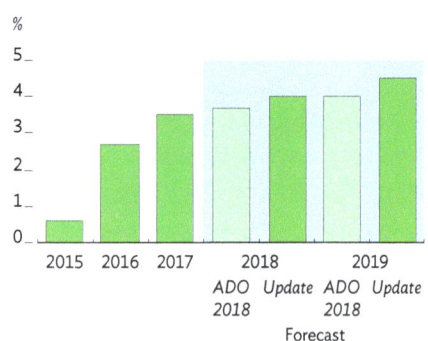

Source: Asian Development Outlook database.

3.4.54 Implemented foreign direct investment

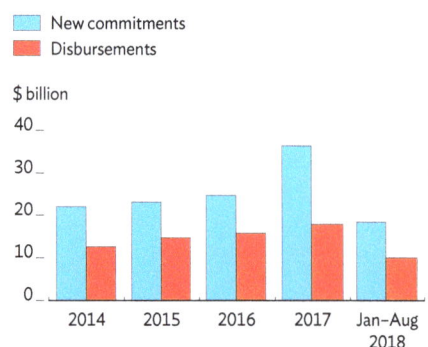

Source: General Statistics Office of Viet Nam.

market interest rate. The central bank has signaled that it intends to pursue a more flexible exchange rate as it gradually shifts its monetary policy from a focus on stabilizing exchange rates and controlling credit to one of targeting inflation. Recent measures and future policy intentions are consistent with tightening monetary policy in the near term to rein in inflation.

Risks to the outlook are mostly on the downside. If escalating trade tensions around the world slow global trade substantially and disrupt global production networks and supply chains, the growth outlook for Viet Nam will be much dimmer. Not only would such developments hurt its export prospects they would also hold back FDI. Heightened volatility in international financial markets is another downside risk.

Other economies

Brunei Darussalam

Driven by higher domestic investment, the economy grew by 2.5% in the first quarter of 2018, reversing 1.3% contraction in the same period of last year. Available indicators suggest that GDP growth was likely more than 2.0% in the first half of the year. Accordingly, growth for the year as a whole is now forecast half a percentage point higher than the *ADO 2018* forecast in April. A similar growth rate is expected in 2019, as earlier forecast.

A 21.0% increase in domestic investment in the first quarter was underpinned by a whopping 25.8% rise in private fixed investment, mostly to expand capacity for oil and gas extraction.

Economic recovery in the first quarter was further assured by a 4.4% rise in oil and gas production, a marked improvement from 3.7% contraction in the corresponding months of last year. Other components of industry also posted strong growth, with output from construction rising by 24.4% and reversing 1.8% contraction in the first quarter of last year. Meanwhile, output in both agriculture and services continued to decline.

Prices were highly stable, with annual inflation averaging just 0.2% in the first half of the year despite a 2.6% rise in prices for food and nonalcoholic beverages, which have a weight of 20% in the consumer price index. Continued government subsidies and a stable exchange rate kept a lid on prices. Inflation in 2018 and 2019 as a whole is still projected to be very low, only marginally higher than forecast in *ADO 2018*.

In the first 5 months of the year, exports rose by 6.4%, much lower than the 11.1% rate recorded in the same period of last year. Meanwhile, the rebound in investment and higher economic growth were accompanied by a surge in imports, as forecast in April. In the first 5 months, imports rose by 16.7%, led by whopping 54.9% growth for manufactured goods and 26.7% for machinery and transport equipment. The current account surplus this year and next is thus likely to narrow substantially, as forecast in *ADO 2018*, from 18.0% in 2017.

Cambodia

Helped in the first half of the year by strong export growth, robust tourist arrivals, and buoyant domestic demand, the economy is on track to achieve annual economic growth of 7.0% this year and next, as forecast in *ADO 2018*.

The dollar value of merchandise exports rose by 13.3% in the first 6 months of the year, against 7.7% in the corresponding period last year. Exports to Europe rose by 13.7% and to the US by 27.4%. A whopping 72.6% rise in tourist arrivals from the PRC in the first 7 months sustained growth in international tourist arrivals at 11.1%, albeit down from 12.8% growth a year earlier.

3.4.6 Selected economic indicators, Brunei Darussalam (%)

	2018		2019	
	ADO 2018	Update 2018	ADO 2018	Update 2018
GDP growth	1.5	2.0	2.0	2.0
Inflation	0.1	0.2	0.1	0.2
Current acct. bal. (share of GDP)	14.0	14.0	14.0	14.0

Source: ADB estimates.

3.4.7 Selected economic indicators, Cambodia (%)

	2018		2019	
	ADO 2018	Update 2018	ADO 2018	Update 2018
GDP growth	7.0	7.0	7.0	7.0
Inflation	3.2	2.6	3.5	3.0
Current acct. bal. (share of GDP)	−11.1	−12.1	−10.8	−11.8

Source: ADB estimates.

Normal weather in the first half seems to have supported robust farm and fishery output, though rubber production was hampered by the low international prices. Industry appears to have posted double-digit growth, while continued strength in tourism indicates brisk service sector expansion.

Despite strong growth, inflation was subdued, averaging 2.4% in the first 6 months of the year, down from 3.4% a year earlier. A stable exchange rate and only modest increases in food prices more than offset inflationary pressures from higher international oil prices, calling for downward revision of inflation forecasts for this year and next.

Despite the strong increases in merchandise exports and tourist arrivals, even faster growth in imports is expected to widen the current account deficit, requiring higher forecasts for these deficits, excluding official transfers, for this year and next. The capital account should continue in surplus, however, buoyed by foreign direct investment worth $1.3 billion in the first half of the year. Gross international reserves stood at $9.1 billion in July 2018 and should reach around $10 billion by year-end, providing 6 months of import cover.

Revenues in the first 6 months of 2018 amounted to 53.3% of the budget target for the year. Meanwhile, disbursements were only 34.5% of the full-year target, though past experience shows expenditure picking up toward the end of the year. The fiscal deficit this year is likely to be close to the budget target, equal to 5.1% of GDP. Monetary and credit conditions remained accommodative with broad money (M2) up by 16.5% year on year in June and credit to the private sector up by 18.4%.

The main external risk to the outlook would be US monetary policy tightening faster than expected and exciting volatility in regional and international financial markets. The major domestic risk would be repeated hikes in the minimum wage.

Lao People's Democratic Republic

Economic growth probably slowed slightly in the first half of 2018 while inflation accelerated. Meanwhile, the first quarter of the year saw the dollar value of exports rise by a whopping 36.6%—the export acceleration likely driven by manufactures and electricity—while imports increased by 15.0%.

Government revenue collected in the first 4 months of 2018 came to 28.6% of budget projections for the full year, while the corresponding figure for expenditure was 26.3%. As these fiscal trends align with original budget proposals, the target of a 2018 fiscal deficit equal to 4.8% of GDP appears to be attainable. Meanwhile, the Lao kip depreciated against the US dollar according to its official exchange rate by 1.6% from the beginning of 2018 to the end of July. On the parallel market, it depreciated by 5.2%, pointing to continued vulnerability to stress from external payments.

3.4.8 Selected economic indicators, Lao People's Democratic Republic (%)

	2018		2019	
	ADO 2018	*Update 2018*	ADO 2018	*Update 2018*
GDP growth	6.8	6.6	7.0	6.9
Inflation	2.0	2.5	2.5	3.1
Current acct. bal. (share of GDP)	–14.9	–13.8	–13.7	–13.0

Source: ADB estimates.

Economic growth is now projected at 6.6% this year, slightly lower than the 6.8% rate forecast in April by *ADO 2018*, with agriculture and mining underperforming forecasts. Further, a series of floods damaged farm output and disrupted transport services. Agriculture is projected to grow by 2.0% this year, slowing from 2.9% growth in 2017. Electricity generation should increase by 8.0% and mining output to decline by 2.0%.

Growth in construction and continued expansion in services are expected to partly cushion the adverse effects on growth from underperformance in agriculture and mining. Construction is benefiting from foreign direct investment in hydropower and transport projects such as the railway line from Vientiane to the border with the People's Republic of China, now under construction. Meanwhile, an advertising campaign to boost visitor arrivals is catalyzing growth in services.

Inflation was higher than foreseen as unexpectedly high international oil prices pushed up prices for a wide range of products. Headline inflation year on year tripled from 0.8% in December 2017 to 2.4% in July. Inflation is now forecast at about half a percentage point higher than *ADO 2018* projections for this year and next.

The current account deficit is likely to be narrower this year and next than forecast in *ADO 2018*. Despite expected improvement in the current account deficit, net official international reserves are forecast to fall below $1 billion by December 2018, providing cover for only 1.5 months of imports. This external payments vulnerability is the main risk clouding the outlook in the near term. Another is the possibility of recurrent disasters.

Myanmar

Available indicators suggest that GDP growth will be slightly below forecast for fiscal year 2018 (FY2018, the 6 months ending on 30 September 2018 as the end of the Myanmar fiscal year shifts from 31 March). While agriculture, which accounts for about 30% of GDP, has held up well, industry and services look less buoyant than earlier forecast as foreign direct investment (FDI) declines and international tourist arrivals appear to languish.

In the 5 months from April to August 2018, the value of merchandise exports rose by 32.0% year on year to reach nearly $7 billion, supported largely by rising international oil prices. However, in the first 4 months to July, FDI plunged to $830 million from $3 billion a year earlier. Isolated communal disturbances seem to have held back growth in international tourist arrivals despite a steady rise in arrivals from Asian markets. Tourism-related services—hotels, restaurants, transportation, and communications—thus underperformed earlier forecasts.

3.4.9 Selected economic indicators, Myanmar (%)

	2018		2019	
	ADO 2018	Update	ADO 2018	Update
GDP growth	6.8	6.6	7.2	7.0
Inflation	6.2	6.2	6.0	6.0
Current acct. bal. (share of GDP)	-5.4	-3.0	-5.5	-4.0

Note: Years are fiscal years ending on 30 September of that year; with a change in the fiscal year, FY2018 is only 6 months long.

Source: ADB estimates.

Average annual inflation from April to July 2018 accelerated to 6.4% from 3.5% in the same period of last year. Inflation has likely remained high at close to 6%, owing to higher international oil prices and continued depreciation of the Myanmar kyat. The 14 August decision of the Central Bank of Myanmar to remove a tight trading band on the kyat temporarily pushed the currency still lower, but a more flexible exchange rate regime without the trading band should help the economy adjust to external shocks.

The trade deficit plunged in April–August 2018 to $1.1 billion from $2.2 billion a year earlier. The current account deficit for FY2018 is therefore likely to be much smaller than the *ADO 2018* forecast. Despite the smaller deficit, slumping FDI seems to have worsened the overall balance of payments, putting more downward pressure on the kyat.

Trends in the 6 months ending in September 2018 suggest mixed economic prospects for FY2019. GDP growth is now envisaged slightly lower than forecast in *ADO 2018*. The inflation forecast is unchanged, as it is for FY2018. Softening oil prices next year will likely crimp export earnings and send the current account deficit wider again but still below the earlier forecast.

Lackluster progress on economic reform continues to be a domestic risk to the outlook. Another would be slow progress in the national peace process. The major external risks are possible worsening of international trade tensions and large swings in regional and global financial markets.

Singapore

Continued strength in exports and domestic demand enabled the economy to grow by 4.2% in the first half of 2018, up from 2.7% in the same period of last year. Exports of goods and services rose by 3.5% by volume, with the dollar value of merchandise exports up by 12.3% and net receipts from service exports up by 10.6%. Domestic demand expanded by 3.3% as private consumption rose at the same rate and fixed investment by 1.3%.

By sector, strong expansion in manufacturing and services more than compensated for continuing contraction in construction. Manufacturing growth at 10.5% was led by electronics, buoyed by strong global demand for semiconductors, and, in the second quarter, by higher production of pharmaceuticals and biotechnology products. Services expanded by 3.4% on strong finance and insurance and trade.

Inflation averaged just 0.3% in the first 7 months of the year. Core inflation, which excludes accommodation and private road transport, was much higher, however, at an average of 1.6% as economic growth continued and the labor market tightened.

3.4.10 Selected economic indicators, Singapore (%)

	2018		2019	
	ADO 2018	Update	ADO 2018	Update
GDP growth	3.1	3.1	2.9	2.9
Inflation	0.9	0.7	1.4	1.4
Current acct. bal. (share of GDP)	19.0	19.0	19.0	19.0

Source: ADB estimates.

With exports growing faster than imports in the first half, the current account surplus widened to $33.1 billion from $29.5 billion a year earlier, reaching the equivalent of 19.2% of GDP. The capital account saw net capital outflows of $22.2 billion, up from $15.9 billion in the first half of 2017. The overall balance of payments was a surplus of $11.0 billion, or 6.4% of GDP.

Monetary policy is expected to tighten in response to fast growth in the first half, and higher domestic interest rates will likely moderate growth in the second half. The 3-month Singapore interbank offered rate rose from 1.1% in January 2018 to 1.6% in July. In the same period, the purchasing managers' index for manufacturing fell from 53.1 to 52.3, indicating slower growth in production. Meanwhile, the government cut public expenditure on security, external relations, and economic development. Despite rapid growth in the first half of 2018, *ADO 2018* forecasts for slowing GDP growth are unchanged.

Even as global commodity prices edge up and domestic inflation pressure builds, the forecast for consumer inflation in 2018 is downgraded because of a continuing decline in prices for accommodation and marginal drop in public transport fares that partly offset higher gasoline prices.

The main risks to Singapore's open economy are rising trade tensions globally and a potential slowdown in trade. Tighter global finances could raise debt-servicing costs to households and businesses alike.

The Pacific

Despite higher growth forecasts for Solomon Islands and Tuvalu, the subregional projection for 2018 is reduced from *ADO 2018* mainly because of weaker prospects for Timor-Leste and for Papua New Guinea, where an expected recovery next year raises the subregional growth projection for 2019. Inflation is now seen to rise with higher taxes and commodity prices in 2018 before falling back in 2019. Larger subregional current account surpluses are projected on strong private remittances, tourism receipts, and fishing license revenue.

Subregional assessment and prospects

Growth in the Pacific is now projected to average 1.1% in 2018, only half the rate forecast in *ADO 2018* in April because of weakness in Papua New Guinea (PNG) and Timor-Leste, the largest and third-largest economies in the subregion. This is a slowdown from 2.4% growth in 2017 and a sharp fall from near double-digit growth just 3 years ago (Figure 3.5.1).

In PNG, damage from an earthquake in February 2018 is greater than initially estimated. Production of liquefied natural gas for export, which accounts for 14% of GDP, is now expected to be at least 10% below 2017. Growth in Timor-Leste is expected to be lower than previously projected as a decline in public spending weakens private consumption and commerce. Activity will likely stay subdued with the government's decision not to provide fiscal stimulus in the second half of 2018. The growth projection for Palau in FY2018 (ending 30 September 2018) is revised down because of curtailed flight connections for tourists from Japan and the PRC.

Conversely, the 2018 outlook for Solomon Islands and Tuvalu has improved. Logging, agriculture, and bauxite and nickel mining have performed above expectations in Solomon Islands, where growth is now seen to hold steady in 2018 rather than slip as projected in April. In Tuvalu, windfall fishing license revenue is being mobilized to provide more fiscal stimulus this year, prompting an upward revision to the 2018 growth projection.

3.5.1 GDP growth, the Pacific

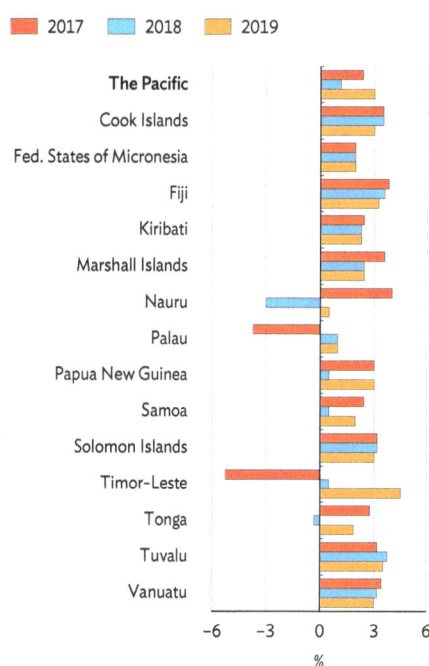

Source: *Asian Development Outlook* database.

The writeup on the Pacific economies was prepared by Jacqueline Connell, Edward Faber, David Freedman, Rommel Rabanal, Shiu Raj Singh, and Cara Tinio of the Pacific Department of ADB, and by Prince Cruz and Noel Del Castillo, consultants to the Pacific Department.

The outlooks for Fiji and Vanuatu remain unchanged, and outcomes in three smaller South Pacific economies in FY2018 (ended 30 June 2018) aligned with April projections.

The subregional growth projection for 2019 is adjusted upward from 3.0% to 3.1% largely in anticipation of a rebound in PNG as full gas production resumes. However, the 2019 outlook for Timor-Leste is downgraded in line with indicative forward spending plans that are less expansionary than initially anticipated. Likewise, the FY2019 growth forecast for Palau is cut as its woes from flight reductions are expected to drag into next year.

Average annual inflation in the subregion is now seen to remain steady at 4.2% in 2018, or 0.1 percentage points higher than projected in April (Figure 3.5.2). Price increases have been sharper than expected in Kiribati, Samoa, and Tuvalu, reflecting elevated costs for imported food and fuel. In Tonga, disruption of local food supply from Tropical Cyclone Gita pushed inflation above expectations. Higher taxes on alcohol and tobacco contribute to inflation in Fiji and Solomon Islands that is higher than anticipated in the year to date. By contrast, the impact of a recent value-added tax hike in Vanuatu has been relatively muted. Inflation projections for PNG, Timor-Leste, and three North Pacific economies are unchanged. Heightened price pressures are seen to persist into next year in Kiribati, Tonga, and Tuvalu but not enough to change the *ADO 2018* subregional inflation projection for 2019.

The aggregate current account balance is expected to remain in surplus, narrowing only slightly to the equivalent of 9.4% of subregional GDP in 2018 from 10.4% in 2017 (Figure 3.5.3). This projection is 2.8 percentage points higher than in *ADO 2018*, mainly because imports of vehicles, construction materials, and other equipment and machinery to Timor-Leste will likely be lower than anticipated as public spending and economic activity stall. Strong remittance inflows and tourism receipts in Samoa and Tonga, as well as unexpectedly high fishing license revenue in Tuvalu, contribute to the improved outlook. Meanwhile, current account deficits are expected to be larger than initially projected in Fiji and Solomon Islands on higher import bills, and in Palau because of weak tourism receipts.

Further narrowing of the aggregate current account surplus to the equivalent of 8.2% of subregional GDP is projected for 2019. This is 1.8 percentage points higher than forecast in *ADO 2018*, the slight upgrade underpinned by a better outlook in Timor-Leste for petroleum revenue, expectations of sustained growth in remittances and tourism receipts in Samoa, and higher fishing license revenue in Tuvalu.

3.5.2 Inflation, the Pacific

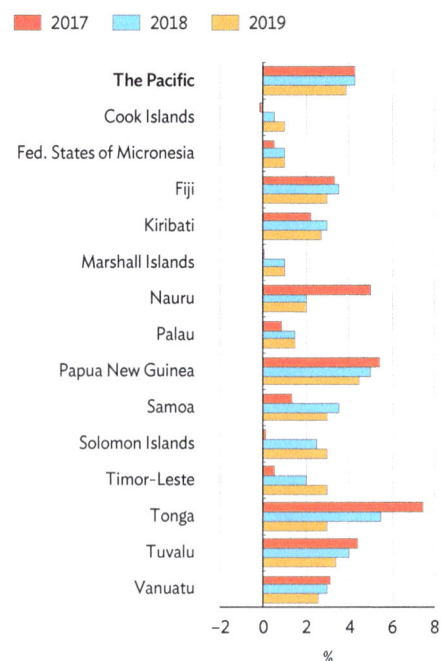

Source: *Asian Development Outlook* database.

3.5.3 Current account balance, the Pacific

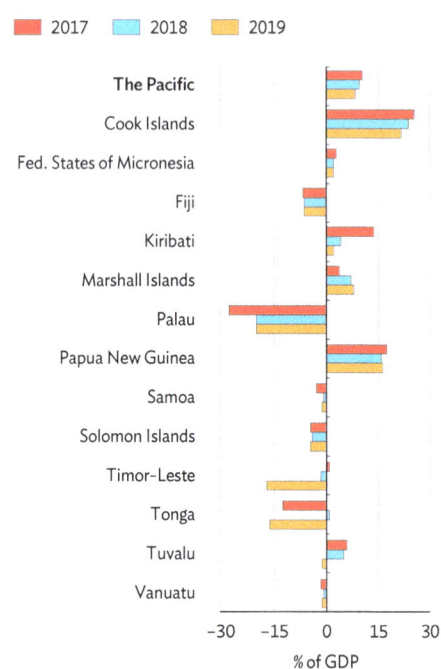

Source: *Asian Development Outlook* database.

Fiji

Growth is expected to meet the *ADO 2018* projection for 2018, with tourism, construction, and agriculture performing in line with expectations. Infrastructure investment continues with higher budgetary allocations for road transport and water-supply and sanitation infrastructure.

Tourist arrivals rose by 3.0% year on year in the first half of 2018, with the largest increase in visitors from New Zealand, followed by the US and India. Arrivals from Asia grew by 3.2% year on year in the same period, in line with broader growth trends. Fiji Airways resumed direct flights to Tokyo in July 2018, and this is expected to boost arrivals from Japan. Further, higher spending is expected from visitors, with tourism earnings having grown by 12.3% in 2017, almost double growth in visitor arrivals at 6.4%. This trend is expected to continue in 2018, with tourism earnings expanding by 4.7% year on year in the first quarter of 2018.

Increases in the number of building permits by 2.2% and their value by 26.9% in the first quarter of 2018 indicate continued growth in construction. Outstanding loans from commercial banks for building and construction were higher by 11.0%, and outstanding loans for real estate and property development were higher by 19.0%, than in the first quarter in 2017. Construction will continue to grow. In addition to new investment, multiple cyclones in 2018 have boosted government spending on infrastructure.

Agriculture grew significantly year on year in the first half of 2018 and will contribute further to growth. The early harvest of sugarcane was better than a year earlier. Meanwhile, gold production grew by 11.6%, reversing an 18.1% decline in the first half of 2017. Production of mahogany, sawn timber, and wood chips also posted marked growth.

The central bank maintained its accommodative monetary policy in the first half of 2018. Interest rates have remained low, with the weighted average lending rate at 5.66%. Meanwhile, a slight reduction in banking system liquidity came from greater payments for imports. Treasury securities were oversubscribed. Credit to the private sector grew by 7.5% in June 2018 over a year earlier. Foreign exchange reserves at the end of July were estimated to provide cover for 5 months of retained imports of goods (not counting reexports) and nonfactor services.

The revised central government budget estimates a deficit equal to 4.5% of GDP in FY2018 (ended 31 July 2018), doubling the deficit of 2.2% in FY2017. Operating revenue is projected to increase from the equivalent of 29.9% of GDP in FY2018 to 32.1% in FY2019 with improved compliance and higher taxes on alcohol and tobacco. Higher operating expenditure is also planned, with greater transfer payments and personnel costs, but an operating surplus equal to 11.6% of GDP is still expected.

3.5.1 Selected economic indicators, Fiji (%)

	2018		2019	
	ADO 2018	Update	ADO 2018	Update
GDP growth	3.6	3.6	3.3	3.3
Inflation	3.0	3.5	3.0	3.0
Current acct. bal. (share of GDP)	–5.0	–6.1	–4.8	–6.0

Source: ADB estimates.

Together with capital spending equal to 15.8% of GDP, to be offset in part by asset sales, an overall fiscal deficit equal to 3.5% of GDP is budgeted for FY2019 to be financed with domestic and concessional external borrowings. In preparation for asset sales, the government has corporatized the former Fiji Electricity Authority into Energy Fiji Limited. It offered 5% as nonvoting shares to domestic customers and still seeks to sell off much of the corporation.

The inflation forecast for 2018 is revised upward in light of further increases in taxes for alcohol and tobacco implemented in June. Higher prices for alcoholic beverages helped push inflation to an average of 3.1% in the year to July 2018. The inflation forecast for 2019 is retained.

Current account figures have been revised from those reported in *ADO 2018*, including a higher deficit in 2017 equivalent to 6.4% of GDP, largely because of increased repatriation of investment income following the central bank's relaxation of exchange controls. Fiji is now expected to incur higher current account deficits in both 2018 and 2019 as outflows of investment income continue and as imports rise to meet demand in a growing economy.

Papua New Guinea

Projected GDP growth is revised down for 2018, largely to accommodate an upward reappraisal of impact from an earthquake in February 2018. Liquefied natural gas production is forecast to be at least 10% below 2017 levels, and production of gold, oil, and condensate will also be lower. The mining and petroleum sector is therefore expected to contract in 2018. However, higher prices for metals and for oil and gas in the first half of 2018 provided a reprieve in export value terms.

Outside of mining and petroleum, the broader economy, which provides three-quarters of GDP, is still forecast to grow by 3% or so in 2018. Construction and demand for goods and services are buoyed by urbanization, population growth, and activity connected with Asia-Pacific Economic Cooperation (APEC) meetings culminating in a November summit. Agriculture is similarly forecast to expand in 2018 on a rebound in coffee production. Reconstruction of public and private infrastructure in the earthquake-affected zone should contribute modestly to growth, though much of the damage was in remote rural areas where the rebuilding of homes may not feature in GDP calculations.

Growth is expected to rebound in 2019 with a return to full production of liquefied natural gas and minerals. Further, confidence may be restored as PNG draws closer to the next round of gas investments, with two large projects expected to commence in early 2020. If commodity prices resume an upward trend, this will further support growth prospects.

3.5.2 Selected economic indicators, Papua New Guinea (%)

	2018		2019	
	ADO 2018	Update	ADO 2018	Update
GDP growth	1.8	0.5	2.7	3.0
Inflation	5.0	5.0	4.5	4.5
Current acct. bal. (share of GDP)	13.4	15.9	13.8	16.2

Source: ADB estimates.

Downside risks include rising US interest rates, which recently sent gold prices lower, and trade tensions between the US and the PRC, which recently reversed increases in copper, nickel, and cobalt prices.

Inflation was 4.6% in the 12 months to the end of March 2018 but is expected to rise over the remainder of the year. The inflation forecasts for 2018 and 2019 remain unchanged. Underlying drivers of rising inflation in 2018 include pass-through from higher oil prices, the recent implementation of tariffs, modest currency depreciation, and some upward pressure on prices from the APEC meetings. Foreign currency shortages have contributed to inflation by constricting the availability of imported goods and thereby pushing up prices.

The current account will remain in surplus thanks to a solid export basket. Latest available data show that the current account surplus in 2017 was higher than initially estimated, necessitating slight upward adjustments to the 2018 and 2019 forecasts. The PNG kina depreciated against the US dollar by 3.8% from August 2017 to July 2018, but the International Monetary Fund recommends faster depreciation to correct a foreign exchange imbalance. Foreign exchange reserves remain static, standing at the end of June 2018 at $1.7 billion, or cover for 5.1 months of imports.

Since June 2018, the government has tapped $290 million in budgetary support and is expected to receive another $150 million in the coming months. Further, a $500 million sovereign bond issue is planned for the third quarter of 2018. These borrowings will finance a projected fiscal deficit in 2018 equal to 2.4% of GDP and may be put toward refinancing existing debt.

The government's cashflow concerns have eased because, according to recent data released by the Treasury in its midyear economic and fiscal outlook, revenue tracked slightly above target in the first 6 months of 2018 as the collection of mining and petroleum taxes was bolstered by higher oil and gas prices. Revenue collection improved as well with reform implemented under the government's medium-term revenue strategy. That said, expenditure in the first half of 2018 also tracked slightly above estimates as personnel emoluments exceeded forecasts.

Solomon Islands

The economy is expected to expand slightly more than forecast in *ADO 2018*, buoyed by strong logging and agriculture in the first half of 2018. Slower growth in logging output, or else the beginning of a gradual decline, is expected to cause growth to moderate in 2019.

Logging production leapt by 30.3% year on year in the first quarter of 2018. The value of logging exports in the quarter equaled 37.5% of the 2017 total. The value of fish and copra exports, by contrast, declined in the quarter despite rising

3.5.3 Selected economic indicators, Solomon Islands (%)

	2018		2019	
	ADO 2018	Update 2018	ADO 2018	Update 2018
GDP growth	3.0	3.2	3.0	3.0
Inflation	2.5	2.5	3.0	3.0
Current acct. bal. (share of GDP)	-2.1	-4.0	-2.5	-4.5

Source: ADB estimates.

production as international prices fell. Bauxite and nickel output was in line with expectations. Looking ahead, the rehabilitation of the country's sole goldmine, Gold Ridge, could provide a new source of growth, though challenges remain. To fully benefit from mineral deposits and encourage inclusive growth, the government needs to improve its regulation and taxation of mining.

The government has made a concerted effort to restore fiscal stability. Although the budget is expected to remain in deficit in 2018, the shortfall will likely be smaller than in 2017, when the deficit equaled 3.8% of GDP. The 2018 budget, approved in April, provided for payment of expenditure arrears incurred last year that amounted to the equivalent of 1.4% of GDP. The government's commitment to clear these arrears by finally paying its suppliers and contractors is a confidence booster for the private sector. Fiscal consolidation has come, however, largely at the expense of development expenditure, with the budget reduced by 42.0% from 2017. This decline was somewhat offset by a rise in recurrent spending.

A supplementary budget, approved in August, is expected to increase expenditure by 4.0%. It is financed mainly by unexpectedly high revenue, especially from taxes, duties, and royalties related to logging and fishing. Spending pressures are likely to mount in the approach to elections in early 2019.

The government recently issued new domestic debt to capitalize its new state-owned enterprise for an undersea telecommunications cable project that aims to improve internet connectivity. The project is majority funded by the Government of Australia and scheduled for completion by the end of 2019. Public debt, both domestic and external, was estimated to equal 11% of GDP in the second quarter of 2018.

Higher visitor arrivals are expected to catalyze economic growth. Arrivals by air grew by 17.8% in the first half of 2018, with the average length of stay rising to 16 days from 13 in 2017.

The inflation forecast for 2018 is retained. After several years of low inflation, inflation rose to 3.4% in the first quarter of 2018 but fell back to 2.5% in the second quarter. It was driven mainly by the domestic component: food, alcoholic drinks and tobacco, and transport and communications. Fuel import duties, which had not been adjusted for more than 20 years, were raised in the first quarter of 2018, contributing to price rises across various sectors. Monetary policy is expected to remain accommodative.

Inflation is projected to pick up in 2019 in line with forecasts made in *ADO 2018*. Higher global fuel prices will likely be moderated by more stable food prices held in check by favorable domestic supply.

Imports were higher than expected in the first quarter of 2018, mainly in line with higher international prices for fuel and food. The projection for the size of the current account deficit is therefore revised up for both 2018 and 2019, reflecting as well an expected gradual decline in logging exports and rising imports to supply infrastructure projects.

Because log output has long been far from sustainable, a risk to the 2019 outlook is an unexpectedly rapid decline in the logging industry, which could be triggered by either environmental or governmental pressures.

Timor-Leste

Growth forecasts for 2018 and 2019 are revised down as continued political uncertainty stymies government spending and private investment. Possible rejection of the budget for 2019 and further political instability pose downside risks to the forecast.

Delays in resolving a political impasse that began in 2017 have sharply curtailed economic activity. Official estimates show the economy outside of the large offshore petroleum sector contracting by 5.3% in 2017 as public expenditure plunged by 25.6%. Public spending continued to decline in 2018, by 27.9% year on year in the first 7 months, with reductions of 25.7% in purchases of goods and services, 57.5% in transfer payments, and 6.8% in spending on salaries and wages. The reduction in transfer payments reflected a scaling back of development in the Special Administrative Region of Oe-Cusse Ambeno and some deferral of personal benefit payments, which were down by 26.4% year on year.

The slowdown in public spending brought more challenging business conditions and reduced private consumption. International air passenger arrivals declined by 30.1% year on year in the first quarter, while vehicle registrations were down by 23.9% and electricity use by businesses slipped by 6.8%. The merchandise trade deficit narrowed in the first half of the year with imports down by 9.8% year on year, notably large reductions for vehicles, construction materials, and other equipment and machinery. Fuel imports rose by 11.4%, reflecting higher oil prices. Food imports were unchanged.

No budget was approved for 2018 before national elections in May. This forced the government to operate under a budget regime in which monthly expenditure was capped at one-twelfth of the appropriation for the previous fiscal year. The elections gave a three-party coalition a clear parliamentary majority, but the formation of a new government has proceeded more slowly than expected, leaving several key positions vacant.

Parliament approved in early September a $1.3 billion budget for 2018, of which 40% had been spent from January to August. The President is expected to promulgate this budget. Although it raises public spending by 6.9% over 2017, the likely stimulus is now seen to be lower than predicted in *ADO 2018*.

3.5.4 Selected economic indicators, Timor-Leste (%)

	2018		2019	
	ADO 2018	Update	ADO 2018	Update
GDP growth	3.0	0.6	5.5	4.5
Inflation	2.0	2.0	3.0	3.0
Current acct. bal. (share of GDP)	–15.2	–1.6	–22.0	–17.1

Source: ADB estimates.

The 2018 budget includes indicative expenditure for 2019–2022. However, a separate budget must be prepared for 2019. Its preparation is under way but with significant uncertainty about how much spending it will propose and its prospects for approval from Parliament and the President. Construction on the Tibar Bay port project began in August and will provide some stimulus. However, other major private investments remain contingent on government support and a conclusive resolution to recent political instability.

Inflation forecasts for 2018 and 2019 are maintained. Higher prices for tradable items such as rice, tobacco, and petroleum products saw inflation rise to 2.2% year on year in the first half of 2018. Prices for non-tradable items such as education also increased moderately. Revised projections for smaller current account deficits, in both 2018 and 2019, reflect expected narrowing of the trade deficit and an improved outlook for petroleum income. Income from petroleum production has improved significantly on higher oil prices and improved extraction with infill drilling on an existing field. Petroleum taxes and royalties were up by 25.9% year on year in the first half of 2018 and are likely to exceed official forecasts.

Petroleum Fund investments were lackluster in the first half of 2018, but the fund still posted a gain to reach a balance of $16.9 billion at the end of June. Official projections for taxes and royalties during 2019–2022 have been revised upward. This has increased Petroleum Fund estimated sustainable income—the amount that can be withdrawn each year without depleting it—by 14.3% to $550.4 million. The development of new petroleum resources such as the Greater Sunrise field could yield significant increases in petroleum wealth but are not reflected in current estimates.

Vanuatu

Growth forecasts for 2018 and 2019 are retained. Expansion in agriculture is likely to be lower than expected because of Tropical Cyclone Hola and volcanic activity in Ambae, but this will be compensated by acceleration in public administration and tourism.

A supplementary budget was approved to raise expenditure by 8.4%. The increase was mainly to cover higher compensation for government employees, but the internally funded allocation for goods and services was also raised, mainly for road construction and airfield upgrades. Meanwhile, less than a third of the government-funded budget for goods and services was disbursed in the first half of 2018, along with an even smaller 12% of funds provided by development partners for goods and services. This may reflect slower project implementation after several years of rapid growth in public construction. By contrast, some 80% of the budget for fixed asset investment funded by partners was spent in the first half of the year.

3.5.5 Selected economic indicators, Vanuatu (%)

	2018		2019	
	ADO 2018	Update	ADO 2018	Update
GDP growth	3.2	3.2	3.0	3.0
Inflation	4.8	3.0	2.5	2.5
Current acct. bal. (share of GDP)	–1.0	–1.0	–1.1	–1.1

Source: ADB estimates.

The government now expects a fiscal deficit equal to 6.7% of GDP in 2018 with higher use of goods and services and the implementation of the Government Remuneration Tribunal decision to increase public service wages. The actual fiscal deficit will likely be lower with unanticipated delays in project execution and with additional revenues from the sale of secondary citizenship, which has become an important source of income in recent years. Revised figures show a fiscal surplus equal to 1.9% of GDP in 2017, not a 2.0% deficit as reported in *ADO 2018*, with revenue revised up and fixed asset investment revised down.

Tourism is on track for a strong recovery in 2018. Visitor arrivals by air rose by 12.4% in the first quarter of 2018, while cruise ship arrivals soared by 25.6%. The recovery follows the rehabilitation and upgrading of wharves in Port Vila and Luganville in 2017.

Tropical Cyclone Hola in March and a volcanic eruption that forced an evacuation of Ambae in July disrupted agriculture, notably copra and cocoa production. Agricultural exports declined slightly by 1.1% in the first half from a year earlier. Massive drops in the export value of copra by 83.6%, beef by 75.6%, and cocoa by 11.8% were only partly compensated by higher exports of kava, by 162.5%.

Inflation was 2.8% in the first half of 2018, mainly reflecting higher prices for food, up 5.1%, and transport, up 3.2%. A value-added tax increase in January 2018 did not stoke inflation as predicted, perhaps because consumers had brought forward purchases to beat the rate hike. Higher global prices for food and fuel in the second half of 2018 may bring slightly higher inflation. However, with inflation in the first half lower than projected, the forecast for 2018 is revised down to 3.0%, now within the target range of 0%–4% set by the Reserve Bank of Vanuatu, the central bank. The inflation forecast for 2019 is retained. The central bank raised its key policy rate from 2.85% to 2.90% in May 2018 in anticipation of higher inflationary pressure.

Higher revenue from tourism is expected to balance the expected fall in agricultural exports, leaving unchanged forecasts for small current account deficits in 2018 and 2019. Risks to the forecasts include lower agricultural exports by value, an unexpectedly sharp spike in fuel prices, or imports for infrastructure projects rising more than foreseen.

North Pacific economies

GDP growth projections are retained for two of the three North Pacific economies in fiscal year 2018 (FY2018, ending 30 September 2018) and FY2019. The outlook for the third, Palau, is weaker as tourism faces further challenges with the discontinuation of two regular flight services.

Although growth forecasts for the Federated States of Micronesia (FSM) and the Marshall Islands are unchanged, long-term prospects remain weak and largely dependent on major public infrastructure projects.

Federated States of Micronesia

In July 2018, the US approved disaster funding under the Compact of Free Association in response to a request from the FSM following floods and landslides caused by heavy rain. Tropical Depression Jelawat hit Pohnpei in late March, but the full extent of its impact was not realized for several weeks, delaying an emergency declaration by the FSM to mid-April.

The impact of the disaster on growth is expected to be largely offset by ongoing reconstruction with US funding and administrative support. The forecasts for growth in FY2018 and FY2019 are therefore unchanged.

Although international food and fuel prices rose faster than expected in the first half of 2018, inflationary pressures in the FSM remain broadly in line with expectations. A bill pending in the Guam legislature to levy fuel transshipment taxes affecting other ports in Micronesia, including the three North Pacific members of ADB, could significantly increase electricity, transport, and associated costs. Pending further developments, this *Update* also retains the *ADO 2018* inflation projection for FY2019.

Fishing license revenues have likely reached a plateau but remain large enough to offset perennial FSM merchandise trade deficits. The current account surplus is seen to narrow slightly in FY2018 and stabilize in FY2019, as forecast in *ADO 2018*.

Marshall Islands

Economic growth projections are unchanged from *ADO 2018*. Expansion remains dependent on continued infrastructure investment funded by development partners and US compact grants, with potential growth tempered by constraints on local capacity to implement projects.

Progress has been slow toward achieving the goal of fiscal self-sufficiency by the time compact grants expire in 2023. Fiscal surpluses have narrowed despite continued high collections from fishing license fees because incremental revenue increases have been channeled into recurrent spending, including subsidies paid to state-owned enterprises. The Compact Trust Fund, whose proceeds are supposed to replace compact grants after 2023, languishes well below target.

In February 2018, a law was approved enabling the country to issue a cryptocurrency, called the sovereign, that would be recognized as legal tender alongside the US dollar. The potential repercussions of this move pose further downside risks to growth. The concern is that cryptocurrency volatility, the lack of appropriate regulatory mechanisms in

3.5.6 Selected economic indicators, Federated States of Micronesia (%)

	2018		2019	
	ADO 2018	Update	ADO 2018	Update
GDP growth	2.0	2.0	2.0	2.0
Inflation	1.0	1.0	1.0	1.0
Current acct. bal. (share of GDP)	2.0	2.0	2.0	2.0

Note: Years are fiscal years ending on 30 September of the same calendar year.
Source: ADB estimates.

3.5.7 Selected economic indicators, Marshall Islands (%)

	2018		2019	
	ADO 2018	Update	ADO 2018	Update
GDP growth	2.5	2.5	2.5	2.5
Inflation	1.0	1.0	1.0	1.0
Current acct. bal. (share of GDP)	7.0	7.0	8.0	8.0

Note: Years are fiscal years ending on 30 September of the same calendar year.
Source: ADB estimates.

the Marshall Islands, and possible violations of US banking regulations could cost the Bank of the Marshall Islands its only remaining correspondent banking relationship, with the First Hawaiian Bank, and cause the Bank of Guam to close its single branch in the country. This could limit the country's access to global financial networks.

Inflation and the current account balance are still expected to meet *ADO 2018* projections. Inflation will continue to track trends for international food and fuel prices but remain low, and the current account surplus will widen as implementation capacity constraints slow capital imports needed for infrastructure investments.

Palau

Recovery from a tourism downturn, which saw visitor numbers drop by almost 30% from FY2015 to FY2017, has been slow and uneven. Visitor arrivals in the first 9 months of FY2018 inched up by only 1.2% from the same period a year earlier. Of late, the recovery appears to have stalled as a 9.8% drop in visitor arrivals year on year in the third quarter of FY2018 reversed solid 6.6% growth in arrivals in the first half. The PRC and Japan—the two largest sources of tourists in Palau—recorded the sharpest declines, with arrivals from Japan hit by the termination of Delta Air Lines flights from Tokyo in May 2018. Further, Palau Pacific Airways indefinitely suspended in July its scheduled charter flights from Hong Kong, China because restrictions on tour groups from the PRC had sharply reduced passenger numbers and caused mounting financial losses for the Koror-based carrier.

These latest developments likely mean a third consecutive year of visitor arrival declines. The growth projection for FY2018 is therefore revised sharply down, but with private and public investments seen sufficient to stave off a second consecutive year of economic contraction. Because of uncertainties surrounding tourism, growth is similarly projected lower in FY2019 than previously forecast.

Inflation in the first 3 quarters of FY2018 averaged 1.7% year on year, pushed up by higher costs for imported food and beverages. However, price pressures in the final quarter are expected to be subdued by a likely slowdown in tourism and economic activity in general. On balance, inflation projections are unchanged from *ADO 2018*.

Weak tourism is seen to widen current account deficits. With tourism receipts likely falling below expectations, surpluses in the service account will offset a smaller fraction of Palau's persistently large merchandise trade deficit. Current account deficit projections from *ADO 2018* are revised up, with Palau now expected to incur current account deficits equal to 20% of GDP in both FY2018 and FY2019.

3.5.8 Selected economic indicators, Palau (%)

	2018		2019	
	ADO 2018	Update	ADO 2018	Update
GDP growth	3.0	1.0	3.0	1.0
Inflation	1.5	1.5	1.5	1.5
Current acct. bal. (share of GDP)	-16.0	-20.0	-16.0	-20.0

Note: Years are fiscal years ending on 30 September of the same calendar year.

Source: ADB estimates.

South Pacific economies

Growth in the South Pacific in fiscal year 2018 (FY2018, ended 30 June 2018) aligned with *ADO 2018* forecasts. Tourism will continue to drive economic expansion in the Cook Islands and Samoa, while the Tongan economy is expected to recover with reconstruction and rehabilitation in the wake of Tropical Cyclone Gita. Similarly, growth forecasts for FY2019 remain unchanged. Inflation was higher than projected for FY2018 in Samoa because of elevated import prices. In Tonga, the cyclone disrupted local food supply, pushing inflation higher than projected in FY2018 and requiring a higher inflation forecast for FY2019.

Cook Islands

Estimated economic growth in the Cook Islands in FY2018 was in line with the April forecast in *ADO 2018*, with a 4.6% increase in visitor arrivals an important contributor. A similar increase in visitor arrivals is expected in FY2019, for which the growth projection is retained. However, historical national accounts data have been revised downward with the recent exclusion of fish offloaded by foreign vessels in the Cook Islands but caught in international waters.

    Inflation is estimated to have met the forecast for FY2018, edging into positive territory for the first time since FY2015 despite continued price declines for housing and household operations and for apparel. The forecast for slightly higher inflation in FY2019 is retained with increased food and transport costs.

    The government realized a fiscal surplus in FY2018 equal to 5.7% of GDP thanks to high revenue collection attributed largely to a tax amnesty, increased tourism-related activity, and recurrent spending and public investment that were significantly below expectations. A deficit equal to 4.6% of GDP is budgeted for FY2019. Gross public debt is estimated to have reached the equivalent of 31.7% of GDP at the end of FY2018. Subtracting cash reserves held for debt service yields a net debt of 26.9%.

    Private sector credit declined by 0.9% year on year in the first 3 quarters of FY2018. Despite this, 14.6% growth in broad money pushed deposit interest rates marginally lower but left lending interest rates unchanged.

    The current account estimate for FY2018 meets the *ADO 2018* projection, and the forecast for FY2019 is retained. However, with the change in the treatment of fish caught by foreign vessels, revisions to current account data are expected.

Samoa

Growth in FY2018 is estimated to have met expectations. Data show the economy shrinking by 0.3% year on year in the first 3 quarters of the fiscal year. While visitor arrivals

3.5.9 Selected economic indicators, Cook Islands (%)

	2018		2019	
	ADO 2018	Update	ADO 2018	Update
GDP growth	3.5	3.5	3.0	3.0
Inflation	0.5	0.5	1.0	1.0
Current acct. bal. (share of GDP)	23.6	23.6	21.7	21.7

Note: Years are fiscal years ending on 30 June of that year.

Source: ADB estimates.

grew by 12.2%, there were notable contractions in fishing, by 36.6%, and nonfood manufacturing, by 33.3%. The economy is estimated to have expanded in the last quarter, however, to realize growth for the whole of FY2018. As the increase in visitor arrivals is expected to continue into FY2019, the projection for higher growth in FY2019 is retained.

Inflation in FY2018 is estimated to have been higher than projected in *ADO 2018* because price increases for imports were substantially greater than anticipated. The inflation forecast for FY2019 is retained in line with initially projected trends.

The fiscal deficit in FY2018 is estimated to have stayed within the budget target, equal to 3.5% of GDP, as expenditure did not exceed allocations. Public debt, which has been declining for the past 2 fiscal years, was equal to 47.4% of GDP at the end of FY2018. A deficit of 3.5% is budgeted again for FY2019.

Despite the Central Bank of Samoa maintaining its accommodative monetary policy to support economic growth, private sector credit was 0.4% lower in May 2018 than in May 2017.

Remittances and income from tourism in the first half of FY2018 outperformed expectations. The estimated current account deficit for the full year is therefore revised down from the forecast in *ADO 2018*, as is the projected deficit for FY2019. Foreign exchange reserves at the end of March 2018 were sufficient to cover 5.4 months of goods imports.

Tonga

Widespread damage from Tropical Cyclone Gita last February is estimated to have caused contraction in FY2018, as anticipated in *ADO 2018*. The cyclone severely affected agriculture, fisheries, electricity supply, and services. Economic activity is expected to pick up in the first half of FY2019, however, so the growth projection for the fiscal year as a whole is retained. Recovery will be driven primarily by government-led cyclone reconstruction and supported by strong growth in private credit, which will spur activity in various sectors of the economy.

Damage caused by the cyclone disrupted local food supply, pushing inflation in FY2018 considerably higher than projected in *ADO 2018*. The inflation forecast for FY2019 is revised up to accommodate lingering impacts from the cyclone and anticipated higher fuel prices in line with global trends.

Government revenue increased only slightly in FY2018 from FY2017 as a substantial contraction in grants offset higher tax revenue. Meanwhile, increased spending driven by higher public sector wages, initial reconstruction expenses, and the maintenance of existing infrastructure is estimated to have narrowed the fiscal surplus. In FY2019, the continuation of government reconstruction and rehabilitation projects is

3.5.10 Selected economic indicators, Samoa (%)

	2018		2019	
	ADO 2018	Update	ADO 2018	Update
GDP growth	0.5	0.5	2.0	2.0
Inflation	2.0	3.5	3.0	3.0
Current acct. bal. (share of GDP)	−4.3	−0.8	−3.2	−1.1

Note: Years are fiscal years ending on 30 June of that year.
Source: ADB estimates.

3.5.11 Selected economic indicators, Tonga (%)

	2018		2019	
	ADO 2018	Update	ADO 2018	Update
GDP growth	−0.3	−0.3	1.9	1.9
Inflation	3.8	5.5	0.5	3.0
Current acct. bal. (share of GDP)	−14.8	0.8	−15.9	−15.9

Note: Years are fiscal years ending on 30 June of that year.
Source: ADB estimates.

expected to further shrink the budget surplus. Additionally, the government intends to start repaying a large loan from a state-owned bank in the PRC.

Tonga's current account is estimated to have recorded a small surprise surplus in FY2018 brought about by tourism-related earnings above expectations in the first half of the fiscal year, and later by emergency assistance. The forecast for a widening deficit in FY2019 is maintained, however, given the higher volume of imports needed for reconstruction and rehabilitation.

Small island economies

Economic prospects for two of three small island economies in the Pacific improve as GDP growth assessments for Nauru and Tuvalu are revised upward. Higher growth in Tuvalu and adjustments to public sector wages in Kiribati contribute to higher inflation. Tuvalu received fishing license revenue that was higher than expected, prompting changes to forecasts for the current account balance, and fishing license revenue was higher in Nauru as well.

Kiribati

Prospects over the short term appear to sustain the growth forecasts presented in *ADO 2018* in April. The implementation of infrastructure projects financed by development partners will support continued expansion in the economy.

The government budget is expected to remain in surplus in the short term despite rising expenditure and falling revenue. While fishing license revenue remains high, a projected decline will reduce government revenue collection by 10.1% in 2018. Meanwhile, operating expenditure is expected to grow in both 2018 and 2019, with public sector wages ballooning by 24.2% in 2018 and increasing by a further 3.4% in 2019. Capital expenditure, by contrast, is expected to decline in each of the next 3 years while debt servicing costs increase over the same period.

The inflation forecast for Kiribati is adjusted upward for 2018 and, to a lesser extent, for 2019 because increases in public wages and global oil prices have exceeded earlier expectations.

The country's external financial position is largely driven by fishing license fees, contributions to the Revenue Equalization Reserve Fund from development partners and income from fund investments, and the importation of capital goods mainly for infrastructure investment. Forecasts for the current account surplus remain unchanged as they already incorporated the expected decline in fishing license revenue this year.

3.5.12 Selected economic indicators, Kiribati (%)

	2018		2019	
	ADO 2018	Update	ADO 2018	Update
GDP growth	2.3	2.3	2.3	2.3
Inflation	2.5	3.0	2.5	2.7
Current acct. bal. (share of GDP)	4.3	4.3	2.3	2.3

Source: ADB estimates.

Nauru

The economy contracted by less than earlier forecast in fiscal year 2018 (FY2018, ended 30 June 2018) because the scaling down of the Regional Processing Centre (RPC), an Australian facility for asylum seekers, and the resettlement overseas of refugees proceeded at a slower pace than expected.

The slower scaling down of RPC activities, combined with higher revenue from fishing license fees, allowed the government to increase expenditure despite its earlier projection of lower expenditure. RPC-related revenue is now estimated to have increased by 7.1% compared with budget projections showing a 23.6% decline. Most of the higher revenue has been channeled to spending. Total expenditure is estimated to have increased by 10.0% in FY2018.

The FY2019 budget provides for expenditure close to actual spending in FY2018. The economy is still projected to reverse contraction in FY2018 with slight expansion in FY2019 as the planned construction of the Nauru seaport gets under way.

Inflation was 2.0%, as forecast in *ADO 2018*, down from 5.0% in FY2017. Inflation is still forecast to continue at this rate in FY2109, despite rising global fuel and food prices, as weaker demand is expected with the resettlement overseas of asylum seekers and the scaling down of the RPC.

As more data on the full impact of scaling down the RPC becomes available, forecasts for FY2019 could change. Other risks to the forecasts would include any sharp changes in global prices for commodities or delays in constructing the Nauru seaport.

3.5.13 Selected economic indicators, Nauru (%)

	2018		2019	
	ADO 2018	Update	ADO 2018	Update
GDP growth	−4.0	−3.0	0.5	0.5
Inflation	2.0	2.0	2.0	2.0
Current acct. bal. (share of GDP)	...	...	...	...

... = not available.
Source: ADB estimates.

Tuvalu

Economic growth forecasts are revised up for both 2018 and 2019. The revisions take into account higher fiscal spending projected in the supplementary budget, which will be supported by fishing license revenue exceeding expectations. A recent one-off payment from a subregional pooling scheme with four other Pacific island economies—Nauru, the Marshall Islands, Solomon Islands, and Tokelau—is expected to boost fishing revenue by 73.1% in 2018. Meanwhile, large infrastructure and housing projects continue in preparation for the Pacific Forum Secretariat Summit in 2019.

Inflation is now expected to be significantly higher in both 2018 and 2019, in line with expectations of stronger economic activity.

Forecasts for the current account balance are revised to reflect the impact of strong fishing license revenue. Instead of steep deficits in both years, Tuvalu is now expected to post a surplus in 2018 and a much narrower deficit in 2019.

3.5.14 Selected economic indicators, Tuvalu (%)

	2018		2019	
	ADO 2018	Update	ADO 2018	Update
GDP growth	3.0	3.8	3.0	3.5
Inflation	2.5	4.0	2.8	3.4
Current acct. bal. (share of GDP)	−31.4	5.0	−29.1	−1.0

Source: ADB estimates.

STATISTICAL APPENDIX

Statistical notes

This statistical appendix presents selected economic indicators for the 45 developing member economies of the Asian Development Bank (ADB) in three tables: gross domestic product (GDP) growth, inflation, and current account balance as a percentage of GDP. The economies are grouped into five subregions: Central Asia, East Asia, South Asia, Southeast Asia, and the Pacific. The tables contain historical data for 2015–2017 and forecasts for 2018 and 2019.

The data were standardized to the degree possible to allow comparability over time and across economies, but differences in statistical methodology, definitions, coverage, and practices make full comparability impossible. The national income accounts section is based on the United Nations System of National Accounts, while the data on balance of payments are based on International Monetary Fund accounting standards. Historical data are obtained from official sources, statistical publications, ADB estimates, and databases, as well as from documents of ADB, the International Monetary Fund, and the World Bank. Projections for 2018 and 2019 are generally ADB estimates made on the bases of available quarterly or monthly data, though some projections are from governments.

Most countries report by calendar year. The following record their government finance data by fiscal year: Brunei Darussalam; Fiji; Hong Kong, China; the Lao People's Democratic Republic; Singapore; Taipei,China; and Thailand. South Asian countries (except for Maldives and Sri Lanka), the Cook Islands, the Federated States of Micronesia, Nauru, Myanmar, Palau, the Republic of Marshall Islands, Samoa, and Tonga report all variables by fiscal year.

Regional and subregional averages are provided in the three tables. The averages are computed using weights derived from gross national income (GNI) in current US dollars following the World Bank Atlas method. The GNI data for 2015–2016 are obtained from the World Bank's World Development Indicators Online. Weights for 2016 are carried over through 2019. The GNI data for the Cook Islands and Taipei,China were estimated using the Atlas conversion factor.

The following paragraphs discuss the three tables in greater detail.

Table A1: Growth rate of GDP (% per year). The table shows annual growth rates of GDP valued at constant market price, factor cost, or basic price. GDP at market price is the aggregation of value added by all resident producers at producers' prices including taxes less subsidies on imports plus all nondeductible value-added or similar taxes. Constant factor cost measures differ from market price measures in that they exclude taxes on production and include subsidies. Basic price valuation is the factor cost plus some taxes on production, such as those on property and payroll taxes, and less some subsidies, such as those on labor-related subsidies but not product-related subsidies. Most countries use constant market price valuation. Pakistan uses constant factor cost, while Fiji, Maldives, and Nepal use basic prices.

Table A2: Inflation (% per year). Data on inflation rates represent period averages. The inflation rates presented are based on consumer price indexes. The consumer price indexes of the following economies are for a given city or group of consumers only: in Cambodia for Phnom Penh, in the Marshall Islands for Majuro, in Solomon Islands for Honiara, and in Nepal for urban consumers. Data for Uzbekistan in 2017 are sourced from the International Monetary Fund's Enhanced General Data Dissemination System.

Table A3: Current account balance (% of GDP). The current account balance is the sum of the balance of trade for merchandise, net trade in services and factor income, and net transfers. The values reported are divided by GDP at current prices in US dollars. In the case of Cambodia, the Lao People's Democratic Republic, and Viet Nam, official transfers are excluded from the current account balance.

Table A1 Growth rate of GDP (% per year)

	2015	2016	2017	2018 ADO2018	2018 Update	2019 ADO2018	2019 Update
Central Asia	3.1	2.7	4.3	4.0	4.1	4.2	4.2
Armenia	3.2	0.2	7.5	4.0	5.3	4.2	4.5
Azerbaijan	1.1	−3.1	0.1	1.7	1.7	2.0	2.0
Georgia	2.9	2.8	5.0	4.5	4.9	4.7	5.0
Kazakhstan	1.2	1.1	4.1	3.2	3.7	3.5	3.9
Kyrgyz Republic	3.9	4.3	4.6	3.5	2.5	4.0	4.0
Tajikistan	6.0	6.9	7.1	6.0	6.0	6.5	6.5
Turkmenistan	6.5	6.2	6.5	6.5	6.2	6.7	6.0
Uzbekistan	7.9	7.8	5.3	5.5	4.9	5.6	5.0
East Asia	6.1	6.0	6.3	6.0	6.0	5.8	5.7
Hong Kong, China	2.4	2.2	3.8	3.2	3.7	3.0	3.0
Mongolia	2.4	1.2	5.3	3.8	6.4	4.3	6.1
People's Republic of China	6.9	6.7	6.9	6.6	6.6	6.4	6.3
Republic of Korea	2.8	2.9	3.1	3.0	2.9	2.9	2.8
Taipei,China	0.8	1.4	2.9	2.9	3.0	2.8	2.8
South Asia	7.4	6.7	6.5	7.0	7.0	7.2	7.2
Afghanistan	1.3	2.4	2.5	2.5	2.2	2.5	2.5
Bangladesh	6.6	7.1	7.3	7.0	7.9	7.2	7.5
Bhutan	6.2	7.3	7.5	7.1	6.7	7.4	7.1
India	8.2	7.1	6.7	7.3	7.3	7.6	7.6
Maldives	2.2	6.2	6.9	6.7	6.7	6.8	6.4
Nepal	3.0	0.2	7.4	4.9	5.9	5.5	5.5
Pakistan	4.1	4.6	5.4	5.6	5.8	5.1	4.8
Sri Lanka	5.0	4.5	3.3	4.2	3.8	4.8	4.5
Southeast Asia	4.7	4.7	5.2	5.2	5.1	5.2	5.2
Brunei Darussalam	−0.4	−2.5	1.3	1.5	2.0	2.0	2.0
Cambodia	7.0	7.0	6.9	7.0	7.0	7.0	7.0
Indonesia	4.9	5.0	5.1	5.3	5.2	5.3	5.3
Lao People's Dem. Rep.	7.3	7.0	6.9	6.8	6.6	7.0	6.9
Malaysia	5.1	4.2	5.9	5.3	5.0	5.0	4.8
Myanmar	7.0	5.9	6.8	6.8	6.6	7.2	7.0
Philippines	6.1	6.9	6.7	6.8	6.4	6.9	6.7
Singapore	2.2	2.4	3.6	3.1	3.1	2.9	2.9
Thailand	3.0	3.3	3.9	4.0	4.5	4.1	4.3
Viet Nam	6.7	6.2	6.8	7.1	6.9	6.8	6.8
The Pacific	8.1	2.4	2.4	2.2	1.1	3.0	3.1
Cook Islands	3.2	8.8	3.5	3.5	3.5	3.0	3.0
Federated States of Micronesia	4.9	−0.1	2.0	2.0	2.0	2.0	2.0
Fiji	3.8	0.4	3.9	3.6	3.6	3.3	3.3
Kiribati	3.5	1.8	2.5	2.3	2.3	2.3	2.3
Marshall Islands	−0.6	1.9	3.6	2.5	2.5	2.5	2.5
Nauru	2.8	10.4	4.0	−4.0	−3.0	0.5	0.5
Palau	10.1	0.1	−3.7	3.0	1.0	3.0	1.0
Papua New Guinea	10.5	2.0	3.0	1.8	0.5	2.7	3.0
Samoa	1.6	7.1	2.5	0.5	0.5	2.0	2.0
Solomon Islands	2.6	3.4	3.2	3.0	3.2	3.0	3.0
Timor-Leste	4.0	5.3	−5.3	3.0	0.6	5.5	4.5
Tonga	3.7	3.1	2.8	−0.3	−0.3	1.9	1.9
Tuvalu	9.1	3.0	3.2	3.0	3.8	3.0	3.5
Vanuatu	0.2	3.5	3.5	3.2	3.2	3.0	3.0
Developing Asia	6.0	5.9	6.1	6.0	6.0	5.9	5.8
Developing Asia excluding the NIEs	6.6	6.4	6.6	6.5	6.5	6.4	6.3

Note: The newly industrialized economies (NIEs) are Hong Kong, China; the Republic of Korea; Singapore; and Taipei,China.

Table A2 Inflation (% per year)

	2015	2016	2017	2018		2019	
				ADO2018	Update	ADO2018	Update
Central Asia	6.4	10.3	9.2	8.5	8.4	7.9	7.7
Armenia	3.7	–1.4	1.0	2.7	2.7	2.2	2.5
Azerbaijan	4.0	12.4	12.9	7.0	4.5	8.0	5.0
Georgia	4.0	2.1	6.0	3.5	3.0	3.0	3.0
Kazakhstan	6.6	14.6	7.4	6.8	7.0	6.2	6.5
Kyrgyz Republic	6.5	0.4	3.2	4.0	3.8	4.5	4.5
Tajikistan	5.1	6.1	6.7	7.5	6.5	7.0	7.0
Turkmenistan	7.4	3.6	8.0	8.0	9.4	8.0	8.2
Uzbekistan	8.5	8.0	14.4	16.0	16.0	14.0	14.0
East Asia	1.3	1.9	1.6	2.3	2.1	2.2	2.1
Hong Kong, China	3.0	2.4	1.5	2.2	2.3	2.1	2.2
Mongolia	6.6	1.1	4.3	8.0	7.2	7.0	7.0
People's Republic of China	1.4	2.0	1.6	2.4	2.2	2.3	2.2
Republic of Korea	0.7	1.0	1.9	1.9	1.8	2.0	1.8
Taipei,China	–0.3	1.4	0.6	1.1	1.4	1.1	1.3
South Asia	4.9	4.5	4.0	4.7	4.9	5.1	5.2
Afghanistan	–0.7	4.4	5.0	5.0	3.5	5.0	5.0
Bangladesh	6.4	5.9	5.4	6.1	5.8	6.3	6.3
Bhutan	6.6	3.3	4.3	4.6	3.6	5.4	4.9
India	4.9	4.5	3.6	4.6	5.0	5.0	5.0
Maldives	1.0	0.5	2.8	3.1	1.2	3.0	1.7
Nepal	7.2	9.9	4.5	5.5	4.2	6.0	6.0
Pakistan	4.5	2.9	4.2	4.5	3.9	4.8	6.5
Sri Lanka	3.8	4.0	7.7	5.2	4.5	5.0	4.7
Southeast Asia	2.7	2.0	2.8	3.0	2.9	3.0	2.9
Brunei Darussalam	–0.4	–0.7	–0.2	0.1	0.2	0.1	0.2
Cambodia	1.2	3.0	2.9	3.2	2.6	3.5	3.0
Indonesia	6.4	3.5	3.8	3.8	3.4	4.0	3.5
Lao People's Dem. Rep.	1.3	1.6	0.8	2.0	2.5	2.5	3.1
Malaysia	2.1	2.1	3.8	2.6	1.4	1.8	2.0
Myanmar	10.0	6.8	4.0	6.2	6.2	6.0	6.0
Philippines	0.7	1.3	2.9	4.0	5.0	3.9	4.0
Singapore	–0.5	–0.5	0.6	0.9	0.7	1.4	1.4
Thailand	–0.9	0.2	0.7	1.2	1.3	1.3	1.4
Viet Nam	0.6	2.7	3.5	3.7	4.0	4.0	4.5
The Pacific	4.3	4.8	4.2	4.1	4.2	3.9	3.9
Cook Islands	3.0	–0.1	–0.1	0.5	0.5	1.0	1.0
Federated States of Micronesia	0.0	–1.0	0.5	1.0	1.0	1.0	1.0
Fiji	1.4	3.9	3.3	3.0	3.5	3.0	3.0
Kiribati	0.6	0.7	2.2	2.5	3.0	2.5	2.7
Marshall Islands	–2.3	–1.5	0.0	1.0	1.0	1.0	1.0
Nauru	11.4	8.2	5.0	2.0	2.0	2.0	2.0
Palau	2.2	–1.3	0.9	1.5	1.5	1.5	1.5
Papua New Guinea	6.0	6.7	5.4	5.0	5.0	4.5	4.5
Samoa	1.9	0.1	1.4	2.0	3.5	3.0	3.0
Solomon Islands	–0.5	1.1	0.1	2.5	2.5	3.0	3.0
Timor-Leste	0.6	–1.3	0.6	2.0	2.0	3.0	3.0
Tonga	–1.0	2.6	7.4	3.8	5.5	0.5	3.0
Tuvalu	4.0	2.6	4.4	2.5	4.0	2.8	3.4
Vanuatu	2.5	0.8	3.1	4.8	3.0	2.5	2.5
Developing Asia	2.1	2.4	2.2	2.9	2.8	2.9	2.8
Developing Asia excluding the NIEs	2.4	2.6	2.3	3.0	2.9	3.0	3.0

Note: The newly industrialized economies (NIEs) are Hong Kong, China; the Republic of Korea; Singapore; and Taipei,China.

Table A3 Current account balance (% of GDP)

	2015	2016	2017	2018 ADO2018	2018 Update	2019 ADO2018	2019 Update
Central Asia	-3.7	-6.2	-2.0	-2.1	-1.3	-2.2	-1.2
Armenia	-2.6	-2.3	-2.8	-3.2	-4.5	-2.8	-4.0
Azerbaijan	-0.4	-3.6	5.5	6.9	7.9	6.2	10.9
Georgia	-11.9	-12.8	-8.9	-9.5	-9.5	-8.5	-8.5
Kazakhstan	-2.8	-6.5	-3.3	-3.3	-1.5	-3.4	-2.5
Kyrgyz Republic	-15.9	-11.6	-6.5	-12.0	-12.0	-10.0	-10.0
Tajikistan	-6.2	-3.8	-0.5	1.1	-2.5	-3.0	-3.0
Turkmenistan	-15.6	-19.9	-11.5	-9.0	-8.5	-8.0	-7.8
Uzbekistan	0.7	0.7	2.8	0.5	0.5	0.1	0.1
East Asia	3.7	2.8	2.4	2.1	1.6	1.9	1.1
Hong Kong, China	3.3	4.0	4.3	3.9	3.7	3.5	3.3
Mongolia	-8.1	-6.3	-10.0	-6.3	-8.9	-7.0	-8.5
People's Republic of China	2.7	1.8	1.4	1.3	0.7	1.2	0.2
Republic of Korea	7.7	7.0	5.1	4.9	4.8	4.8	4.7
Taipei,China	14.3	13.7	14.5	10.0	12.0	9.0	10.0
South Asia	-0.8	-0.6	-2.0	-2.5	-2.9	-2.6	-2.9
Afghanistan	7.5	7.1	1.6	3.3	0.4	2.6	-0.5
Bangladesh	1.8	1.9	-0.5	-2.2	-3.6	-1.9	-3.5
Bhutan	-28.3	-31.2	-23.0	-22.2	-19.0	-18.8	-16.5
India	-1.0	-0.6	-1.9	-2.2	-2.4	-2.4	-2.5
Maldives	-7.6	-24.5	-18.9	-17.3	-17.5	-17.1	-17.7
Nepal	5.1	6.2	-0.4	-3.5	-8.2	-5.8	-8.7
Pakistan	-1.0	-1.7	-4.1	-4.9	-5.8	-4.5	-5.0
Sri Lanka	-2.3	-2.4	-3.0	-2.7	-2.9	-2.5	-3.1
Southeast Asia	3.2	3.6	3.6	2.7	2.5	2.5	2.4
Brunei Darussalam	16.7	15.5	18.0	14.0	14.0	14.0	14.0
Cambodia	-11.9	-11.2	-10.9	-11.1	-12.1	-10.8	-11.8
Indonesia	-2.0	-1.8	-1.7	-2.2	-2.6	-2.2	-2.6
Lao People's Dem. Rep.	-18.0	-14.1	-13.0	-14.9	-13.8	-13.7	-13.0
Malaysia	3.0	2.4	3.0	2.4	2.0	2.1	2.4
Myanmar	-5.0	-3.9	-5.0	-5.4	-3.0	-5.5	-4.0
Philippines	2.5	-0.4	-0.8	-1.0	-1.8	-1.4	-2.0
Singapore	18.6	19.0	18.8	19.0	19.0	19.0	19.0
Thailand	8.0	11.7	11.2	8.0	8.0	7.5	7.5
Viet Nam	0.5	3.0	2.9	2.5	2.3	2.0	2.0
The Pacific	9.8	6.6	10.4	6.6	9.4	6.4	8.2
Cook Islands	22.5	25.8	25.5	23.6	23.6	21.7	21.7
Federated States of Micronesia	3.0	3.9	2.8	2.0	2.0	2.0	2.0
Fiji	-3.1	-5.0	-6.4	-5.0	-6.1	-4.8	-6.0
Kiribati	47.4	18.9	13.8	4.3	4.3	2.3	2.3
Marshall Islands	14.3	7.4	3.7	7.0	7.0	8.0	8.0
Nauru	-9.4	1.7	0.5	...	...	...	...
Palau	-16.5	-21.0	-27.6	-16.0	-20.0	-16.0	-20.0
Papua New Guinea	13.6	15.2	17.6	13.4	15.9	13.8	16.2
Samoa	-2.7	-4.5	-3.0	-4.3	-0.8	-3.2	-1.1
Solomon Islands	-3.4	-4.5	-4.4	-2.1	-4.0	-2.5	-4.5
Timor-Leste	14.9	-30.7	0.8	-15.2	-1.6	-22.0	-17.1
Tonga	-14.8	-13.9	-12.2	-14.8	0.8	-15.9	-15.9
Tuvalu	-53.0	23.0	6.0	-31.4	5.0	-29.1	-1.0
Vanuatu	-8.9	-4.6	-1.5	-1.0	-1.0	-1.1	-1.1
Developing Asia	2.9	2.3	1.8	1.4	1.0	1.3	0.7
Developing Asia excluding the NIEs	1.8	1.2	0.8	0.5	0.0	0.4	-0.3

... = data not available.

Note: The newly industrialized economies (NIEs) are Hong Kong, China; the Republic of Korea; Singapore; and Taipei,China.

www.ingramcontent.com/pod-product-compliance
Lightning Source LLC
Chambersburg PA
CBHW061219270326
41926CB00032B/4779